TEACHING THE ARTS
Early Childhood and Primary Education

Teaching the Arts: Early Childhood and Primary Education foregrounds the importance of Arts education to children's development and learning while connecting each Arts area to the Australian Curriculum. The third edition provides the same comprehensive coverage and exciting introduction to Arts education in Australia as previous editions, with updated content and new, interactive features. The book covers the key areas of dance, drama, media arts, music and visual arts, with chapters full of teacher tips, practical examples and suggestions for classroom activities.

This new edition's enhanced eBook content includes:

- interactive questions and answers
- links to videos of Arts activities
- over 30 downloadable lesson plans
- links to online resources to support students in their learning.

This book is a vital resource for all pre-service early childhood and primary teachers, emphasising the often-overlooked yet fundamental nature of the Arts in schools. Through the Arts, if we can instill a love of learning, then we can all learn to love.

David Roy is Lecturer in Arts Education at the University of Newcastle.

William Baker is Lecturer in Arts Education at the University of Tasmania.

Amy Hamilton is Associate Professor in Visual Arts and Arts Education at Flinders University.

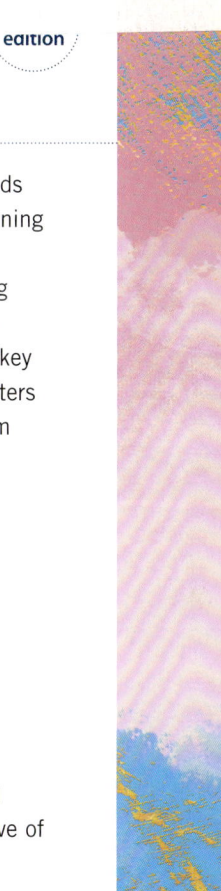

TEACHING THE ARTS

THIRD EDITION

Early Childhood and Primary Education

David **ROY**
William **BAKER**
Amy **HAMILTON**

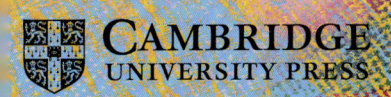

CAMBRIDGE UNIVERSITY PRESS

CAMBRIDGE
UNIVERSITY PRESS

University Printing House, Cambridge CB2 8BS, United Kingdom

One Liberty Plaza, 20th Floor, New York, NY 10006, USA

477 Williamstown Road, Port Melbourne, VIC 3207, Australia

314–321, 3rd Floor, Plot 3, Splendor Forum, Jasola District Centre, New Delhi – 110025, India

79 Anson Road, #06–04/06, Singapore 079906

Cambridge University Press is part of the University of Cambridge.

It furthers the University's mission by disseminating knowledge in the pursuit of education, learning and research at the highest international levels of excellence.

www.cambridge.org
Information on this title: www.cambridge.org/9781108552363

© Cambridge University Press 2012, 2015, 2019

This publication is copyright. Subject to statutory exception and to the provisions of relevant collective licensing agreements, no reproduction of any part may take place without the written permission of Cambridge University Press.

First published 2012
Second edition 2015
Third edition 2019

Cover designed by Cate Furey
Typeset by Integra Software Services Pvt. Ltd
Printed in China by C & C Offset Printing Co. Ltd, May 2019

A catalogue record for this publication is available from the British Library

A catalogue record for this book is available from the National Library of Australia

ISBN 978-1-108-55236-3 Paperback

Additional resources for this publication at www.cambridge.edu.au/academic/teachingarts

Reproduction and communication for educational purposes
The Australian *Copyright Act 1968* (the Act) allows a maximum of one chapter or 10% of the pages of this work, whichever is the greater, to be reproduced and/or communicated by any educational institution for its educational purposes provided that the educational institution (or the body that administers it) has given a remuneration notice to Copyright Agency Limited (CAL) under the Act.

For details of the CAL licence for educational institutions contact:

Copyright Agency Limited
Level 12, 66 Goulburn Street
Sydney NSW 2000
Telephone: (02) 9394 7600
Facsimile: (02) 9394 7601
E-mail: memberservices@copyright.com.au

Cambridge University Press has no responsibility for the persistence or accuracy of URLs for external or third-party internet websites referred to in this publication and does not guarantee that any content on such websites is, or will remain, accurate or appropriate.

Please be aware that this publication may contain several variations of Aboriginal and Torres Strait Islander terms and spellings; no disrespect is intended. Please note that the terms 'Indigenous Australians' and 'Aboriginal and Torres Strait Islander peoples' may be used interchangeably in this publication.

For
Fraser,
Janine
&
Ben

Contents

PREFACE	xi
ACKNOWLEDGEMENTS	xiii
USING YOUR VITALSOURCE EBOOK	xiv
Introduction	1

PART 1 WHY: THE ARTS IN EDUCATION AND SOCIETY — 4

Chapter 1 A vision for the Arts in education — 6

Introduction	7
What are the Arts and what do they 'do'?	11
Access and equity in Arts education	14
Learner agency and cultural diversity in Arts education	17
Sustained, sequential and 'quality' Arts education	19
A 'praxial' vision for the Arts in education	22
Your role: the Arts in early childhood and primary education	23
Conclusion	27
Review questions	28
Recommended reading	28

Chapter 2 Why the Arts are fundamental — 30

Introduction	31
Arts education in 21st-century lives	34
What we know about Arts education, its value and effects	37
Learning 'in' and 'through' the Arts and your role as an educator	54
Conclusion	58
Review questions	59
Recommended reading	59

Chapter 3 The Arts and cross-curriculum priorities — 60

Introduction	61
The meaning of cross-curriculum priorities	62
Aboriginal and Torres Strait Islander histories and cultures	63
Asia and Australia's engagement with Asia	74
The Arts and sustainability	81
Conclusion	89
Review questions	89
Recommended reading	90

PART 2   WHAT: THE ARTS LEARNING AREAS   92

Chapter 4   Learning in dance   94

Introduction   95
Engaging with dance in education   96
The elements and principles of dance education   98
Dance in early childhood settings   99
Dance in primary education   103
Making and responding in dance   107
The context of dance in the Arts and in education   115
Conclusion   118
Review questions   119
Recommended reading   119

Chapter 5   Learning in drama   120

Introduction   121
What is drama?   121
Engaging with drama in education   124
Drama in early childhood and primary settings   126
The elements of drama   130
Making and responding in drama   142
Theatre arts   149
The context of drama in the Arts and in education   151
Conclusion   153
Review questions   153
Recommended reading   153

Chapter 6   Learning in media arts   155

Introduction   156
Engaging with media arts in education   156
The elements and principles of media in education   159
Media arts in early childhood settings   165
Media arts in primary settings   169
Media texts   173
Making and responding in media arts   176
The context of media in the Arts and in education   181
Conclusion   182
Review questions   183
Recommended reading   183

Chapter 7   Learning in music   184

Introduction   185
Engaging with music in education   188

The elements and principles of music in education	190
Music in early childhood settings	194
Music in primary settings	197
Making and responding in music	201
The context of music in the Arts and in education	212
Conclusion	214
Review questions	214
Recommended reading	214

Chapter 8 Learning in visual arts — 216

Introduction	217
Engaging with visual arts in education	217
Elements and principles of visual arts in education	218
Visual arts in early childhood settings	223
Visual arts in primary settings	224
Visual arts practices	226
Making and responding in visual arts	239
The context of visual arts in the Arts and in education	244
Conclusion	248
Review questions	248
Recommended reading	248

PART 3 HOW: EMBEDDING THE ARTS IN EDUCATION — 250

Chapter 9 Integration and general capabilities — 252

Introduction	253
Programming the Arts curriculum	253
The elements and principles of general capabilities	255
Integration of the Arts with other Learning Areas	261
Curriculum integration	264
Conclusion	273
Review questions	274
Recommended reading	274

Chapter 10 Organisation — 275

Introduction	276
Planning for learning and teaching in the Arts	276
Approaches to learning and teaching in the Arts	282
Assessment in learning and teaching in the Arts	288
Organisation for Arts learning in early childhood settings	298
Organisation for Arts learning in primary settings	300
Conclusion	304
Review questions	305
Recommended reading	305

Chapter 11 Diverse learners, pedagogy and the Arts — 306

- Introduction — 307
- Reflective teaching — 307
- Recent history of curriculum ideologies — 309
- Implementing reflective practices — 311
- Observation — 312
- Understanding quality teaching and reflective learning — 313
- Equity in the classroom and diverse learners — 318
- How to T.E.A.C.H. — 329
- Other pedagogical approaches — 331
- Conclusion — 332
- Review questions — 333
- Recommended reading — 333

Chapter 12 Quality Arts education and rich learning — 334

- Introduction — 335
- Characteristics of quality Arts education — 336
- Arts-rich learning — 343
- Partnerships and the contributions of colleagues, parents and the community — 345
- Arts-rich learning contexts for early childhood and primary — 348
- Arts-rich teaching — 351
- Conclusion — 354
- Review questions — 354
- Recommended reading — 355

REFERENCES — 356
INDEX — 371

Preface

In the 21st century, the educational landscape is changing quickly. With changing global economic priorities, population shifts and demographics, education is once again being recognised as a leading agent of change. The Arts, more so than ever before, are needed for creative solutions, shared communication and social and personal development. STEM may well develop technologies, but it is the Creative Arts that will discover them first.

Too often, the Arts have been marginalised, or perceived to be elite. This third edition is significantly updated to further empower all teachers and Initial Teacher Education (ITE) students to not only have knowledge of teaching the Arts, but security and confidence in doing so successfully, to allow their students to be successful, ongoing learners. At the time of writing this third edition there is a call to educate more Mathematics and Science teachers for secondary schools from the highest education official in Australia. There is a quote misattributed to Albert Einstein that states the definition of insanity is doing the same thing over and over expecting a different outcome. Yet this is where many Western education systems are at the moment. Rather than attempting bold moves to enable imaginative and creative solutions to seemingly intractable problems they merely seek to give us more of the same.

How very sad.

Australia has developed the Australian Curriculum, with individual State and Territory implementation and adaptation. This edition takes that into account and additionally recognises the core Arts practices that apply internationally as well, allowing teachers across multiple international jurisdictions to use this text to support their classroom practice.

In this third edition we have undertaken to unify the chapter sections, with a multitude of practical supports and resources, both within the text and online. *Teaching the Arts* draws important links to the Australian Curriculum and the Early Years Learning Framework while including substantial references to Indigenous histories and cultures, relationships with Asia, and sustainability. New to the text is a widened focus on diversity and inclusion for all students.

Generously illustrated and featuring excellent online resources, *Teaching the Arts* is an indispensable resource for pre-service teachers.

The third edition also features enhanced and updated content:
- significant extension to each chapter particularly on the five art forms of dance, drama, media, music and visual arts
- additional practical activities
- additional current research and theory
- additional curriculum information linked to the Australian Curriculum: The Arts, while still maintaining the depth of content for the Early Years Learning Framework and individual State curricula
- additional online resources, including lecture PowerPoints for academics.

We would particularly like to recognise the students and academics who have engaged with and supported this text. Without their support, usage and helpful feedback the text would not have been so successful and widely used. Indeed, it is because of the positive feedback and requests for additional content that we have been able to create this third edition. We aim to even further support the needs of teachers in training across Australia and elsewhere, as well as our academic colleagues.

There is a growing recognition that for our children to be successful in society we need to have innovative and creative thinkers who see education as an opportunity to explore possibilities rather than confirm probabilities. It is our sincere hope that this greatly expanded third edition will support us all in recognising and implementing the Arts and their importance in education. Water is the giver of life. We need STEAM in academia and education, not just a STEM that will never grow.

David, Bill and Amy

Acknowledgements

The authors would like to thank the following:

All our families and friends for their support and advice. Michael Spurr, Georgina Lowe, Vilija Stephens and the editorial staff at Cambridge University Press. The staff and pupils of Eleebana Public School, the Universities of Newcastle, Tasmania, and Flinders, Caroline Dock, Gracie, Hannah and Liam for their work. Visual artist Angelina Parfitt for allowing us to publish her painting *Big Mob together to learn* and visual artist Rebecca Hastings for allowing us to publish her painting *Smell This*. Thank you to Theresa Sainty, Dr Sarah Jane Moore and Dyan and Ronnie Summers. Finally, may we thank the reviewers and colleagues from many universities who have offered valuable, constructive criticism.

We are grateful to the following individuals and organisations for permission to use their material in *Teaching the Arts*.

Page 7: © Getty Images/G. Mazzarini; **9**: © Getty Images/Kelly Sillaste; **15, 34**: Pixabay.com; **19**: © Getty Images/Portra; **21**: © Getty Images/Adam Taylor; **24, 27, 39, 47, 156, 173, 177, 201, 281**: © Getty Images/Hero Images; **32**: © Getty Images/Steve Debenport; **41**: © Getty Images/KidStock; **55**: © Getty Images/Jonathan Gelber; **58**: © Getty Images/Westend61; **76**: © Getty Images/Ernesto r. Ageitos; **77**: © Getty Images/SuradechK; **82**: © Getty Images/SeppFriedhuber; **83**: © Getty Images/Wavebreakmedia; **88**: © Getty Images/Jeff Greenberg; **95, 253, 262, 264, 265, 268, 271, 273, 307, 312, 315, 317, 319, 321, 323 (top), 325, 330, Figures 4.2, 5.1–5.13**: David Roy; **100**: © Getty Images/Highwaystarz-Photography; **112**: © Getty Images/JackF; **116**: © Getty Images/photobac; **159**: © Getty Images/Flashpop; **180**: © Getty images/Vstock LLC; **185**: © Getty Images/Yaorusheng; **187**: © Getty Images/Tara Moore; **196**: © Getty Images/Manabu Jike/EyeEm; **210**: © Getty Images/Marius Faust/EyeEm; **217**: © Getty Images/waldru; **222**: © Getty Images/Richard Bailey/SPL; **226**: © Getty Images/DenKuvaiev; **233**: © Getty Images/Carol Yepes; **235**: © Getty Images/Bonfanti Diego; **241**: © Getty Images/Fuse; **298**: © Getty Images/Jasmin Merdan; **323** (bottom): Wikimedia Commons; **324**: © Getty Images/Chalabala; **328**: © Getty Images/gbrundin; **332**: © Getty Images/lostinbids; **335**: © Getty Images/Jupiterimages; **338**: © Getty Images/Jose Luis Pelaez Inc; **340**: © Getty Images/Artur Debat; **345**: © Getty Images/adamkaz; **349**: © Getty Images/Bjarte Rettedal; **354**: © Getty Images/JohnnyGreig.Figure 3.1**: © The State of Queensland 2018. The Queensland Government supports and encourages the distribution of its material. Unless otherwise noted, all copyright material available on or through this website is licensed under a Creative Commons Attribution 4.0 International licence (CC BY 4.0); **Figure 3.4**: Reproduced with permission of Angelina Parfitt; **3.6**: © Getty Images/Rosa Furtado; **4.1**: © Getty Images/K-King Photography Media Co. Ltd; **4.3**: © Getty Images/Darcy Spowart; **6.1–6.3, 8.1–8.8**: Amy Hamilton; **7.1**: Photographer: Daniela-Maria Brandt. Orff-Zentrum Munchen; **7.2**: Courtesy of Photographie Institut Jacques-Dalcroze, Geneve; **7.3**: Reproduced with permission from the Canada Council for the Arts; **8.9**: Reproduced with permission of Rebecca Hastings.

Every effort has been made to trace and acknowledge copyright. The publisher apologises for any accidental infringement and welcomes information that would redress this situation.

Using your VitalSource eBook

Once you have registered your VitalSource access code (see the inside front cover for instructions), you will have access to the interactive eBook via your VitalSource Bookshelf. The below navigation instructions provide a general overview of the main features used within the interactive eBook.

Icons This icon is used throughout the textbook to indicate the presence of an interactive component in the eBook. A descriptor below indicates the type of content available.

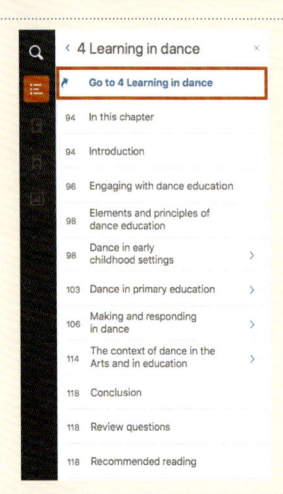

← Navigation and search

Move between pages and sections in multiple ways, including via the linked table of contents and the search tool.

Highlight →

Highlight text in your choice of colours with one click. Add notes to highlighted passages.

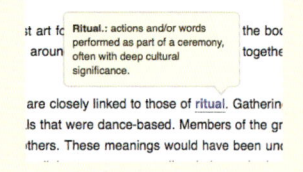

← Key terms

Click on bold terms to display pop-up definitions of key concepts.

Questions and activities →

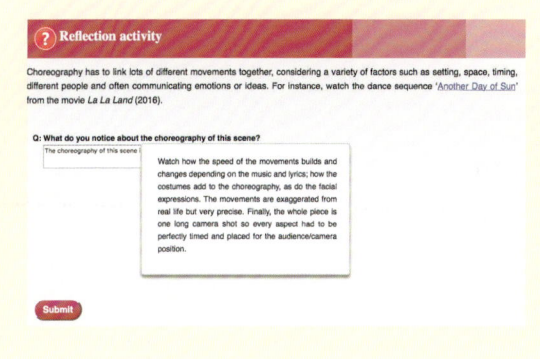

Spotlight on Arts education boxes explore theory to practice through looking at artists or aspects of arts history, while **In the classroom** boxes provide suggestions for activities that can be used in the classroom. **Reflection activity** boxes enable students to contemplate arts teaching and learning, and **Teacher tip** boxes offer practical, experience-based hints for pre-service teachers

Read the question and type your answer in the box. Submit your answers to view the guided solutions and assess your results. Note that the solution pop-ups can be moved about the page.

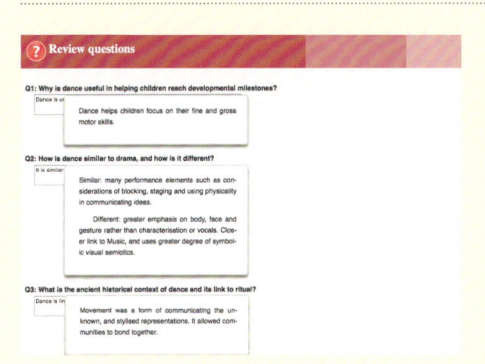

← Review questions

At the end of the chapter, respond to the review questions and use the prompts to assess your responses. Note that the solution pop-ups can be moved about the page.

Videos and links →

View relevant video and online content to extend your knowledge on the topics presented in the book. Click the icon, which links to the video or website.

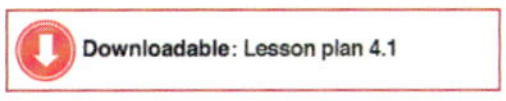

← Downloadable lesson plans and additional resources

Throughout the book there are over 30 lesson plans featuring aims, overviews, intended outcomes and links to the curriculum that can be conveniently downloaded as Word documents.

Using your VitalSource eBook   XV

Introduction

Wherever we are in society, we are surrounded by the Arts. This text has been designed by artists, and the words you read are but visual artworks representing the oral storytelling foundation of all societies. Its layout was designed by artists, using multiple media forms. You are reading it in an environment where the soundscape will hopefully allow you to concentrate. Your body is probably positioned to minimise discomfort and maximise efficiency, while communicating to all those around you your current state of thought (whether consciously or not). Surrounding you may be posters, objects, noises, people interacting with facial expressions, probably some communicating via Facebook, Instagram or other social media using increasingly advanced technologies. The Arts power our lives, yet too often we power down children as they enter formal education (preschool and upwards), stifle their natural forms of communication and interaction, and slowly destroy their ability to be creative and to think diversely.

This text aims to demonstrate the power of each of the five Art forms in the Australian Curriculum as a discrete source of knowledge and also as a pedagogical tool to access other Learning Areas. *Teaching the Arts: Early childhood and primary education* is a book born out of the requests of children and teachers. As authors and educators of Initial Teacher Education students and also as consultants in schools, we were continually met by colleagues and children who were frustrated by the fact that, while there were excellent texts out there, none seemed to fit their requirements. This text aims to meet that need. This is not the ultimate answer to how to teach the Arts; it represents just one of many ways. There is, however, a dichotomy in its title. By its very definition, the title condones and possibly promotes the idea that the Arts are separate from other forms of knowledge and, indeed, from society. However, one of the key threads running through the text is that the Arts are embedded in life and in all aspects of education.

Imagine (a key process for the Arts) a newborn child. Newborn children gaze at all the new faces that surround them. They observe and mimic facial expressions (drama); they listen to the sounds around them – their pitch, tone colour and rhythm – and develop their language skills (music). They engage with shapes and designs and explore the world through their eyes and through creating new shapes with objects (visual arts). They try to sit – and fall; they learn control of their arm movements, their bodies and their balance with fine and gross motor skills (dance). Before long they are playing on smartphones, tablets, computers and televisions (media). Babies learn through the Arts and with the Arts. Often, through our focus on isolated formal learning and, let's be honest, our own feelings of inability, we slowly come to ignore the value of the various art forms as educational tools, even though they are the very forms of learning that everyone initially engages with.

From our earliest beginnings, we humans have used the Arts to understand and explore our world, both physical and spiritual, for the Arts create meaning within us.

This is done all around the world. Let us consider the mask – an aesthetic artefact and a performance device. There are few, if any, societies in the world where we do not find references to, or images of, masks. Sometimes we are even given clues, recorded for example in ancient rock carvings and paintings, as to how they might have been used. These clues tell us that masks have been with us from prehistoric times through to the current era (Edson, 2005). There is no definitive time when they were first introduced; however, their purpose is and has always been to transport and transform the user and the observer (Foreman, 2000). Masks have an audience, whether in entertainment or in ritual. The difference between these two functions can cross boundaries. Ritual is fascinating for the individuals who participate in it, as they are actively engaged in it while still being able to glorify and observe the spectacle around them (Campbell, 1969).

Masks, like the Arts themselves, challenge the identity of the individual. This fact is clear in the definition of the Arabic word *maskhahra* (to falsify or transform) and of the English word *mask* (to conceal). The human mind focuses clearly on the face of the individual and thus, through the concealment of this core identifier, the mask allows the individual to be separated from their identity and their movements to be interpreted as separate from the individual. Shamans were able to use this function of masks to allow them to represent and embody the spirit world, as is represented in the Mesolithic rock art at Trois Frères, France or at Aunanrat, Tassili in Algeria (Lévi-Strauss, 1982).

Throughout history the mask has allowed a freedom and licence for individuals to adopt personae and roles other than their own. In medieval masquerades, the individual was relieved of responsibility and the moral certitude of the times and was able to revel in their society's perceptions of immorality without fear of retribution.

All the Arts have this power to surprise. How can we separate the Arts from each other, let alone divide them into separate Learning Areas? In a world where there are developing crises concerning the environment, energy, human resources and basic foods, and fundamental political polarisations regarding these, even in established societies, can we ignore the Arts and the creativity they cultivate? Someone has to find new ways to create sustainable resource applications; ways to engage our society and bridge the equity gaps in all areas. This won't happen unless the next generation embraces creative ways of thinking. As a human race we can't survive without the Arts; therefore, we must be confident in passing on their power to the next generation. Indeed, as drama is often about the transformation of the individual into the 'other' to explore aspects of the human condition, there can be no question that the role transformation plays in the lives of all schoolchildren needs to be identified and explored. Eisner, for one (Eisner, 1998), uses the Arts in education as a focus for this.

When coupled with the idea of the Arts as a social, anthropological or ethnographic study, the possible value in delivering them to children is apparent. The use of the Arts within the classroom gives children the freedom to explore and establish their identities in their childhood years, thus fulfilling the purposes of schooling on multiple levels. This both meets curricular needs and addresses the wider 'hidden curriculum' of creating individuals with skills to embrace society.

This text is divided into three distinct areas of educational development: why the Arts (the purpose and the past); the Arts Learning Areas (the knowledge, the skills and the present); and embedding the Arts (the application and the future). In each chapter, we have tried to model good teaching practice by offering a knowledge download, practical activities, opportunities to demonstrate understanding, methodologies of application and significance and purpose as to why. For educators and their students it is a win–win situation. For early childhood and primary educators, the issue is not so much about when we should engage with the Arts, but more when we should not.

We hope you enjoy reading and applying the ideas and concepts in this text as much as we do, and aim to continue doing so, for many years to come. If we do not teach the Arts across the curriculum, we deny children the most basic abilities to communicate, explore and share. If we teach them the Arts, we empower them and, as a bonus, introduce them to a great source of joy and pleasure.

PART 1

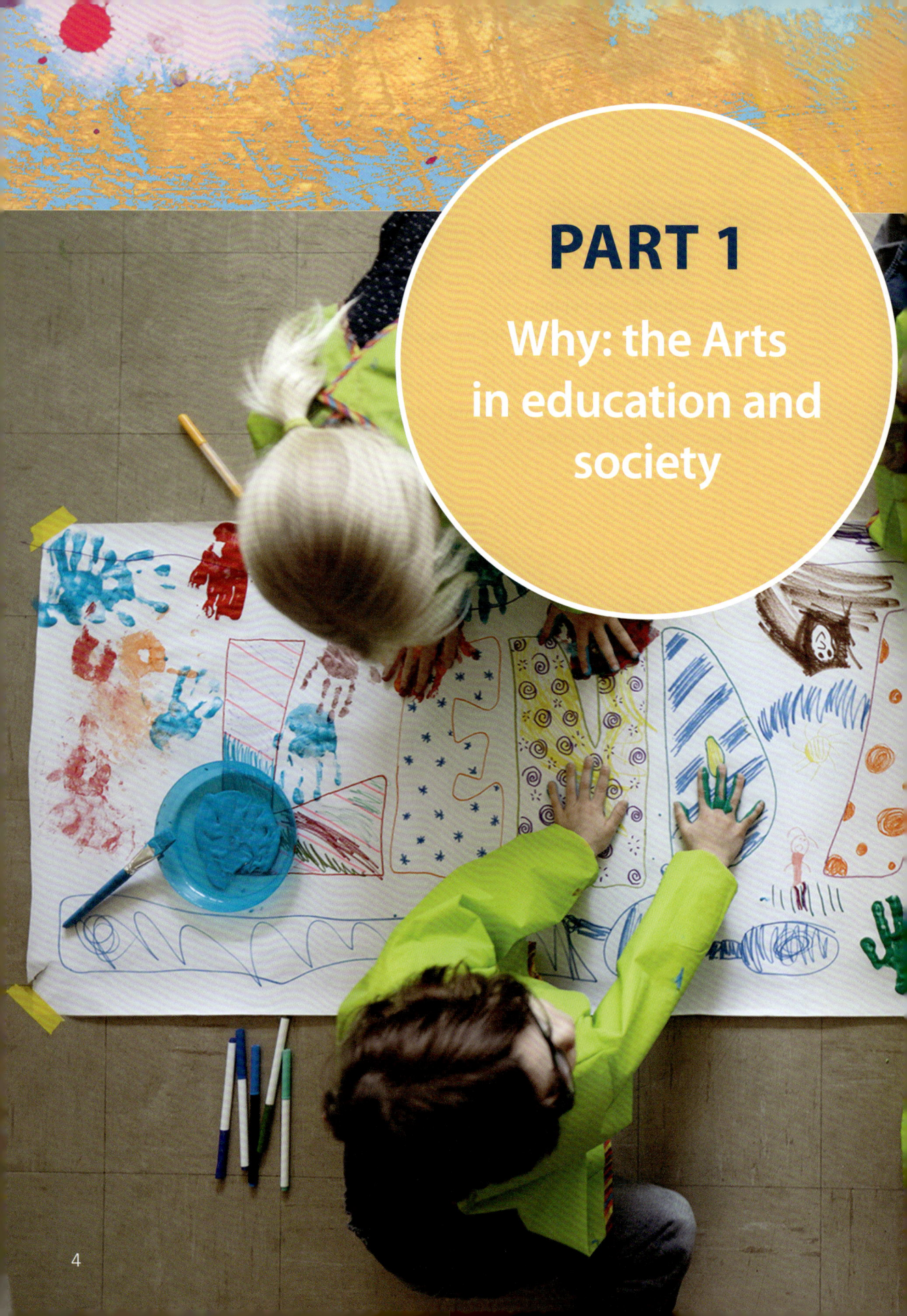

Why: the Arts in education and society

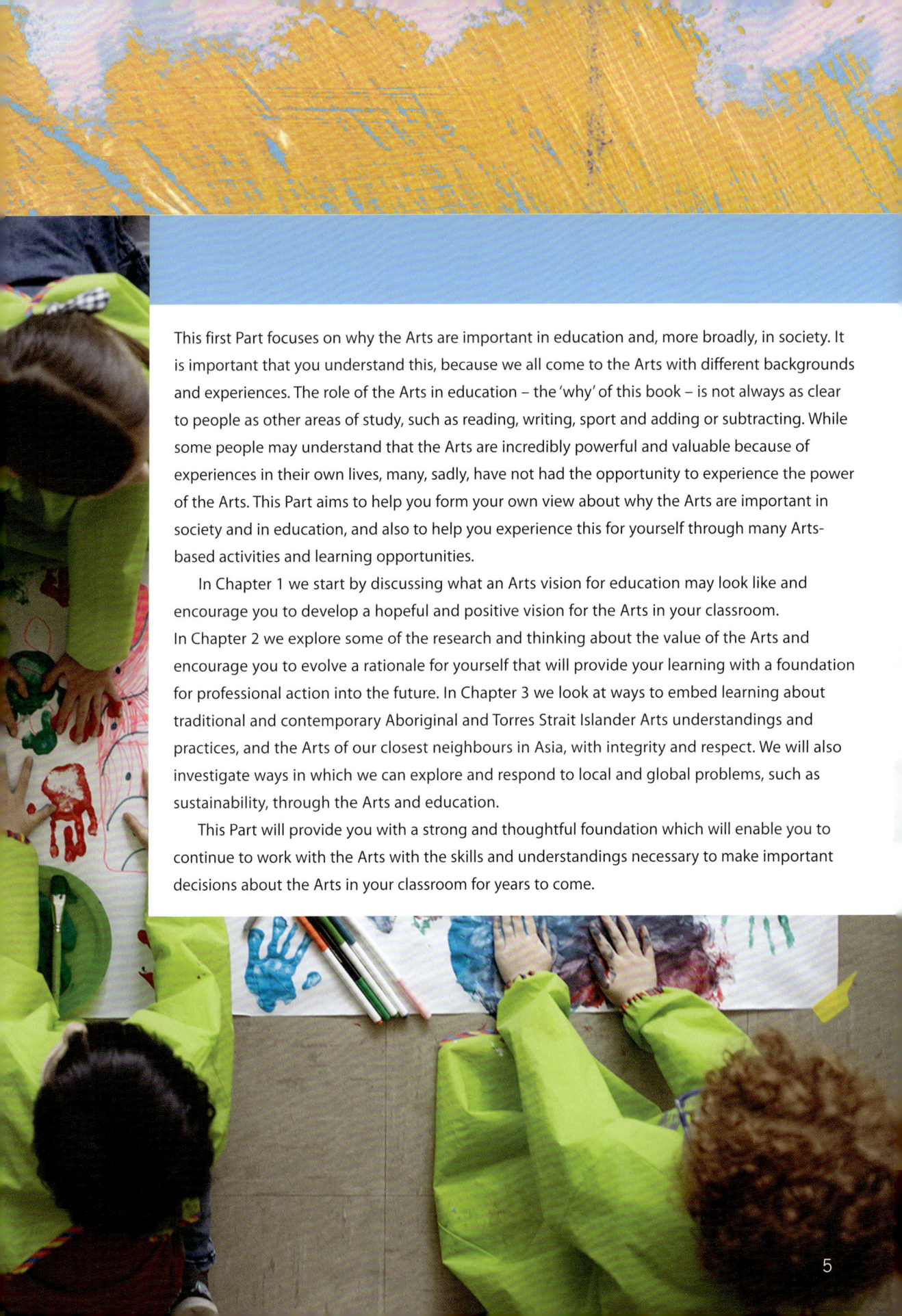

This first Part focuses on why the Arts are important in education and, more broadly, in society. It is important that you understand this, because we all come to the Arts with different backgrounds and experiences. The role of the Arts in education – the 'why' of this book – is not always as clear to people as other areas of study, such as reading, writing, sport and adding or subtracting. While some people may understand that the Arts are incredibly powerful and valuable because of experiences in their own lives, many, sadly, have not had the opportunity to experience the power of the Arts. This Part aims to help you form your own view about why the Arts are important in society and in education, and also to help you experience this for yourself through many Arts-based activities and learning opportunities.

In Chapter 1 we start by discussing what an Arts vision for education may look like and encourage you to develop a hopeful and positive vision for the Arts in your classroom.
In Chapter 2 we explore some of the research and thinking about the value of the Arts and encourage you to evolve a rationale for yourself that will provide your learning with a foundation for professional action into the future. In Chapter 3 we look at ways to embed learning about traditional and contemporary Aboriginal and Torres Strait Islander Arts understandings and practices, and the Arts of our closest neighbours in Asia, with integrity and respect. We will also investigate ways in which we can explore and respond to local and global problems, such as sustainability, through the Arts and education.

This Part will provide you with a strong and thoughtful foundation which will enable you to continue to work with the Arts with the skills and understandings necessary to make important decisions about the Arts in your classroom for years to come.

A vision for the Arts in education

> We have a clear choice, we can choose to passively accept the education system we have been 'gifted' or we can choose to change it to meet the needs of young people facing the challenges of an uncertain world.

From *Transforming Schools: Creativity, critical reflection, communication, collaboration* by Miranda Jefferson and Michael Anderson

In this chapter

In this chapter we will explore the unique nature of the Arts along with what the Arts 'do' for people. The differences between Arts education policy and its actual provision will be presented with particular reference to the need for broad access to, and equity in, Arts education in primary and early childhood settings. The importance of an approach to Arts education that encourages and embeds learner agency and cultural diversity is discussed, and the benefits of sustained 'quality' Arts education are presented. Your role in the provision of the Arts in early childhood and primary education is discussed and a 'praxial' vision for the Arts in education is presented.

By the end of this chapter you should have a clear understanding of:

- what the Arts are and what they 'do'
- the need for access and equity in Arts education and the 'gap' between policy and provision
- learner agency and cultural diversity in Arts education
- sustained, sequential and 'quality' Arts education
- a 'praxial' vision for the Arts in education
- your role as an educator in Arts education.

Introduction

> Remember when you were a child? Remember what it felt like to 'squish' paint around a piece of paper? What it felt like to dance and sing along to your favourite TV characters, whether they were bears, birds or dinosaurs? Remember what it felt like to make something new out of playdough, or to wonder what playdough might 'taste' like? Remember what it felt like to be totally 'wrapped up' in the moment of painting a picture or of 'being' a pirate? (Baker, 2012)

Those sensational experiences did not feel like 'learning' to you at that moment, did they? As adults we so often forget what those experiences felt like, and can continue to feel like. As John Lennon said, 'Every child is an artist until he's told he's not an artist' (Fawcett, 1976, p. 55). Those sensations were central to exploring your world, expressing yourself, sharing your expressions with others and just having great fun. These are some of the things that the Arts 'do' for us.

We believe that the Arts are everywhere. Everyone has artistic potential, and we all have a right to explore our individual identities and cultures through the Arts (Bamford, 2006; UNESCO, 2006). For millennia the Arts have been a part of what it means to be human, to express and communicate our individual and shared perceptions of our world, what it is like to live in a particular culture and what it is like to express personal and shared emotions (Robinson, 1999). The United Nations Educational, Scientific and Cultural Organization (UNESCO) considers Arts education to be a 'universal human right' for *all* children (2006) and highlights the importance of Arts education in cultivating creative potential and cognitive development.

As a central part of human existence, the Arts are a natural part of children's worlds, and children enjoy and value them in their daily lives (Barrett & Smigiel, 2003). Quality Arts education enables children to learn valuable Arts skills and understandings (Hunter, 2005; McCarthy et al., 2004) in addition to cultivating many of the important dispositions that are of value in life and in other areas of learning (Bryce et al., 2004; Deasy, 2002; Ewing, 2010). The Arts have a unique capacity to help all children to reach their creative potential and to engage in genuine, lifelong learning. These observations about the fundamental role of the Arts in education will be explored in much greater detail in Chapter 2, but it is also important for you to be aware of them as you read this chapter.

Embodied learning: holistic, cognate, kinaesthetic learning that occurs when using our whole bodies to fully express ourselves. Mind and body work in unison in the moment.

The Arts are central to the education of children because they occur through our senses, rather than linguistically or mathematically; or, as O'Toole (2012, p. 7) writes, 'We make sense through our senses, and thus we give meaning to our reality'. Learning through all of our senses and with our whole body is generally referred to as **embodied learning**. Jefferson and Anderson (2017, p. 109) write that 'Cognition is embodied when the physical body plays a significant and causal role in cognitive processing'.

TEACHER TIP

Watch the video 'It's Time to Invest in Embodied Learning' by Tommaso Lana on YouTube. What are people learning and how are they learning in this video?

Teacher tip

The central premise of this book is that children must first think and act through their senses *as* artists in order for them to value and engage meaningfully with the Arts as a central part of their daily lives. Our vision for Arts education, based on this premise, is that early childhood and primary settings provide children with a rich education in the Arts that gives them genuine agency (discussed later in this chapter); that includes each of the five art forms of dance, drama, media arts, music and visual arts; that is culturally situated (discussed later in this chapter); and that is sustained over time.

In the classroom

When you are next working with children, take notice. Notice how much of their learning is 'embodied' during any given day. Notice what sort of learning is embodied and how. When you next teach children plan to give them an opportunity to embody their learning in some way.

As digital technologies rapidly develop, the concept of 'audience' has begun to change and Arts content, such as music, paintings and movies, have become increasingly portable and flexible, providing new ways to access the Arts for more people, in lots of different locations (Biasutti, 2017; Cayari, 2011; Cremata & Powell, 2017; Webb, 2007). At the same time, artists are employing new technologies that invite audiences to become actively involved in responding to or even creating Arts, forcing them to move beyond passive consumption of an artistic 'product'. Artist and audience are key terms used throughout the Australian Curriculum: The Arts. Children therefore need skills and understandings *as* artists and *as* audiences to prepare them to be able to navigate Arts practices, content and forms in the 21st century. We ask you to reflect on and consider, throughout this book, how you can achieve this critical outcome, for the children in your care, through your beliefs and practices as a teacher.

Reflection activity

She lies in bed in her room filled with pink Swedish-designed furniture, which is child-sized and covered in images of music, flowers and fluffy animals. The clock radio alarm clicks on and she opens her eyes and smiles as she recognises her favourite song and singer. Her mum is downstairs practising Zumba; her dad is already on his laptop sending emails. The wardrobe is full of logo-stamped kids' gear, but she selects her eco-friendly school uniform.

She switches on the TV, flicking through the channels of children's shows, sitcoms, cartoons and movies as she listens to music on her tablet through her earphones. Her favourite song comes on again and she jumps up to dance along with the images on the screen. Soon she joins her parents,

Reflection activity
Video: Tate Britain Art Gallery

who are perched on handcrafted bar stools in the kitchen, chatting via Skype to Grandma in Scotland. With the digital screen in the corner of the kitchen announcing the top news stories of the day, she selects from the different, bright, gift-promising boxes of cereal, and eats from her theme-designed dish. Her lunch is packed into her popstar lunchbox, cleverly matching her brightly decorated schoolbag and shoes. Popping her tablet in, she heads for the car … all this before leaving the house. The Arts are everywhere.

We have all had different experiences with the Arts in our lives. Some of us have had full, rich and rewarding encounters with them; but sadly, some have had little experience of them at all. However, we have all had some contact with the Arts. The Arts are a part of our individual worlds regardless of our formal experiences of them.

Bearing in mind the widespread nature of the Arts in society, as described above, reflect on the role the Arts have played in your life and play in your life today. Share your reflections with a colleague. It is important for you to know that this is not a judgmental process; rather it is about you reflecting on the Arts in your life and what that means for you today as you start reading this book.

What role have the Arts played in your life?

Creativity, critical reflection, communication and collaboration

The 4Cs (creativity, critical reflection, communication and collaboration) were developed by the Partnership for 21st Century Skills (now the Partnership for 21st Century Learning) around the turn of the century. This organisation, based in Washington DC in the United States, brings together business, education and government leaders with the aim of ensuring students have the skills necessary for life in the 21st century. The 4Cs are part of an overall strategy or framework for 21st-century learning called P21. The 4Cs offer a way of viewing or thinking about learning and teaching that has the potential to challenge and alter entrenched structures and attitudes about education.

Recently the Grattan Institute released a discussion paper entitled *Towards an adaptive education system in Australia* (Goss, 2017). This paper stated that:

> Our current education system is not fit for purpose given the complex challenges it faces. These challenges show up in flat or declining performance in national and international tests; in the unacceptable number of students who are not ready for life after school; and in the persistent equity gaps among our schools, despite increased needs-based funding (p. 3).

Jefferson and Anderson (2017, p.10) likewise note that:

> The testing and reporting regimes imposed on schools by governments in western economies such as Australia and the United Kingdom have created a market-driven schooling system that is much more about training for rapidly disappearing types of work than it is about imagined futures.

This is not a new discovery by any means; our education system continually struggles to be a place of inspiration, flexibility and creativity. Jefferson and Anderson (2017) propose that part of the transformation of schools in Australia should be prioritisation of the 4Cs: creativity, critical reflection, communication and collaboration, all of which are resident in the Arts (although not exclusively of course).

Creativity: Creativity as a term is often overused and misused. According to the National Advisory Committee on Creative and Cultural Education (1999) creativity is a capacity that everyone has, is something that can be learned and features above all the production of something original for the maker. For Jefferson and Anderson (2017) creativity involves 'Noticing … Asking why? Really why? … Playing with possibility … and then Selecting and evaluating' (p. 83). The Arts do these things intrinsically.

Critical reflection: In this book we feature critical reflection as a characteristic of quality Arts education. It is an essential characteristic that can enable educators to grow and develop over time. Jefferson and Anderson (2017) state that critical reflection 'is for all voices to question, elaborate and explain ideas. It is to develop thinking processes beyond asking "what?" to asking "why, how, what if and when?"' (p. 34). The Arts do this intrinsically.

Communication: The Arts are vehicles for communication of our inner worlds; however, communication 'encompasses all forms of human expression' (Jefferson & Anderson, 2017, p. 107). Communication happens in many different ways or modes, and reflects our identities. Jefferson and Anderson maintain that communication evolves through being 'alert to messaging' (p. 117), enabling everyone to have a 'voice' (p. 120), 'conveying meaning and purpose' (p. 122) or shared understanding, and 'generating action and agency' (p. 124) or the positive outcomes of communication. The Arts *are* means of communication.

Collaboration: Jefferson and Anderson (2017) state that collaboration suggests 'an intense synergy of ideas, goals, trust and relationships between people'. They also ask the question that if collaboration is such an important part of human development then why is it not a feature of school education? The Arts are forms of collaboration.

Imagine now a school where the 4Cs infused and surrounded all learning and teaching. In which creativity was the dominant feature of learning. In which collaboration produced amazing outcomes across domains of learning!

What are the Arts and what do they 'do'?

Spotlight on Arts education

Watch the video 'Student Voices: Becoming Engaged through the Arts', by CAPE videos on YouTube.

Next time you are working with children remember these voices and plan to include the Arts in your classroom every day.

What do these students tell us about the way the Arts have changed their lives?

The Arts are culturally determined

The Arts are a part of the educational curricula of almost every country in the world, yet they are defined differently according to the culture in which they are created; indeed, the Arts are culture and context specific, and their meaning varies from country to country (Bamford, 2006). The Arts are fundamentally means of expression and communication and by their nature they are also intensely personal. In some cultures, literature and poetry are strongly associated with the Arts, yet in others they are not; in some cultures, the Arts include the creation of utilitarian objects, such as baskets or pots, whereas in others these activities may be defined as 'crafts'. The 'Arts' cannot be neatly tied up in a box with a bow and a label; they are culturally determined, personally and communally constructed, and open to a multitude of interpretations and meanings.

In the classroom

Ask students to talk to their parents or grandparents about what they think the Arts are. Students can ask their parents or grandparents to share an example of the Arts from their home; they could ask them if the object selected has a 'story' behind it. Students can then bring these items to class and talk about what their parents or grandparents said about the object they selected.

Because Australia is such a multicultural society, including Aboriginal and Torres Strait Islander peoples and generations of immigrants from all over the world, this should produce a diversity of Arts objects and ideas for discussion. Likewise, the 'meaning' embodied in the selected objects should elucidate children's cultural backgrounds. It is really important that this activity is inclusive not exclusive. So, children should be made aware that the Arts are everywhere and can include anything from furniture or posters to instruments and music or photos.

The Arts and aesthetics

Aesthetics: 'critical reflection on art, culture and nature' (Kelly, 1998, p. ix). Judgments of aesthetic value rely on our ability to discriminate at a sensory and intellectual level. The word comes from the Greek *aisthetikos*, meaning 'of sense perception'.

Viewing, talking about, writing about and investigating the Arts involves 'aesthetic' appreciation. The traditional focus of **aesthetics** is the experience of beauty, but the contemporary view of beauty is not based on innate qualities but rather on ideas that are specific and unique to particular cultures and individual interpretations; for example, in New Mexico non-Native American collectors of silver value signs of age ('patina' or 'tarnish'), but Native Americans generally keep even heirloom pieces highly polished (Smith et al., 1993). Aesthetics offers one way of understanding and engaging with music. Reimer (1989) asserts that the value of the artistic experience is to be found in making what is essentially subjective (our inner world), tangible through art. Music is an expression of an inner world. He reflects that:

Aesthetics is the study of that about art which is the essence of art and that about people which has throughout history caused them to need art as an essential part of their lives. So among all the disciplines of thought that are interested in the arts, aesthetics is the one devoted to an explanation of their intrinsic nature (p. 2).

The Arts in curriculum

As mentioned earlier, Arts education is context specific (Bamford, 2006). In Australia the Arts Learning Areas consist of dance, drama, media arts, music and visual arts (ACARA, 2017). Each art form is a different means of expression and communication, each with distinct 'language' and processes. By 'language' we do not mean to imply that an art form can communicate specific linguistic meanings, such as 'The sky is beautiful'; this is what our different spoken and written languages such as English or Mandarin do. Rather, we mean that each art form communicates meaning in different ways; for example, music communicates through sound and silence and visual arts communicate through spatial, symbolic and visual means.

TEACHER TIP

Watch the video 'A World Without Art – Spoken Word' by PHOCO on YouTube. Imagine ways in which you can integrate the Arts into your next teaching experience.

Video: A world without art

- What art forms do you remember from the past that had an impact on you?
- Why do you remember it?
- How did it influence you?
- Where do you enjoy different types of Art (such as music or media or acting or images)?

The Arts as 'language'

Take the sentence, 'The sky is beautiful.' Communicating this through visual means might include a visual representation of a sky rich in deep layers of colour that exudes a sense of beauty. Or, through the elements of music a composer may attempt to communicate a sense of natural beauty and calm. It is important to note here that the Arts are not some form of inferior linguistic communication, but rather that they have different objectives. They enable expression and communication in different ways and in so doing can alert the audience to those aspects of an object, person, place or emotion that are impossible to convey through language alone.

The Arts communicate in non-linguistic, expressive ways (Wright, 2003a), culturally and through symbol (O'Toole, 2012; Wright, 2003a) and metaphor (Wiggins, 2009). Wright (2003a, p. 17) highlights the non-linguistic nature of artistic expression and communication stating that the Arts:

involve expressive and symbolic modes of thinking, understanding and knowing, and communicate ideas in a unique manner ... they enable us to 'say' things to each other that cannot be expressed in any other way.

Most importantly, they communicate something 'other', something valuable that is 'beyond' words. This is what the Arts 'do' for us, and therein lies their real value to adults and children alike.

> **Reflection activity**
>
> Listen to a recording of Polish composer and conductor Krzysztof Penderecki's *hrenody for the Victims of Hiroshima* (1960) and view Pablo Picasso's painting *Guernica* (1936).
>
> Both works explored in this activity are an individual's response to war. One is auditory and one is visual; one is a piece of music and one is a painting. Both express and communicate feelings, ideas, thoughts and emotions about war; yet both are different. As human beings we also respond to each artwork differently. *This is what the Arts share.* They are all non-linguistic means of communication and expression, but they speak in their own ways and with their own 'languages'.
>
> Reflect on the ways in which the music communicated a certain 'mood', and the ways in which the painting communicated through certain symbols. Share your responses to both of these pieces with a colleague. What kind of questions can you use to help understand these responses?

Access and equity in Arts education

The Arts, as noted, are a defining aspect of human experience. In fact, they are deemed so important that UNESCO regards access to the Arts as a 'fundamental human right'. Unsurprisingly then, the Arts are 'a compulsory part of school education in 84% of countries' (Bamford, 2006, p. 59). While considered fundamental and important, access and equity in Arts education is problematic in practice because access to 'quality' Arts education is inconsistent (for further discussion of quality Arts education see p. 115). Access to quality Arts education varies from system to system, school to school, teacher to teacher and student to student. The Australian Curriculum includes the Arts as discrete, core Learning Areas and provides important guidance about the ways in which Arts education should occur; but curriculum 'presence' is really only one aspect of genuine access to quality Arts education.

TEACHER TIP

Set up a learning corner in your classroom that includes learning in at least two of the core areas of Arts education. Change the Arts focus every day and encourage students to engage with the corner regularly.

The Arts and 'hierarchies' of curricula

One reason for the inconsistency in the delivery of Arts education is a tendency in schools to consider the Arts peripherally rather than centrally, despite the evidence that the Arts actually contribute to learning in other areas, provide valuable skills in and of themselves, and have important benefits for children, such as improved self-esteem, self-confidence and motivation to learn (see Chapter 2). Jefferson and Anderson (2017) provide exceptional coverage of this problem, with attention given to the particularly disturbing recent focus on testing at all costs in schools. They state:

> We know from the overwhelming weight of research that large and frequent testing does not sustainably enhance student learning. Yet testing regimes persist in schools, which effectively makes the goal of learning, testing (p. 12).

Robinson (1999, p. 38) emphasises the importance of multiple ways of knowing when he states that:

> our primary perceptions of the world are through the senses: through light, sound, shape, texture, smell and movement ... Conventional education tends to emphasise verbal and mathematical reasoning. These are vital to the intellectual development of all young people *but they are not the whole of intelligence* (emphasis added).

In the classroom

When next engaged with children, reflect on what learning you intend to focus on. Does this learning give children opportunities to learn in non-linguistic ways? If not, can you think about ways to include embodied learning in the experience and what this learning might actually be?

One reason for the inconsistent provision of Arts education in the schools context is what is frequently described as the 'hierarchy' of Arts education domains which means that some Arts disciplines are valued or privileged above others (Anderson & Gibson, 2004; Bamford, 2006; O'Toole, 2012; Robinson, 2005). This structure tends to rank music and the visual arts at the apex, and drama and dance as less valuable, and frequently neglects the media arts altogether. There are a range of reasons for this 'hierarchy' and they vary according to cultural context. The hierarchy also reflects systemic, societal and individual biases. Some observers of Arts education in Australia have argued that the grouping of five Arts domains as one Learning Area called 'the Arts' has unintentionally contributed to a devaluing of individual Arts domains (Davis, 2008; Pascoe et al., 2005). This may be because grouping the Arts as a single domain inadvertently allows schools and early childhood providers to choose to include only one of the five art forms in their curriculum at the expense of others. By doing this they satisfy a requirement to provide an 'Arts' education despite the fact that this education is, by any measure, incomplete (Davis, 2008; Pascoe et al., 2005).

The Arts domains are all different

To understand why this is problematic for early childhood and primary education, you must understand that 'the Arts' are not an amorphic mass, but rather, individual domains of human activity, each with its own 'language', while also sharing attributes, as you will have understood from the Reflection activity about Penderecki and Picasso. To claim that experience in one Arts area equates to learning in all Arts areas is definitely problematic. Please think about what quality Arts education is: 'quality' Arts education is education that occurs in and across *all* five of the art forms.

The problem of time

The lack of sufficient time for pre-service educators to adequately explore all five art forms is also an important reason for the inconsistent provision of Arts education across Australia. Reviews of pre-service teacher training in the Arts in Australia, such as *First We See: The National Review of Visual Education* (Davis, 2008) and the *National Review of School Music Education: Augmenting the Diminished* (Pascoe et al., 2005), highlight the lack of adequate time for the Arts in Education degrees and the resultant lack of confidence and skills for teachers (see also Bamford, 2006). These reports also indicate a lack of systemic-level professional learning in the Arts for practising educators, suggesting that there are too few opportunities for teachers to improve their use of the Arts in the curriculum. There is absolutely no reason for general primary or early childhood educators not engaging in professional learning activities. Professional learning organisations in all five Arts education domains provide regular and quality opportunities for professional learning.

The Arts and equity

Equity of access to Arts education is a very serious issue in Australia, not only because organisations such as UNESCO maintain that access to Arts education is a fundamental right, but also because, unless all children have equal access to Arts education in our country, entrenched socioeconomic disadvantages will be perpetuated. Bamford (2006, p. 39) found that:

> poor quality arts education may be particularly evident within 'at risk' school communities, where there is a perception that literacy and vocational education take precedence over the arts. Extensive arts-rich programmes tend to be most prevalent in affluent and high-achieving schools.

This highlights an inherent inequality for children in schools and early childhood centres in low socioeconomic status (SES) areas. So, children in less financially prosperous schools actually miss out on quality education because of the schools' mandated, misguided focus on literacy and numeracy. In Australia, where we are renowned for declaring our privileging (no pun intended) of meritocracy, this is absolutely extraordinary.

In the music domain, the problem of equity is referred to by Pascoe et al. (2005, p. xi) as 'Those who play music are those who can pay for music'. This is shameful, and is particularly ironic when one considers a study undertaken in the United States using National Educational Longitudinal Survey (NELS) data that found significant improvement in achievement, attitudes and behaviours for children who were highly involved in music or drama activities *regardless of their* SES (Catterall, Chapleau & Iwanaga, 1999). This means that Arts education may be a great 'leveller' for children from low SES areas, as in this study they improved in their achievements, attitudes and behaviours in the same way as children from high SES areas did. Your role as an early childhood or primary educator is to ensure that *all* children in your care have equal access to quality Arts learning experiences regardless of their demographic.

> **Reflection activity**
>
> Watch the video 'Historic flashmob in Antwerp train station, do re mi' by The Ad Show on YouTube.
>
> This video is a simple demonstration of the power of music, dance and media arts to touch the daily lives of people as makers and responders. What do you notice about the ways in which people are engaged in this event? Reflect on what is unique about this event. Think about such things as the ways in which these creators are engaged in Arts making, and the pure joy of their engagement.

Video: Flashmob in Antwerp train station

Learner agency and cultural diversity in Arts education

Learner agency

Learner agency is a critical component of quality Arts education. Gallagher (2000) defines 'agency' as a self-aware action, stating that it is the 'sense that I am the one who is causing or generating an action'. Waller and Bitou (2011, p. 103) write that agency 'seeks to understand the

Learner agency: a learner's awareness of their own ability to affect an outcome. It is critical to engaged learning and to the ownership of learning, as Wiggins (2009, p. 23) writes: 'To be willing and able to learn, learners must have a sense of personal agency'.

definitions and meaning children give to their own lives and recognises children's competence and capacity to understand and act upon their world'.

Because the Arts are fundamentally vehicles for personal and shared expression and communication, learner agency is critical if genuine artistic learning is to be achieved in your classroom. Ewing (2010, p. 41) highlights the power of drama as a means of increasing children's agency by 'authentically sharing power and risk-taking' between teachers and children. All of the Arts have the potential to increase learner agency, because they enable children to engage through authentic processes *as* artists, *as* makers and *as* responders. As an early childhood or primary educator, your role is to enable your students to experiment with the Arts without fear of failure, because all failures are creative vehicles for learning, and to take risks, to make and to respond to the Arts as they find them.

Cultural diversity

As stated earlier, the Arts occur within specific cultural traditions and not only respond to these cultures but also shape them. The Arts are vehicles for exploring other cultures and traditions, because engagement in making and responding to the Arts requires understanding the cultures and traditions in which these Arts occur. The Arts can therefore be important vehicles for cross-cultural understanding (Australian Government, DEEWR, 2009; MCEETYA, 2007; UNESCO, 2006), or understanding between cultures (Nakata, 2002). The importance of the Arts and education in creating cross-cultural understanding is emphasised in the *National Education and the Arts Statement* (MCEETYA, 2007, pp. 4–5), which states:

> Arts and culture can enrich our lives by building mutual respect and understanding. An arts-rich education can help young people make sense of the world and enhance their awareness of diverse cultures and traditions and the wider global context in which they live.

This is something that is a foundational aspect of Arts engagement – the Arts encourage understanding and respect.

The Arts have been a part of Australian Aboriginal and Torres Strait Islander cultures long before the arrival of European cultures, and as such they provide a link to some of the oldest cultural traditions known to humanity (Rudd, 2008). It is essential that any Arts education curriculum in early childhood and primary contexts includes substantial and respectful exploration of these First Nations peoples' arts practices. The Arts offer a unique vehicle for this exploration to take place, and your role is to ensure that this happens for your students.

Reflection activity

What is Country? According to Professor Deborah Rose (1996, p. 7),

it is a place that gives and receives life. Not just imagined or represented, it is lived in and lived with. Country in Aboriginal English is not only a common noun but also a proper noun. People talk about country in the same way that they would talk about a person:

they speak to country, sing to country, visit country, worry about country, feel sorry for country, and long for country. People say that country knows, hears, smells, takes notice, takes care, is sorry or happy. Country is not a generalised or undifferentiated type of place, such as one might indicate with terms like 'spending a day in the country' or 'going up the country'. Rather, country is a living entity with a yesterday, today and tomorrow, with a consciousness, and a will toward life. Because of this richness, country is home, and peace; nourishment for body, mind, and spirit; heart's ease.

Watch the video '*liyini milaythina rrala*' ('Singing Country Strong') by Tasmanian Aboriginal Centre on YouTube; it concerns about Country and what this means to Aboriginal and Torres Strait Islander peoples.

Video: liyini milaythina rrala

Reflect now on what you think the meaning of the lyric 'Singing Country Strong' is for Aboriginal and Torres Strait Islander peoples. Hint: Country lives and hears.

Sustained, sequential and 'quality' Arts education
Time matters

Like any area of the curriculum, from numeracy to literacy, children's engagement and achievement in the Arts is in part determined by their exposure to ongoing and evolving learning experiences over time. Unfortunately, for some of the reasons outlined earlier, and due to differences in state-based Arts curriculum, children often do not receive such exposure in Australia (Davis, 2008; Pascoe et al., 2005). It is hoped that the introduction of the Australian Curriculum: The Arts and the Early Years Learning Framework may overcome some of the issues associated with this systemic fragmentation.

UNESCO (2006, p. 5) highlights the importance of sequential and sustained Arts education, stating that it should 'be systematic and be provided over a number of years as it is a long term process'. Sustained and sequential Arts education refers to education which continues from preschool years to the end of formal compulsory education. It is education that provides learning experiences that enable students to progress in making and responding in the Arts over time, culminating in children who are confident, aware and engaged in their Arts making and responding. Our approach is that Arts education also needs to be 'substantial'; this means that it needs to be of substance or 'quality', and ideally to provide for progression over time.

'Quality' Arts education

So what does 'quality' Arts education mean? UNESCO (2006, p. 6) highlights the importance of the individual learner in Arts education, stating that:

> 'Quality education' is learner-centred and can be defined by three principles: education that is relevant to the learner but also promotes universal values, education which is equitable in terms of access and outcomes and guarantees social inclusion rather than exclusion, and education which reflects and helps to fulfil individual rights.

As in other curriculum areas, quality Arts education is learner-centred.

The characteristics of 'high-quality' Arts education programs, according to Bamford (2006, pp. 88–9), include: partnerships with the community and Arts organisations; shared responsibilities between stakeholders; opportunities for performance and exhibition; critical reflection, problem-solving and risk-taking; collaboration; inclusivity; assessment and reporting; professional learning for teachers; and flexible school organisational structures.

Bryce et al. (2004), through their investigation of four Australian Arts-based programs, highlight three characteristics of Arts education programs that enhance children's learning: the use of positive reinforcement, engagement with 'authentic' activities, and consistent procedures and processes.

In the classroom

When you are next in a classroom or childcare setting make regular notes in your journal about any times you see evidence of collaboration, risk-taking or critical reflection.

Authentic Arts learning

Engagement with 'authentic' Arts activities in authentic ways is central to quality Arts education. An 'authentic' Arts activity is one that may be found in the 'real world' of Arts practice. Examples would be creating an original dance piece for performance to a community audience; painting a self-portrait that highlights an aspect of the artist's identity, to be exhibited to an intended audience; composing a piece of music to accompany an original film; or devising a drama that is to be performed for a school audience. These are all authentic activities because they are the types of activities that occur in the 'real world'; also, each of these includes an opportunity for exhibition or performance of the completed art to an intended audience, another important aspect of 'real world' Arts making.

Note also that these activities all present opportunities to both 'make' and 'respond' to the Arts, thus including learning that is authentic to the art form. For example, the self-portrait may contain learning about colour, space and line that is explicitly taught as such. The ways in which these activities occur are also important in identifying them as authentic; the process must be similar to the 'real world'. For example, in the music activity, children should be given opportunities to storyboard the film, to match the storyboard to the music, to explore ways in which music can represent characters and emotions, and to experiment with the elements of music to achieve their musical goal. Notice that this is a child-centred approach wherein the musical composition evolves in response to the children's own ideas.

Quality Arts education programs include:

- the Arts taught as praxis (see below)
- sequential learning planned to enable growth/progression in both Arts making and responding
- sustained learning from preschool
- substantial learning in each of the five Arts domains of dance, drama, media arts, music and visual arts
- child-centred teaching
- active learning
- authentic activities and processes

- access for children of all abilities
- inclusion of Arts from diverse cultural perspectives including Asian countries and Aboriginal and Torres Strait Islander peoples.
- continuous teacher reflection about the effectiveness of learning Arts opportunities provided for children.

A 'praxial' vision for the Arts in education

Praxis: in the context of Arts education, understanding through making and responding; children are perceived as artists with genuine agency, who understand each of the Arts as a unique and culturally diverse vehicle for expression and communication.

Praxis refers to action or practice in an area of human activity. It refers to 'doing' a human activity and all that this involves. In the Arts, this means understanding the Arts as a particular form of human endeavour in all of its different contexts, meanings and practices. According to Bernstein (1999):

> [The Greek term] 'praxis' has an ordinary meaning that roughly corresponds to the ways in which we now commonly speak of 'action' or 'doing'; it is frequently translated into English as 'practice' (p. xii) ... and corresponds to 'a form of truly human activity' (p. xv).

The use of the term 'praxis' may be traced back to the ancient Greeks and Aristotle, and questions surrounding praxis have been considered by philosophers, including Hegel, Marx and Dewey (Bernstein, 1999). Praxis has been associated specifically with education through the work of Paulo Freire (1993) in the context of education as a means of human transformation and liberation. For Regelski (1998), praxis also includes a distinct ethical element, wherein the purpose is to ensure good outcomes for participants.

Freire saw education as liberation through dialogue. He wrote: 'Liberation is a praxis: the action and reflection of men and women upon their world in order to transform it ... Liberating education consists in acts of cognition, not transferrals of information' (1993, p. 60). For Freire, 'action and reflection occur simultaneously' (1993, p. 109), and 'human activity consists of action and reflection: it is praxis; it is transformation of the world. And as praxis, it requires theory to illuminate it. Human activity is theory and practice; it is reflection and action' (1993, p. 106). This symbiotic relationship between action and reflection is the critical component of praxis.

Alperson (1991) relates praxis to art, and maintains that it is an attempt 'to understand art in terms of the variety of meaning and values evidenced in actual practice in particular cultures' (p. 233). For Alperson, cultural context relates to the actual 'practice' of art in specific cultures. Elliott (1995), writing about music education, maintains that music as praxis revolves around music as 'particular kinds of human doing-and-making that are purposeful, contextual and socially-embedded'. For these authors, praxis refers to 'action' in the sense that the action is an intentional, conscious and culturally determined human activity. Regelski (1998) adds to this understanding of praxis by foregrounding the importance of praxis bringing 'about "right results" for people' (p. 28), in an educational setting meaning that praxis should result in the best curricular outcomes for students.

Arts education as praxis

We believe that a praxial approach to Arts education includes the following characteristics. It:

- reflects the 'real' world of Arts practice and authentic Arts processes; learning occurs through making and responding in the Arts, the same way as this occurs in the 'real world'
- occurs as a distinct human activity through all of the senses; it is fundamentally an activity that is intentionally 'done' (in the sense of being a practical and conscious action) by learners
- is situated in and explores the Arts of many cultures and their diverse forms of expression and communication; in this sense it is both a process and an end (as cultural understanding)
- involves the learner as an active Arts 'maker' and 'responder'
- is both a means for and the result of learner agency.

Reflection activity

Take a moment to read back over the points above and note elements of our vision that may or may not resonate with you. Write your own five-point vision for the Arts in your practice, and share this with a colleague.

Your vision should be based on what you have learned so far in this chapter and should, where possible, be written in your own voice. Aspects of your vision may include, for example: learner agency, cultural diversity, making and responding opportunities. This is about you checking on your personal values in relation to the evidence we have presented about the importance of the Arts in education.

Your role: the Arts in early childhood and primary education

Early childhood

When discussing early childhood Arts education, we are referring to children up to school age (which varies from state to state). The approach to Arts education in early childhood settings in this book is consistent with Outcome 5 'Children are Effective Communicators' in the Early Years Learning Framework.

Primary

The Australian Curriculum provides 'organisers', which make a consistent structure for the Arts in primary years. 'Making' and 'responding' are the broad organisers and each subject (dance, drama, media arts, music and visual arts) has its own specific language, concepts and processes.

Your role in Arts education

Before we discuss your role in the provision of Arts education in early childhood and primary contexts in more detail, it is important to make three points.

- First, your role needs to be grounded in the approach outlined throughout this book, starting with the notion of praxis, which includes learner agency, cultural diversity and quality, as discussed in this chapter. Further chapters will also provide you with essential understandings about the value of the Arts in education, the individual art forms, and areas such as general capabilities that will further inform your understanding of your role.
- Secondly, your attitude to the Arts in education will determine the scope of your role. As we have stated, curriculum 'presence' is but one factor in the provision of quality Arts education; your valuing of the Arts in your classroom is crucial to your enacting of that curriculum.
- Thirdly, your role in the provision of Arts education may be determined in part by your own self-efficacy, or beliefs about your own competence to teach the Arts. As an early childhood and primary educator, you have a unique role in the delivery of quality Arts education experiences to the children in your care. It is you who will allow the Arts to make a difference in these lives.

The role of early childhood and primary educators in Arts education is far more complex than you may at first expect. As discussed earlier, one of the problems is a lack of substantive time in Education degrees to enable pre-service teachers to develop the skills and understandings they need. This situation is further complicated by the general lack of background experience in Arts education among many pre-service teachers, and the resultant beliefs about their own competence in the Arts. Garvis and Pendergast (2011, p. 1) state that 'Teacher self-efficacy is defined as teacher beliefs in their ability to perform a teaching task'. In their study of early childhood teachers in Queensland, Garvis and Pendergast (2011, p. 2) found – perhaps not surprisingly when one considers our first point – that 'early childhood teachers had greater perceived competence for teaching maths and English *compared to any of the arts strands*' (emphasis added). Bamford (2006, p. 80) supports both of these points, stating that 'the lack of time dedicated to art[s] education, especially in generalist teacher training, is compounded by the lack of entering ability possessed by students'. In a survey of 936 pre-service primary teachers in Australia, Namibia, South Africa, the United States and Ireland, Russell-Bowie and Dowson (2005) found similarly that 'in every creative arts area background is very strongly, and positively, predictive of confidence and enjoyment in teaching'. 'Background' in this study refers to previous experience with the Arts.

TEACHER TIP

Confidence in teaching the Arts can be developed through practice. Preparation is key. So when you next go into a classroom or childcare setting, make sure you have practised an activity using one of the Arts. For example, find a children's action song, such as the Hokey Pokey, on YouTube and practise it at home until you are confident you can teach children to sing and dance to it.

You are uniquely placed to provide Arts education

One of the most important features of early childhood and primary settings is that they are uniquely placed to enable children to experiment with the diversity of Arts making and responding. As McCarthy et al. (2004, p. 55) write:

> Of central importance to an individual's inclination to continue future involvement is his or her reaction to the initial arts experience. Those who find their initial experience positive are very likely to be willing to continue their involvement … Many young people's first hands-on involvement with the arts is when they learn to draw, to play an instrument, to sing in a choir, or, perhaps, to act in a play.

In this respect you are the **gatekeeper** to many initial Arts experiences, with an opportunity to inspire your students to engage with the Arts. This is a critical role.

According to Bamford (2006, p. 75), 'the majority of art[s] teaching in primary schools is done by generalist teachers', and this assertion is

Gatekeeper: in an educational sense, someone who has the power to decide what resources or opportunities are given to a group, in order to meet their abilities or learning goals.

also true of early childhood settings. Most early childhood settings do not employ Arts specialists, although this does sometimes happen. Some primary schools do employ Arts specialists, but more often than not this is usually a specialist in one Arts area only, such as music or visual arts. It is far less common to find a dance, drama or media arts specialist in either of these contexts. As a practising or pre-service teacher, it is your responsibility to ensure Arts provision for the children in your care, even when a specialist may teach one or two of the art forms.

Lesson plan 1.1

AIM
Learning through play using sounds to tell a story.

OVERVIEW
In this activity students are enabled to learn through play.

OUTLINE/DESCRIPTION
A music learning corner is set up in the childcare centre. Musical instruments located at this learning corner include a variety of tuned and non-tuned percussion instruments such as claves, tambourines, xylophones, glockenspiels and drums. Other stimuli at the learning corner include a selection of favourite children's picture books. Students are asked to select their favourite picture book. Together with the teacher children experiment with creating sound to accompany the story. For example, each character could have their own sound. Children could be encouraged to use what they know about the elements of music to portray characters in the best way they can. One way of doing this is to focus on selected elements such as pitch (high and low sounds), rhythm (long and short sounds) and dynamics (loud and soft sounds).

INTENDED OUTCOMES
Children identify
- ways to use music to represent a character.

Children understand
- that music can be used to tell a story.

Children are able to
- use instruments to express personal preferences for sound.

LINKS TO CURRICULUM
Children:
- 'express ideas and make meaning using a range of media' (DEEWR, 2009, p. 42).
- 'begin to understand how symbols and pattern systems work' (DEEWR, 2009, p. 43).

> **ASSESSMENT**
>
> Students should be provided with positive, formative feedback throughout their engagement

Conclusion

When determining your role, it is important to identify what strengths and weaknesses you and any specialist teachers may possess. The Arts specialist has expert Arts knowledge, expertise in making Arts and a vision for the scope and knowledge for the sequence of Arts education over time. Arts specialists, however, usually only see children for a short period each week, and tend not to have a breadth of curriculum knowledge. You, the early childhood or primary educator, are a learning and curriculum specialist with a breadth and depth of knowledge about the curriculum and its connections, and expertise in the ways in which children learn. Furthermore, you have expertise in the individual learning styles and idiosyncrasies of each child, and teach these children as a group over an extended period of time.

The roles for specialists and early childhood or primary educators have the potential to be re-imagined to ensure that the strengths of both are recognised and used. We suggest that, in the near future, the specialist may become more of an Arts consultant to the classroom teacher, providing expertise in Arts learning, teaching and assessment. In this model, education in the Arts is far more of a shared responsibility, embedding the Arts within daily learning, and enabling natural thematic and conceptual connections between areas of learning already occurring. This is a powerful, holistic and collaborative model that has much potential to ensure that the evolving needs of our students are best met and that quality Arts education is provided for all.

The Arts are not for a select few whom we label as gifted or talented; they are for all children. Arts education is about providing them with opportunities to explore and develop their natural Arts potential as part of their broad education, to reach the end of primary school knowing and valuing the Arts in their lives. The Arts enable us to express and communicate our individual and shared perceptions of what it means to be human, what it is like to live in a particular culture and to promote intercultural understanding. Despite the disconnect between policy and practice, as an early childhood or primary educator you have a unique and important role to play in the delivery of quality Arts education experiences to the children in your care; it is you who will allow the Arts to make a difference in these lives. A praxial approach to the Arts in education that emphasises authentic practices and processes, is reflective of diverse and unique cultures, and that positions the learner as an active Arts 'maker' and 'responder', will make a difference to you as a professional and, most importantly, to the children in your care.

REVIEW QUESTIONS

1. UNESCO (2006) places great value on Arts education. How does it express this value?
2. The Australian Curriculum includes five Arts domains. List these.
3. All the Arts are fundamentally vehicles for … (two points)?
4. 'The Arts are non-linguistic forms of communication.' What does this mean?
5. 'The Arts are sensorial forms of communication.' What does this mean?
6. Define 'learner agency'.
7. 'The Arts make meaning in specific cultural contexts.' What does this mean?
8. What are the characteristics of a praxial approach to Arts education?
9. Any role for early childhood or primary educators should include an understanding of three main assumptions. Describe these.

RECOMMENDED READING

Anderson, M. and Gibson, R. (2004). 'Connecting the silos: Developing Arts rich education'. *Change: Transformations in education*, 7(2), 1–11.

Bamford, A. (2006). *The Wow Factor: Global Research Compendium on the Impact of the Arts in Education*. Berlin: Waxmann Verlag.

Davis, D. (2008). *First We See: The National Review of Visual Education*. Canberra: Department of Education, Science and Training. Retrieved from http://2014.australiacouncil.gov.au/__data/assets/pdf_file/0003/36372/NRVE_Final_Report.pdf

Freire, P. (1993). *Pedagogy of the Oppressed*, 3rd edn. London, UK: Pearson.

Goss, P. (2017). *Towards an adaptive education system in Australia*. Grattan Institute Discussion paper No 2017–01, November 2017. Grattan Institute. Retrieved from https://grattan.edu.au/report/towards-an-adaptive-education-system-in-australia/

Jefferson, M. and Anderson, M. (2017). *Transforming Schools: Creativity, critical reflection, communication, collaboration*. London: Bloomsbury.

Pascoe, R., Leong, S., McCallum, J., Mackinlay, E., Marsh, K., Smith, B., Church, T. and Winterton, A. (2005). *National Review of Music Education: Augmenting the Diminished*. Canberra: Department of Education, Science and Training.

Robinson, K. (2006). *How Schools Kill Creativity*. Retrieved from http://www.ted.com/talks/ken_robinson_says_schools_kill_creativity.html.

Seidl, S., Tishman, S., Winner, E., Hetland, L. and Palmer, P. (2009). *The qualities of quality: Understanding excellence in Arts education*. Cambridge, MASS: Project Zero. Retrieved from http://www.wallacefoundation.org/knowledge-center/Documents/Understanding-Excellence-in-Arts-Education.pdf.

Wright, S. (2003). *Children, Meaning-making and the Arts*. Frenchs Forest, NSW: Pearson.

2

Why the Arts are fundamental

> Through the arts we learn to see what we had not noticed, to feel what we had not felt, and to employ forms of thinking that are indigenous to the arts. These experiences are consequential, for through them we engage in a process through which the self is remade.

Elliot Eisner

In this chapter

This chapter explores much of the current research concerning the value and effect of Arts education and aims to assist you as you develop your own thinking about the importance of the Arts in education. This research is framed by an understanding of developing modes of engagement in Arts education, and a discussion of the importance of personal agency and Arts education as 'praxis' (see Chapter 1). Finally, the notions of learning 'in' and 'through' the Arts are explored so that you understand the types of learning in which your students engage.

By the end of this chapter you should have a clear understanding of:

- Arts education in 21st-century lives: how technology has changed Arts production and distribution and the impact of this on learners and learning

- what we know about Arts education, its value and effects: 'intrinsic' and 'instrumental' reasons for the inclusion of the Arts in education

- learning 'in' and 'through' the Arts and your role as an educator.

Introduction

Access to the Arts and Arts education is regarded by UNESCO as a 'universal human right', and under the Convention on the Rights of the Child full participation in the Arts is a right for all children (UNESCO, 2006). The Arts are a natural part of children's lives, whether through dancing and singing a song, playing as a pirate or making colourful marks on a piece of scrap paper (Barrett & Smigiel, 2003; Barrett, Everett & Smigiel, 2012). As a central part of human existence the Arts are a part of a child's world, and according to Barrett and Smigiel (2003): 'Australian children do see the Arts as part of their daily lives, and … they understand and enjoy their participation in these activities.' Barrett et al. (2012) state that in their study of 570 Australian children, those 5 to 8 years of age 'tended to prioritise active "making" in the arts rather than audience-participation' (p. 194), and that these children also 'spoke about the ways their engagement in the arts helped them "feel good about yourself, proud of what you have done"' (p. 198). Thus children prioritised active Arts making in their worlds and wellbeing as a positive outcome from participation. The Arts have been an intrinsic part of human culture and society for millennia and can be found in every culture around the world. The Arts are everywhere; everyone has the potential to be artistic and the right to explore their culture and arts (Bamford, 2006; UNESCO, 2006; Wright, 2003a).

For centuries the Arts have been a part of what it means to be human (Ewing 2010; Gibson & Ewing, 2011; Wright, 2003a), to express our humanity, and to communicate and share this planet with others (UNESCO, 2006). The Arts have been a central means for the transmission and preservation of cultural knowledge among Indigenous peoples, and Judeo-Christian Western and Asian cultures for millennia. All societies in the world engage in the Arts, albeit in unique and culturally specific ways (Bamford, 2006). The Arts enable us to express and communicate our individual and shared perceptions of what it means to be human, what it is like to live in a particular culture (ACARA, 2017; MCEETYA, 2007), and what it is like to express personal feelings and emotions (Robinson, 1999). As Wright (2003a, p. 10) puts it: 'The Arts can help us to place our objects, our activities and ourselves in a larger existential framework – to participate in something greater than our individual selves and our individual "realities".'

Spotlight on Arts education

MUSIC AND NEUROSCIENCE

Research over the last two decades has indicated that there are differences between the brains of musicians and non-musicians. However, until recently it has not been possible to determine if these differences are the result of engaging in music or because of pre-existing, anatomical differences between musicians' and non-musicians' brains. Likewise, there has been no research undertaken to establish if changes in the brain structure of musicians may result from engagement in other types of activities, such as sport.

In a continuing project, researchers at the University of Southern California (Habibi et al., 2017) investigated a possible relationship between changes in brain anatomy and engagement in instrumental music making. They tested 75 participants aged between 6 and 7 years, with similar IQs and from similar socioeconomic backgrounds in the Los Angeles area of the United States. These researchers used one control group alongside two experimental groups of children. After initial Magnetic Resonance Imaging (MRI) testing, one experimental group commenced musical training based around the El Sistema orchestra education system, the other experimental group commenced participation in soccer or swimming training, and the control group was engaged in neither music nor sport. This particular project structure allowed researchers to investigate if changes in brain structure were due exclusively to music-specific activities.

The researchers re-measured brain anatomy in participants after two years of intensive music or sport activity, and will repeat these measures after another two years. The results of this study so far show that there was a difference between the 'rate of cortical thickness maturation' (Habibi et al., 2017, p. 1) for the musical group and for that of the other groups, and increased connections between the left and right sides of the brain in the music group compared to the other groups in the first two years of the study.

This project, one of the few longitudinal studies in this area, may be the first to provide evidence of the impact of early musical training on brain development across time. The significance of this research is that early musical training does have an impact on brain development, confirming the importance of music education in the early years. For primary and early childhood educators this confirms the value of musical engagement to young brains.

Link: Art Facts

The Australia Council for the Arts is Australia's peak body responsible for much of the Federal Government's funding and support for the Arts. The Australia Council for the Arts has released 'Art Facts', a website dedicated to reporting statistics about the Arts in Australia. These statistics will be extremely useful for you as you develop your understanding of why the Arts are important in society and education. Some of these key facts are as follows:

1. Nine in 10 Australians think the Arts are an important part of education.
2. Nine in 10 Australians think Indigenous arts are important.
3. Seven in 10 Australians think there are plenty of opportunities to get involved with the Arts.
4. One in three artists bring their creative skills to other industries.
5. More children play an instrument than soccer.

Australia Council (2014)

TEACHER TIP

Ask children to bring their devices to class for the purpose of sharing their favourite piece of art or music. This could involve anything from a song to a cartoon and everything in between. They should be prepared to share this with other children, talking about why their choice is important to them. Once they have shared with a partner, children could then share with a larger group. Children thus begin to 'own', share and talk about their Arts choices.

We all have different backgrounds in and experience with the Arts and hence different understandings of the role of the Arts in education. Take some time to reflect on what you think the purpose of the Arts is in education and write your thoughts down.

Using these thoughts as a starting point, share your ideas with a colleague.

Watch the TED Talk 'Do Schools Kill Creativity? | Sir Ken Robinson' on YouTube.

Between the two of you, can you agree on five points about the role of the Arts in education? These should be mutually agreed and understood points. Now share this with a larger group.

Reflection activity

Video: Do schools kill creativity? Reflection activity

In the classroom

When you are next working with children ask students to 'find' and record the Arts in their immediate vicinity. Students should be provided with a selection of drawing materials, sound recording devices and video recording devices. Working in pairs students select their materials or devices and spend time in and around the classroom or outside space recording, in whatever way they choose, something that 'speaks' to them in some way. For example, this may be a recording of bird sounds, or a photograph of concrete or pavers that form a pattern, or a drawing of a branch or a leaf. Children should be encouraged to really take their time with this, taking time to observe and pay attention to their chosen subjects. Children should then return to the classroom where they can share and discuss their work with others.

Arts education in 21st-century lives
Technology has changed both the game and the rules

Since the development of the internet, ways of engaging with the Arts have changed radically, and interactive technologies have ensured that the Arts are now far more accessible than ever before (Cayari, 2011; O'Toole, 2012; Robinson, 1999). According to Cayari (2011), 'Educators and artists alike are seeing new ways to express their art though technological means. Digital technology has brought with it new media'. This evolving and dynamic mode of engagement has been characterised as leading to 'a renaissance of interest in the Arts' (Bamford, 2006, p. 19). It is one of the single most important developments to impact upon participation and engagement in the Arts in recent years, and thus also upon classrooms and learning.

Prior to 19th- and 20th-century technologies, such as photographic and mechanical sound reproduction, an artist might have exhibited a work or a composer performed an original piece of music in a single city or region. These artists may also have 'toured' their works to other locations; however, the audiences for these works were temporally and geographically limited. In the 21st century, nothing could be further from the truth. A musician may record an original piece of music in their bedroom, upload this to the internet, and then receive critical feedback from locations across the world within minutes. The cycle of creating new works and reflecting critically upon them has been reduced to seconds and geographical location is no longer a barrier to this transaction.

One way that the internet has changed music education is through the proliferation of sites dedicated to sharing musical practice. Fontana (2018) estimates that there are 'hundreds of thousands of guitar related websites', with hundreds more coming online each month, and this has impacted music education in two main ways. First, it has helped many people to learn to play an instrument such as the guitar, and secondly, it has impacted the ways in which people learn. The proliferation of sites has meant that people often learn through 'working it out' in an informal way and this has changed the role of the teacher from a traditional master and apprentice model to one more akin to mentor and colleague. In a sense this aligns with the notion of a 'flipped' classroom, where students learn content outside the classroom (online in this case) and refine and apply that knowledge in the classroom. Lo and Hew (2017, p. 1) describe the flipped classroom as an 'instructional approach [that] combines video-based learning outside the classroom and interactive group learning activities inside the classroom'.

The impact of the internet is similar for other art forms also. A simple Google search conducted in January 2018, using the terms 'drawing + how to', resulted in 882 million results. As was the case in guitar education, these resources have had a major impact on learners through the availability of instruction, and on teachers and classrooms through resultant changes in pedagogy, such as a more nuanced or flipped approach. The internet has also enabled mass sharing of finished artworks in ways that were simply not possible before. Sites like 'behance' and 'Art Web' enable artists to upload and share their artwork easily, having an educational and multiplier effect on the refinement and development of styles and genres of art.

What this means for the Arts in education

The impact of these changes has been profound and we see both advantages and disadvantages for Arts education and children. The immediacy and availability of the Arts through new media can be incredibly stimulating when making, responding to and sharing these new forms. However, the potential downside is the evolution of a generation of passive consumers. By this we mean that the proliferation of artistic creations and their immediate availability on the internet may result in these being viewed as consumer 'products', with children 'consuming' them rather than taking part in their creation. Robinson (1999, pp. 55–6) argues that 'young people are not simply passive consumers of cultural products: they appropriate and adapt them to their own urgent need for a sense of personal and group identity'. We agree with this point of view, that children can use and adapt their artistic choices and even curate them through media such as Google Play Music. So a child can 'own' a variety of songs and store them on a platform, creating playlists of personal meaning and continually updating these. We suggest though that this does not take the place of Arts making and children's own artistic practice – it is just one part of it. New media offer new opportunities for children to make and respond in the Arts, and schools are uniquely placed to enable a new generation of Arts making and responding. Gibson and Ewing (2011, p. 9) emphasise the importance of the Arts in this environment, stating:

> In our increasingly digital world, Arts processes can enable us to select, analyse and reflect in order to interpret information effectively, and, at the same time, be more conscious of our own social and cultural biases.

When thinking about the place of new media it is worth noting that the paradigm in which many schools still operate is a 19th-century one of **domain-centred learning**, classrooms and rigid time constraints. This archaic system of rigid timetables and separate learning areas does not serve our students well (Gibson & Ewing, 2011; Jefferson & Anderson, 2017; O'Toole, 2012; Robinson, 1999, 2005). We argue that at this time in educational history nothing is more important than providing children with Arts-rich possibilities for learning, because such possibilities enable students to be genuinely creative and to embrace the potential risk of criticism or failure, rather than fearing it. This is true for many reasons, but perhaps most of all because we are all individuals who have an intrinsic need to express ourselves and communicate with others in unique ways. The Arts enable this to occur (Robinson, 1999), and for this reason alone they should be regarded as central to learning. Sadly this is not the case however.

> **Domain-centred learning:** multidisciplinary learning in which children learn the different subjects of the curriculum in isolation from one another; that is, learning in which there is no attempt to integrate learning areas.

In a digital environment, what is important for the education of children is to move away from the mere purchase or consumption of artistic 'products', such as mp4s, to authentic engagement in the Arts through active and meaningful participation. This is a central tenet of this book – children must think and act as artists in order for them to gain genuine understanding of what the Arts are and what they can do for them. This approach is sometimes referred to as 'praxis' or a 'praxial' approach (see Chapter 1). In a praxial approach to Arts education, the Arts are 'done' as a part of *everyday activity*. In a praxial approach, making and responding in the Arts are, at their heart, human activities that are culturally and socially located and heavily invested with personal agency. It is worth noting that technology can now be used as a key enabler of Arts making and responding in classrooms and can provide learners with opportunities to develop their sense of agency, sharing their Art creations and their learning across geographical boundaries.

Reflection activity

Spend a couple of minutes listing the technologies that you use in your everyday life. This may include such technologies as Facebook, Twitter, YouTube, tablets, smartphones, computer software and apps, or email, to list a few. List as many as you can think of.

If you haven't included Arts technologies in your list, do a quick search for one music and one visual arts technology that you could incorporate into your teaching.

Describe one advantage of using one of these technologies in your future classroom. Put yourself in the shoes of the learner using this technology and think about the ways in which the technology could empower you to learn.

You may choose any number of technologies. As an example, let's look at *MuseScore*. This is a free music technology application with the capacity to enhance and impact quality music education. This technology has different uses, one of which is the ability for users to record and notate music in a simple and easily shareable format. It is also a repository for many great children's songs and rhymes. This enables users with or without music notation skills to press the play icon and sing along to a favourite nursery rhyme.

Link: MuseScore

What we know about Arts education, its value and effects

Many of us have developed skills in one or other Arts domains through our personal interests, such as playing an instrument, painting pictures, joining a dance class or engaging with the local theatre company. We have consequently experienced the pure enjoyment and transformative power of the Arts and thus have reasons to include and value them in our teaching. Aside from these compelling personal reasons, there is also a constantly evolving and compelling body of research regarding the value and effects of the Arts in education, which will be discussed in this section. Familiarity with this body of research is essential for you to fully understand the importance of the Arts, and thus to value it within your own practice. It is also important to note that we can only present a small fraction of the research that is now available in support of the Arts in education and you should be encouraged to use your own institution's library site to further investigate the research. Websites like ArtsEdSearch are a great place to start your search. When using these sites, it is important to focus your research terms to ensure that you find the resources you are seeking, as in any Boolean search.

In the classroom

When next engaged with children, bring a plan to engage them in one of the Arts domains. If you already have an area that interests you, or with which you are familiar, then plan to incorporate this in some way. If not, do some basic research on the internet. Think about an area or art form that you would like to experiment with and plan a simple five-minute interaction.

If you are interested in exploring drama a little more, then you might plan to use a picture book as a basis for exploring characters with children.

Lesson plan 2.1

AIM

Using visual art to express emotional responses to different styles of music.

OUTLINE/DESCRIPTION

In this lesson students listen to music (without lyrics) while drawing or painting in response. Following their response they share their artwork with a friend, reflecting on and discussing each other's use of the elements of visual art (see Chapter 9). As teacher it is your responsibility to select appropriate music for students to respond to. The requirement for this music to have no lyrics is important, because lyrics will induce responses that are necessarily related to the words. The point of this task is for children to respond

Videos: Suggested music

to the music only. It is also really important that you do not have any screen operating while the music is playing, again because we want children to respond to the music only. When selecting music you should select works that are of a duration that will, in your opinion, suit your students. Here are some suggestions you may like to try, but feel free to use any other music that you think may be appropriate. Please note timings are approximate.

- Jean-Michel Jarre – Oxygène Part 1 (8 minutes)
- Johann Sebastian Bach – Prelude and Fugue in D Minor (9 minutes)
- He Zhanhao and Chen Gang – The Butterfly Lovers (10 minutes)
- Camille Saint-Saëns – Danse Macabre (7 minutes)
- Claude Debussy – La Mer (23 minutes)
- Mikis Theodorakis – Zorba the Greek (4 minutes)
- Richard Wagner – Ride of the Valkyries (5 minutes)
- Dave Brubeck – Take Five (5 minutes 30)
- Edvard Grieg – In the Hall of the Mountain King from Peer Gynt (2 minutes 30)
- Zakir Hussain – Peshkar Concerto for Tabla and Orchestra (3 minutes)

INTENDED OUTCOMES

Students identify
- visual elements used in their own and others' artworks.

Students understand
- that people respond to music in different ways – no one response will be exactly the same as another
- that one way of engaging with music is to paint or draw our emotional response.

Students are able to
- listen to different styles of music
- draw or paint in response to different styles of music
- talk about their completed artworks.

LINKS TO CURRICULUM

Years 1 and 2 content descriptors
- Explore ideas, experiences, observations and imagination to create visual artworks and design, including considering ideas in artworks by Aboriginal and Torres Strait Islander artists (ACAVAM106).
- Use and experiment with different materials, techniques, technologies and processes to make artworks (ACAVAM107).
- Create and display artworks to communicate ideas to an audience (ACAVAM108).

Early Years Learning Framework
Children:
- 'express ideas and make meaning using a range of media' (DEEWR, 2009, p. 45)

- 'begin to understand how symbols and pattern systems work' (DEEWR, 2009, p. 46).

ASSESSMENT
- Students complete a visual response and talk about it.

EXTENSION
Please note the musical pieces used above can also be used as inspiration for dramatic or dance-based responses.

The body of research discussed in the following sections reports on the benefits and value of Arts participation, but it is important to understand that people usually do not engage in the Arts because they think it will make them 'smarter' (McCarthy et al., 2004). Rather, people engage in the Arts for diverse and highly personal reasons, including enjoyment and feelings of self-accomplishment (Barrett, Everett & Smigiel, 2012). This point is noted in an article by Rickard, Bambrick and Gill (2012), who emphasise that the value of music in education lies in its benefits to students as a unique area of learning; rather than 'on the basis that it may enhance ability in other domains' (p. 58). For example, children who play a simple singing and clapping game in the playground do this because it is enjoyable and stimulating for them to do so; or a young child who finds a small broom in the dress-up box and imaginatively plays with this as a 'wand' does so because it allows them to enjoy 'being' a fairy.

> **TEACHER TIP**
>
> Set up a dress-up box in one corner of your classroom. This could include anything that you think children could use to imagine or make-believe with. Encourage children to use this resource as an imaginative adjunct to any learning activity, allowing them to explore, for example, characters in a story, play or piece of music. This enables embodied learning to occur – learning that focuses on using the whole of our mind and body to solve a problem or express a point of view.
>
> Ways to explore such 'play' in an educational context might be for children to choose a jacket and list the number of different characters/jobs/settings the jacket could be used for (for example, a black trench coat could represent a spy, soldier, business woman/man, a homeless person, someone out in the rain/snow, a politician or a television news reporter).

Intrinsic benefits: refer to the direct benefits of participation in the Arts, such as visual art making skills or singing skills. Intrinsic benefits also include such outcomes as feeling a sense of 'flow' (Nakamura & Csikszentmihalyi, 2002), 'flowtion' (Barrett et al., 2012) or 'captivation' (McCarthy et al., 2004) in the moment of making art.

Instrumental benefits: refer to the impact of Arts learning on other areas, such as academic, personal and social skills.

The research around the importance of the Arts in education is presented in two main sections: '**intrinsic benefits**' and '**instrumental benefits**'. In this chapter we also discuss the ideas of learning 'in' and learning 'through' the Arts. Learning 'in' the Arts is associated with the research regarding 'intrinsic' benefits, and learning 'through' the Arts is associated with the 'instrumental' benefits. Understanding these concepts will assist you to better understand what it is that your Arts teaching is doing for your children.

Intrinsic benefits

The Arts are unquestionably important enough in and of themselves to be of value in student learning. In fact, Robinson (1999, 2005) and Jefferson and Anderson (2017) argue that children need the diversity provided by Arts participation *because* of recent educational trends that focus on quantifiable, reportable outcomes in areas such as literacy and numeracy.

Ewing (2010), O'Toole (2012) and Robinson (2005) all make the point that there is a hierarchy of learning evidenced in curricula around the world that places a premium on traditional verbal and mathematical reasoning. This is one of the most compelling reasons for arts-rich education in schools and childcare centres. Human endeavour at its best is multifaceted, not just verbal and mathematical, and likewise children are diverse in their capabilities and dispositions rather than just uni-dispositional. It is therefore vital that all children have access to diverse ways of understanding their worlds, such as through the Arts.

The intrinsic benefits of Arts participation are, according to McCarthy et al. (2004, p. 37), 'intangible and difficult to define. They lie beyond the traditional quantitative tools of the social sciences, and often beyond the language of common experience'. This is true because of the nature of the Arts as intensely personal reflections and translations of individual human experiences, the inability of language to authentically communicate the impact of a multisensory experience, and because of the limitations of quantitative means to report on these experiences in a world that places a premium on facts and figures. However, it is clear that the Arts do something 'different' for people; they enable the expression and communication of thoughts, ideas and emotions in ways that other forms of communication simply cannot. Central to this premise is the fact that the Arts intrinsically communicate in non-verbal ways (Barrett, 2003; McCarthy et al., 2004; Wright, 2003a).

Wright (2003a, pp. 16–17) states: 'Language is inadequate for the expression of everything we feel and sense.' Non-verbal communication refers to that which is non-language-based, such as through visual mark-making, dramatic gesture and movement or through sound. This is perhaps one of the most important functions of the Arts in our lives: they are not an inferior form of verbal communication; rather, they are *unique* forms of expression.

McCarthy et al. (2004, p. 14) report the following intrinsic benefits of Arts participation:

- the pleasure and emotional stimulation of a personal, 'felt' response
- captivation by an imaginative experience
- an expanded capacity for empathy, leading to the potential for creating social bonds and shared experiences of art
- cognitive growth in being able to make sense of art
- the ability to find a voice to express communal meaning through art.

Hunter (2005, p. 4) refers to two intrinsic benefits of Arts participation, these being 'arts knowledge and skills [and] enjoyment and value of the Arts'. We argue that the very human sense of enjoyment through engaging in an art form is not an instrumental benefit, but rather something that is fundamental to why people 'do' the Arts in the first place. McCarthy et al. (2004, p. xv) refer to this benefit as a 'distinctive type of pleasure and emotional stimulation'.

Reflection activity

INTRINSIC BENEFITS

Think for a moment about when you may have seen children deeply engrossed in an Arts activity – such as dress-ups, singing, painting or dancing. How do you know that they are so engrossed? What in their behavior tells you this? Is this an example of intrinsic benefit?

Table 2.1 summarises the intrinsic benefits of Arts participation and provides you with some useful examples. As you read the examples in Table 2.1 think about how and when these behaviours may be exhibited. When you are next in a position to observe child behaviour and see evidence of these, take some notes and then refer back to this table, reflecting on the significance of this.

TABLE 2.1 EXAMPLES OF THE INTRINSIC BENEFITS OF THE ARTS

Benefit	Example
Arts knowledge and skills	Singing or playing a piece of music, drawing a picture, acting a role, making a movie or dancing all enable children to develop important skills such as rhythm, harmony, spatial orientation or imagination.
Non-verbal expression	A child paints a picture, performs a self-devised dance or creates a soundscape. None of these activities express linguistically; they allow the child to use their senses.
Pleasure and captivation	The rapt involvement of a child singing a song or acting a role, when they forget the world around them and just enjoy the moment. The Arts captivate children and can be intensely pleasurable.
Emotional stimulation	Listening to a beautiful, emotionally stimulating piece of music or gazing at a piece of art can evoke intense emotional responses in children.
Finding a 'voice'	Children learn in many ways, involving all of the senses. For some children this will be particularly important as 'their' way of expressing their 'self'.
Expressing shared meaning	Singing in a choir, dancing a story or acting in a role-play allows children to express something shared, such as understanding or identity, in ways that no other activity can. These opportunities can greatly increase empathy between children.

Video: I'm yours (ukulele)

Instrumental benefits

The instrumental benefits of Arts education refer to the ways in which participating in the Arts can assist other curriculum or cross-curriculum areas. An example is the ways that singing a song may assist literacy development or social learning. Intrinsic and instrumental benefits are basically two sides of the same coin – they are both important. Gardner (1999) does however provide a cautionary note when considering the instrumental benefits of Arts participation, stating:

> If arts live by instrumental arguments, they may also die should those arguments be proved faulty – or should someone find a less expensive way to raise IQ or spawn imaginative business people (np).

In other words, while the instrumental benefits of Arts participation offer us sound extrinsic reasons for including the Arts in our practice, the most important reasons for the Arts in education are intrinsic because they are actually about the Arts themselves. When using instrumental arguments for the inclusion of the Arts we also need to be aware of the contested notion of 'transfer' of skills or dispositions from one area of learning to another. Hallam (2010, p. 271) addresses the notion of transfer when discussing music education, noting:

> The transfer of learning from one domain to another depends on the similarities between the processes involved. Transfer between tasks is a function of the degree to which the tasks share cognitive processes.

In other words, transfer is more likely when the skills being 'transferred' are similar, such as in decoding written music and decoding written language. Transfer is closely related to the notion of 'causation', that participation in one art form 'causes' effects in another Learning Area. This notion is contested, and we do need to be careful in the claims that we make about the instrumental impacts of Arts participation. We have tried to do so in this chapter.

Spotlight on Arts education

IMPROVING ENGLISH AND LITERACY USING DRAMA STRATEGIES

'School Drama' is a professional learning program developed by Sydney Theatre Company in 2009, involving the pairing of a teaching artist with a teacher for a school term. The teaching artist models ways to use drama-based strategies with children's story books to improve English and literacy learning.

Links: Sydney Theatre Company; State Theatre Company

Evaluation of drama programs such as School Drama and the State Theatre Company SA Education Program has shown a high level of success in changed teacher beliefs, professional learning, in their use of drama in literacy, and drama strategies across the curriculum. Evidence of increased achievement in student literacy outcomes has also been clearly demonstrated. The drama activities engage students on many levels, and it is generally not just improvement in literacy skills that can be observed, but improvement in many other aspects of student wellbeing as well.

Students are engaged by the drama activities and strategies, which leads to them gaining a better understanding of what literacy actually is; and students are often surprised when they realise they are actually learning literacy while participating in activities they enjoy. Teachers recognise that the drama techniques can make a difference to student interest and enjoyment in their learning.

These are some quotes from one such evaluation of the South Australian School Drama program by Hamilton (2014):

> one of my kids just turned around and said 'we're in literacy aren't we?'. He'd just made that connection in his head that because we were talking about words and

> how we can put a bit more detail into our writing the task wasn't to write something the task was to do some sort of acting and it was fun yeah! (Teacher)
>
> Oh I'm learning but I'm having fun. (Student)
>
> This was particularly effective with previously unmotivated students. Teachers related how disengaged children slowly came around and became interested.

The most common instrumental benefit asserted is that participation in the Arts improves academic performance. In her review of the Arts in Australian education, Ewing (2010, p. 13) refers to this, writing:

> It is now widely documented in the United States of America, Canada and Europe, including the United Kingdom, that those students whose learning is embedded in the Arts … achieve better grades and overall test scores, are less likely to leave school early, rarely report boredom and have a more positive self concept than those students who are deprived of arts experiences.

In a study of Arts education in over 40 countries, Bamford (2006, p. 20) also suggests that participation in quality Arts education leads to improved academic achievement, particularly enhanced literacy and language learning. Brouillette et al. (2014) found that attendance rates increased and speaking and listening performance improved among K–2 students who participated in drama, dance and visual programs. Another study by Thomas, Singh and Klopfenstein (2015) found that consistent engagement in Arts education had a positive impact on attendance at high school. Bamford (2006) also draws attention to the social benefits of Arts participation in building a 'sense of community through a shared spirit and encourage[ing] student motivation to learn', and refers to improved perceptions of schools by stakeholders. The attitudinal benefits of Arts participation, such as 'risk-taking, confidence, and ownership of learning' (p. 20), are also noted, as are 'increased co-operation, respect, responsibility, tolerance, and appreciation' (p. 115).

Of particular significance in this research is the attention drawn to the importance of 'quality' Arts education in achieving these outcomes; Bamford maintains that the benefits are only evident when programs of quality are functioning. Duma and Silverstein (2014) reported on the John F. Kennedy Center for the Performing Arts 'Changing Education through the Arts' (CETA) program. They reported that, through programs that focused on Arts integration, students were more engaged, had improved cognitive and social skills and improved marks. There have also been recent studies that focused on the impact of music on language development (Lorenzo et al., 2014; Pitts, 2016), and of theatre arts on literacy and numeracy (Inoa, Weltsek & Tabone, 2014).

> **TEACHER TIP**
>
> Arts integration is what general primary and early childhood teachers do. As you begin to plan for learning in your classrooms and spaces, continue to ask the question: 'Have I integrated the Arts into this lesson?'. Thus, you become more aware of the extent to which you can use your understandings to make student learning more exciting and rewarding – through the Arts. Read the article 'Integrating Arts and Science in the Classroom' by David Roy at teachermagazine.com.au.
>
> Think about the activities listed and the potential for use within the classroom.
>
> Link: *Teacher* magazine

In an overview of six research studies of mostly 'at-risk' children aged 9–15 years, Hunter (2005) emphasised the importance of professional support for teachers and for partnerships between schools, families and community Arts organisations in achieving benefits for children. Referring to both the intrinsic and the instrumental benefits, Hunter (2005, p. 4) states that:

> There is evidence in the research reports to indicate that arts participation, to varying degrees, positively impacts on students':
>
> - social and personal [instrumental]
> - attitude to learning [instrumental]
> - literacy [instrumental]
> - numeracy [instrumental]
> - arts knowledge and skills [intrinsic]
> - generic competencies (writing, communicating, problem-solving, planning, organising, perseverance) [instrumental]
> - enjoyment and value of the arts [intrinsic].

Bryce et al. (2004) studied four Australian Arts programs (two music and two drama) and found that these programs enhanced children's engagement with learning through increased self-esteem, improved cooperation in learning, and goal-setting. Interestingly, as was the case in Hunter (2005), this study also mentions the value of Arts programs in bringing together stakeholders, such as families and community groups, with schools also being a feature of the *Seoul Agenda: Goals for the Development of Arts Education* (UNESCO, 2010). Bryce et al. (2004) also comment on the role played by these Arts programs for children who seem not to 'fit' with more traditional learning programs in schools, and on the positive value of Arts learning for children who may struggle with literacy. Finally, Bryce et al. (2004) make particular reference to the advantages demonstrated by programs in respect of improvements in student teamwork skills and in using the Arts to express emotions.

Despite the fact that the Arts contribute to social development and educational impact, as seen in the work of Geese Theatre (Baim, Brookes & Mountford, 2002), for example, along with the potential implication for wider school engagement and success for children, it is surprising that empirical examination of the implementation of the Arts as a pedagogical tool still remains a developing area. A key exemplar of this is the methodology of using drama with offenders who have been institutionalised, and the impact it has had upon those individuals and their sense of identity and place in society (Baim, Brookes & Mountford, 2002; Wilsher, 2007).

Critical Links: Learning in the Arts and Student Academic and Social Development (Deasy, 2002) is a compendium of 62 studies regarding the instrumental benefits of Arts education. In this compendium, a UK-based mixed-method study examining the relationship between Arts education and performance on national exams (Harland et al., 2000, p. 76) indicated that participants reported many benefits from Arts study, but there was no significant improvement for these children in exam results in non-Arts areas of study.

> [Children] reported that arts classes resulted in enjoyment, relief of tension, learning about social and cultural issues, development of creativity and thinking skills, enriched expressive skills, self confidence, and personal and social development.

This study, along with observations by Horowitz and Webb-Dempsey (2002), adds to the growing body of evidence regarding the cognitive, attitudinal and social benefits of Arts participation.

In another *Critical Links* study, Burton, Horowitz and Abeles (2000) examined 2406 children from grades 4, 5, 7 and 8 in a mix of 18 Arts-rich and Arts-poor schools, exploring the transfer of creativity and self-concept through Arts education. Using a variety of tools, the researchers 'found that children in Arts-rich schools scored higher in creativity and several measures of academic self-concept than students in schools without that level of arts' (p. 66). This study adds further weight to the argument that Arts participation has an impact on personal and cognitive development.

In her meta-analysis of existing studies, Vaughn (2000) found that there was '[a] significant relationship between music study and mathematics achievement. Students who take music classes in high school are more likely to score higher on standardized mathematics tests'. In another *Critical Links* study, Butzlaff (2000, p. 106) found that a meta-analysis 'demonstrated a strong and reliable association between music instruction and standardised measures of reading ability'.

Champions of Change: The Impact of the Arts on Learning (Fiske, 1999) was a ground-breaking report on the impact of Arts education. It reports on the findings of seven research teams over several years into seven different Arts education programs in the United States, using a mix of research methodologies. In this report, a study by Catterall, Chapleau and Iwanaga (1999) into intense involvement in music and drama and its effects on achievement revealed powerful relationships, particularly in relation to socioeconomic status (SES). The study used National Educational Longitudinal Survey (NELS) data from 25 000 grade 8–12 students, analysing data at grades 8, 10 and 12. The study:

> found substantial and significant differences in achievement and in important attitudes and behaviours between youths highly involved in the Arts on the one hand, and those with little or no arts engagement on the other hand (p. 3).

Most importantly, this was irrespective of SES. This is extremely significant, because it suggests that Arts participation can 'value-add' to the education of children regardless of their SES. Two specific findings are worthy of particular note. The study found that involvement in 'band' activities doubled the maths proficiency of children; and those children engaged in drama studies outperformed others in reading proficiency, in addition to demonstrating greater levels of tolerance. A more recent study by Phillips et al. (2014) found that participation in an integrated Arts program in Mississippi (USA) substantially reduced the gap in achievement between higher and lower SES students. The same study found that participation also increased achievement in mathematics, literacy and science.

Catterall and Waldorf (1999) conducted a six-year investigation of the Chicago Arts Partnerships in Education (CAPE) program, in which the focus was on Arts curriculum integration in low SES public schools and partnerships between teachers and community artists. In one finding from this study, those schools involved in the CAPE program outperformed non-CAPE schools on every one of 52 measures. Importantly, the research found a 'very strong case' to support the effects of the Arts program on reading and mathematics at grade 6 and a 'moderate case' for reading and mathematics at grade 3 (p. 54). Scripp and Paradis (2014) investigated the CAPE Partnerships in Arts Integration Research (PAIR) project in which Arts integration sites were compared to sites where no Arts integration was occurring, and determined that 'students at schools with an arts focus combined with arts integration programming scored higher on state academic tests than did students who received exclusively academic or conventional arts learning instruction' (p. 1).

Also adding to the growing body of support for the impact of the Arts on young people is a report (Martin et al., 2013) of a two-year study involving 643 primary (grades 5 and 6) and high school (grades 7–12) students in 15 schools by the University of Sydney's Faculty of Education and Social Work and the Australia Council for the Arts. This study found that active Arts participation in school, home and the community impacts on academic and non-academic outcomes for students, with school-based Arts participation having the greatest impact on academic outcomes (p. 722). Academic outcomes included such things as motivation, engagement, academic intentions, enjoyment of school, participation in class and academic resilience. Non-academic outcomes included such effects as 'self-esteem, life satisfaction, and sense of meaning and purpose' (p. 713). According to the study students who are involved in the arts have higher school motivation, engagement in class, self-esteem, and life satisfaction. Also of significance from this study is the author's statement that 'The findings suggest that practice should not simply be focused on the quantity of arts participation; rather, there is a need to ensure quality factors such as engagement' (Martin et al., 2013, p. 723). This is consistent with the findings of other researchers such as Bamford (2006), who emphasises the importance of quality, not just curriculum presence.

The research reported above contributes to the claim that Arts engagement has effects on student learning in many ways. These include:

- academic performance (literacy and numeracy), with particular evidence of the effect of music and drama on learning
- personal dispositions and habits, such as improved self-concept, increased school engagement, personal organisation and perseverance
- social functions, such as teamwork and increased tolerance.

Finally, the research also suggests that the Arts provide avenues for children who may not respond well to traditional curricula and school structures, and that the Arts provide valuable opportunities for partnerships between schools and communities. Hallam (2010) also makes an interesting observation in respect of the benefits of engagement in music education, stating that 'the positive effects of engagement with music on personal and social development only occur if it is an enjoyable and rewarding experience' (p. 269). This suggests, along with Bamford (2006), that it is the quality of Arts experiences that has the potential to assist student learning.

Reflection activity

In this section, we have reviewed much of the research about the intrinsic and instrumental benefits of Arts participation.

Read the article 'Science classes won't future-proof our children. But dance might' by Christina Patterson in *The Guardian* and list the intrinsic and instrumental benefits referred to.

Read the article 'Music is good for your health and wellbeing, researchers say' by Siobhan Ryan in *The Argus* about the benefits of singing, and list the claims made by the authors.

How many of these are intrinsic and how many are instrumental?

Links
Reflection activity

Lesson plan 2.2

Please note that this lesson would be part of a longer unit or series of lessons, and that it can be adapted for use with any age group.

AIM

Using drama strategies to improve student literacy and engagement.

OUTLINE/DESCRIPTION

Students will identify characters and activities in an artwork. They will learn drama strategies to explore roles and situations relating to the artwork. They will also develop skills in using descriptive words and creating short stories. A suggested artwork is *Australian Beach Pattern* by Charles Meere, which was painted in 1940.

Students begin by describing the scene, starting a list of words that can be added to over time. Teacher: What words can you use to describe a beach? Imagine a beach you have visited and describe what you see and hear and feel. Then students identify different characters and groups of characters in the painting, for example the woman and two children (left). Students work in small groups discussing the characters in one of the groups. How are they feeling? Who are they with? Why are they there? What are they doing? What is going to happen next? Students develop personal empathy by getting into character using voice, movement and facial expression to create a believable character. They then choose a role and form a tableau (dramatic picture).

EXTENSIONS – OVER A SERIES OF LESSONS

Each student could write a story including the person whose role they took. There is a lot of action in the painting so you could use the drama strategy of 'body sculpting', whereby students work in pairs taking turns to be the sculptor or the lump of clay. In this strategy, using words only without any physical touching, the 'sculptor' has to direct the piece of clay into an action figure from the painting. For example: 'lift your right arm up and make a curved shape. Then make your face look excited by widening your eyes and smiling'.

Once the 'sculptures' are finished, the sculptors can wander around and admire their work. Students can then write a description of what they did, and then the pairs swap roles and choose another character. Students can also write a script to 'bring the painting to life' through drama elements.

INTENDED OUTCOMES – DRAMA

Students identify
- characters and roles

Students understand
- that elements of drama communicate meaning

Students are able to
- use voice, body and movement to create character
- feel empathy for characters and engage in play building

> ## LINKS TO CURRICULUM
>
> ### Foundation to year 2 content descriptors
> - Explore role and dramatic action in dramatic play, improvisation and process drama (ACADRM027).
> - Use voice, facial expression, movement and space to imagine and establish role and situation (ACADRM028).
>
> ### Early Years Learning Framework
> Children:
> - 'are effective communicators' (DEEWR, 2009, p. 41)
> - 'engage with a range of texts and gain meaning from these texts' (DEEWR, 2009, p. 44).
>
> ## ASSESSMENT
> Students are asked to explain how they used drama elements to create their character.

Table 2.2 provides an overview of much of the research around the instrumental benefits of Arts participation that have been presented in this section. This is intended to provide you with a quick reference and may be useful as you advocate for the Arts in your teaching context.

TABLE 2.2 INSTRUMENTAL BENEFITS OF THE ARTS

Benefits	Research
The Arts, self-esteem, cooperation, goal-setting and inclusion: • children's self-esteem is increased • children are better able to work cooperatively with others • children learn to plan and set goals • the Arts can provide learning opportunities for children who do not fit the conventional mould of institutional learning	**Reference:** Bryce, J. et al. (2004). *Evaluation of School-based Arts Education Programmes in Australian Schools*. Camberwell, Vic: Australian Council for Educational Research. **Research questions:** • What is the impact of each Arts program on participating children's academic progress, engagement with learning and attendance at school? • Are empirical or anecdotal examples of improved learning outcomes substantiated? • What are the attributes of Arts programs that are of particular benefit to the children? **Overview:** Investigation of four Australian school-based Arts programs: Arts@Direk in South Australia; Northern Territory Music Programs – Boys' Business program; Northern Territory Music Program, Indigenous Music Education Program; SCRAYP – Youth Arts with an Edge (Melbourne).

TABLE 2.2 (Cont.)

Benefits	Research
Broad impacts: Positive impacts on: • social and personal development • attitude to learning • literacy • numeracy • Arts knowledge and skills • generic competencies (writing, communicating, problem-solving, planning, organising, perseverance).	**Reference:** Hunter, M. (2005). *Education and the Arts Research Overview*. Sydney: Australia Council. **Research questions:** This is an overview of studies. **Overview:** Summarises the scope and results of six education and the Arts research projects commissioned by the Australia Council that researched mostly 'at-risk' children aged 9–15 years.
The Arts, creativity and self-concept: Children in Arts-rich schools scored higher than children in schools without that level of Arts in: • creativity • measures of academic self-concept • more innovative teachers.	**Reference:** Burton, J. M., Horowitz, R. and Abeles, H. (2000). 'Learning in and through the Arts: the question of transfer', *Studies in Art Education*, 41(3), 228–57. In R. Deasy (ed.), *Critical Links: Learning in the Arts and Student Academic and Social Development*, pp. 106–7. Washington, DC: Arts Education Partnership. **Research questions:** • Do children in Arts-rich schools show more creativity and higher academic self-concept than those in Arts-poor schools? • Do Arts-rich schools have different climates from Arts-poor schools? **Overview:** Explored 2406 grade 4, 5 7 and 8 students in a mix of 18 Arts-rich and Arts-poor schools, exploring the transfer of creativity and self-concept through Arts education.
Music and reading: • The study found a 'strong and reliable association between music instruction and standardised measures of reading ability'.	**Reference:** Butzlaff, R. (2000). 'Can music be used to teach reading?' *The Journal of Aesthetic Education*, 34(3),167–78. In R. Deasy (ed.), *Critical Links: Learning in the Arts and Student Academic and Social Development*, pp. 106–7. Washington, DC: Arts Education Partnership. **Research question(s):** • Is there a relationship between music instruction and performance in reading? • Does music instruction lead to enhanced reading ability? **Overview:** This research was conducted as a meta-analysis of 30 studies that used a standardised measure of reading performance and were used after a period of music instruction.

TABLE 2.2 (Cont.)

Benefits	Research
Music and mathematics: • There is a relationship between music study and mathematics achievement. • There is a 'small causal relationship showing that music training enhances math performance'. • 'Students who take music classes in high school are more likely to score higher on standardised mathematics tests.' • 'Listening to some kinds of music may aid performance on mathematics tests.'	**Reference:** Vaughn, K. (2000). 'Music and mathematics: Modest support for the oft-claimed relationship.' In R. Deasy (ed.), *Critical Links: Learning in the Arts and Student Academic and Social Development*, pp. 130–1. Washington, DC: Arts Education Partnership. **Research questions:** • Is there a relationship between music study and mathematics achievement? • Does music instruction cause increases in mathematics achievement? • Does listening to background music while thinking about mathematics problems enhance mathematics ability? **Overview:** A meta-analysis of existing research studies – initially 4000 studies.
Music and mathematics: • There is a 'very strong case' to support the effects of the Arts program on reading and mathematics at grade 6. • There is a 'moderate case' for mathematics at grade 3. **Music and reading:** • There is a 'moderate case' for reading at grade 3.	**Reference:** Catterall, J. S. and Waldorf, L. (1999). 'Chicago Arts Partnerships in Education Summary Evaluation'. In E. Fiske (ed.), *Champions of Change: The Impact of the Arts on Learning*, pp. 47–62. Washington, DC: The Arts Partnership and the President's Committee on the Arts and Humanities. **Research question:** Do low-SES urban public school children in schools that integrate Arts and academics (through partnerships with teachers and artists) perform better on standardised tests than children who are in schools that do not integrate Arts with academics? **Overview:** A six-year investigation of the Chicago Arts Partnerships in Education (CAPE) program.
The Arts and academic achievement: No evidence that the Arts boost general academic performance. Children reported benefits such as: • enjoyment • relief of tension • learning about social and cultural issues • development of creativity and thinking skills • enriched expressive skills • self-confidence • personal and social development.	**Reference:** Harland, J. et al., with Cusworth, L., White, R. and Paola, R. (2000). 'Arts education in secondary schools: Effects and effectiveness'. In R. Deasy (ed.), *Critical Links: Learning in the Arts and Student Academic and Social Development*, pp. 76–7. Washington, DC: Arts Education Partnership and National Endowment for the Arts. **Research question:** Does involvement in the Arts in secondary school boost general academic performance? **Overview:** This was primarily a qualitative study based on student self-report, but it also included a quantitative examination of the relationship between Arts concentration in secondary school and performance in national exams.

TABLE 2.2 (Cont.)

Benefits	Research
Music and drama and academic achievement: • Music and mathematics: highly engaged music students performed better in mathematics in year 12. • Drama and reading: highly engaged drama students performed better in reading. • Music, drama and reading: highly engaged Arts year 8–12 students scored higher in reading. • Music, drama and history, geography and citizenship: highly engaged Arts year 8–12 students scored higher in history, geography and citizenship tests. Note: The study 'found substantial and significant differences in achievement and in important attitudes and behaviours between youths highly involved in the Arts on the one hand, and those with little or no Arts engagement on the other hand' (Catterall, Chapleau & Iwanaga, 1999, p. 3).	**Reference:** Catterall, J. S., Chapleau, R. and Iwanaga, J. (1999). 'Involvement in the Arts and human development: General involvement and intensive involvement in music and theater arts'. In E. Fiske (ed.), *Champions of Change: The Impact of the Arts on Learning*, pp. 1–18. Washington, DC: The Arts Partnership and the President's Committee on the Arts and Humanities. **Research questions:** • Do high school seniors who have been highly involved in the Arts at least since eighth grade perform better academically than students who have not been involved in the Arts? • What academic achievement patterns are associated with intensive involvement in theatre and in music? **Overview:** The study used National Educational Longitudinal Survey (NELS) data from 25 000 grade 8–12 students, analysing data at grades 8, 10 and 12. It included data on music and drama participation and relationships to SES and standardised test results.
Music and spatial–temporal reasoning: • A medium-sized causal link was found between listening to music and temporary improvement in spatial–temporal reasoning • A large causal relationship was found between making music and spatial–temporal reasoning. **Classroom drama and verbal skills:** A causal link was found between drama and a variety of verbal areas.	**Reference:** Hetland, L. and Winner. E. (2001). 'The Arts and academic achievement: What the evidence shows'. *Arts Education Policy Review*, 102(5), 3–6. **Research question:** No research question is stated; however, this is a meta-analysis that investigated the relationship between the Arts and academic achievement. **Overview:** This project reported on 188 reports, written between 1950 and 1999, which examined the notion of the Arts and academic achievement.

In the classroom

Next time you are working with children observe the ways in which using the Arts help such outcomes as self-esteem, communication, teamwork and enjoyment. Just make up an observation sheet with the names of children down one side of the page and the various behaviours you are looking for along the top. Every time you see one of the behaviours demonstrated by a student put a tick in the appropriate box. Once the activity is finished, count the ticks and reflect on the ways in which you could continue to assist these children through the Arts.

Learning 'in' and 'through' the Arts and your role as an educator

Learning 'in' the Arts: associated with the 'intrinsic' benefits – it is about the Arts learning.

Learning 'through' the Arts: associated with the 'instrumental' benefits – it is about the 'other' things that learning in the Arts helps with.

What is the distinction between **learning 'in' the Arts** and **learning 'through' the Arts**, and why is this distinction important? These are both important concepts to understand in relation to the value of the Arts in education, and in your practice as an early childhood or primary educator. When you include, structure and enable learning using the Arts, it is important that you can also articulate the areas of learning that you are thus having an impact upon.

Much of the literature refers to the importance of the distinction between learning 'in' and learning 'through' the Arts. Bamford (2006, p. 12) writes:

> [Education in the arts] can be described as being sustained and systematic learning in the skills, ways of thinking and presentation of each of the art forms … Concurrently, education which uses creative and artistic pedagogies to teach all curricula – i.e. education through the arts – enhances overall academic attainment, reduces school disaffection and promotes positive cognitive transfer.

Importantly, Bamford (2006, p. 70) adds to our understanding of these two notions by stating that they 'should be considered in a complementary but separate manner'. The complementary nature of these two notions is significant when understanding the types of learning you are encouraging in your children and your role in this process. Learning 'in' and 'through' the Arts most commonly occur *simultaneously*.

Learning 'in' the Arts

Learning 'in' the Arts refers to specific and unique learning in each art form. For example, when children sing a song they learn about pitch, harmony and rhythm (see Chapter 7); or when children paint a self-portrait they learn about colour, composition and mark-making (see Chapter 8). Learning 'in' the Arts is characterised by:

- art form specific skills and understandings usually determined through codes and conventions, such as elements, principles and processes of the particular art form

- art form specific views of the world, paradigms or ways of creating and communicating meaning (while these five art forms are all 'Arts', each implies a different way of looking at and responding to our past and present worlds)
- the actual works that are created in each art form, such as a sculpture, a piece of music or a ballet.

Learning 'through' the Arts

Learning 'through' the Arts refers to what children learn in other areas as a result of Arts making and responding. For example, when children sing a song they also learn about the lyrics and poetry of that song; or when children paint a self-portrait they also learn about identity and culturally specific modes of representation. Learning 'through' the Arts is characterised by:
- specific academic learning in another learning area, such as decoding in literacy, drugs awareness in health or multiplication in numeracy
- cognitive or emotional dispositions, such as collaboration skills, improved self-esteem or an increased desire to learn.

Table 2.3 outlines five example tasks that include learning 'in' and 'through' the Arts. Each task represents one of the Arts areas. As you read the table, think about the ideas of learning 'in' and 'through' and the ways in which a task can embed these types of learning. Also note the ways in which these types of learning occur simultaneously in the same task. Understanding these two different types of learning is important when considering your role in your school or childcare centre, as you need to be able to identify, select, structure and implement learning in both 'types' of Arts-related learning.

TABLE 2.3 LEARNING IN AND THROUGH THE ARTS: EXAMPLES

Example	Learning in the Arts	Learning through the Arts
1 Music Year 6 children compose and rehearse a song based on a piece of poetry.	- Pitch – writing a melody for the words. - Harmony – working out chords to go with the tune. - Tempo – finding the correct speed for the song. - Dynamics – what volumes suit certain moments in the song. - Notation – writing the finished song down or recording it for others. - Ensemble – children rehearsing the song as a group. - Composition – composing a piece of music that expresses a point of view or emotional state.	- Speech and language skills – matching melody and lyrics. - Mathematical skills – matching the correct number of beats per bar of music; 'feeling' and counting the pulse or beat. - Thinking skills – conceiving a song that illustrates an emotional state of being by the combination of language and music. - Social skills – working and rehearsing as a team to compose and perform the song. - Motivation to learn – children feeling 'successful' having completed their song, and this feeling of success motivating them to learn more. - Positive school environment – the children get so good at performing their song, that they compose and perform other songs; other children view this success and realise that they too can be successful.
2 Drama Children develop a performance based upon the stimulus of the poem and the song they have created.	- Creating – developing a performance idea that re-enacts the ideas of the poem/song. - Role – adopting a character to reflect the mood/tone of the poem/song. - Relationship – exploring how the different roles in the created performance interact with each other. - Tension – using the performance area to demonstrate the tensions and relationships between characters/roles.	- Literacy skills – structuring a performance, considering the narrative structure of introduction, complication, development and resolution. - Social competence – planning through group work. - Health and PE – using bodies in a healthy, safe manner to represent roles. - Numeracy – planning sight lines and measuring for a suitable performance area.
3 Dance Children explore movements that reflect the emotions of the poem/song.	- Body – using hands, wrists and arms to reflect the tone of music through gestures. - Space – children in groups using the area to move in, exploring different heights and positioning to communicate the core emotion of the poem as they interpret it. - Energy – exploring pace and size of movements to show changes in tempo/mood of the poem/song. - Choreography – watching a video of rehearsed movements and suggesting ways to change individual and group movements to enhance the visual literacy of their performance.	- ICT – using video as a tool for recording work. - Literacy – writing expository text to justify movement decisions and representations. - Critical thinking – discussing and sharing ideas of how movements represent emotion concepts. - Intercultural understanding – exploring movements and meanings from a variety of cultures that demonstrate their intended meanings. - Self-confidence – experiencing success as they demonstrate their ideas to others in the class and potentially outside the classroom, recognising that there is no right or wrong method of expression.

4 Visual arts Year 6 children design a CD cover and poster to promote their song.	• Target audience – designing a cover to appeal to a target audience. • Art/design elements and principles – colour, space, line, composition, focal point, harmony/ discord etc. • Exploring media such as acrylic paint, watercolours, digital photographs. • Printing posters and CD covers.	• Cognitive skills – thinking about the target audience; how to catch their attention. • Mathematics – working out ratios fitting the image to the cover; golden mean (rule of thirds). • English – writing an introduction. • Literacy – labelling, contents, etc. • Social skills – working as a team to promote their song. • Motivation to learn – successful promotion of the song they are proud of.
5 Media arts Year 6 children create a video clip of their song.	• Movie making and editing, writing a script, using props, camera angles, transitions. • Sound – using GarageBand, adding music to the movie. • Marketing – target audience.	• Cognitive skills – matching visuals to the song, making the meaning visible to others through images. • Self and group confidence in their abilities – having control of editing, being creative. • Mathematics – marketing, costing, budgeting. • English/literacy – creating a storyline to match the song. • Positive school and community environment – pride in their achievements.

> **Reflection activity**
>
> You are to present an argument to your school or childcare centre principal for the centrality of the Arts in the curriculum. Having reflected upon the intrinsic and instrumental benefits of Arts education and the notions of learning 'in' and 'through' the Arts, compile your own rationale for the Arts in education to use for this purpose. Try to relate your reading and thinking to what you know about the ways in which children learn.
>
> Present this to a colleague.
>
> *Statement:* The Arts are important in education because …
>
> *Rationale:* The research about the Arts in education includes intrinsic and instrumental studies, such as …
>
> The Arts can impact on student learning in multiple ways, including …
>
> *New media:* New media can impact on Arts participation in my classroom by …
>
> *My students:* My students will be given opportunities to learn 'in' and 'through' the Arts by …
>
> What should your rationale include?

Conclusion

The Arts have been an important part of human existence for millennia. They allow us to express and communicate our perspectives on life, our cultures and what it means to share this planet with others. The Arts have enormous value in their own right as unique and deeply engaging expressions of our individuality and shared values; indeed, they are deeply personal expressions of the human condition. As such, they are an intrinsic and important component of any curriculum. They also have a unique instrumental curriculum position for the ways in which they stimulate and enable learning, cognitive and academic development, and important personal and social dispositions. Importantly, children value and enjoy participating in the Arts.

Understanding the argument for the Arts in education is important for you in your teaching contexts because, despite the raft of research and the power of the Arts as pedagogy, unlike other curriculum areas such as literacy or numeracy, the Arts seem to require that the argument be regularly made. As an early childhood and primary educator, you have a unique role in the delivery of quality Arts education experiences to the children in your care; it is you who will allow the Arts to make a difference in their lives.

REVIEW QUESTIONS

1. What have new media changed about Arts engagement in recent years?
2. The Arts are unique forms of expression and …
3. What do the Arts have in common and do uniquely?
4. What elements does a praxial approach to Arts education include?
5. In a praxial approach to Arts education, children must …
6. Why should we be careful when making claims about 'transfer' and 'causation'?

RECOMMENDED READING

Eisner, E. (2002). *The Arts and the Creation of Mind*. New Haven, CT: Yale University Press.

Elliott, D. J. (1995). *Music Matters: A New Philosophy of Music Education*. New York: Oxford University Press.

Robinson, K. (2006). *How Schools Kill Creativity*. Retrieved from http://www.ted.com/talks/ken_robinson_says_schools_kill_creativity.html.

Wright, S. (2003). *Children, Meaning-making and the Arts*. Frenchs Forest, NSW: Pearson.

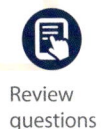

3

The Arts and cross-curriculum priorities

> We are living on this planet as if we had another one to go to.

Terry Swearingen (1997)

In this chapter

In this chapter we will discuss the important role of the Arts in addressing the cross-curriculum priorities of the Australian Curriculum. The cross-curriculum priorities serve a number of functions, including fostering intercultural understanding. We will also explore ways the Arts can be used to respond to issues of sustainability. The chapter includes innovative and practical suggestions for developing continuous and sequential cross-curriculum learning in the Arts.

By the end of this chapter you should have a clear understanding of the way the Arts link to:

- cross-curriculum and Arts learning
- Aboriginal and Torres Strait Islander histories and cultures
- Australia's engagement with Asia
- the Arts and sustainability.

Introduction

The Australian Curriculum's three cross-curriculum priorities have their origins in the educational priorities identified in the Melbourne Declaration on Educational Goals for Young Australians (MCEETYA, 2008). At the highest level the Melbourne Declaration is a commitment to schooling that 'promotes equity and excellence' and ensures that:

> All young Australians become:
> - successful learners
> - confident and creative individuals
> - active and informed citizens. (MCEETYA, 2008, p. 7)

In committing to the Declaration, the education ministers recognised the importance of equity and access to schooling, the need to foster cultural understanding, respect, and representation, and the importance of preparing students to face the challenges of the 21st century, which includes the issue of sustainability.

Within the Australian Curriculum three cross-curriculum priorities have been defined:

- Aboriginal and Torres Strait Islander Histories and Cultures
- Asia and Australia's Engagement with Asia
- Sustainability.

These three topics are not intended to be taught as separate Learning Areas; instead, they are about exploring relationships of subjects to one another. They enable the delivery of learning area content at the same time as developing knowledge, understanding and skills relating to the three priorities (ACARA, 2014).

Donelan (2012) suggests that Australia is one of the most ethnically diverse countries in the world. Classrooms could include children and teachers from a wide range of backgrounds. One of the professional standards for teachers (AITSL, 2017) is to 'know students' and be able to demonstrate knowledge of strategies that respond to the learning needs of students from diverse ethnic, religious, linguistic, cultural and socioeconomic backgrounds (Moloney & Saltmarsh, 2016).

In the past Australian educators have tended to focus on European examples in the Arts, but looking at Arts from diverse cultures enables children to see their histories more clearly and to reflect on their own. This text promotes the importance of learning about diverse cultures, especially those of Australia and Asia, and aims to support teachers in the development of related quality teaching materials.

In this chapter we propose ways to imbue traditional and contemporary Aboriginal and Torres Strait Islander Arts understandings and practices with integrity and respect. We include and acknowledge the Arts of our closest neighbours in Asia, providing you with knowledge and understanding that will guide you in your own preparation of appropriate learning materials. We also focus on ways to engage students in the concept of sustainability both locally and globally.

The meaning of cross-curriculum priorities

Cross-curriculum: connecting different subjects to develop a deeper knowledge and understanding of a particular topic.

The term **cross-curriculum** refers to the linking of subjects with a conceptual focus of developing a deeper knowledge and understanding of a particular topic (Parker, Heywood & Jolley, 2012). This approach has been shown to develop understanding and critical thinking skills as well as promoting connections between subject areas (Voogt & Pareja Roblin, 2012). The Australian Curriculum, Assessment and Reporting Authority (ACARA) gives equal significance to all three cross-curriculum priority areas. They are to be embedded in the curriculum, not taught as discrete areas, and vary in the degree of depth of integration depending on the degree of relevance to the subject. This approach was developed with the educational goals of the Melbourne Declaration in mind (ACARA, 2014). The goals are to make learning both relevant to the lives of students and address the contemporary issues they face.

> The priorities provide national, regional and global dimensions which will enrich the curriculum through development of considered and focused content that fits naturally within learning areas. They enable the delivery of learning area content at the same time as developing knowledge, understanding and skills relating to Aboriginal and Torres Strait Islander Histories and Cultures, Asia and Australia's Engagement with Asia and/or Sustainability. Incorporation of the priorities will encourage conversations between students, teachers and the wider community (ACARA, 2014, CCP Introduction).

For each cross curriculum priority, ACARA suggests ways that each Learning Area can contribute to Aboriginal and Torres Strait Islander histories and cultures, Asia and Australia's engagement with Asia, and sustainability.

The Arts

Students' exploration of traditional and contemporary artworks by Aboriginal and Torres Strait Islander Peoples provides insight into the way the relationships between People, Culture and Country/Place for Aboriginal and Torres Strait Islander Peoples can be conveyed through the arts, their expression in living communities, and the way these build Identity.

In the Australian Curriculum: The Arts, students can examine art forms that have arisen from the rich and diverse belief systems and traditions of the Asia region. Students can consider the aesthetic qualities of these art forms as well as their local, regional and global influence. This learning area provides opportunities to investigate the role of the arts in developing, maintaining and transforming cultural beliefs and practices and communicating an understanding of the rich cultural diversity of the Asia region. Students can engage with a variety of art forms, media, instruments and technologies of the Asia region. They can reflect on the intrinsic value of these artworks and artists' practices as well as their place and value within broader social, cultural, historical and political contexts.

The Australian Curriculum: The Arts provides engaging and thought-provoking contexts in which to explore the nature of art making and responding. It enables the exploration of the role of The Arts in maintaining and transforming cultural practices, social systems and the relationships of people to their environment. Through making and responding in The Arts, students consider issues of sustainability in relation to resource use and traditions in each of the Arts subjects. The Arts provides opportunities for students to express and develop world views, and to appreciate the need for collaboration within and between communities to implement more sustainable patterns of living. In this learning area, students use the exploratory and creative platform of the Arts to advocate effective action for sustainability (ACARA, 2014, CCP).

Cross-curriculum priorities provide an opportunity to foster cross-cultural understanding and respect. The Arts provide a particularly rich way to promote understanding and sensitivity to cultural and social diversity and to promote inclusivity for children who are marginalised or have special needs. The Arts are a means to explore other cultures through deep engagement through both process and product with culturally situated artistic practice, so they are also a means to cross-cultural understanding. The Arts provide ways to express ideas about sustainability and to consider local and global practices and contribute ways to influence audiences in order to change behaviours.

Cross-curriculum priorities and the early years

The Early Years Learning Framework (EYLF) does not include cross-curriculum priorities in the same way as the Australian Curriculum. Nonetheless there are similarities because the framework, like the Australian Curriculum, supports Goal 2 of the Melbourne Declaration, that:

> All young Australians become:
> - successful learners
> - confident and creative individuals
> - active and informed citizens. (MCEETYA, 2008, p. 7)

As a result, the EYLF's principles emphasise respect for diversity, which has obvious implications for Aboriginal and Torres Strait Islander peoples and for Australians of Asian backgrounds, and active citizenship. Furthermore, the learning outcomes articulated in the EYLF stress underlying themes closely associated with the cross-curriculum priorities of the Australian Curriculum. The most obvious illustrations of these aims are:

- Outcome 1: the development of knowledgeable and confident self-identity (Who I am? How I belong?)
- Outcome 2: Children respond to diversity with respect; and children become socially responsible and show respect for the environment.

So while the EYLF does not have the same cross-curriculum priorities of the Australian Curriculum, it shares the same impetus, values and aims.

Aboriginal and Torres Strait Islander histories and cultures

We, as the authors, must acknowledge that we are not of Aboriginal or Torres Strait Islander heritage, and are therefore keenly aware of this in approaching pedagogical methodologies on this topic. We have consulted widely with Indigenous peoples and with texts (many of which are linked in this chapter). We provide examples of work that we have used effectively in the classroom and hope that they will be useful starting points for teachers from any background.

One of the objectives set out in the Melbourne Declaration is for Australian students to understand and value the knowledge and skills of Indigenous cultures and to contribute to reconciliation between Indigenous and non-Indigenous Australians (MCEETYA, 2008).

This is a role entrusted to teachers. The AITSL Professional Standards for Teachers (2017), which is a public statement of what is expected of teachers in Australia, states strongly that it is everyone's responsibility to understand and respect Aboriginal and Strait Islander peoples to promote reconciliation between Indigenous and non-Indigenous Australians. This means that as a teacher, regardless of whether you are an Aboriginal Australian or a non-Aboriginal Australian, and regardless of whether or not your classes have Aboriginal or Torres Strait Islander students, there is a responsibility and expectation that you teach with respect and sensitivity.

The aim is to give all children the opportunity to learn about Indigenous cultures and languages and develop an understanding of and respect for Indigenous past, present and future. Learning to recognise and value Indigenous viewpoints on social, cultural and historical issues makes it harder for racism and exclusion to persist and helps foster a shared pride in the story of the land. Through learning about Aboriginal and Torres Strait Islander history, cultures and perspectives, students also learn about our national history and heritage, the experience of our First Nations peoples, the impact of **colonialism** and how we have become the society we are today. This aim seeks to ensure that all Australian children engage in reconciliation, respect and recognition of the histories of Aboriginal and Torres Strait Islander peoples' unique and long-lived history.

> **Colonialism:** one country controlling another country and benefitting from its wealth and resources. Within an Australian context, colonialism primarily refers to Britain's invasion and settlement of Australia and its subsequent effects lasting through to the present day.

Another key aspect of this cross-curriculum priority is to address concerns of equity and representation. The inclusion of Aboriginal and Torres Strait Islander histories and cultures across the curriculum means that Aboriginal and Torres Strait Islander students 'see themselves, their identities and their cultures' represented and reflected in their educational experience. By doing this they are supported in the curriculum and, through being seen, present and valued, 'can build their self-esteem'. As the noted Aboriginal educationalist Mark Rose observed, this cross-curriculum priority area is the 'best opportunity since the Education Acts of the 1880s to influence the national psyche around Indigenous issues' (Rose, 2015).

> The Aboriginal and Torres Strait Islander histories and cultures cross-curriculum priority area has been developed around the three key concepts of Country/Place, Peoples and Cultures. Each of these key concepts has a number of organising ideas which are imbedded in each learning area according to the relevance to the content (ACARA, 2014).

ACARA explicitly notes that through the Arts students examine and explore the artworks of traditional and contemporary Aboriginal and Torres Strait Islander peoples to gain insight into the 'ways the relationship between People, Culture and Country/Place … can be conveyed through the arts, their expression of living communities, and the way these build identity' (ACARA, 2014).

In this section of the chapter we identify a number of teaching ideas and classroom strategies to assist you in addressing the Aboriginal and Torres Strait Islander Histories and Cultures cross-curriculum priority. These examples include the idea of culture and cultural identity, the reticence some teachers feel when approaching Indigenous topics, the diversity of Aboriginal and Torres Strait Islander cultures, cultural respect and some strategies for bringing to life Aboriginal perspectives through the Arts.

> Before you start reading the rest of this chapter reflect on your beliefs:
>
> What is culture?
>
> What is cultural identity?
>
> Make some notes about what you 'know' about people from a culture other than your own. Of these, what might be your assumptions and what are actually facts?

Reflection activity

Link: *The Little Red, Yellow, Black Book*

TEACHER TIP

Dr Peter Anderson, the Director of Indigenous Education and Leadership at Monash University, said that, 'Most teachers are a little tentative about engaging with this space … They don't want to cause any offence, or say the wrong thing' (Mokak, 2017).

Recent research shows that, in many cases, generalist teachers know very little about Aboriginal and Torres Strait Islander peoples and have little confidence in teaching about their cultures (Moreton-Robinson et al., 2012; McDowall, 2018).

Some non-Indigenous pre-service teachers claim that they are afraid of being offensive, and so avoid addressing issues associated with Aboriginal and Torres Strait Islander peoples in their teaching. The best way to overcome this fear is to become familiar with the many available resources – just as you would for any subject area you are not familiar with. Get to know your local community and its history. Engage with Aboriginal culture by attending cultural events such as art exhibitions, dances and movies. Seek out books and articles written by Aboriginal and Torres Strait Islander authors and commentators. If you were to go to China to teach wouldn't you research Chinese customs, history, language and popular culture?

Other non-Indigenous pre-service teachers offer up lesson plans for 'dot painting' or 'boomerang decorating' without considering what their students will actually learn about Aboriginal and Torres Strait Islander peoples. Will students in these instances understand what boomerangs are used for? Which people use them? Will students appreciate the technology of the boomerang, the application of physics, or the origin of the name? Have these activities considered the fact that some students in the class may be Aboriginal and Torres Strait Islander, or are they assuming that all students are non-Indigenous?

An activity could either be a meaningless, fun task (decorating an object) or a rich experience that increases students' intercultural understanding.

It is also important to note that Aboriginal and Torres Strait Islander peoples are not culturally homogeneous. The most obvious distinction is between the cultures of the Torres Strait Islanders, who inhabit around 270 small islands off Northern Queensland, and the Aboriginal peoples of mainland Australia and Tasmania. The cultures of Aboriginal peoples of mainland Australia and Tasmania are also shaped by, among many things, location, linguistic groupings, the timing of their first encounters with white colonisers and their experiences of the Stolen Generations. It is for this reason that terms such as 'people' and 'culture' are referred to as plural, as in 'Aboriginal peoples and cultures'. This diversity means that there are differences in the materials used and the themes portrayed in artworks and storytelling.

In the classroom

Artwork made by people from the Torres Strait Islands has been influenced by many years of interaction with close neighbours in the Pacific region. It is stylistically different from mainland Aboriginal artwork. The Art Gallery of NSW website has an excellent article called 'Art Sets: Art of the Torres Strait Islands' focusing on Torres Strait Islander artists Ken Thaiday, Destiny Deacon, and Ellen José with videos and questions for discussion.

Link: Art of the Torres Strait Islands

Reflection activity

Look up some of Yvonne Koolmatrie's artwork and think about it through the following questions.

What sorts of materials does she use?

What objects or animals does she depict?

Explore different artworks from other Aboriginal and Torres Strait Islander artists. Look through the websites of the Art Gallery of NSW, Japingka Aboriginal Art, and Erub Arts.

Much of Torres Strait Islander culture has strong links to the ocean. How has this influenced the artwork? Compare the use of materials and themes in the work.

How do the materials link to the sea? Compare the sculptures and consider: what differences about the way they are made do you notice between islander sculptures and mainland sculptures?

What are the key themes in the artworks? How do they differ from mainland art?

Ricky Maynard is an Indigenous artist. He uses photography to represent his people and uses his photographs as a catalyst for social change. Look up some of his work on the Stills Gallery website and watch the video of him talking, 'Saddened Were the Hearts of Many Men', on the Art Gallery of South Australia's YouTube channel.

What is the intent of Ricky Maynard's work? Why is he making these portraits?

Links
Reflection activity

Indigenous communities have distinct, deep cultural and world views – views that are different from those of their colonisers – and it is important that both sets of views be treated with equal respect. The Queensland government has produced a guide for embedding these perspectives (EATSIPS, 2011). A diagram included in the guide illustrates its recommended approach to teaching in this area (see Figure 3.1). This diagram has two distinct rings, representing Western and Indigenous cultures, and a central circle, representing a new way of educating children. It illustrates the fact that there are two communities, each with its own distinct and deep cultural world view, but also shows how a 'third cultural space' can be created when both systems are acknowledged and valued equally. Teachers are encouraged to reflect on their practice and look at ways in which their teaching provides a balanced, inclusive perspective. The guide explains that it is not a one-way view of the world. Aboriginal and Torres Strait Islander perspectives are inclusive of non-Indigenous peoples' perspectives.

> Perspectives on Australian history, local and national developments should not be viewed as separate to Indigenous perspectives on Australian history. Each event and circumstance has impacted on another; for example, colonisation has impacted on Indigenous peoples and Indigenous peoples have impacted on local and regional development. EATSIPS encourages schools to rethink the ways in which Indigenous perspectives are conceptualised, and in particular, the way in which Indigenous perspectives have been positioned as something that exists at the margins of mainstream education policy and programs (EATSIPS, 2011 p. 22).

The third cultural space

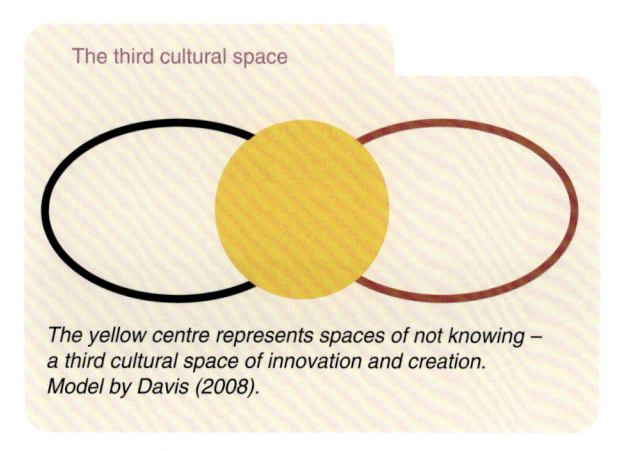

The yellow centre represents spaces of not knowing – a third cultural space of innovation and creation. Model by Davis (2008).

Figure 3.1 The third cultural space

Reflection activity

Read the article 'The stolen Wandjina totem takes Cultural Appropriation to a new level' on the Sovereign Union – First Nations Asserting Sovereignty website. It outlines the following story.

A Croatian-born artist 'appropriated' an image of Wandjina which is sacred to the Worrara, Ngarinyin and Wunambal peoples from the North Eastern coastal region of Kimberley, Western Australia. According to Adrian Newstead, owner of the Coo-ee Aboriginal Art Gallery in Bondi: 'Only a few Aboriginal artists ever win the right to depict Wandjina, and only then after years of initiations and ceremonies'.

The leading elder of the Kimberley Worora tribe found out about the Wandjina being misused and was shocked, and he travelled to Katoomba in March 2010 to express his concern to the artist over the 'inappropriate use' of Wandjina images but the artist argues that because it is art anything goes.

1. What do you understand cultural appropriation to mean?
2. Do you think it is appropriate for children to copy sacred Aboriginal images or symbols because they are art?

Link: article
Reflection activity

We should also value all cultures and groupings as equal to the dominant culture of the school classroom. In the context of Indigenous communities, as classroom teachers we should recognise the land on which the class is taking place. For example, we should always start the day or week with an Acknowledgement of Country. This act however need not be limited to when you are teaching in an Aboriginal community. An Acknowledgement of Country is a powerful way to convey respect, understanding and appreciation to an audience regardless of the setting.

We all have different ways of seeing the world and interacting with the environment. The Indigenous approach is through the interconnected aspects of Country/Place and People and Culture. This often means that a particular Aboriginal culture is closely linked to a particular area or environment, and this affects the way in which the land is perceived.

A good starting point would be to access your local Indigenous community or Aboriginal Education Consultative Group, such as the Living Kaurna Cultural Centre in the City of Marion, South Australia. Create links between the local Indigenous community and the school and invite members of the community to share their creative understandings with your students.

Lesson plan 3.1

Lesson plan 3.1

AIM

For children to understand that particular histories can be interpreted in different ways.

OVERVIEW

Children will study two different representations of Cook's landing at Botany Bay. They will develop an understanding about the lives of people in Australia's colonial past.

OUTLINE/DESCRIPTION

This integrated unit will use visual arts questioning to create a media arts product.

OUTCOMES

- Children will study two interpretations of European settlement: one from the point of view of the European settlers and one from the Indigenous perspective.
- They will understand that we have different ways of seeing the world.
- They will learn to appreciate the impact of colonisation on Indigenous peoples.

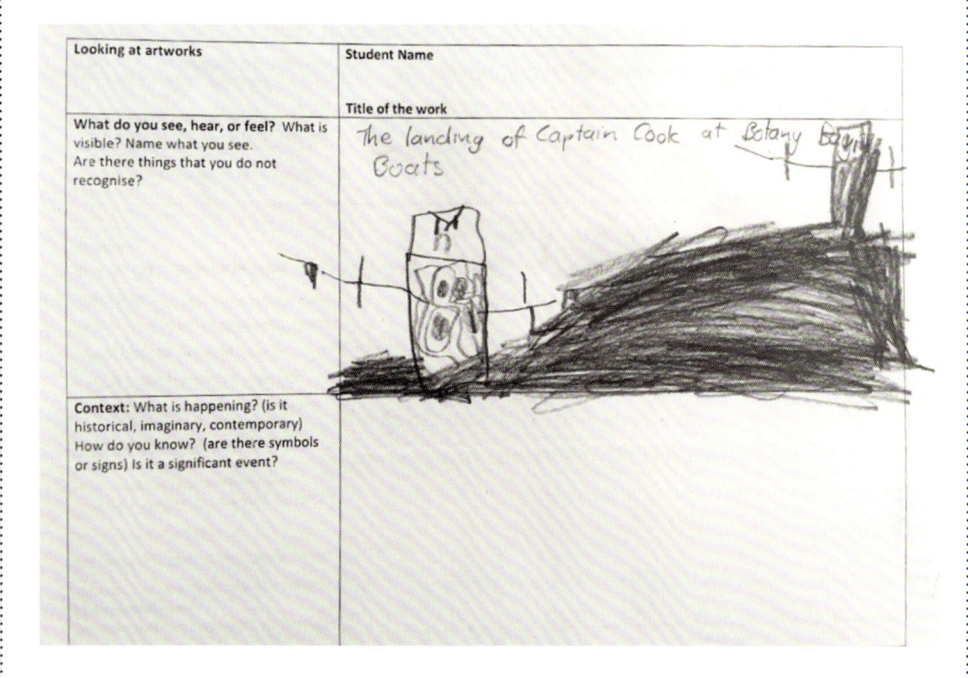

Figure 3.2 A 5-year-old's interpretation of Cook's landing (writing by teacher)

Figure 3.3 An example of a year 3's response to the artwork

> - They will use their imaginations to create a story about aliens from another planet moving into their town. They decide which viewpoint to take (the view of the aliens or the view of the people already living in the town) and present these ideas and feelings through a media art form (creating a digital presentation using images and sound to tell their story).
>
> Show the children the painting *The Landing of Captain Cook at Botany Bay, 1770* by E. Phillips Fox (National Gallery of Victoria).
>
> Then compare Fox's painting to Daniel Boyd's *We Call them Pirates Out Here,* 2006 oil on canvas located at the Museum of Contemporary Art, Sydney.

Links: Cook's landing

Learning in and through the Arts (see Chapter 2) is a powerful way to communicate cultural knowledge, values and perspectives. According to the Early Years Learning Framework, belonging, being and becoming are fundamental in children's lives (DEEWR, 2009). Indigenous artists have used the Arts as a way to communicate their understandings of their land, country and belonging. By experiencing different perspectives, children build connections with other people's stories and experiences. Children can play and create with alternative versions of stories, making comparisons and looking for differences and similarities, and thereby begin to develop their own cross-cultural understandings.

As teachers we need to consider the content we are engaging with. This means presenting Indigenous and non-Indigenous ways of knowing in a respectful way and involves using a critical lens. Research shows that:

> culturally responsive teaching needs a transformative curriculum in schools. Students become agents for social change by being provided with opportunities to develop critical thinking skills that enable them to analyse situations (Perso, 2012).

Lesson plan 3.2

Lesson plan 3.2

This can be adapted for use with early childhood or primary years (see the example below of a response from a 5-year-old child).

AIM

Learning about cultural practices by responding to art.

OVERVIEW

Students use structured inquiry to investigate an artwork and then make their own artwork in response.

OUTLINE/DESCRIPTION

Students use the 'questions to ask' table (refer to Table 8.3 in Chapter 8) or a simplified version for young children to respond to this artwork by Angelina Parfitt, an Eastern Arrernte woman of the remote community of Santa Teresa. It is called *Big Mob Together to Learn* and it hangs in the foyer of the Education building at Flinders University.

Students should investigate the artist's intention of telling a story through the artwork. They design symbols to create their own artwork to tell a personal story.

Figure 3.4 Angelina Parfitt, *Big Mob Together to Learn*, 2010–11

Angelina's artist statement:

> The university is a big place. It was therefore important for me to represent our coming to this place as a large artwork.
>
> It was my intention to represent the university, the people who work and study there, and the journey that we take by going to university, but I also wanted to recognise that we leave.
>
> The dot style art is particular to Aboriginal groups of the greater Central Australia region, which extends south to the APY Lands and into the western desert and north to lajamanu (Walpiri country).
>
> I have incorporated traditional colours of ochre red, ochre yellow, brown, grey and white, but I have also included more contemporary colours such as green and orange.
>
> The paints used are commercially produced.
>
> At the centre of the artwork is the largest circle (light brown) representing the university framed by people/students in faculties, study groups and social groups.
>
> The smaller circles painted in yellow and red depict the campus landscape. The landscape is painted from an aerial view showing the environment.
>
> Six pathways painted in smaller white circles/dots frame the larger central circle of the artwork, three on the left and three on the right. These white dot paths hold the tracks of those people who have entered into the university to gather and learn and those who have completed their study and left for work with a degree in hand.
>
> The university is a large and complex place. It can be overwhelming but it can also be a place where your learning grows. The journey into and out of the university is a rewarding experience.

INTENDED OUTCOMES

Students identify
- visual conventions used in artworks (their own and others) (colour, shape, line, space and the use of symbols)
- the artist and the artist's cultural identity
- the intention of the artist to tell a story about a journey.

Students understand
- Aboriginal and Torres Strait Islander peoples use artworks for telling stories
- that Aboriginal and Torres Strait Islander art styles differ across Australia
- that artists use visual conventions when they make their work.

Students are able to
- design personal symbols for important people, places and objects to tell a personal story about a journey
- create an artwork using their personal symbols to tell their story
- talk about their artworks using visual art language.

LINKS TO CURRICULUM

This could be achieved at all primary school age levels, for example for Years 3 and 4.

Years 3 and 4 content descriptors
- Explore ideas and artworks from different cultures and times, including artwork by Aboriginal and Torres Strait Islander artists, to use as inspiration for their own representations (ACAVAM110).
- Identify intended purposes and meanings of artworks using visual arts terminology to compare artworks, starting with visual artworks in Australia including visual artworks of Aboriginal and Torres Strait Islander Peoples (ACAVAR113).

ASSESSMENT

Students complete a worksheet identifying visual conventions used in artworks (their own and others). They identify the artist and the artist's cultural identity and can talk about why the artwork was made.

SHORT PRESENTATION

Students can talk about:
- how Aboriginal and Torres Strait Islander peoples use artworks to tell stories
- how Aboriginal and Torres Strait Islander art styles differ across Australia.

ARTWORK
- Design personal symbols for important people, places and objects to tell a personal story about a journey and create a key to the symbols.
- Create an artwork using these personal symbols to tell a personal story.
- Written reflection on the success of their artwork.
- Explain how they used visual conventions such as symbols, colour, shape to tell the story.

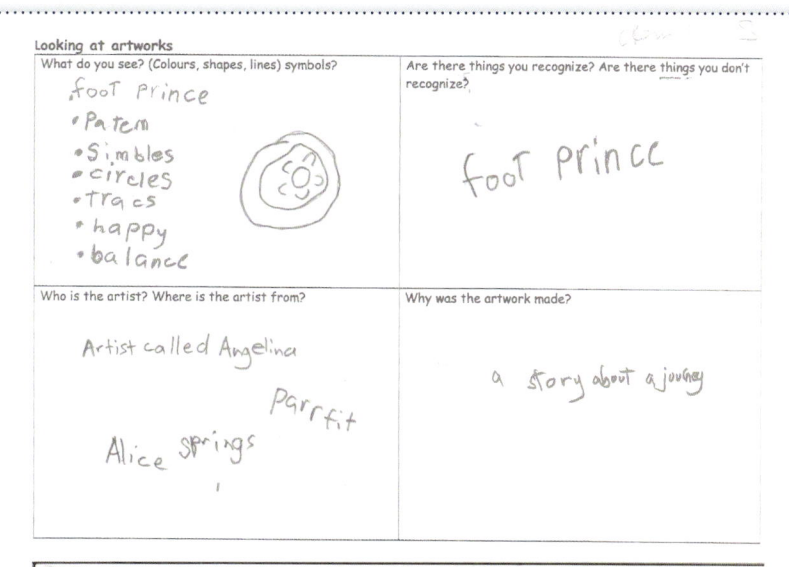

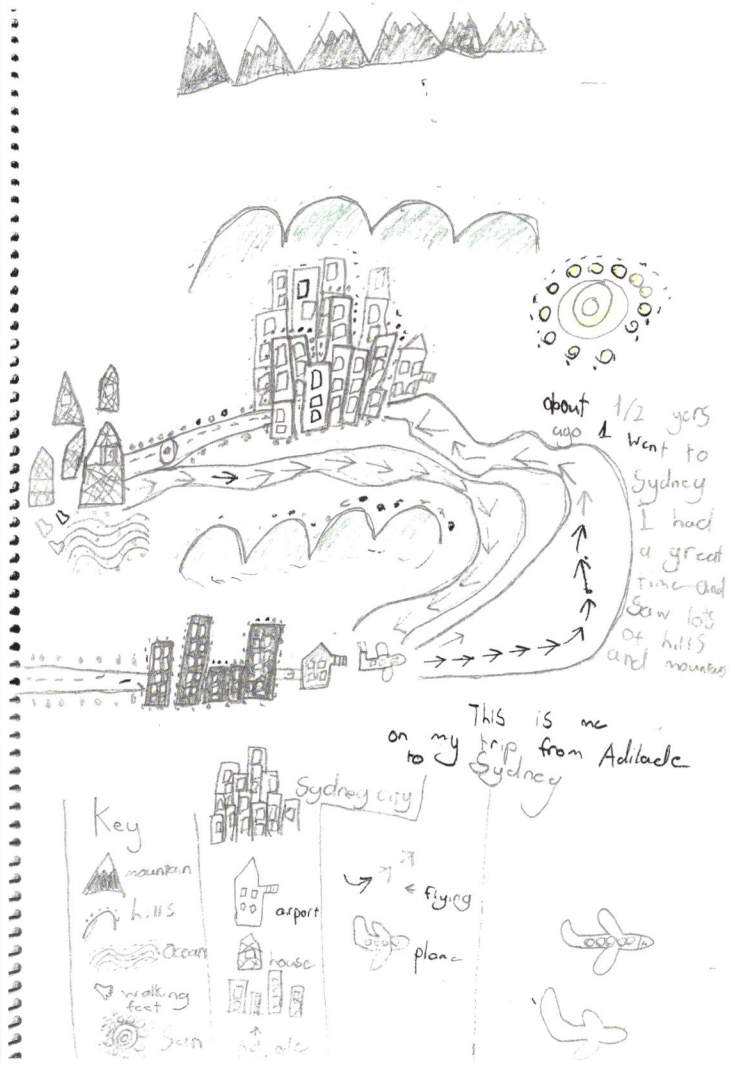

Figure 3.5 A child's response to the artwork and their own story of a journey using their own symbols

In the classroom

LOOKING FOR MEANING IN ARTWORKS

Looking at works of art can be a useful starting point for learning in other subject areas. This is an example of a unit of work that starts by looking very closely at a **contemporary** work of art and then leads to exploration of social and historical studies. Children learn authentic visual arts concepts and language and at the same time develop an understanding of issues, such as colonisation and the impact that it has on Indigenous peoples.

Contemporary: of this time. In the Arts, usually referring to art made since 1970.

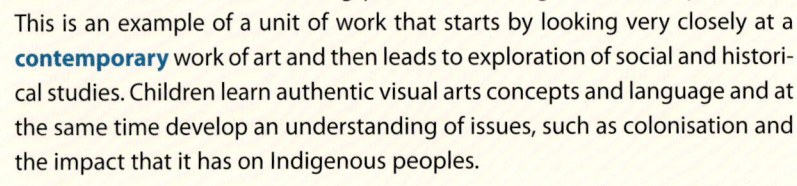

Locate an image of Gordon Bennett's *Triptych: Requiem, of Grandeur, Empire*, 1989 (Queensland Art Gallery).

Gordon Bennett is one of Australia's leading contemporary artists. According to the education notes for Bennett on the National Gallery of Victoria website, he prefers to be known as 'an artist first and not a "professional Aborigine"' in order to free himself from any preconceptions associated with his Aboriginal heritage.

Links: Gordon Bennett

Most of his work is concerned with looking at the history of Australia from various viewpoints. He looks at the way social and cultural structures, such as language, religion and history, shape experiences and perceptions of race and identity. For example, he paints about the way that Australia's education system has in the past reinforced a history of Australia built on the stories of exploration, colonisation and settlement. This history has failed to recognise the effect on Aboriginal people or their rights to the land.

QUESTIONS

- What are the important symbols that you can see?
- Bennett is representing his mother in the middle panel. What is she doing? Who are the other characters that are represented?
- What visual conventions has Bennett used?
- How has Bennett used colour? What mood does this express?
- What other conventions (perspective, use of photographs and paint) has Bennett used?
  - Compare Bennett's *Triptych* to *The Pioneer* by Frederick McCubbin, 1904. They both are **narrative artworks.**
  Compare the stories. What are some similarities/differences?

Narrative artworks: artworks that tell a story.

Links: Additional resources for Aboriginal and Torres Strait Islander histories and cultures

Asia and Australia's engagement with Asia

As home to two-thirds of the world's population, Asia is the most densely populated region of the world. Over recent decades the region has revived as a global economic force. In 2018, of the world ten largest economies, China was ranked 2, Japan 3 and India 7. The changes in economic power have also led to enhanced political and cultural influence of these nations. Unsurprisingly Australia's proximity to Asia means that employment and lifestyle opportunities in Australia are becoming increasingly influenced by these developments. Given the Melbourne Declaration's commitment to fostering the ability to understand the contemporary world,

Asia literacy has become a key goal of the Australian education system and for this reason constitutes the second of the cross-curriculum priorities: Asia and Australia's Engagement with Asia. It is, in many respects, recognition that, until the implementation of Australian Curriculum, the nation's educational approach to this region was haphazard and fragmented. This reflected a rather European-centred outlook that neglected the cultural richness and diversity of Asian societies and their relevance to Australia, and tended to cast Asia as 'other'.

> **Asia literacy:** the knowledge, skills and understandings necessary to enable students to engage with the peoples of Asia.

As an element of the Australian Curriculum this priority area considers three central concepts:

1. Asia and its diversity
2. achievements and contributions of the peoples of Asia
3. Asia–Australian engagement.

As with Aboriginal and Torres Strait Islander Histories and Cultures, the 'Asia' priority is not a standalone learning area but a topic to be addressed through the various Learning Areas. ACARA notes that the Arts can be used to illuminate key aspects of the three concepts. More specifically it notes:

> students can examine art forms that have arisen from the rich and diverse belief systems and traditions of the Asia region. Students can consider the aesthetic qualities of these art forms as well as their local, regional and global influence. This learning area provides opportunities to investigate the role of the arts in developing, maintaining and transforming cultural beliefs and practices and communicating an understanding of the rich cultural diversity of the Asia region. Students can engage with a variety of art forms, media, instruments and technologies of the Asia region. They can reflect on the intrinsic value of these artworks and artists' practices as well as their place and value within broader social, cultural, historical and political contexts (ACARA, 2014).

The Arts, then, are a rich vein when it comes to fostering Asia literacy. In this section of the chapter we will provide some ideas from the visual arts, music and drama that you can use or adapt to your school setting. These examples address the key concepts identified in the Australian Curriculum relevant to the Arts including Asian diversity and achievements and contributions of the peoples of Asia.

Lesson plan 3.3

AIM

Introduce students to cross-cultural influences between Japan and the rest of the world.

OVERVIEW

Children will be introduced to the cross-cultural connections between Japan and the rest of the world from the 1600s to now. They will focus on Manga and its influence today.

OUTLINE/DESCRIPTION

Children will research cultural connections between Japan and the rest of the world and present their findings. They will develop skills in the Manga art form and create their own Manga comic.

INTENDED OUTCOMES

Children will understand that:
- art forms from a particular culture can have global influence
- cultures have influenced each other throughout history
- Japanese Manga is a traditional art form of Japan but its development has been influenced by other cultures.

Children will be able to:
- identify traditional and contemporary artworks from Japan
- talk about visual conventions used in the artworks
- talk about cultural influences
- make their own Manga comic.

LINKS TO CURRICULUM

Years 5 and 6 content descriptors
- Explore ideas and practices used by artists, including practices of Aboriginal and Torres Strait Islander artists, to represent different views, beliefs and opinions (ACAVAM114).
- Develop and apply techniques and processes when making their artworks (ACAVAM115).
- Explain how visual arts conventions communicate meaning by comparing artworks from different social, cultural and historical contexts, including Aboriginal and Torres Strait Islander artworks (ACAVAR117).

Learning Area statement for the Arts cross-curriculum priorities

In the Australian Curriculum: The Arts ... Students can examine art forms that have arisen from the rich and diverse belief systems and traditions of the Asia region. Students can consider the aesthetic qualities of these art forms as well as their local, regional and global influence.

ASSESSMENT

- Children choose a decade between 1600 and 2017 and research cultural connections between Japan and the rest of the world. They make a short presentation to the class showing artworks from that time.
- Children make their own Manga comic and are able to talk about visual conventions used to make it (such as distortion of eyes).

Lesson plan 3.4

AIM

Introducing and identifying different styles of Asian music.

OUTLINE/DESCRIPTION

In this lesson students listen to music from three different Asian countries – Indonesia, China and Japan – and identify some of the musical characteristics of each style of music. Present students with the following for each country: a map that locates the country; a brief history of the country; a description of the instruments used in the style of music; and a listening example of each style of music. For example: Indonesia – focus on Gamelan music – music that mostly uses gongs, metallophones and drums and has set scales (sets of notes); each instrument has a set role.

Links: Indonesian, Chinese and Japenese music

You may like to use the BBC World Music website to start your research.

YouTube is another great resource for finding music from around the world. Find the video 'Traditional Chinese Music: "Fisherman's Song at Dusk," Chinese Zither Performance' by NTDonMusic. The instrument in the video is an example of the deep history of Chinese music – it is thought to be over 2500 years old. The music combines melody (pitch) and chords (vertical pitch). The music is narrative in nature, telling the story of a fisherman returning with his catch.

Watch the video 'Taiko-performance – 25 years TENTEKKO-Taiko – Taiko drummers – Taiko-drumming' by Kaiser Drums on YouTube. Taiko drumming has a long history in Japan. There are a variety of drum sizes and, as is the case with Gamelan, each size of drum has a different role to play in the group. As there is no pitch in Taiko drumming, the importance of layers of rhythm and changes in tempo is highlighted as you listen.

Please note these are just examples of single styles within cultures. There are many, many different styles of music within each culture. Once students are aware of these different styles, make up a playlist of further examples and ask students to listen and identify each style, which country it represents, and how they know. This can be made even more interesting for students by dividing into teams and running the lesson as a game.

INTENDED OUTCOMES

Students identify
- different styles of music from different Asian countries
- how different styles of music use the elements of music differently.

Students understand
- that Asian countries have deep and old musical cultures and traditions.

Students are able to
- identify different styles of music
- describe how they identify different types of music from Asia.

LINKS TO CURRICULUM

Year 5 and 6 content descriptors
- Explain how the elements of music communicate meaning by comparing music from different social, cultural and historical contexts, including Aboriginal and Torres Strait Islander music (ACAMUR091).

Cross-curriculum priority: Asia and Australia's Engagement with Asia
- OI1: The peoples and countries of Asia are diverse in ethnic background, traditions, cultures, belief systems and religions.
- OI4: The arts and literature of Asia influence aesthetic and creative pursuits within Australia, the region and globally.

ASSESSMENT
- Students demonstrate depth of understanding through the depth of their explanations of how they identify different styles of music.
- Students could do this in teams or by worksheets.

CHAPTER 3 THE ARTS AND CROSS-CURRICULUM PRIORITIES ■ 79

The EYLF describes cultural competence as: 'Much more than awareness of cultural differences. It is the ability to understand, communicate with, and effectively interact with people across cultures' (DEEWR, 2009, p. 16). One way to increase this awareness is to compare different ways that people in diverse communities tell stories. All cultures have specific ways of telling stories and passing on information; even if the story is the same it is told in different ways. Stories are effective pedagogical tools as students become engaged through listening, observing and participating, and are more likely to remember the meaning of the story.

Lesson plan 3.5

AIM

To introduce the diverse traditions, cultures and beliefs of Asia and make comparisons to Australian cultures using puppetry, music and drama.

OVERVIEW – PART 1

The concept of puppetry will be used to compare traditional storytelling from different cultures.

Figure 3.6 A Vietnamese water puppet in Hanoi

OUTLINE/DESCRIPTION

Display a range of Asian puppets (perhaps children bring from home) and European puppets, e.g. Punch and Judy (from the UK) or Pulcinella (from Italy).

Link: puppetry.info

The website puppetry.info has links to information about puppets from different countries.

Read traditional stories and discuss the ways the puppets could be used to 'act out' the stories. Children make their own puppets using found objects.

OVERVIEW – PART 2

Comparing music from different cultures.

OUTLINE/DESCRIPTION

Listen to and watch movies showing popular songs from Asian and Australian cultures. Listen for different sounds; talk about likes and dislikes and differences.

OVERVIEW – PART 3

Comparing stories from different cultures by role play.

OUTLINE/DESCRIPTION

Act out in response to a traditional story such as 'The Rainbow Serpent' or Panchatantra to deepen the understanding of the meaning of the story 'The Lion and the Rabbit'

INTENDED OUTCOMES

Children will understand that there are broad categories of art forms that are common across Asian and Australian cultures.

LINKS TO CURRICULUM

Foundation to Year 2 Achievement Standard

- By the end of year 2, students describe artworks they make and those to which they respond. They consider where and why people make artworks.
- Students use the elements and processes of arts subjects to make and share artworks that represent ideas.
- Develop intercultural understanding.
- Recognise culture and develop respect.
- Develop respect for cultural diversity.
- Explore and compare cultural knowledge, beliefs and practices.
- Asia and its diversity
    - OI.1 The peoples and countries of Asia are diverse in ethnic background, traditions, cultures, belief systems and religions.
    - OI.4 The arts and literature of Asia influence aesthetic and creative pursuits within Australia, the region and globally.

Early Years Learning Framework

Children:
- are confident and involved learners (DEEWR, 2009, p. 36).

ASSESSMENT

Part 1: Children identify puppets from different cultures and talk about how they are used to tell stories. Successfully make their own puppet.

Part 2: Children can identify sounds from different forms of music and state opinions about likes and dislikes.

Part 3: Children are able to act out characters from a simple story.

Overall: Students are able to identify artworks from different cultures and talk about similarities and differences.

In the classroom

Read the children's book *The Gift of the Crocodile: An Indonesian Cinderella Story* by J. Sierra (2000). Compare that story to the traditional European version of Cinderella. Have the children act out the play or create another version from an Australian point of view.

In Australia, there are several programs that can be accessed online for teaching materials. One is the Asia Education Foundation, which is an initiative of 'AsiaLink' at the University of Melbourne. It aims to provide curriculum resources and professional learning opportunities for schools.

Link: Asia Education Foundation

The Arts and sustainability

The Sustainability cross-curriculum priority of the Australian Curriculum takes a threefold approach to the topic that includes the capacity of Earth to maintain all life, patterns of living and their implications for the future, and sustainability education. This approach fosters the 'knowledge, skills, values and world views necessary to contribute to more **sustainable** patterns of living' (ACARA, 2014) and is framed by three key concepts: systems, world views and futures. The aim of this cross-curriculum priority is therefore fundamentally linked to the Melbourne Declaration's commitment to fostering an active and contemporary informed citizenship.

Sustainable: able to be maintained. In relation to the environment, it means minimising harm to the Earth and not using natural resources past the point that they can be replenished.

There is little doubt that sustainability is a global and a local issue. In 2017 the United Nations adopted a new sustainable development agenda. The agenda called for all countries to improve lives of people globally. António Guterres, the Secretary-General of the United Nations, stated at its introduction that world leaders had resolved to free humanity from poverty, secure a healthy planet for future generations, and build peaceful, inclusive societies as a foundation for ensuring lives of dignity for all by 2030. He observed that although this process has begun, the Sustainable Development Goals Report (Guterres, 2017) showed that the rate of progress in many areas was far slower than needed to meet the targets by 2030. The ranking of Australia as twentieth in the world in national performance on the Sustainable Development Goals highlights that locally we have a long way to go to reach our clean energy and climate change goals (Thwaites, 2016). This situation will only change if the general community understands the issues and is supportive of change. Many see the role of the Arts as the best way to communicate issues, influence and educate, and challenge the dominant paradigms (Curtis, Reid & Ballard, 2012).

ACARA also mentions a special place for the Arts in cultivating sustainability literacies, noting that the Australian Curriculum:

> enables the exploration of the role of The Arts in maintaining and transforming cultural practices, social systems and the relationships of people to their environment. Through making and responding in The Arts, students consider issues of sustainability in relation to resource use and traditions in each of The Arts subjects. The Arts provides opportunities for students to express and develop world views, and to appreciate the need for collaboration within and between communities to implement more sustainable patterns of living. In this learning area, students use the exploratory and creative platform of The Arts to advocate effective action for sustainability (ACARA, 2014).

TEACHER TIP

A starting point in your classroom could be designing a 'recycle, reuse, reduce' system. The class could work collaboratively to design the area and then make posters to promote sustainability at school. The Australian Government Department of Education and Training has set up a website called 'Getting Started with Sustainability in Schools' that offers many more ways to introduce sustainability into the classroom.

Link: Sustainability in schools

The Arts fosters and sustains confident communicators, imaginative thinkers, and active and informed citizens who reflect and comment on the state of our society and the natural environment. Learning in the Arts develops awareness of the natural, human and urban environments and of the ways in which the Arts have also been a catalyst for change. Action to improve sustainability is both individual and collective and can start locally and develop into a global outlook: 'Think global – act local'. The Arts are a powerful means by which humans can interact with the environment.

Arts education for sustainability develops knowledge and skills in children that prepare them to contribute to the future by valuing environmental and social sustainability and to develop an ability to communicate information about sustainability and to advocate action to achieve improved sustainability. Through the Arts, children have an important and effective means of challenging and changing behaviour and expressing ideas and suggestions for meeting their own needs without compromising the ability of future generations to maintain all life.

As in previous discussions of the cross-curriculum priorities, we offer some ideas, strategies and reflections that can shape and inform your practice as Arts educators in the contemporary context.

Sustainability in and through the Arts

There are three approaches to sustainability in the Arts: one that considers the degree of sustainability of the Arts and artists, and the question of how artists support themselves and how, for example, performing arts companies can remain viable; one that is concerned with the environment, and one that encourages sustainable art practices.

> **Spotlight on Arts education**
>
> The World's Largest Lesson is a part of the focus on sustainability. It introduces the Sustainable Development Goals and aims to inspire action among children and young people around the world.
>
> Link: The World's Largest Lesson
>
> 1 What are the 17 global goals?
> 2 Why do some people think they are important?
> 3 Are some more important than others?
> 4 Are some more relevant this year than in past years?
> 5 Do some have to be met before others can be?
> 6 Which ones are most relevant to children?
> 7 Which ones might be harder for children to engage with?

Sustainability of the Arts

Competition in the marketplace has increased and the development of new technologies and platforms such as YouTube (Cayari, 2016) changes the size and scope of the audience. By lowering the costs of distribution to negligible levels, technology makes the Arts market more open to all, which has simultaneously fostered an atmosphere of intense competition. According to Grishin (2015), although public art galleries are sustaining visitation numbers, major commercial art galleries are experiencing poor visitation rates and the number of art galleries in Australia has halved over the past 20 years. There seems to be a growing number of art collectors who purchase globally rather than investing in local artworks, meaning that Australian artists face increased competition from international artists.

New technologies can be used to enhance the Arts experience, but if children only experience the Arts 'remotely' and digitally without being able to participate in live Arts activities, they may lose or never achieve a sense of engagement with active participation. Learning in and through the Arts inspires and engages children and gives them confidence to experience the Arts both as artists and as audience. Without authentic engagement, how will children be prepared to sustain Arts practice in the future? Teachers, no matter where they are or what technology they have at hand, can provide real-life, authentic Arts experiences by ensuring that all children have access to learning in and through active engagement with all of the Arts.

The environment and the Arts

The Arts are an excellent vehicle for raising awareness of environmental sustainability, able to reach a global audience through technology (see Cayari, 2016). The key concepts of systems, world views and futures can be realised through the arts. Through art making, students can consider systems in relation to resources and environmental protection. They explore world views as they compare and develop world views and understand reasons for collaboration in order to transform relationships between people

Figure 3.7 Child's representation of our carbon footprints

and the environment. They think critically and creatively as they explore ideas for future action.

The Arts have the potential to develop skills, knowledge and dispositions for children to act in ways that contribute to environmental sustainability. Many contemporary artists around the world are working to make us think more deeply about the environment. There are many ways that teachers can teach about the environment in and through the Arts.

Spotlight on Arts education

Pre-service teachers in a compulsory art curriculum course for primary school teachers are asked to research the role of the zoo in the 21st century. Zoos today act as sites of wildlife conservation and have a role in connecting people with nature, research, education, threatened species protection, and recreation.

They are asked to work in groups to use all five arts of the Australian Curriculum to present one of the zoo themes to an audience of primary school children. Through this they gain an understanding of the ways the Arts can be utilised to express strong messages to an audience. They also understand that by learning through the Arts they develop a deep understanding of their chosen theme.

Some schools have developed a whole-school approach, involving the wider community and support organisations such as AuSSI (Australian Sustainable Schools Initiative), which provides case studies and outlines steps to take to achieve this aim.

Spotlight on Arts education

An article from SBS News online called 'Teaching sustainability in Australian schools: who's missing out?' claimed that even though sustainability is supposed to be a priority across the national curriculum the reality varies greatly between schools nationwide. A survey has shown that teachers are not aware of ways to embed cross-curriculum priorities in their teaching.

The Arts provide a unique way to explain environmental challenges. They can motivate people to work towards solutions by communicating ideas and creating empathy.

We suggest that you start simple. Find a simple message or issue and brainstorm ways that Arts learning can focus on that; for example, looking at ways that artists reuse materials to create work; writing and presenting a play about the environment; observing and analysing powerful images; and music that changes the way people think about issues. A good starting point would be to search 'global warming poster' on Pinterest, or to search for protest songs about climate change.

Links: SBS News; protest songs

Sustainability practices and the Arts

Teachers can model sustainability practices in the classroom. There can be a focus on using recycled materials; asking parents to collect supplies of paper, containers and other materials; and reusing packaging and wrappers as well as small containers, plastic and paper plates, spoons, and trays. Containers can be used for musical instruments or props for drama or media arts. Having separate bins for different waste and being aware of environmentally friendly disposal of paints, inks and other materials will develop awareness in children. Teach children not to waste materials like paint and paper by demonstrating economical practices like using sauce containers to dispense small amounts of paint (they can always go back for more) rather than dispensers that are difficult to control and tend to deposit excess amounts. Found objects such as branches and rocks can be exciting starting points for 3D work or musical instruments.

Reflection activity

Look at a catalogue of school art materials (for example, Modern Teaching Aids).

Think of ways in which you could substitute recycled materials for some of the 'highly enticing' alternatives on offer. Make a list of environmentally friendly materials you could collect (e.g. from parents or local businesses) and a list of materials that are essential and 'nice to have' but not really vital.

Link: Eco friendly art and craft supplies

Spotlight on Arts education

TOMÁS SARACENO

Tomás Saraceno, an Argentinian architect-artist, was one of many who contributed to an exhibition held before the Climate Change Summit in Copenhagen. His work, entitled *Aerocene*, is a floating plastic bubble. It's hi-tech enough that it is lighter than air, and so has to be attached by ropes to the walls of the National Gallery of Denmark in Copenhagen. Madeleine Bunting, writing for the *Guardian UK*, described the experience of entering the bubble thus:

> As I step gingerly on to its see-through floor, I can peer down at the gallery 100ft below. When I'm joined by one of the museum staff, I become unsteady. We crawl around this airborne plastic yurt like babies and then, feeling giddy, stop to sit and talk about how our children might end up living in a city of such bubbles, sealed off from a contaminated earth; about who might be lucky enough to have such a refuge; how they might sing their children lullabies of a lost earth (Bunting, 2009).

Saraceno (in Bunting, 2009) suggests that the role art has to play in discussing climate change is to make people feel unsteady and to push them to talk to strangers about our uncertain future. 'Art is about trying to rethink the things you take for granted' (Bunting, 2009).

Link: Tomás Saraceno profile

Lesson plan 3.6

This lesson is aimed at years 3 and 4 but could be adapted for older or younger children.

AIM

Children will explore the idea that the arts can be used to influence people to act in sustainable ways.

OVERVIEW

Visual arts: Children will explore the way recycled materials can be used to make artworks with a sustainability message.

OUTLINE/DESCRIPTION

Introduce children to artists who use recyclable material to create their artworks.

Artists such as:
1. Ritchie Ares Doña (assemblage)
2. Tiffany Ownbey (papier-mâché sculpture)
3. Michelle Reader (sculpture)
4. Adam Frezza and Terri Chaio (sculpture)

Links: Artists

→ Discuss the artists' aims. Why are they doing this? Who is their intended audience? What is the message? Children then sort their collected 'rubbish' and brainstorm the monster. Where should it be placed for maximum impact? How will it influence other children? What joining techniques need to be learned? What framework is needed to make it strong? What shape will it be? What colour? What texture? Is it meant to be scary or cute?

Children will collect recyclable materials from their food wrappers collected over a few weeks and create a 'rubbish monster' to influence other children to recycle their rubbish. The Rubbish Monsters will be displayed publicly.

INTENDED OUTCOMES

Children will understand that
- artworks can be used to influence people to act
- some artists use recycled materials to make artworks.

The children will be able to
- identify artworks made from recycled materials
- identify artworks with a message
- identify visual conventions used in artworks they see and make
- use a range of recycled materials to create a 'monster'.

LINKS TO CURRICULUM

Years 3 and 4 content descriptors
- Explore ideas and artworks from different cultures and times, including artwork by Aboriginal and Torres Strait Islander artists, to use as inspiration for their own representations (ACAVAM110).

- Use materials, techniques and processes to explore visual conventions when making artworks (ACAVAM111).
- Present artworks and describe how they have used visual conventions to represent their ideas (ACAVAM112).
- Identify intended purposes and meanings of artworks using visual arts terminology to compare artworks, starting with visual artworks in Australia including visual artworks of Aboriginal and Torres Strait Islander peoples (ACAVAR113).

Cross-curricular priorities
- Through the priority of sustainability, students develop the knowledge, skills, values and world views necessary to contribute to more sustainable patterns of living. This learning is future-oriented, focusing on protecting environments through informed action.

ASSESSMENT
- Children will keep a journal of annotated examples of artworks made of recycled materials and intended to influence people.
- They will record ways that visual conventions are used in artworks.
- They will be able to select and join a range of materials to make an artwork.
- They are able to talk about their intentions and to reflect on the outcome of their artwork.

Links: Sustainable artwork

Conclusion

Cross-curriculum priorities focus on different human perspectives in life through sustainability, Aboriginal and Torres Strait Islander peoples, knowledges and Asian/Pacific knowledges, as well as providing opportunities to foster cross-cultural understanding and respect. By learning in and through the Arts, children learn respect for and value the traditions, histories and beliefs of other cultures and celebrate similarities and differences. The rich cultures of all people of Australia and Asia have much to offer each other and to sustain living well through aesthetic resolutions and solutions.

By learning to make and critically respond to artworks, children develop skills that enable them to maintain Arts practices and traditions in the future, as well as prepare for future technologies. They develop skills to enhance broader understanding of sustainability and climate change through the Arts as they learn about sustainable process in the Arts. They also learn to recognise the need for social justice, healthy ecosystems and effective action for sustainability.

REVIEW QUESTIONS
1. What strategies could you employ to ensure cross-cultural understanding and respect in your classroom?
2. What role can the Arts play in achieving this?

Review questions

3   How important do you think images are in promoting sustainability?
4   What are the challenges for non-Aboriginal teachers and children engaging with Aboriginal and Torres Strait Islander peoples' cultural knowledges?
5   Where is Australia's place in Asian/Pacific culture?
6   As well as shared knowledges, how else can the Arts support sustainability goals?

RECOMMENDED READING

Bentley, T. and Savage, G. C. (eds) (2017). *Educating Australia Challenges for the Decade Ahead*. Carlton, Vic: Melbourne University Press.

Cayari, C. (2011). 'The YouTube effect: How YouTube has provided new ways to consume, create, and share music'. *International Journal of Education & the Arts*, 12(6). Retrieved from http://www.ijea.org/v12n6.

EATSIPS (2011). *Embedding Aboriginal and Torres Strait Islander Perspectives in Schools: A Guide for School Learning Communities*. Retrieved from deta.qld.gov.au/indigenous/pdfs/eatsips_2011.pdf.

Garg, K. (2017). 'Teaching sustainability in Australian schools: who's missing out?'. *SBS News*. Retrieved from www.sbs.com.au/news/teaching-sustainability-in-australian-schools-who-s-missing-out

Harrison, N. (2008). *Teaching and Learning in Indigenous Education*. Melbourne: Oxford University Press.

Kapoor, D. (2009). *Education, Decolonization and Development: Perspectives from Asia, Africa and the Americas*. Rotterdam: Sense Publishers.

Ministerial Council on Education, Early Childhood Development and Youth Affairs (MCEECDYA) (2010). *Aboriginal and Torres Strait Islander Education Action Plan 2010–2014*. Melbourne: MCEECDYA.

Muthersbaugh, D. and Kern, A. (2012). 'Pre-service teachers' use of images in integrating environmental sustainability lessons', *Journal of Teacher Education for Sustainability*, 14(1), 67–79.

Nicholls, C. (2009). 'The Australian Aboriginal visual art of the Central and Western Deserts: A comparative approach'. *Australian Art Education*, 32 (Special Edition), 1–20.

PART 2

What: the Arts Learning Areas

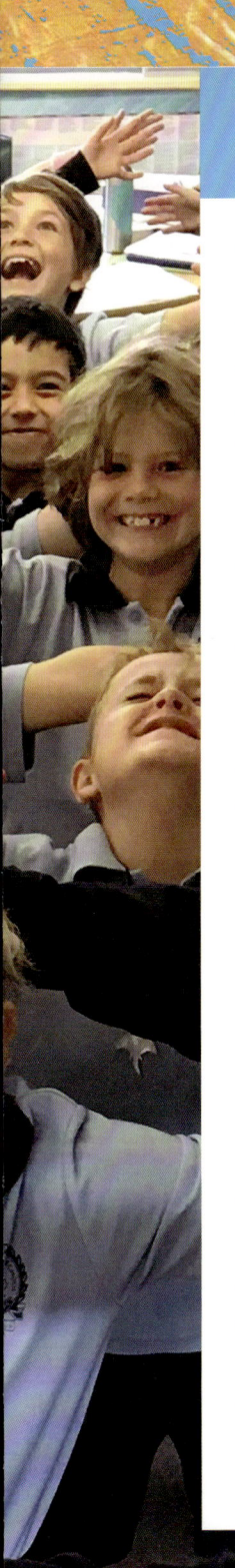

Parents and teachers are aware of the enjoyment that young children, with their spontaneous creativity, experience in the Arts. They happily sing, dance and paint and enjoy the Arts for their own sake. The quality of these early experiences will have a powerful influence on their adult attitudes towards the Arts. Teachers themselves have their own beliefs about the Arts, based on their past experiences, and this is likely to affect what they teach. The literature shows that attitudes are formed and shaped by experience and these attitudes drive motivation for behaviour. It is important, then, that teachers provide children with a high-quality Arts education from an early age. If children's only experiences in the Arts are as 'play', or as a treat, then they are unlikely to value them as a discrete Learning Area.

Each chapter in this Part defines an art form in depth, as set out in the Australian Curriculum. We will explore the theoretical underpinnings that are core to an engagement with the art form and suggest further avenues for professional development for the reader. All of these art forms have a set of principles and core theoretical elements. These are explained in clear language with suggested developmentally appropriate approaches to teaching in and through each of the art forms.

The Australian Curriculum, which all the states are adapting their curricula to align with, is addressed, with a focus on the two organising strands of 'making' and 'responding'. 'Making' is defined as the way in which art makers use Arts elements to imagine, invent or design an idea or expression and then make that artwork 'real' and tangible for an audience to experience. 'Responding' refers to the ability to recognise one's perceptive response to the artwork and the ability to experience the work in a critically reflective manner.

Rather than separate early childhood from primary years, the book is organised so as to describe progression in quality Arts education from early childhood to the final years of primary schooling, acknowledging that many of the exemplars offered apply equally to all levels of learning. Each chapter provides suggestions and examples of continuous and sequential progression in Arts education. Glossary definitions and website resources appear throughout the text where they are relevant to the content in the chapter. These provide additional information for you regarding appropriate theory, additional practical ideas and definitions of key terms.

This Part aims to provide a theoretically sound foundation with a practical framework that can be built upon as you become experts through application. There are recommended readings and resources and helpful guiding questions at the end of each chapter.

4

Learning in dance

> To watch us dance is to hear our hearts speak.
>
> Hopi Indian saying

In this chapter

Dance – often left to specialists outside the classroom – is a means by which children can explore the world through their whole bodies. For many learners who lack the ability or the interest to pursue more academic subjects, this is where they need to be given opportunities to demonstrate their potential for success.

This chapter will focus on forms and skills of dance and movement, methods for engaging children and the theoretical knowledge behind dance, as well as practical activities to use in the early childhood and primary classrooms. Linking to other Knowledge Learning Areas, as well as to wider school and curricular issues, this chapter aims to equip both the novice and the experienced educator in dance to confidently and knowledgeably facilitate the learning and development of children. Personal and environmental health and safety issues will also be explored.

By the end of this chapter you should have a clear understanding of:

- engaging with dance in education
- the elements and principles of dance education
- dance in early childhood settings
- dance in primary education
- making and responding in dance
- the context of dance in the Arts and in education.

Introduction

Many of the most important and fundamental milestones we look for in child development involve their gross and **fine motor skills** and balance. For many children, the mastery of these skills takes precedence over mastery of speech. It is clear that this is not a measure of intellectual capability, but without these key motor skills there will be barriers to the child's development in future years. However, children of all abilities can develop control in their physicality, no matter what special needs they have. Indeed, those children with gross motor skill developmental delays will benefit from dance as a form of therapy. Engaging in dance enables a multitude of cognitive growths linked to literacy and numeracy.

> **Fine motor skills:** a child's ability to use smaller muscles effectively, such as those in the fingers and toes. These develop continuously throughout a child's growth.

Dance is defined in the Australian Curriculum as:

> expressive movement with purpose and form. Through dance, students represent, question and celebrate human experience, using the body as the instrument and movement as the medium for personal, social, emotional, spiritual and physical communication. Like all art forms, dance has the capacity to engage, inspire and enrich all students, exciting the imagination and encouraging students to reach their creative and expressive potential.
>
> Dance enables students to develop a movement vocabulary with which to explore and refine imaginative ways of moving both individually and collaboratively. They choreograph, rehearse, perform and respond as they engage with dance practice and practitioners in their own and others' cultures and communities.
>
> Students use the elements of dance to explore choreography and performance and to practise choreographic, technical and expressive skills. Students respond to their own and others' dances using physical and verbal communication.

Active participation as dancers, choreographers and audiences promotes wellbeing and social inclusion. Learning in and through dance enhances students' knowledge and understanding of diverse cultures and contexts and develops their personal, social and cultural identity (ACARA, 2015, p. 31).

Engaging with dance in education

Dance, like drama, is an ephemeral subject. Each takes two major forms in the classroom – child-centered learning and education – and has some particular requirements as to organisation and resourcing. However, unlike drama, dance is connected to music by the fact that it is rare for dance not to use music in the processes of making and responding. Music, rather than being an add-on, is a complementary Learning Area, as it uses aspects such as interpretation and rhythm. Dance also embeds interpretation and rhythm both explicitly and implicitly in the learner. As individuals, we undertake forms of dance and movement every day, and as teachers we should find this helpful in demystifying some of the more challenging initial aspects of approaching dance.

Reflection activity

Listen to some music and go for a walk. Most music has a clear rhythm. Start to be conscious of how you are walking. For most of us, our pace and even our stride will vary according to the music we are listening to. In the simplest of ways, our movements have become a form of dance movement.

A suggested piece is 'All I Can Think About Is You' by Coldplay.

Note how your pace/movements change as the music changes halfway though the piece. What changed in the music and how did this change your movements? This activity can also be undertaken in a classroom.

Video: 'All I can think about is you'

Dance is one of the oldest art forms. It was through the use of the body and its expression that we first communicated to give sense and meaning to the world around us. Dance and drama merge together through movement; the purpose and distinction of drama are defined in Chapter 5.

Ritual: actions and/or words performed as part of a ceremony, often with deep cultural significance.

The origins of dance are closely linked to those of **ritual**. Gatherings of early humans depicted in cave paintings seem to suggest that they took part in rituals that were dance-based. Members of the group would enact particular movements that had developed significant meaning for the others. These meanings would have been understood by all and passed down to following generations. The dances would have had a religious purpose as well as being a sharing of knowledge (Lévi-Strauss, 1995). Meanings are conveyed in the same way in Indian Kathakali or Balinese performances today. Again, the distinction between dance and drama is blurred, since in some societies dialogue also entered the performance so that it

Figure 4.1 The character Mu Gui Ying, a heroine of Chinese opera

became a dance-drama, rather than a dance in itself. Chinese opera is a clear example of this, as are Aboriginal corroborees.

It is young people, and children in particular, who can become most easily engaged in dance and movement. Preschool children taking part in child-centred dance, unhindered by dialogue and with the diverse thinking skills that haven't yet been eroded by formal education, find freedom of expression and the freedom to create a language of movement that is an emotional release. Dance education also uses the historical elements of learning with folk dance. When the origins of such dances are explained, the meaning of movements engages the children further and allows them to demonstrate deep understanding (Davies, 2003).

There are some key organisational requirements that need to be met before dance activities can take place. As with drama, children doing dance need to understand that they are in a safe environment both mentally and physically. Warm-ups are essential, as are rules about notification of injury. These matters are explained in further detail in Chapter 5 as it is often harder in the drama classroom to recognise injuries, due to the children 'pretending' in role, but this is an equally important consideration with dance.

TEACHER TIP

To prevent personal injury just through movement alone, stretch the muscles to prepare the mind and body. Set out clear safety words and instructions, remove potentially dangerous objects, furniture and jewellery and ensure that social support is high. There can be no mocking of children or 'put-downs' from either the other children or the staff. Children will make mistakes and will struggle with movements and timing. They must be reassured that it is fine to develop skills and to have limitations. It is the willingness to try, and develop, that is important. Children with dyspraxia and other diverse learning needs will often give up on an activity if they do not sense a potential for achievement. As the teacher, you need to create a safe environment (Hattie, 2008).

A suggested way to do this is ask students to stand up straight. Students should raise their hands above their heads as high as they can go. Now ask the children to stretch as high as they can going on the tips of their toes. Students then need to slowly lower their hands to the side. Point out that the more they try this, the better they will get at stretching.

The elements and principles of dance education

Dance education is shaped by the two organising principles of the Australian Curriculum: 'making' and 'responding'.

- Making: Children will make artworks by using the elements of an art form. They will work from an idea, an intention, an expressive or imaginative impulse, or an external stimulus. They will imagine, create and design artworks. Through disciplined practice, children will learn to use and manage the materials, instruments and skills of the art form to prepare, develop, produce and present art.
- Responding: Children will respond to artworks through their senses, thoughts and emotions. They will come to understand and appreciate artworks through critical and contextual study. As children begin to learn in the Arts they will respond to what they see or hear in an artwork, and express what they feel personally about it (ACARA, 2013).

While the key concepts can appear generalist in some areas, to fully understand how to engage with dance in the classroom, an understanding is needed of what dance actually is. Dance is different to movement and action, in that it is a deliberate choice of these forms of praxis to create an effect in an audience and/or performer, to communicate meaning. There may be a technical aspect to an appreciation of dance but there is also an aesthetic that is being communicated. There is no clear definition of what the difference between action and aesthetic nature is, but the philosopher Frank Sibley expands that

> there is a sharp distinction between descriptive phrases such as 'moved to the left' and 'raised his arm' and the aesthetic terms such as 'graceful' and 'unified.'

Sibley allows that the qualities denoted by aesthetic terms are 'in' the perceived object and hence are not subjective, and also allows that these objective aesthetic qualities are 'dependent' upon descriptive qualities (Snoeyenbos & Knapp, 1979, p. 20).

Dance in early childhood settings

As with drama, for the early childhood classroom the connection to play will be embedded in the learning through dance education. However, for the basic skills to be implemented successfully, the teacher needs to impose an element of structure. Very young children need to develop basic rhythm and movement skills. Using simple climbing equipment and having the children walk to a beat allows them to practise responding to rhythm, which can then be applied in dance. This needs to be a conscious response, as opposed to an innate one, so that children can recognise success in their learning. To complement this, free play with climbing equipment and music played in the background will support the learning through subconscious cognition (Kirby & Peters, 2007). Young children's awareness of the kinaesthetic and their communication through this will support the learning. Allowing children to emotionally respond to excitement through small jumps and hand flapping lets them know that self-expression is valued (Edwards, Gandini & Forman, 1993).

Reflection activity

Knowing and understanding the starting point of movement for different children is important. For instance, watch the video 'Halloween 2014 – Kindy Kids: Thriller Video' by Grow International Pre-School on YouTube.

This a long, complex dance for very young children. Watch it several times, focusing on different children each time.

Which children keep time with the music even if movements are wrong?

Which children have the correct movements even if the timing is out?

Which children are unsure of their movements?

Which children check the movements of their peers and which children follow the teaching staff's movements?

Are the children enjoying themselves?

You will notice a multitude of different ways the children learn and interact. That is the joy of a class, developing each individual child.

Video: 'Halloween 2014 – Kindy Kids: Thriller Video'

As teachers, we should start to adapt these behaviours to develop control and deliberation. We must also remember that some children with diverse needs will be challenged in controlling these movements and for autistic children, or those with speech apraxia, such movements may be their norm for communication and should not be stopped completely, yet neither should they be left uncontrolled. Instead, children should be supported in finding additional methods to share their emotional responses (Agin, Geng & Nicholl, 2003). Dance, along with drama, is therefore a powerful art form to enable children to achieve control and deliberation, as well as to share emotional responses. Chapters 9 and 11 expand upon the support for children with diverse needs.

For good body awareness, the brain must receive messages from the senses and thus create a good map of the body and its relationship to space. This awareness is gained through activities that stimulate the inner ear, where balance is developed. Without good body awareness motor planning is affected, leading to poor thinking and moving. If children have to concentrate on moving their fingers to draw or write, then their spelling will be affected and their access to other Key Learning Areas will be delayed. Despite their intelligence, their academic progress will suffer. All activities that involve body mapping and body awareness, such as forcing movements to cross the midline of the body, will support all learning in early childhood and beyond (Pink, 2006).

Lesson plan 4.1 Video: If you're happy and you know it

Lesson plan 4.1

AIM

Students are to develop awareness of movement, **coordination** and spatial awareness.

OVERVIEW

Students are given instructions to follow, each time being a different movement that builds on the previous one, therefore allowing repetition to support mastery of movements.

Coordination: the ability of a person to use different parts of their body harmoniously and/or effectively.

OUTLINE/DESCRIPTION

In a circle, play/sing the song 'If You're Happy and You Know It' by The Wiggles.

Act out each verse with the children to develop special coordination; for example, clap your hands, turn around and touch your toes. Model the movements for those children who have a particular focus on visual learning (as many children with a neurological disability do), as these children will choose to observe multiple times before undertaking activities (see Chapter 11). Do not force them to take part but praise their observation. There are a multitude of other songs that can support body awareness, such as 'Head and Shoulders, Knees and Toes' and 'Put Your Finger On Your Nose'.

Each movement can also be added to the previous one so an ongoing list develops, assisting the students with memory skills. It can be made even more challenging by speeding up and slowing down the pace of the activity.

INTENDED OUTCOMES

Students identify
- elements of dance: action and dynamics
- successes and challenges of movement

Students understand
- body movement and interaction
- body space area
- coordination

LINKS TO CURRICULUM

Foundation to Year 2 content descriptors
- Use fundamental movement skills to develop technical skills when practising dance sequences (ACADAM002).

ASSESSMENT
- Students explore movements.
- Assessment undertaken through observation and discussion.

Moving to rhythm

An important aspect to develop early in children is becoming aware of the beat or rhythm of music if we are to respond expressively with dance. This area comes under the element of tempo in music, but is equally important to dance. It may seem that some people, children included, find moving to a beat a challenge but our bodies are naturally built to keep a constant rhythm when we are healthy. This happens through our regular breathing, our pulse and heartbeat that keep our bodies working in time. The key for young children is to make them conscious of their innate ability to keep a rhythm without making them so self-conscious of it that they overthink 'keeping to a beat' and then become unable to maintain a rhythm. Like all activities, there will be those who find it easier to engage with but again, like all activities, everyone is capable of developing the skills required.

In the classroom

Play a simple repetitive beat (in 4/4 time). This could be most modern music played or easily found on an app or website if you don't have an electronic instrument to maintain a constant rhythm. As a class, have the students start to walk around the room. If the beat playing is loud enough, students will gradually move to the time of the beat – though if they are directed to move in time, by becoming self-conscious of their initial movements, they will 'overthink' their movements and lose natural rhythm. It is better to let them just walk for a minute or two then stop the class. As a class discussion, ask the students if they noticed anything about their movements. As the class realise they were walking in time to the beat, praise them for recognising their natural ability to spot a rhythm, thus offering positive re-enforcement of their abilities. Any students who have limitations on their walking can undertake this activity from a seated position using any part of their body, from facial expressions to hands or even just fingers, in different movements.

Now play the beat again and ask them to walk slowly to the beat or quickly (no running). Vary their movements as well, to large or tiny steps. You can add in as many variables as possible including speed, size or even styles of movement (locomotion). In this way, confidence is built and the concept of deliberate movements to express an idea is introduced. At the end discuss what the different movements suggest, such as large movements being confident or 'giants', small movement being careful or small-animal like.

Link: Examples of 4/4 and 3/4 beats

By using rhythm and moving to a specific tempo and beat, children start to consider deliberate movements. It is this usage of deliberate movements in a steady rhythm, which are chosen to convey an idea or expression, that is the basis of all dance activities. Developing self-awareness and control of movements supports children who at times demonstrate their emotions through less controlled movements such as hand flapping.

To further develop body kinaesthetic awareness, it is useful to use a slower beat to develop the movements and then as the muscle memory develops, increase the tempo to the level finally desired by the dancers/choreographers. At this point, the introduction of rehearsal and practice, it is always useful to link such disciplined skill development to other areas of learning, such as sport. Not only will transferable skill awareness be created but such connections will encourage more reluctant children who might have developed barriers to engaging with dance through societal pressures such as their own physicality or gender stereotypes.

In the classroom

Through creating a group performance, with students taking the roles of objects and representing the natural world, students can develop an understanding that the simplest of movements can become dance.

Take, for instance, being in the rain. Ask the children what they do with their shoulders when it rains. The majority will 'symmetrically' bring their shoulders forward in a rolling motion and create a 'closed' shape. Have the children repeat this movement, rhythmically.

Now add a 'locomotion' to this, each child choosing their own locomotion, whether walking or crawling, repeating a stand up/sit down, or even a non-locomotion – remaining still.

Now add Tchaikovsky's 'Dance of the Sugar Plum Fairy' from 'The Nutcracker Suite'. The students are creating an aesthetic representation of rain, in a non-gender stereotyped manner, using their variety of physicalities without judgment.

Video: Dance of the Sugar Plum Fairy

Figure 4.2 Children in expansion/growing movement

Dance in primary education

Within the primary setting, dance education becomes more important and specific dance activities become more teacher-driven and controlled. It is at this stage that folk dances and formal movement styles with specific meaning are developed. That does not mean that child-centred dance should be discouraged. The learning should, however, be more structured as children expand their learning foundations.

Lessons will be more structured as a result. As with all activities, there needs to be a purpose to the learning.

- What do you want the children to learn?
- Why does that learning matter?
- What are you going to get the children to do (or to produce)?
- How well do you expect them to do it?

As a lesson plan, therefore, consider the following six basic steps. Some of these may be predetermined by the teacher and others by the children themselves. As the teacher, you choose the element of child direction to apply.

- Stimulus: What is the dance about? Concept: a possible link to other learning, such as literacy or the environment; or any other stimulus to support understanding of ideas?
- Style: What kind of dance is it? Traditional, improvised/free form, folk, formal, expressionistic/impressionistic?

- Structure: How will it be organised: in pairs, groups, whole class, inclusion of all? Are other non-dance roles required, such as music?
- Skills: What movements are required? Are there particular techniques that need to be introduced or refined, such as hand gestures and torso movements?
- Space: Where will the dance be performed/rehearsed? The final performance area needs to be known, so that boundaries are understood, and potential movement/visual opportunities and limitations should be taken into account.
- Sound: What musical support will be used: silence, from a recording, live. What instruments will be played and who will play them?

In the classroom

Read to the class the poem 'Benjamin Bandicoot' by Banjo Paterson (Paterson & Lindsay, 1970). Have the class discuss how they could represent night, the bandicoot and the environment through movement. Rehearse these ideas by having children show the movement of ferns, flickering lanterns, worms and anything else they can consider. Then introduce the idea of fire, and how the different parts of the environment might react, finally leaving stillness at the end (with smoke moving like the ferns). The children may wish to introduce the stillness before the fire arrives. Such ideas are full of movement. How does the bandicoot move when searching for worms? How does the bandicoot react to the fire? Does the bandicoot return and, if so, how would the movements have changed now the ground is hot?

Link: Benjamin Bandicoot

Figure 4.3 Bandicoot

> There will be a variety of different answers that can be given. It is always good to recognise there is not one set of correct answers and if the children are able, have them explain the reasons for their choices.

There are many ways to explore various movements that also allow the children to explore comprehension activities for literacy in a physical and practical way, which leads to a purposeful product, creating connectedness.

Traditional dance styles

Dance, as has been previously explored, is the physical demonstration of the expression and imaginative power of the mover. Traditional dance forms are no different to this, and while there are specific areas that are useful to cover, there are clear similarities to traditional dance forms developed throughout multiple and diverse cultures on multiple continents. Often schools explore these through the concept of social dances. Many traditional forms of dance have an aspect of socialisation attached to them, whether they derive from ritual or celebrations. All were, and still are, used to bring a community together in some form. The key difference in the types of dance is the purpose. Social dances tend to be less formal, relaxed and often have partners. School discos are included in this form, as are dance games such as for the X-box and other games platforms.

Social and traditional dance not only reinforces the bonds between people but also can be a demonstration of the uniqueness of a culture. Often this is not only represented in the dance movements but also in the costumes and dress worn by the dancers.

Reflection activity

Source the countries/regions of origin of the dances listed in Table 4.1.

TABLE 4.1 SOCIAL AND TRADITIONAL DANCE STYLES

Social dance	Traditional dance
Waltz	Corroboree
Foxtrot	Poi dance
Mambo	Haka
Tango	Bhangra
Rumba	Sema dance
Charleston	Nuo dance
Bush dancing	Buyō
Highland dancing (Céilidh)	Schuhplattling dance
Macarena	Kolo
Line dancing	Baile folklórico

Lesson plan 4.2
Videos: Dance forms

Lesson plan 4.2

AIM
Students to identify elements of dance found in different 'named' dance forms.

OBJECTIVE
Have the children choose one type of dance and present a brief information report on it, or even try to demonstrate four simple movements for it.

OUTLINE/DESCRIPTION
Students are to watch two videos of different dance forms, observing and considering the similarities and differences in the type of dance.

Have the class watch the two short clips and then ask the students to list as many similarities and differences between the two types of dance as they can. It may include foot movements, partners and costumes. As a class you can create a mind map to show the differences.

Having undertaken this, in pairs students then choose a different dance form from Table 4.1 and research it using Google, YouTube or any other reference platform. They then provide a brief information report, presentation or actual re-enactment of the dance form that demonstrates unique features of the dance form and similarities to other dance forms.

INTENDED OUTCOMES
Students identify
- fundamental technical skills
- fundamental movement skills
- why people dance.

Students understand
- key elements of movement to create meaning
- unique elements of dance from cultural groups.

LINKS TO CURRICULUM

Foundation to Year 2 content descriptors
- Use fundamental movement skills to develop technical skills when practising dance sequences (ACADAM002).
- Present dance that communicates ideas to an audience, including dance used by cultural groups in the community (ACADAM003).

ASSESSMENT
- Students explore and develop ideas.
- Students describe/demonstrate the effect of the elements of dance used by a cultural group.
- Students view and understand where and why people dance.

Making and responding in dance

In its simplest form, dance can communicate form, movement and feelings. The human body is the material basis for all dance activities. Through the combination of joint and muscle movements, the only limit to communication in dance is the control and flexibility of the performers in their artworks. This however is fundamental for children in their developmental processes and indeed for those children with diverse needs for whom traditional forms of communication are challenging or who have coordination developmental needs. Rather than being a barrier for many children with diverse needs, the fact that dance encourages children to explore using their bodies as a tool for communication and control, without competition, often results in their embracing of the pedagogy of dance in the classroom.

This is a key difference for dance in 'The Arts' as opposed to a 'Physical Education' class. In the Physical Education curriculum, dance is a technical skill. In the Arts, it is a form of 'praxis' communication. The theoretical concepts of dance are under-represented in Philosophical Arts aesthetics; however there is general agreement that dance can be both representational, as in the Greek 'mimesis', where there is imitation of reality, as well as symbolic.

Spotlight on Arts education

Chris was a new teacher with little experience of the Arts, but very good at sports. Thinking carefully, Chris decided to encourage a year 3 class in dance. First Chris had the students think about the way their bodies could bend and move, and what parts could not. The class practised technical skills. Chris then showed the class a video clip of trees blowing in a strong wind, how they bent and moved in the wind. The class discussed how a wind builds up and then slowly goes away.

Finally, the class started to bend their bodies slowly, then built up in speed and made larger movements until eventually slowing down. They became trees in the wind. This was more than technical movement; it was being creative in the movement representing the lived environment, considering it in a mindful way.

Making in dance

The principles of movement are the control of the body through six areas: the head and neck, the torso, the arms, the legs, the feet and the hands. These are where the most important joints are. Each area has its own scope of movement. There are 360 joints in the body. With the aid of the muscles, which allow the joints to turn and hinge, there are over one million possible movement combinations. It is useful to turn to the ideas of Rudolf Laban, who codified movement.

> **Spotlight on Arts education**
>
> Rudolf Laban was a Hungarian choreographer and theorist of dance, born at the end of the 19th century. He originally trained to be a sculptor, but his work led him to consider the way the body moved. He developed means of codifying movement for understanding and analysis, which he called kinetography. This is still used today as the basis for expressionistic dance. It describes body, effort, shape and space with a multitude of sub-categories. For early childhood and primary levels, this can be simplified into a study of three types of contrasting body shapes (Bradley, 2009): open or closed, angular or curved, and symmetrical or asymmetrical (see Figures 4.4, 4.5 and 4.6).
>
> You can read more about Rudolf Laban and his theories of movement at the Laban Eurolab website.

Link: Eurolab

Figure 4.4 Two figures, closed and open

Figure 4.5 Two figures, angular and curved

Figure 4.6 Two figures, symmetrical and asymmetrical

Each shape can also be given a height: low, middle or high. These concepts of shapes allow children to explore the immediate space of their bodies.

In the classroom

Have the children rehearse making three different Laban shapes, open or closed, angular or curved, and symmetrical or asymmetrical, each one at a different level. Once these shapes have been planned, the children can rehearse the following sequence. They start by standing straight up, looking ahead. As four slow beats are given, they 'morph' or change position into the first shape. They hold the first position to the count of four beats.

Then, during the next four slow beats, they change to their second shape in slow motion. They hold this shape for four beats and then change to the third position.

Finally, on the last fourth beat, they change into the starting upright position.

As an extension activity, they can begin to add a different sound to each shape.

To extend the movement, three children can stand in a line together and make their shapes in unison. They are starting to create a movement piece. Many children will think it looks like a machine. They have taken part in a piece of collective choreography for which the leader/teacher has given instructions, but in which they have developed the movements themselves.

Choreography: planning the movements

When **choreography** is added to movement through a defined performance space (see the section on body and space in Chapter 5 under 'The elements of drama'), an infinite variety of movements can be applied, particularly if you consider the above activity and all the factors listed below:

Choreography: planning of the movements in dancing.

- **locomotion** (how you travel across an area): crawl, walk, jump, etc.
- **speed**: slow, normal, fast
- **level**: low, medium, high
- **size**: large, small, normal
- **style**: open, closed, angular, curved, symmetrical, asymmetrical.

This will take time, but remember that the more children practise, the better they will become.

TABLE 4.2 DANCE CONCEPTS

Concept	Explanation	Dance example
Convention	Conventions are habits or accepted ways of doing things.	Irish dancing: straight upper torso and arms, head movement for gesture and tapping legs.
Form	'Form' refers to the type of art material used.	Dance type, such as jazz, traditional or 'modern'.
Materials	'Materials' refers to the origins, structure, characteristics, properties and uses of natural and fabricated materials. Materials are used to create products, services or environments (Technologies Initial Advice Paper).	In dance, 'materials' often refers to the body and how it is used; for example, the arm being outstretched with a flat hand and closed fingers to create a product, such as a gesture communicating 'Stop'.
Language	Each Arts subject has its own way of looking at the world. Each uses a specialised language: visual, written or performed. Each Arts subject has distinctive ways of telling stories.	Dance uses repeated/similar if extended and rhythmic movements that can often have specific meaning for the audience or performers. This is the language of performance.
Audience	Each art form requires an audience for the artwork to communicate the artist's intent. This includes audiences for: • performances in dance, drama and music • exhibitions of visual artworks and media artworks.	An audience in dance can be the actual performer, performing in front of a mirror, or a full auditorium of observers.
Aesthetic/ artistic value	Aesthetic/artistic value is the intrinsic value of something.	Dance has an intrinsic value to the performer, through the release of endorphins in performance, and to the audience through the beauty of technically skilled or visually appealing movements and communication.
Play	Play-based learning is a context for learning through which children organise and make sense of their social worlds as they engage actively with people, objects and representations. Play is a context for learning that: • allows for the expression of personality and uniqueness • enhances dispositions such as curiosity and creativity • enables children to make connections between prior experiences and new learning • assists children to develop relationships and concepts • stimulates a sense of wellbeing (Early Years Learning Framework, p. 9).	In early childhood and primary levels, the ability to play through self-devised and teacher-led activities is important. In dance, to have freedom to experiment with movements, and to develop special awareness and awareness of oneself in an area is important for children. It is taught through children experimenting and making mistakes in a safe area where they cannot be injured. The role of the teacher in dance is to facilitate rather than intrude.

TABLE 4.2 (cont.)

Concept	Explanation	Dance example
Performance	Performance is the presentation of products.	In dance, this can be the rehearsal or the final product. With mirrors present to allow the children to observe their activities, the process becomes performance at the same time.
Processes of design	Processes of design are a subset of technology processes and typically involve identifying, exploring and critiquing needs or opportunities; generating, researching and developing ideas; and planning, producing and evaluating to produce a best-fit solution (Technologies Initial Advice Paper).	In dance, it is important to experiment, but also to sometimes plan. This becomes choreography, in which movements are organised in a particular way to create meaning.

Responding in dance

For children to respond to stimulus they have to consider the basic elements of dance. These elements allow students to explore movement and planning through the use of their bodies and expression, working collaboratively or individually. Key to using the elements and choreography (making in dance) effectively is the need for students also to reflect on the processes and performances of themselves and others. As with all the art forms in the Arts curriculum, students' ability to state not only what they think but why, developing skills in reflection and evidence, is fundamental.

> Choreography has to link lots of different movements together, considering a variety of factors such as setting, space, timing, different people and often communicating emotions or ideas. For instance, watch the dance sequence 'Another Day of Sun' from the movie *La La Land* (2016).
>
> What do you notice about the choreography of this scene?

Reflection activity

A balanced approach to engaging with all the elements of dance is required, as each element supports the others equally. There is no hierarchy in the elements, and while they are often most easily applied sequentially, this is not a requirement. What is important for the teacher is to remember is that the diversity of learners means that all elements need to be engaged with equally, and for the teacher to continually reflect on practice to ensure certain elements are not given dominance. By giving one particular element preference over others, an imbalance in technique, skill and/or creativity could develop.

The elements of dance

- Action – what
- Dynamics – how

- Time – when
- Space – where
- Relationships – who

Action: what?

The **'what'** a body is doing, the action, is the specific movement. This includes the parts of the body moving and their interaction together to create a wider, overarching movement. This can include:

- locomotion – the body travelling over an area. Examples of locomotion include: running, crawling, hopping, walking or even stillness.
- non-locomotion – the movement of the body in itself. Examples of non-locomotion include: bending, squatting, twisting, stretching, contracting.
- shape – the bodies overall shape created by action. Examples of shape include: curved, twisted, symmetrical, asymmetrical, closed, open.
- body parts – the different articulated body parts that are in action, either in isolation or in conjunction with other body parts. Examples of body parts include: head, limbs, wrists, fingers, hands, shoulders, neck, knees.

Dynamics: how?

The **'how'**, or dynamics, is a description of the action, similar to literacy usage of adjectives and adverbs. It is a physical form of the literary technique as part of the visual literacy of dance.

Children need to consider not only if they are 'walking' or 'stretching', but the quality of the movement such as with force, or the emotion/feeling such as with pain. The aspect of tension should also be considered here. Is there a pause, stillness, followed by a change in movement quality? All these aspects create meaning for the audience as well as the performer.

Concepts/descriptions to consider might be as follows: lightly, delicate, rough, quickly, softly, carefully, rushed, exaggerated, etc. as well as force, size and weight of a movement. In planning the dynamics, it is of potential benefit to link the concepts to literacy and descriptive techniques/vocabulary. Students can then explore the literary, abstract idea in a concrete physical exploration through 'action'.

Time: when?

The **'when'**, or time, of a movement refers specifically to the body and movements itself, rather than the setting of performances/movements which is explored in 'space'. The 'when' refers to the speed at which movements take place, either in conjunction with accompanying music or in silence, which is an aural soundscape in itself – the absence of sound creates meaning.

Similar to music (as explored in Chapter 7), movements have a speed and a pace. Our natural movements have a tempo and a rhythm to them, and varying these aspects helps create or change the meaning of a movement. For children who struggle to understand these aspects and indeed those children developing coordination in fine and gross motor skills, such a focus on movement timing can be beneficial.

Aspects to consider are acceleration/deceleration of movements; rhythm and beat of movements; contrasting tempos; gradual change in speed; and unified speed between multiple movements. There is an additional complementary comparison that dance supports in this area, with the role of the chorus in drama, which is explored in Chapter 5.

Space: where?

The **'where'**, or space, refers to three different aspects of movement. It defines the area used by the body as part of the dance, the creation of the place the dance is representing, but also the time in which the dance is taking place (as opposed to the 'timing' of the movements).

When the body undertakes action, where the action travels the body to, and the stretch of area that the body covers, is the space used to create meaning. Central to this is the effect that this will have upon other bodies, on movement with the dance, and the 'blocking' or choreography of the dance. One individual body can create a meaning but when there are other performers the meaning changes, similar to the way that individual words change when placed in context with other words. Again, the use of performance space is explored in greater detail in Chapter 5, where staging in drama is detailed. Other aspects in space to consider include height (high, medium, low levels used in movement), eye focus and direction of movements.

The other two aspects of space are the actual environment/place of the dance created by movements, and the period of time, whether time of day or indeed year. Movements can demonstrate place, through their formality or freedom, to allow the audience and performers to experience a variety of settings (such as a market place, home, open field). Varying the dynamics can also communicate the time of day (night/morning, etc.) and temperature (warm, frosty, etc.). Time period, such as the future, medieval times, etc. can also be demonstrated through the action and the dynamics of the movements.

Relationships: who?

Linked to space, is the '**who**', or relationships, in regard to how the body interrelates with objects and others in the performance and the performance area. This creates the context for meaning in a similar way that words in literacy placed together create new meanings.

Through contrasting the movement of different parts of their own body, or in partner with another, students can explore the semiotics of meaning with dance.

Audience and performer relationships also create meaning, as do students working in unison as part of a group or in time with others, or being continually aware of the space between other dancers or objects, and using that so show power or relationships and meaning in a manner similar to drama, which is explored in detail in Chapter 5.

Structure

The five elements of action, dynamics, time, space and relationships work together with structure to create meaning and intention, which is key to creative dance.

Structure refers to how the different elements are put together, in a similar manner to the way that a building 'structure' is created through beams, walls, and piping etc. It is through a unified, considered application of all the elements that a complex and engaging structure can be created. This can include repetition of movements or ideas, which then have contrast and variety. All together these variations and similarities create meaning and intention. All forms of dance can have these parts and they are for a particular purpose. In many traditional dances, repetition is key to allow the performers to feel successful in engaging in the dance, but also to unite them as part of a wider community in said engagement.

There is a similarity to music in that as well as using music to support a dance, dance often contains repetition of certain actions, body shapes or rhythms to provide unity. Dances are made from movement patterns (motifs), or sequences. The emphasis placed upon these through the varying elements creates additional intentional meaning. Chapter 7 supports further the idea of structure in performance composition.

Facilitating storytelling through dance is common to the origins of most forms of traditional dance, in Australia and elsewhere. Traditional Highland dances from Scotland, as well as many other cultural dances, impart a similar context. Modern contemporary styles of dance, such as hip hop, have been developed in one culture but then popularised globally and adopted by other cultural groups who identify with the stories within that dance style. Often these dances reflect traditional forms but embrace a contemporary style. Through dance, students can develop a way of knowing and expressing culture in a contemporary continuation from the past.

The context of dance in the Arts and in education

Dance is an important subject for engaging with the Australian Curriculum general capabilities. In particular, dance offers an opportunity to apply embodied learning – with literacy. The lyrics of songs will often give guidance to movements and through developing a dance based upon lyrics and music, the students acquire the skills to analyse and deconstruct poetry. In addition, the lyrics may express an ethical or moral position that may lead to further discussion and analysis.

Many songs have 'interesting' lyrics as well as rhythms that can be used as stimulus. We need to ensure that songs are used which are age appropriate in lyrical content, when used as stimulus for students to generate self-developed dances. By allowing the class to choose a song, and thus empowering them, there is likely to be deeper engagement from the students in the developing of skills and knowledge (see Chapter 11). Be very aware that as the teacher, you must ensure that the song is appropriate in content and that any movements the class choreograph are also appropriate. Young children will often imitate dancing from music videos and have no real depth of awareness of the meaning of particular gestures or movements. The class should always know that you, as the teacher, have the right to veto choices on the grounds of appropriate content, but where possible allow the students to choose a different song.

In the classroom

Use the lyrics video version of the song 'The Boy Does Nothing' by Alesha Dixon, as the official video may not be suitable, and the lyric version supports understanding of the words. Play the song from 2.30 minutes onwards. The lyrics contain many movements, such as 'wash up', 'brush up' and 'clean up'. The students can develop movements to reflect the lyrics. Each line of the song should get a specific movement that the group performs in unison. As the lines are repeated, there are only a few basic movements to learn. Students create movements for each different line. Each line is individually rehearsed. The group of students then rehearses all the movements together and performs. You can choose to choreograph the movements for the whole class or have individual groups have their own interpretation.

After performing there can be a discussion about what the song says about gender roles and the singer's attitude to the fact that 'the boy does nothing' in relation to household duties.

Video: The boy does nothing

Physical education and gender stereotypes

As stated in the introduction to this chapter, ensuring that students physically warm up before undertaking dance activities is of paramount importance. Dance is a physical activity. In many schools, dance is taught as part of the physical education curriculum and the two Knowledge Learning Areas (dance and physical education) can be integrated very successfully. It has to be remembered, though, that while physical education is important for health and wellbeing, dance is an expressive art and therefore offers more than just a physical skill base. It offers a methodology for students to communicate their inner self, thoughts and feelings, as well as having an aesthetic element. It engages with the 'arts praxis' of Chapter 1. Indeed, it is this link between physical education and dance that can engage students who are reticent in partaking in dance-based activities.

Often there is a presumption that *girls* do dance. Society does seem to promote such ideas. When you look at dance classes offered outside of school, girls significantly outnumber boys in participation. The Arts generally suffer from **gender stereotyping** and imbalance, and part of the role of the teacher is to encourage gender equality in participation and understanding of the Arts. Dance suffers more so in this inequity expectation than other art forms, and this misconception is actually false in reality. Dance is not just for girls, and indeed many girls also have a reticence to partake in dance, whether due to a lack of confidence in themselves, society created body self-consciousness, or even a lack of interest.

Gender stereotyping: the association of certain roles and activities with particular genders, often due to prejudice and ignorance.

As a teacher, we can role model alternative views of dance. As well as making the links between sports, gymnastics and dance, the simple strength and athleticism required for dance can help dispel barriers.

> **TEACHER TIP**
>
> Showing clips of television dance competitions such as 'So You Think You Can Dance' or music videos such as Justin Timberlake's 'Can't Stop the Feeling' can demonstrate the wide variety of male and female dancers.
>
> Video: Can't stop the feeling
>
> Exploring some of the purposes of ritual dance, such as the Maori war dance 'the Haka', can also support challenging the gender stereotype of dance.
>
> Looking at modern forms of dance such as hip hop, with a variety of male and female body shapes, as well as circus dance troupes such as Cirque du Soleil, reveals the wider gender performativity possibilities of dance and multiple gender inclusions.

Literacy and numeracy

Dance is a physical and visual literacy, where the performers and the audience form an agreed language of understanding in meaning. Often this has a cultural linguistic basis. The specific movements of Balinese dance have a depth of meaning often lost in Australia if you do not have a background knowledge of the subtleties. However, to meet the increasing curriculum demands of literacy within the context of standardised testing, dance can be used to teach both in and through for literacy. Students can use literacy texts as the stimulus for developing dance, or indeed as a methodology to represent understanding of literacy ideas and concepts.

> **TEACHER TIP**
>
> Using poetry with dance is methodology both to unlock the imagery of poetry in a physical representation, and to create clear conceptual ideas to be applied in performance for dance, allowing children to focus on the movements, rather than being lost in developing original ideas to then choreograph. 'Home Among the Gum Trees' by B. Brown and W. Johnston is one such poem that can be used. Children can consider the movements of clothes on the washing line, the movement of wind around the house, and the various flora and fauna – all of which represent an image of Australia. The performance can also be used to extend consideration of the stereotypes of Australia and whether these images are a reality for the children's experiences.
>
> Link: Home among the gum trees

Science, numeracy and dance

Science and dance are not as disparate as could first be considered. As dance focuses on the use of the body as a performative object, science concepts such as how our body works will give a clear understanding of its use in dance for many children. If we are going to ask children to vary the use of muscles and joints, we can explore with children how muscles and joints work. Similarly, students can represent the natural world and the various cycles of life and the environment through dance representing objects, movement and change; whether it be the rain cycle, blood flow in the body or salmon spawning.

In the classroom

For numeracy, start with a simple pop quiz: basic addition. Then pause with the class and ask who does not enjoy such quizzes, because they feel pressure. Rest assured there will be some children. Now change the context. Say you will be asking more questions of basic addition, but this time place the children into groups of four (preferably) or threes depending on the class size. Students are to answer the question you write on the board but working as a group and forming the number shapes with their bodies. First to answer correctly wins, but the students have to create exact shapes. This leads the students to think about the positioning of arms and legs in juxtaposition to each other. Many will get it wrong, but hopefully they will have fun.

One of the answers you ask for should have a '0' in it. Students will struggle to form this shape as legs can only bend in one direction, to create an outward curved shape. Use this to discuss human body imitations and how better to form the '0', such as with curved arms.

Conclusion

Dance is a core skill, not just for the Arts but also for controlling coordination and balance skills, the gross motor skills that allow children to meet their developmental goals. In early childhood and primary education, the focus is more on the creative dance elements through dance education, rather than on traditional dances or folk dances taught within the curriculum. There are also gender associations a teacher needs to debunk – that dance is not just for girls, but for everyone. Dance needs to be more than the school performance for parents at the end of the year (Sinclair, Jeanneret & O'Toole, 2009).

Children need to be given the freedom to create dance movements, rather than be controlled like puppets by the teacher and have no control. Edward Gordon Craig referred to this situation as 'über-marionettes' (Craig, 1956). Dance is fun for children. It enhances their physical education, and in some countries is part of the physical education curriculum rather than one of the Arts. Dance is, however, an aesthetic, rather than a cold skill; one that applies the Arts praxial model introduced in Chapter 1, with 'praxis' referring to 'action' in the sense that the action is an intentional, conscious and culturally determined human activity (Dewey, 2007). Is dance a form that, in the context of education, allows human transformation and liberation? For the 4-year-old obliviously dancing with happiness at the rain stopping so they can enjoy the glorious sun of the southern hemisphere, the answer has to be an emphatic *yes*.

REVIEW QUESTIONS

1. Why is dance useful in helping children reach developmental milestones?
2. How is dance similar to drama, and how is it different?
3. What is the ancient historical context of dance and its link to ritual?
4. What organisational features for the dance classroom need to be in place to allow authentic dance learning to occur?
5. Why is 'play' important for dance as a 'key concept'?
6. What was Laban's kinetography?
7. What elements of dance support 'responding'?
8. Why do we have to be careful about controlling movements for children with diverse learning needs?
9. How does body awareness support academic achievement?

RECOMMENDED READING

Allen, A. and Coley, J. (1995). *Dance for All*. London: David Fulton Publishers.

Biasutti, P. (2013) 'Improvisation in dance education: Teacher views'. *Research in Dance Education*, 14(2), 120–40.

Bradley, K. K. (2009). *Rudolf Laban*. Abingdon: Routledge.

Davies, M. (2003). *Movement and Dance in Early Childhood*. Thousand Oaks, CA: Sage Publications.

Smith-Autard, J. M. (2001). *The Art of Dance in Education*. London: A&C Black.

Snook, B. (2004). *Count Me In*. Sydney: McGraw Hill.

5

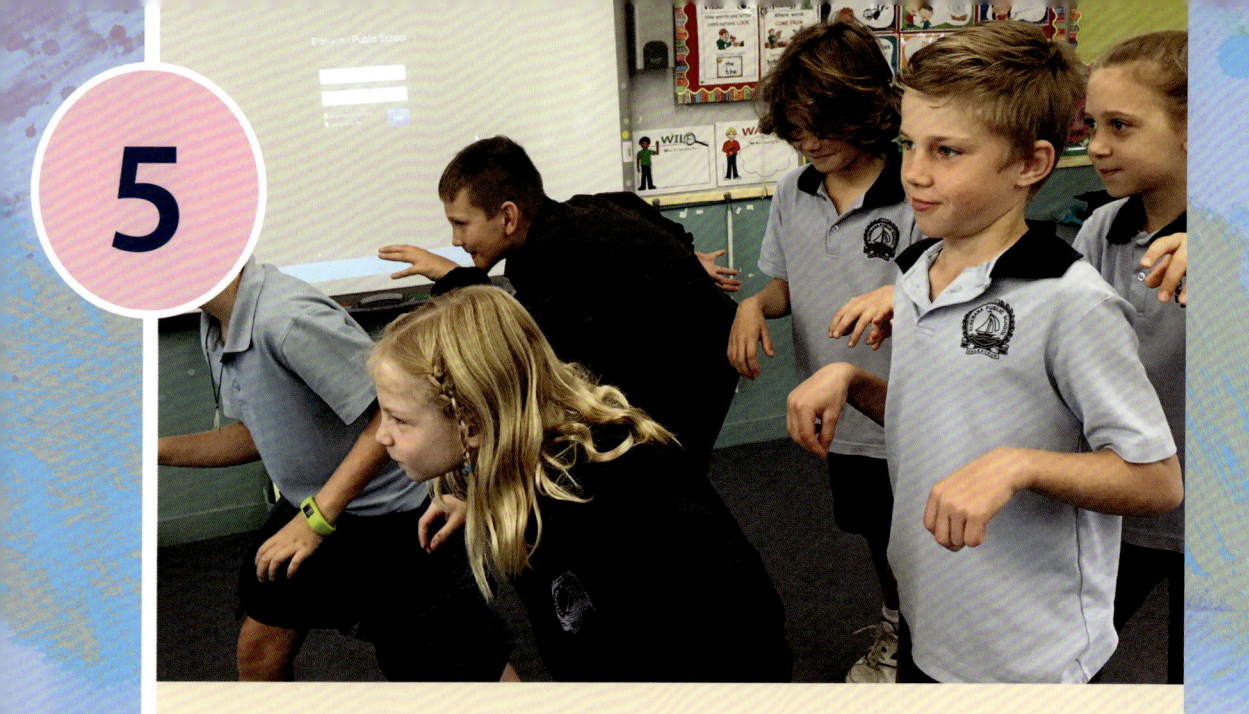

Learning in drama

> I love acting. It is so much more real than life.
>
> Oscar Wilde

In this chapter

This chapter will explore the fundamentals of drama, both as a skill and as a methodology for teaching other curricular requirements. It also offers practical activities and assessment practices, as well as theoretical underpinnings and methods to further develop teaching methodologies beyond this text. You will have the confidence and knowledge to engage learners of all ages and abilities to explore their own ideas through dramatic performance and to evaluate the performance of others. The key to drama is not only the development of skills, but also the ability to apply processes and value these processes as equal to the end product of a drama activity. The application of drama in literacy, numeracy and other areas of learning will be embedded throughout. A great deal of the focus on drama in the classroom, in Australia, is from a Western perspective.

By the end of this chapter you should have a clear understanding of:

- engaging with drama in education
- the elements and principles of drama education
- drama in early childhood settings
- drama in primary education
- making and responding in drama
- the context of drama in the Arts and in education.

Introduction

Drama as an expressive force can be formidable. Drama allows children to address taboo topics, or ideas of emotional depth, and issues such as discrimination, bullying and exclusion. Through the use of cultural forms of Arts expression and stimuli, differing cultural knowledge can be valued and shared equal to the predominate culture of the classroom. It can be as simple as students planning the number of roles to equally include all. Through the organisation and planning of performances, students need to consider angles and sight line, height and depth. As noted in the Australian Curriculum, through drama 'students learn to reflect critically on their own experiences and responses and further their own aesthetic knowledge and preferences. They learn with growing sophistication to express and communicate experiences through and about drama' (ACARA, 2017).

What is drama?

Drama, as a term from the original ancient Greek, means to do or to act. In education we use the term drama in classes to refer to the performance skills in acting and also the associated activities such as directing and designing for the stage. What is important is that drama is not just about the skills of acting such as voice and body movements, but the whole process leading to a product. Encompassed within that is therefore the developing ideas stage, usually from a variety of stimulus. It involves planning, collaboration, decision-making, refining ideas and rehearsing. It usually includes group work and usually involves teacher facilitation of children to extend their creative ideas. Often it is pushing through the limits of the physical in drama that allows the innovative ideas to flourish.

In many drama experiences, children need to be made aware of the explicit skills they are learning while too often having fun in the learning environment. From early childhood, to the final year of senior school, drama has a progression of learning. Drama is not simply about embodied learning through the physical. There is academic theory and knowledge that must be developed along with practical and technical skill if students are to truly succeed. You could potentially describe drama as the practical literacy class. You can give the same activity to a 17-year-old as you give to a 7-year-old, but it is the level of engagement and skill and the product that results that can be differentiated by response and level.

> The arts inform as well as stimulate; they challenge as well as satisfy. Their location is not limited to galleries, concert halls, and theatres. Their home can be found whenever humans choose to have attentive and vital intercourse with life itself. This is, perhaps, the largest lesson that the arts education can teach, the lesson that life itself can be led as work of art. In so doing, the maker himself is remade. This remaking, this re-creation is at the heart of the process of education (Eisner, 1998, p. 59).

> **Spotlight on Arts education**

THEORIES AND THEORISTS OF DRAMA

A lot of people have thought about what acting and performance are and have had a great deal to say. One of the first to write down his ideas about acting was Konstantin Stanislavski. Essentially, he wanted actors to think like the characters they were portraying and then reflect this in their movements (Stanislavski, 1981). Others, like Vsevolod Meyerhold, suggested that a movement would create an emotion (Braun, 1995). It is important that theorists in drama be introduced to children, in the same way as we mention great painters, such as Van Gogh and Degas, in visual arts and great composers, such as Mozart and Beethoven, in music.

Stanislavski

Stanislavski was a Russian director at the beginning of the 20th century. He changed the way we think about drama and acting by creating new ways of rehearsing and teaching acting. He wanted actors to be more realistic in conveying themselves through emotions. Rather than the exaggerated, melodramatic acting that had been used for the last few hundred years, he wanted actors to internalise emotions, then reflect those 'emotional memories' in performing. As obvious as it seems now, his method was revolutionary in helping to develop characterisation in performance.

Meyerhold

Meyerhold was a student, colleague and competitor of Stanislavski. He chose to focus on the physical aspects of performance as well as the staging. He eventually developed a system of rehearsal where instead of internalising the emotion and then representing it, actors had to represent an emotion to allow them to feel it. He tried to create a 'language' for physical acting and had a rehearsal system called 'bio-mechanics'.

Figure 5.1 17th-century Italian commedia dell'arte half-mask

As educators, we can use these principles to encourage and develop children's acceptance of diverse ways of looking at objects and interacting with them. Thus creativity can be further enhanced and developed (Roy, 2012).

Ariane Mnouchkine

Ariane Mnouchkine is a French director who initially explored mask work in her early production *Capitaine Fracasse*, using **Commedia dell'arte** masks. Inspired by Meyerhold, she included not only the elements of the grotesque but also innovative use of theatre spaces. It is in rehearsal rather than performance that the mask is a core device for Mnouchkine.

Julie Taymor

Julie Taymor's work uses aesthetic images, with masked and ritualistic performances exemplified in her most publicly successful work, the Broadway version of *The Lion King* (Blumenthal, Taymor & Monda, 2007). Taymor deliberately allows the audience to see the construction behind set designs and costumes. She wants the audience to be very aware that they are watching something that is not real.

> **Commedia dell'arte:** 17th-century Italian half-mask theatre. Many of the characters have animal attributes; for example, Arlecchino (Harlequin) is catlike. Many of our character stereotypes can be traced back to commedia dell'arte.

Figure 5.2 Full face neutral mask

Engaging with drama in education

Many teachers in early childhood and primary school are wary of teaching drama (Winston & Tandy, 2009). Drama often seems an ephemeral, intangible thing: it happens and then is gone. There is no lasting product. Further, in the history of the Arts in Australia, drama seems to lack the serious academic status that some of the other Arts have managed to gain, although all the Arts often lack status in education in comparison to certain other areas of learning (Anderson, 2012).

If we pause and consider the process of teaching, many teachers in early childhood and primary school engage in drama throughout every lesson and in all subjects. As people, we have been using drama from birth, with children mimicking their carers' vocalisations, movements and expressions as they develop.

> Not only does drama give students permission and opportunity to talk a lot, but it demands practice in speaking like others, people within and beyond their experience, experimenting with and developing a range of registers from outside the classroom, new vocabulary, new gestural signals (Sinclair, Jeanneret & O'Toole, 2009, p. 32).

It is nothing to be scared of and it is something that most individuals are highly competent at; they just don't recognise this. Teachers, more than most other professionals, are performers. They often stand in, before or among an audience and perform whilst entertaining and educating. This is the essence of drama. There are, of course, other skills that are just as important in drama as performance, and these too will be looked at in this chapter; however, we all act at every moment of our lives. The difference is in the development of specific skills for drama and knowing how to implement them successfully. It is very easy to use drama in any context in the classroom, but too often its use is trivial and lacking in depth, unless drama is consciously embedded in multiple Knowledge Learning Areas, as well as being used as a Knowledge Learning Area in its own right.

There are many ways to approach drama, and some methods conflict. Like all forms of knowledge, there is no single set way to teach drama. However, there are key methodologies that have been demonstrated to work with children of all ages. This chapter aims to introduce and explore the core methodologies of teaching drama and then examine alternative concepts that can be applied and extended.

The first recorded play to be performed in colonial Australia was the 1789 staging of *The Recruiting Officer*. The oral histories of Aboriginal and Torres Strait Islander peoples show that drama has been a part of Australia's history and culture for tens of thousands of years. Through rituals and corroborees, drama, dance, music and visual arts have been inextricably linked. It is important that Australians do not forget this heritage.

For many, drama as an educational subject started officially in Australia in the 1990s. The Australian Curriculum is underpinned by the methods of the British drama educator Dorothy Heathcote, who promoted the change in drama in schools from product-based to process-based, so that the end result of work was not the goal, but the learning that took place in the development of a performance (Heathcote & Bolton, 1994). She developed the idea of the teacher as facilitator rather than instructor, with the teacher having the mantle of the expert. The principles she set in place have been embedded in drama education ever since.

> Mantle of the Expert creates roles for students that cast them as the 'ones who know' (instead of the teacher). For example, a student may take on the role of a scientist whose expertise is required to solve a problem in outer space. The expertise role shifts the power from the teacher to the student (Anderson, 2012, p. 36).

Of course there have been a multitude of further developments in classroom educational drama thought, including the work of individuals such as Cecily O'Neill, Jonothan Neelands, Norah Morgan and Juliana Saxton. In Australia the work of John O'Toole and John Carroll has been highly influential, focusing on the process and product being interlinked.

21st-century drama

If schools wish to prepare children for success in the 21st century, we have to rethink the place of educational drama in the curriculum. The Melbourne Declaration on Educational Goals for Young Australians (MCEETYA, 2008), created on behalf of all Australian Ministers for Education, states the over-arching aims and goals for education in Australia for stages, levels and curriculum. It was released in 2008 and superseded similar documents, such as the Adelaide Declaration of 1999. The national Australian Curriculum has its basis in the foundation statements of the document.

The Melbourne Declaration stated two goals:

> Goal 1: Australian schooling promotes equity and excellence.
> Goal 2: All young Australians become:
> – successful learners
> – confident and creative individuals
> – active and informed citizens (MCEETYA, 2008).

The DICE study (see next Spotlight) argues that to meet these aims, which are similar to European educational goals, drama should be given a higher status in the curriculum. At the time of writing, drama often features only in 'prestige' events in primary schools – that is, as a means of promoting the school, but with little day-to-day engagement with it as a consistent Learning Area. To change this situation, we need to offer comprehensive drama training to teachers and support the use of drama methodologies to enhance other curricular subjects. This will support child-centred teaching methodologies and, through the collaborative nature of drama teaching and learning, encourage sharing of best practice.

> **Spotlight on Arts education**
>
> Review the results of the European study *Drama Improves Lisbon Key Competencies in Education* (DICE).
>
> DICE was a two-year research study that involved 12 countries, 111 different drama programs and 4445 students. The study measured the impact drama had on the educational attainment of students.
>
> What did the results of this study show?

Spotlight on Arts education

Drama in early childhood and primary settings

In Australia, the Early Years Learning Framework identifies five learning outcomes, including 'children are effective communicators' (Outcome 5). Drama can be an excellent way of facilitating learning about verbal and non-verbal communication. The Framework suggests a number of ways that educators can promote this learning, such as 'engage in enjoyable interactions with babies as they make and play with sounds' and 'model language and encourage children to express themselves through language in a range of contexts and for a range of purposes'.

For any teacher, whether in early childhood or primary, the control of the elements of learning will always be a source of conflict in classroom planning. In drama there are two core types of drama activity: child-centred dramatic play and drama education. It must be made clear that child-centred dramatic play is different from the early childhood concept of 'play'. The notion of 'play' as allowing a sense of freedom for children to explore their environments is a core educational concept, though the valuing of it as such is often diminished. However, play is a key learning tool that fits within the educational drama language as child-centred dramatic play in which children are given space and materials to create their own dramatic responses. Such ideas are important and happen both within and outside the educational establishment. With drama education the teacher undertakes a more active role, controlling the process and often leading both as teacher and as an observer. In drama education, there are clear roles and processes.

There of course has to be a balance in the freedoms of the child, with the need for the teacher to be in control. It is important that children have freedom to play within a dramatic process under their own control and choosing, while still developing specific skills and techniques identified by the teacher for successful curriculum requirements. As teachers, our role is to facilitate both so that children can apply rules-based knowledge structures, such as curriculum-mandated outcomes and indicators, and still encourage children to harness their divergent thinking and creative abilities; these latter concepts are further elaborated on in Chapter 12. This chapter aims to offer strategies to allow both forms of drama learning to take place.

In the Australian Curriculum, as Chapters 4 to 8 demonstrate, each Arts strand is explored in two key areas: 'making' and 'responding' (ACARA, 2013). For drama, these areas are expanded upon in each level of achievement. The different levels are achieved by the student response. For teachers, the same tasks can be offered to a year 1 student or a year 12 student. It is the complexity of response that demonstrates the level of achievement. As teachers, it is our role to facilitate the responses through the development of skills. These objectives and principles apply internationally to all Arts curricula. It is not the titles that matter, but the content contained in each area that links to the classroom tasks and thus to student achievement (Anderson & Dunn, 2013).

Figure 5.3 Teacher/students focused

As the teacher, you need to manage the drama lesson. Applying the following principles will help make the teaching of drama more successful. These basic principles apply both for early childhood and primary teaching, though as a teacher you will decide how explicitly or implicitly these concepts should be communicated to your students, depending on each individual in the class.

- Treat drama as a serious subject.
- Establish specific rules for the drama lesson – stick to them – and be prepared to stop the drama and the lesson itself if behaviour expectations are not met.
- Make the focus of the lesson clear.
- Break the concepts and tasks into sequential steps – make sure that each step is achievable and builds on previous knowledge.

- Make time for reflection throughout the lesson – redirect attention to the lesson focus and give honest feedback.
- Know your students – expect and acknowledge 100 per cent application to the task.

Children need to feel safe to explore theatrical ideas and movements. They need to be willing to make mistakes and to realise that the classroom is an environment that embraces learning through mistakes and improvement. It is therefore important that you, as the teacher, role model this by being willing to undertake all activities that you want to encourage the children to do, and being willing to look foolish in the process. This not only releases the children to attempt activities, but also creates a unifying bond between all members of the class. The first rule should therefore be that, unless there are issues that arise that you must pass on, what children do in the class activities should remain in the class. The classroom should be a place of fun and safety, where ideas can be explored and rejected in a positive environment. Like all classes, there should be no mocking or gossiping among children or staff outside the classroom. For this reason, very clear guidelines of behaviour must be laid down, not in a punitive sense but in a positive, mindful way for all children to feel acceptance and freedom in the adventure of creative exploration and learning.

Reflection activity

To facilitate ownership of the classroom by the children, it is useful to sit with the class and spend time agreeing on rules and the purposes behind them. The children may also add their own rules that all agree on. The rules should apply to all members of the class, including teachers. The sense of respect and trust that such an activity generates is core to establishing a successful drama learning environment.

Children should not be able to opt in or out of activities just because it is drama. In mathematics, if a child said they didn't like the number seven, would they be allowed to not use it? The same principle must be applied to all knowledge areas. If there is a physical reason not to take part (and there is no way to adapt activities to include the child), then discretion on the part of the teacher is of course advised.

One way to undertake this is to introduce icebreaking games where activity and fun are important. Books such as *Jumpstart Drama: Games and Activities for Ages 5–11* (Cremin et al., 2009) are useful starting places but there are many games and activities to be found just through basic internet searches.

Initially, you need to allow the children to explore roles by using their bodies, space, sound and movement and, as the teacher, you will decide which area to focus on. Often small exercises can be employed to develop each area, as well as activities that use all areas, though you may guide the children to focus on particular ones. Games are often useful tools for developing a sense of trust in the classroom (Boal, 2002). The children do not always realise that they are learning while undertaking these activities.

For early childhood settings in particular, drama meets the needs of taking a holistic approach to the students' development. A holistic approach is when the physical, personal, social, emotional and spiritual wellbeing is supported alongside the cognitive forms. With drama all these aspects are continually engaged. Drama has no set answer, or solution and so the learning must be responsive as children learn through play. Children in early childhood settings will engage with drama and theatre in imaginary role-play directly through dress up, or through third-person manipulation of toys that interact with each other. Such skills are important for very young children not only to explore imagined and real situations and relationships, but also to learn to control and find solutions non-dependent on their caregivers. For intentional teaching to take place, teachers need at times to encourage these activities or direct them to particular areas such as 'sharing' or 'saying no'. At other times children should be observed to allow improvisation and unfettered creativity to happen (Vygotsky, 1986). What we therefore need to be doing is continually ensuring that students are undertaking activities independently and not relying on others.

Actual development is determined through both independent problem-solving and adult guidance or collaboration with peers (Kozulin et al., 2003). Drama is key within this as a collaborative act, which can be independent and also directed to solve problems. Early childhood teachers must engage with children and the dramatic play they seek if we are to fully meet their needs.

TEACHER TIP

STIMULUS

Every piece of drama has to start somewhere. Stimulus is exactly what it states. It is something to stimulate your imagination; to give you a starting point for thinking of lots of ideas. It can be a colour.

Figure 5.4 Picture of stimulus

Stimulus can be:

- a script
- a photograph
- a picture
- an object
- a piece of clothing
- a phrase
- a sound
- a piece of music
- a poem
- a topic
- a toy.

In fact, anything that gets you thinking.

Figure 5.5 Students playing with toy figurines

The elements of drama

The elements and principles of drama are enduring topics of deliberation. The ancient Greek philosopher Aristotle, for example, argued that there were six elements of drama: plot, character, thought, diction, spectacle and song. More recently the Australian Curriculum defined the elements of drama as 'role and character, relationships, situation, voice, movement, focus, tension, space, time, language, symbol, audience, mood and atmosphere' (ACARA, 2017). The elements alone, however, do not create theatre; theatre is the combination of the elements of drama with the appropriate use of narrative, perspective and form, skills, techniques and processes of drama. The elements of drama determine how and why dramatic action is shaped to create meaning. They are fundamental to making and responding across all stages of drama learning. The action of drama involves an interrelationship between drama forms and the elements of drama. This is the language of drama (Edwards, 2014; Neelands, 2004; Posten-Anderson, 2008). In this section the following elements are explored in detail:

- voice
- body and space
- tension
- contrast
- symbol
- time
- space
- focus
- mood and atmosphere.

Voice

The voice is one of the elements of drama and so in the teaching of drama we need to develop skills and techniques for children to become confident and able vocal performers. Children need to develop their voice usage as early as possible, bearing in mind that some children will have special needs, such as apraxia/dyspraxia, and will have vocal usage challenges (Roy, 2011). Many of the techniques mentioned here are also applicable in music and are developed further in Chapter 7.

TABLE 5.1 SOME TERMS RELEVANT TO VOICE USAGE

Voice usage	Meaning
Accent	Way of speaking used in a local area or country
Articulation	Clear pronunciation of words
Clarity	Clearness of the voice
Dialogue	A conversation between two or more characters
Emphasis	Stress on a word or phrase
Fluency	Natural, flowing speech
Intonation	Rising and falling of the voice in speech
Pace	Speed of speech or movement
Pause	A break in speaking; a period of silence
Pitch	How high or low the voice is
Register	Appropriate speech for the person being spoken to, or for the situation
Stage whisper	A loud whisper intended to be heard by the audience
Timing	Speaking, moving or pausing at exactly the right moment
Tone	Changing the voice to express emotion
Volume	Loudness or quietness of the voice

Do not focus on accents when looking at voice in drama; the real purpose of the voice is for children to communicate their inner thoughts rather than their place of origin. Accents can be practised later but are often a barrier to learning in the drama classroom. Your voice tells a lot about how you are feeling. In fact, there are a whole lot of things that can vary in the voice (Morgan & Saxton, 1987).

In the classroom

This is an activity for Stage 1 and beyond.

In pairs, children consider the following situation. A guard has rushed to see the Ruler of the land with bad news. The law has been broken and the sentry has discovered it. The guard has done nothing wrong but is scared that the queen/king will take her/his anger out on them. The children are to act out the scenario, but need to think about the following characterisation for the guard. The pace is fast because the guard is nervous. The volume is louder than normal, but not too loud, as the sentry is speaking to the Ruler. The register is polite and submissive. The tone is worried and fearful. The intonation starts high on every sentence to show fear.

The Ruler is silent at first. Does the Ruler shout at the guard or use a quiet volume? Is the tone low? Is the pace quick and sharp or slow and calm, and possibly dangerous?

Body and space

A core element of drama is the development of the control of the body in the space around it. Many of the skills and techniques used in drama in this respect are shared with dance (see Chapter 4). It is in the way such knowledges and skills are applied that they can be differentiated within their art forms.

All theories of physical performance recognise the need to control the body so as to communicate meaning. Children can use drama as non-threatening methodology to develop fine and gross motor skills and explore shape and space.

No person acts exactly the same way as another. While stereotypes can be useful as a starting point, they often limit skill development in drama. Movements can be isolated, in that certain forms can create specific, subconscious meanings and children should be encouraged to explore these, with concepts based on the work of Rudolf Laban (Bradley, 2009). As explored in Chapter 4 there are a variety of forms of movement.

- Open/closed – reflecting the emotions of an individual being open or closed off to others, e.g. wide arms or folded arms.
- Angular/curved – this can be interpreted to reflect cold or warm individuals and therefore whom might be trusted more (by an audience or other characters).

- Symmetrical/asymmetrical – this can be used in many ways to reflect beauty, youth and an audience's interpretation of a character. Students can be encouraged to explore these movements and then subvert them.

Your face shows a lot of emotions and reactions. A large amount of our brain is focused on understanding other people's faces so as an actor how you use your face is important. Similar to the body, students can start to control the different parts of the face, again using Laban's theories, which are explored in Chapter 4.

- The eyes – open/closed/screwed up.
- The eyebrows – amazed, frowning, etc.
- The mouth – wide, closed, tight, smiling, sad, etc.

Lesson plan 5.1

AIM

To explore stereotypes and ways of movement.

OUTLINE/DESCRIPTION

In this activity students will be exploring different ways of moving based on background knowledge and supporting ideas from the teacher.

Have the children walk around the room at a normal pace. They should look for places where there are no other children. This should cause them to continually change direction and not all walk in a circle.

In all activities, emphasise the need for safety and no touching of others. Only with clear and enforced classroom rules can safety and challenge be achieved.

Introduce the idea of freezing on command. This teaches focus and attention as well as awareness. A whistle is often useful for this, as it saves the teacher having to shout when the classroom is purposefully noisy.

Now introduce stereotypes. Suggest that the children walk like old people. After a minute, stop the class. Have one or two children demonstrate their movement and then discuss with the class what was good, what could be improved and why the child chose to change their movements.

INTENDED OUTCOMES

Students identify
- how their ideas can be expressed through role
- role and situation as they listen and respond
- how movement can create a role

Students understand
- improvisation
- movement and space to imagine and establish a role

> ## LINKS TO CURRICULUM
>
> ### Foundation to Year 2 content descriptors
> - Explore role and dramatic action in dramatic play, improvisation and process drama (ACADRM027).
> - Use voice, facial expression, movement and space to imagine and establish role and situation (ACADRM028).
> - Present drama that communicates ideas, including stories from their community, to an audience (ACADRM029).
>
> ## ASSESSMENT
> - Students explore and develop ideas.
> - Assessment undertaken through observation and discussion.

Figure 5.6 Students character walking

TEACHER TIP

CLASS DISCUSSION

Class discussion of activities needs to be continual. Always start by encouraging positive comments, and then introduce ways to challenge or improve what children are doing. This develops self-reflection in the children. Depending on the age of the class, you can explore different ages, jobs, emotions and even animals. Animals are excellent for all ages. Children can identify with them, they can use their own background knowledge (introducing a sense of belonging) and they can explore the anthropomorphic relationship between animals and human emotions.

Tension

Tension is a force that drives the drama and gives it meaning, such as the unexpected, mystery and conflict. It is tension that engages the audience in the dramatic action. It is what makes you want to keep watching – you want to know what happens next, how it will all turn out – it makes you care.

- It may be something that is very hard to do.
- It may be a surprise waiting to happen that the audience knows about but one of the characters does not know about.
- It may be a difficult problem that has to be solved.
- It may have something to do with danger or a threat.
- It may be an argument or a difference of opinion between characters.

Without the element of tension, the story of Jack and the Beanstalk would just be a simple recount of a family with no food. However, a simple recount changes to a narrative when a complication is added. Jack makes a mistake when he ignores his mother's advice and sells their cow for magic beans. This sets off a sequence of events that keeps the viewer waiting to see what happens next. Moments of tension within the story keep an audience guessing and glued to their seats (hopefully!).

Contrast

Contrast contains opposites, the use of opposing forces at work in the drama. This can be demonstrated, for example, through movement and stillness, sound and silence, dark and light, loud and soft, tall and thin, short and fat, and good and evil.

The story of Cinderella contrasts the poverty and loneliness of Cinderella, who is made to work hard, with the wealth and unkindness of the two ugly sisters.

In the classroom

Have children work in pairs as an ugly sister and Cinderella eating their lunch. One group could be made up of three children, two of whom are the ugly sisters.

Children need to think about what food each of them would have and how much. How would they sit, and where would they sit? (Think about height and space.) This also introduces the concept of status. They need to think about how they would eat the food, including noises. Once they have rehearsed, have some groups show their performances to the class and discuss.

Symbol

Items are symbolic when something is used (such as an object, gesture, word, sound or person) to represent a meaning beyond the literal:

- the basket of food is heavy/the burden of being responsible
- props/costume – crown, halo, axe, white dress, red cloak, dark forest.

TABLE 5.2 TYPES OF STAGE SETTINGS

End-on stage	Often rectangular in shape, it has an invisible wall between the actors and the audience. Stanislavski called this the **fourth wall**. It is a good stage, as it allows the actors to have a simply placed audience, which allows for easier blocking. The audience is clearly separated from them. That said, this form of stage can also keep an audience at a distance and can limit the performance, as the audience is always fixed in one place. This is the most common default type of stage used by children.
Thrust stage	Here the actors push out into the audience. It can create a more intimate performance and break down the barriers between actor and audience. Meyerhold liked this kind of stage. However, it can cause some viewing problems for audience members if the actors are not careful with blocking.
Extended stage	With this stage the actors can slightly surround the audience and really break down the barriers between the audience and performers. The performers can almost intimidate the audience. However, some audience members will have difficulty viewing the performance unless they swing round in their seats.
Avenue stage	With the audience sitting on both sides, the performers are very close and the audience are always reminded that they are watching theatre. The audience will always have the back of an actor to them and the set can be limited.
Theatre-in-the-round	With the audience surrounding the performance, this is the most intimate form of staging. It allows for audience–performer interaction. The performers have to work hard to allow the audience to have clear sight lines and the set is very limited.

Fourth wall: an imaginary wall that the audience observes the action through, unseen by the actors, who perform as if there is no-one there. Meyerhold (Braun, 1995) deliberately broke this convention by having the actors interact with the audience, an idea that Brecht and others applied in Western theatre (Hodge, 2010).

In the classroom

Set up an end-on stage and place a chair in the centre at the front. Have a child sit on the chair. Have two other children stand at the side of the chair. Ask the rest of the class who is the most important character on stage. Now move the chair to the back of the acting area and ask where the focus is. Keep changing the placing of actors and the chair and ask the class what they think each time. You can also vary the heights of the characters to see how the status/power changes.

Focus

Focus is the frame that directs attention to what is most significant and most intensifies the dramatic meaning; for example, the central issue or theme of the drama ('Little Red Riding Hood': stranger danger).

Figure 5.8 End-on stage

Focus can also be a moment in drama that directs attention to a particular part of the drama to make it significant, such as role groupings, an action, a sound, a gesture, a movement or a pause. In 'Little Red Riding Hood', it might be the entrance of the Wolf, which moves the focus from Red Riding Hood to the Wolf. What would be a more powerful, grand entrance and what would be a more subversive, slow, sneaking entrance?

Mood

This is the overall feeling, tone or atmosphere of the drama. The purpose of mood is to concentrate the actions and *move* the audience emotionally. While movements and voices are major factors in creating mood, the theatre arts of lighting, music and sound can also be used to play a very significant role in changing the mood.

TEACHER TIP

Using the children's background knowledge from the other Arts, show various colour cards and ask the children what emotions those colours make them feel. Then try to think of what type of person would wear those colours.

Figure 5.9 Mood created with lighting

In the classroom

Choose various pieces of soundtrack music or classical music and ask the children to decide what they think is happening, or the emotion they think the music reminds them of, as they listen to each piece.

Videos: Soundtrack music examples

TEACHER TIP

SAFETY

One of the best ways to ensure that children do not challenge taking part is to first deal with non-optional safety issues. If you do this, the children will recognise the importance you place on physical activities and drama. So that they do not inadvertently hurt each other, ensure that they all remove footwear. Where possible, socks should also be removed so that children do not slip. Shorts and trousers should be worn, not skirts, and where possible clothing should be loose fitting. Jewellery should also be removed or covered with tape if it cannot be removed. Ensure that reasonable adjustments are made to activities for students with physical limitations.

BASIC WARM-UP TECHNIQUES

For all practical drama activities, it is a good idea to start with a warm-up. This allows the body to flex and gets the blood flowing. Not only will it help to focus children on activities, but it will also prepare the body so that it is less likely to get strained and thus injured.

Figure 5.10 Students warming up

BODY

- Shoulder rolls, hip swivel, knee swivel, foot swivel (basic joints: please note not to do exercises involving the neck as these are potentially dangerous).
- Gentle spinal roll.
- Stretching – legs/arms.
- In pairs, monkey grip row action.
- Lying down and getting up – start by giving children 10 seconds to get up to a standing position reaching for the stars, then ask them to do it again in 8 seconds (reducing by 2 seconds each time) until they only have 2 seconds to stand (a good settling technique to 'shake the sillies out'!).

VOICE

- This exercise explores voice, movement and imagination: Ahh (the Sun), Ohh (the Moon), Ooo (draw in energy), Aayy (split the Earth), Eee (gather energy in own body).
- Elevator: using various vowels.
- Tongue twisters: red leather/yellow leather etc.

Link: Tongue twisters

BREATHING

Lying on the back (knees raised if all of the back is not flat on the floor), eyes closed, hands palm down. Instruct the children as follows: 'Become aware of your breath as it slides in and out of your lungs. Become aware of your abdomen rising as you take an inward breath and dropping as the breath leaves your body. Now, the next inward breath you take, take it in on the count of five (through the nose). Count five on the outward breath (out through the lips). Repeat three times. Now, increase the count to eight. Once the breath is deep and comfortable on the count of eight, begin to visualise (see) your breath as a colour filling your lungs. The inward breath may be blue, and change to red as you blow it gently from your lips. This exercise may include sound – add the vowel AHH, or OH, and imagine the sound as a laser punching a hole through the ceiling, or that you are sending a sound stream up into the universe.'

Again, vary the amount of warm-up exercises depending on the focus of the children and the requirements of the lesson. Sometimes basic stretching exercises are all that are needed.

In the classroom

Tableau: a still image created on the stage, similar to mise en scène in media.

In groups of three, have the children create a tableau of two adults and a child. One of the adults is saying, 'Don't speak to your parent like that'. In one **tableau**, have the children close together. Try the scene far apart. Now in their groups the children should try to make tableaux indicating status and relationships through the use of space. The scenes could include a family, a court, a gang, an argument, a peace treaty. Discuss the differences of each with the class after they have tried them out.

Making and responding in drama

Drama as an art builds on the principles of drama to create a theatrical work. This making of art, and indeed responding to it, requires the ability to understand the nature of dramatic texts. In many respects this metalanguage of drama is as closely related to that of the subject English as it is to the other Arts of dance, visual media and music. Using this language of drama requires an understanding of structures, viewpoints, forms and conventions of dramatic texts. It is only then that a student can move to playbuilding and the execution of the theatre arts.

Within the process of developing a scene, the concept of viewpoints and the possible impacts and resonances of a student's concept for performance have to be explored. Students need to consider the purpose of their work beyond the narrative of the piece. In applying the multiple skills of inquiry and understanding how they function as a whole to create meaning, students can evaluate and expand their skills and goals through reflection of self and others. Developing a clear sense of criteria for quality is important within this, although students will often already have an implicit or undefined set of quality criteria. Within the teaching of the Arts there needs to be a balance of having criteria to develop knowledge and a pedagogy that does not limit creativity by imposing explicit criteria, yet scaffolds the students (Bourdieu & Passeron, 1977).

Viewpoints

An understanding of viewpoint is integral to making and responding in drama. Through an appreciation of viewpoints:

> students learn that meanings can be generated from different viewpoints and that these shift according to different world encounters. As students make, investigate or critique drama as actors, directors and audiences, they may ask and answer questions to interrogate the playwrights' and actors' meanings and the audiences' interpretations. Meanings and interpretations are informed by social, cultural and historical contexts, and an understanding of how elements, materials, skills and processes are used (ACARA, 2017).

Forms

Form, in drama, means the structural and genre characteristics of devised and scripted drama. This of course reflects that drama, like any cultural text, is shaped by the historical, cultural and social contexts of its creation, reproduction and staging. The dramatic works of Shakespeare readily demonstrate the relationship between creation and staging. Shakespeare's plays were written in Elizabethan England and so embody historical, cultural and social aspects of the late 16th and early 17th centuries. When a Shakespearian play is staged today it can be presented in a manner that reflects early 20th-century values. Context is therefore an important aspect of shaping form and responses to that form.

Genre and forms of drama also vary considerably. Forms of drama include:

- play, scripted or improvised: a drama involving dialogue, characters and a narrative
- comedy: a play that is funny
- dance-drama: a drama presented through dance movements
- docu-drama: a documentary style of drama with a reconstruction of events
- forum theatre: a drama in which the audience suggests changes to affect the outcomes
- musical: a drama that involves music and songs
- pantomime: a Christmas theatrical entertainment, usually based on a fairy tale
- tragedy: a play with a sad ending.

Structure is the way in which time, place and action are sequenced. In a linear or chronological structure, the action unfolds from beginning to end. In a non-linear structure, the action unfolds through shifts in time and/or place.

Conventions

Conventions are the language of each art form. In music, for example, the elements of music such as pitch and rhythm are used to create a piece of music. In visual arts elements such as line and shape are used to communicate certain ideas or to convey a message. In drama there are a range of conventions that can be used to present part(s) of a drama. These include:

- aside – a remark addressed only to the audience
- flashback – the acting out of an event from the past
- flash forward – the acting out of a future or imagined event
- freeze frame – an action frozen in time
- frozen picture – an image, created on stage, held without movement
- mime – stylised movement that creates an illusion of reality
- monologue – a speech made by a lone character speaking their thoughts aloud
- movement – use of the body as the sole means of communication
- narration – parts of the story told by a narrator
- slow motion – movement performed at a slowed-down speed
- soliloquy – a lengthy speech made when no other characters are on stage
- tableau – an alternative, more advanced term for the frozen picture
- voice-over – a recorded speech played during a drama.

Playbuilding

All the aforementioned components lead to a core element of drama: playbuilding. This involves the teacher using the various knowledges listed earlier and selecting, adapting and arranging them to create dramatic play and experiences. There are key elements to playbuilding to be applied within the classroom setting. The teacher and children need to work together in groups or as a class, and using the process listed below engage successfully with drama. Several of the steps will be repeated throughout. Children in the early childhood years will take these steps at a very basic level, while year 6 children should be taking them in detail.

1. Select the topic/objective (such as a theme or idea to perform).
2. Find a focus for the performance.
3. Narrow the focus to what, where and why.
4. Research the concept/idea/focus.
5. Develop roles (through characters and challenging stereotypes).
6. Reflect on the process so far.
7. Select a staging type.
8. Improvise and experiment with performance ideas.
9. Stop and discuss what has been done.
10. Further develop the characters, blocking and narrative.
11. Record the process in logbooks throughout.
12. Repeat steps 8 to 11 several times at rehearsal, responding to and changing items as needed.
13. Perform the ideas to an audience.
14. Share/record feelings/reactions and evaluate the experience, including strategies for the next steps.

Improvisation

Part of the playbuilding experience is to improvise and experiment with ideas. Improvisation is both a tool and a performance technique in its own right (Pierse, 2006). When used as a rehearsal tool, it is described as a prepared improvisation.

In improvisation, children need to be taught to accept offers. This involves reacting to and incorporating ideas made by other members of the group. It requires fast, flexible thinking, the ability to make connections between what you want to do, or think should be happening, and what is actually happening. In order to accept an offer, you first need to be aware of what that offer is. This entails an ability to read the signals contained in action and speech and relies heavily on the skills of other members in making offers.

Making offers involves initiating action and dialogue. It allows individuals to make their own contribution to the development of the drama. It is most useful when it incorporates the acceptance of an offer, because it enables the story or the action to move forward.

Making a successful offer requires the performer to clearly communicate not only their own role and action but also those of other members. This involves an ability to incorporate signals in speech and action that indicate what the actor expects other members to be and to do.

The following skills need to be taught and practised:
- listening and speaking
- exercising focus
- flexibility
- quick thinking
- cooperation
- lateral thinking
- responding spontaneously to thought through speech and action.

As improvisation, especially speech improvisation, can be a daunting and sometimes quite confronting experience, it is often best to start with movement improvisations.

In the classroom

In this activity, children need to work silently to create a tableau or a frozen picture or a frieze that illustrates a particular scene. Various sizes of groups can be created. Not all the children need to represent people; they can also represent inanimate objects. A possible list of images to use could be: beach cricket, gardening, the first Australian on the moon, changing a light bulb, the school playground, or an argument. Remind the children that they must respond to offers or it doesn't work.

Lesson plan 5.2

AIM

To use voice, body, movement and language to sustain role and relationships and create dramatic action with a sense of time and space.

OUTLINE/DESCRIPTION

In this lesson students will explore space and movement through rehearsed improvisation.

Divide the class into two groups. Group A is secretly given a place, such as a library, and sits in a line in front of Group B, whose job it is to identify the place. One at a time, members of Group A take up a position as part of the frozen scene. They can represent people or objects. The purpose of the exercise is to 'read' what the previous members are portraying and build on that. For example, if the scene is a library, one child may take the role of a table and the next child may take the role of a chair. Another may freeze a gesture of taking a book from a shelf and the next may be the shelf. When the entire group is in place, a signal is given for the scene to come to life and all participants to interact. This may involve only movement, or movement and sound, or speech. A variation is to limit group members to only one sound, word or phrase that best signals their roles. Members of Group B can simply identify the place or demonstrate their understanding of the signals by joining the scene in an appropriate role. Reflection should include discussion of the importance of reading signals, of the importance of working as a team, and of how making and accepting offers contributes to the creation of 'the big picture'.

INTENDED OUTCOME

Students identify
- representations of people/ideas
- appropriate and inappropriate use if images/visuals in performance

Students understand
- structure, intent, character and settings
- composition/performance elements (ACADRM032)

ASSESSMENT

- Students explore and develop ideas.
- Students present artworks using conventions of art form to represent their ideas.
- Assessment undertaken through observation and discussion.

Masks

Another tool to use in drama rehearsals is the mask. Masks isolate the body from the face, so we can use masks to develop how we control our bodies. Masks can be full-face, half-face or even just covering your eyes. Each mask has a different purpose, which we will explore. Your class may have many types of masks to use. If they do not, there are many simple solutions that are effective.

You can buy masks in most theatrical costume shops, as well as in many craft stores and even some 'dollar' stores. The best masks are made of leather or hardened cloth. Plastic masks are cheap but uncomfortable. Remember, wearing a mask can be tiring and you need to let it breathe.

Figure 5.11 Noh mask

> **Reflection activity**
>
> Take a brown paper bag and place it over your whole head. With a marker pen, gently mark where your eyes are. Now remove the bag and cut very small holes for your eyes. Draw a straight line where the mouth should be. You now have a mask that has no expression. This is called a neutral mask.

Before you use any mask, or indeed perform, you need to learn a type of stance called the neutral position. This is a way of standing that allows you to show as little emotion as possible.

Figure 5.12 Paper bag mask

Figure 5.13 Child wearing mask

> **Reflection activity**
>
> Find your neutral position. Stand with your feet in line with your shoulders. Keep your arms relaxed at your sides. Stand straight. Keep your legs straight but relaxed. Keep your shoulders straight but relaxed and look directly ahead with no emotion.

In the classroom

A number of children from your class each choose a full-face mask. The mask can be neutral or have a character. Each child looks at their mask for a moment. They think about how that mask may stand. Then they turn their backs to the rest of the class. Standing in the neutral position, they put their masks on. Now each child moves their legs, body and arms into a stance that they think suits their mask. Then they all turn around and face the rest of the class. They hold this position for a few moments, then turn their backs to the class. Standing in the neutral position, they remove their masks. Now ask the rest of the class what character they thought each of the masked children was.

This task can be repeated several times, with the masked children changing their body position each time. There will be many surprising and differing responses about what kind of character children thought each mask represented. There are no right or wrong responses in this task.

A couple of important points that the children will need to know about masks:
- You should never touch a mask when wearing it and facing any audience. Every mask makes an audience focus on your body position. By touching the mask, you remind the audience that your 'real' face is covered and it destroys their acceptance that you're someone else. Masks have a 'power', which touching can destroy.
- The same applies to putting on the mask. Always put it on and take it off with your back to the audience. Try never to turn your head away from the audience when wearing a mask, whether in performance or rehearsal, and never to turn your back to the audience.

When wearing masks, children become very aware of what each part of their bodies does. How do they place their feet? How do they bend their knees? How do they move their hips? How do they swing their arms? How do they move their shoulders? Because masks separate the image of the person from the performance, many children develop a sense of confidence when they use them; they feel they can hide behind the mask but still explore their own self-identity through it (Wilsher, 2007).

Theatre arts

While there is a rightful focus on acting performance skills, as part of the playbuilding process, to apply the multitude of forms and structures available we need to introduce other roles within the theatre arts. Such roles may also have the added benefit of engaging those children who, for whatever reasons, struggle with physical, public performance. Such a variety of roles allows for drama to be fully inclusive.

Production skills/theatre arts roles

The director is the person who makes the overall creative decisions about the performance, deciding on the basic ideas for acting and design (set/lighting/sound). The director has ultimate responsibility for the all the aspects of the performance, and works closely with all the people involved in the performance.

The set designer literally designs the set – how the staging will look, including items such as props. This is separate from the costumes, which are the responsibility of the costume designer, who can design new clothing and have it made, or design costumes based on items that can be found or bought. The set designer and stage designer work closely together so the designs complement each other (taking advice from the director).

There are people responsible for the lighting and sound, making sure that these effects add to the performance and act complement the creative ideas of all the others, and ensure that it support she actors.

Make-up is another responsibility (including hairstyles) and can be as simple or complex as needed. Once again there is a need for collaboration, particularly with the costume designer.

All the items used on the stage are the responsibility of the stage props manager. They help source or design the items used (props). While working closely with the stage designer before the performance, during the performance the props manager has to work with the stage manager who ensures all aspects of the performance (acting, set changes, lighting and sound and props) work together to create a wonderfully collaborative piece of art.

Props are important tools to use to create a transformative place, facilitating the actors' imagination and the audience's suspension of disbelief. Indeed, this is the real power of theatre and drama, when ordinary objects are transformed. Having natural items such as cloths, poles, pieces of wood and sand in the rehearsal process is useful. You use them to explore objects and space, and the idea of transformation.

Drama assessment

Drama is often assessed using continual evaluation. The teacher can monitor the children's progress by observation and by using a checklist based upon curricula guidelines. A key point of this assessment is how children demonstrate deep understanding not only through their rehearsal and performances, but also in their oral reflections on activities. As they develop skill in writing, opportunities for extended writing in the children's evaluations of activities should also be taken, including giving their own personal opinions on performances. Additional useful tools for the classroom are digital cameras and video recording. These maintain a record of classwork and performance and are a valid assessment tool for both the teacher and the children.

In the classroom

This is an example of a limited evaluation from a child aged eight:

> I liked the play, it was really well acted and the actors really suited their roles. The lighting was exciting and the costumes really colourful.

This is an example of a more developed evaluation from a child aged nine:

> The play really made me think about the issue of loneliness. It involved a child being evacuated from the city and having to cope with being away from her parents. Julie Smith was very believable as the 12-year-old girl even although she was much older. She moved like a scared teenager and her language made me believe she was both young and she was in 1941. The set was simple with two wooden crates but the performers managed to make me believe there were different areas just by how they used them and how they were placed on the stage. The sound effects really helped in this by creating areas that suddenly made me feel I was on a train or in an old shed. This made up for the fact that there were no lighting effects as the performance was put on in the school gym. The costumes were kept very simple with characters dressed in black and adding one piece of costume to become a character. One character had a jacket on to show they were an official, and then changed into a simple woollen jumper to become a farmer. I would have liked to see more detailed costumes from the period but the simple costumes meant there were quick scene changes. I have never really been that interested in history. The play though gave me a better understanding of how hard it must have been for young people during the Second World War. While the play was not my style, it was well acted and very clear in its message. This was shown by the full attention given by my whole year group as we watched it.

The context of drama in the Arts and in education

As stated, in this process we need to be engaging with theories in order to contextualise the learning for children, creating a depth of knowledge in the understanding of drama through the unveiling of the 'why' certain performance practices are applied in drama.

Children are required to explore their emotions through physical and aural presentation when engaging with drama. There are times when we encourage children to empathise with an emotion and reflect that in the behaviour of their roles, yet we ignore the context of such a dramatic technique originating from Stanislavski. Children may explore different staging types when presenting their product in drama, but there is little evidence that the foundational ideas of Craig, Meyerhold and Brecht are known.

For some children it is through a clear understanding of the social construction of knowledge that embedded learning can be undertaken. If we want children to understand that a movement can communicate an emotion, but there is not necessarily a need to feel the emotion first, then mustn't we also inform them that this is the opposite approach to

Stanislavski's concept of emotional memory, and is in fact a Meyerhold technique and theory?

We present science learning with the knowledge of the physicists, chemists and biologists who 'discovered' such knowledge. Albert Einstein, Charles Darwin and Sir Isaac Newton are not unknown names within the primary classroom, yet ask an adult, let alone a seven-year-old, who Stanislavski or Meyerhold are, and there will be a blank response. The ideas and concepts of performance may be appreciated every day by children through their viewing of acting in films and television, but we are doing them a great disservice by holding back on the knowledge that developed our modern performance concepts. Referencing the specialist knowledge of Meyerhold and many other theatre practitioners in drama education should not be limited only to secondary students but should be shared from early childhood upward. Skills and knowledge should be contextualised, as students are able to grasp the most complex theatrical ideas (McLennan, 2008; Posten-Anderson, 2008; Roy, 2009; Sinclair, Jeanneret & O'Toole, 2009).

TEACHER TIP

Have the students sitting on chairs. The students need to remember a time when they were excited about something that was about to happen (such as getting a present or going on a trip). Have them act this, without words. Now encourage the students to remember a time they were worried (about a competition or a time they were caught doing something wrong, for example). The students then act this out in their chair again without words. Take two students and have them sit in chairs, with there being five chairs in a row. First, one student re-enacts the first memory and then the other student re-enacts the second memory. As they are doing so, announce to the class that this is the airport waiting room. Now ask the other students what each of the performers is feeling and why. We are using the 'emotional memory' technique from Stanislavski to play-build.

The challenge is for us as teachers to link techniques and activities to a theoretical grounding. There is no need for a dry lesson of theory. Instead, by drip-feeding snippets of theory in embodied practice the students will develop an appreciation of knowledge and applied techniques (Anderson, 2012).

> Students should be able to make judgments about the work from a critical perspective based upon her aesthetic understanding which incorporates the ways the social and historical context have been incorporated into the development of meaning in the work (Anderson, 2012).

For the teacher, this means we must have an understanding of the different theories behind the skills and activities we use within the classroom. Our own theory knowledge base must be developed to support this. Through developing students' knowledge of practitioners and theories we not only develop a deep knowledge that should lead to deep understanding, but we offer tools for appreciation of skills. An added support is that by demonstrating the academic validity of drama (and theatre studies) we negate the need to continually justify drama in the curriculum through only the skills it offers, and places us in a level playing field with our fellow Arts subjects and the wider curriculum. Too often drama has had to fight from a deficit model of justification. Instead, let's celebrate the depth and diversity of knowledge in the subject.

Conclusion

Drama is not something to shy away from. We engage with it in every moment of our waking lives in the way we interact with others and the 'roles' we adopt. It is easy to introduce drama into the classroom, but it takes effort and focus to offer meaningful learning experiences in drama that go beyond it merely playing the role of 'handmaiden' to other subjects. The principles and practices of drama apply from 0–18 years and thus resources that are targeted at specific age groups or stages can be easily adapted to support younger or older children. It is the context for application that the teacher needs to be flexible with. Drama opens intellectual spaces that give highly articulate and able children the freedom to stretch and question. Children who undertake educational drama often outperform their peers in other academic areas, due to the variety of skills and opportunities drama offers.

REVIEW QUESTIONS

1. What is the Melbourne Declaration?
2. Why is it suggested that teachers should find drama easy to apply in the classroom?
3. Who was Dorothy Heathcote and why is she important in relation to teaching drama?
4. Why should a class undertake a 'warm-up' before practical activities?
5. What area of basic skill/awareness do dance and drama share?
6. Why are class discussions of activities important?
7. Name the seven elements of drama.
8. What is stimulus and what can be a source for it?

RECOMMENDED READING

Anderson, M. (2012). *Master Class in Drama Education*. London: Continuum.

Anderson, M. and Dunn, J. (eds) (2013). *How Drama Activates Learning: Contemporary Research and Practice*. London: Bloomsbury.

Banks, R. A. and Marson, P. (1998). *Drama and Theatre Arts*, 2nd edn. London: Hodder & Stoughton.

Berry, C. (1992). *The Actor and the Text*. London: Virgin.

Blumenthal, E., Taymor, J. and Monda, A. (2007). *Julie Taymor*, 3rd edn. New York: Abrams.

Bordieu, P. and Passeron, J. P. (1977). *Reproduction in Education, Society and Culture*. Beverly Hills: Sage.

Bradley, K. K. (2009). *Rudolf Laban*. Abingdon: Routledge.

Braun, E. (1995). *Meyerhold: A Revolution in Theatre*. London: Methuen.

Cremin, T., McDonald, R., Goff, E. and Blakemore, L. (2009). *Jumpstart! Drama: Games & Activities for Ages 5–11*. London: Routledge.

Edwards, L. (2014). *The Creative Arts: A Process Approach for Teachers and Children*. Harlow, Essex: Pearson.

Heathcote, D. and Bolton, G. (1994). *Drama for Learning: Dorothy Heathcote's Mantle of the Expert Approach to Education*. Portsmouth, New Hampshire: Heinemann.

Hodge, A. (ed.) (2010). *Actor Training*, 2nd edn. Abingdon, Oxon: Routledge.

Kozulin, A., Gindis, B., Ageyev, V. S. and Miller, S. M. (eds) (2003). *Vygotsky's Educational Theory in Cultural Context*. New York: Cambridge University Press.

Lewis, M. and Rainer, J. (2005). *Teaching Classroom Drama and Theatre*. Abingdon: Routledge.

McLennan, D. P. (2008). 'Kinder-caring: Exploring the use and effects of sociodrama in a kindergarten classroom'. *Journal of Student Wellbeing*, 2(1), 74–88.

Ministerial Council on Education, Employment, Training and Youth Affairs and the Cultural Ministers Council. (MCEETYA) (2008). *Melbourne Declaration on Educational Goals for Young Australians*.

Morgan, N. and Saxton, J. (1987). *Teaching Drama: A Mind of Many Wonders*. Cheltenham: Stanley Thornes.

Neelands, J. (2002). *Making Sense of Drama*. Oxford: Heinemann.

—— (2004). *Beginning Drama 11–14*, 2nd edn. London: David Fulton.

Neelands J. and Goode, T. (2000). *Structuring Drama Work*, 2nd edn. Cambridge: Cambridge University Press.

Posten-Anderson, B. (2008). *Drama: Learning Connections in Primary Schools*. Melbourne: Oxford University Press.

Roy, D. (2008). *How to Pass Standard Grade Drama*. Paisley: Hodder Gibson.

—— (2009). *Nelson Drama for Secondary Students*. Melbourne: Cengage.

—— (2012). 'Opening the curtains to thinking'. *Education Review* (February), 19.

Sinclair, C., Jeanneret, N. and O'Toole, J. (eds). (2009). *Education in the Arts*. Melbourne: Oxford University Press.

Somers, J. (1994). *Drama in the Curriculum*. London: Cassell.

Vygotsky, L. S. (1986). *Thought and Learning*. Cambridge, MA: The MIT Press.

Winston, J. and Tandy, M. (2009). *Beginning Drama 4–11*, 3rd edn. Abbingdon: Routledge.

6

Learning in media arts

> Whoever controls the media – the images – controls the culture.
>
> Allen Ginsberg

In this chapter

This chapter will explore the diverse technologies that can be used to purposefully communicate ideas, stories and information to an audience. The skills and knowledge involved in using and viewing media will be discussed in a way that will guide educators in their planning for quality media arts education, regardless of availability of equipment and technical support.

By the end of this chapter you should have a clear understanding of:

- engaging with media in education
- the elements and principles of media in education
- media in early childhood settings
- media in primary settings
- making and responding in media education
- the context of media in the arts and in education.

Concepts and genres will be explained and suggestions made for links to the other art forms as well as to other Learning Areas. Tools for analysing media and for creating media will be defined and explained in a way that demonstrates a sequential progression from early childhood to primary school. As in other chapters, glossary definitions and website information are provided throughout to define and explain technological terms and indicate available resources for further professional development.

Introduction

Media technologies: technology used to produce media such as film, television, the internet, video games, print and audio.

Media arts: the creative use of media technologies.

Now more than ever before we are surrounded by many forms of **media technologies**, including film, television, the internet, games, print and audio. The Australian Curriculum focuses on **media arts**, which incorporates the creative use of these technologies as an art form. The aims according to ACARA (2015) are that students develop:

- enjoyment and confidence to participate in, experiment with and interpret the media-rich culture and communications practices that surround them
- creative and critical thinking, and exploring perspectives in media as producers and consumers
- aesthetic knowledge and a sense of curiosity and discovery as they explore imagery, text and sound to express ideas, concepts and stories for different audiences
- knowledge and understanding of their active participation in existing and evolving local and global media cultures.

Engaging with media arts in education

In the context of visual arts, 'media' refers to the materials and techniques used to create an artwork; for example, in *The Boating Party* by Renoir the medium is oil paint on canvas. Media arts, however, refers to artworks that depend on a technological component to function. Students use technologies that produce images, sounds and text to create and analyse a broad range of forms such as animations, news reports, music videos in different media contexts such as print, internet, television and new and mobile devices. This is a space that is constantly changing with a range of existing and emerging technologies. The Australian Curriculum: The Arts (ACARA, 2015) describes learning in media arts as involving:

> students learning to engage with communications technologies and cross-disciplinary art forms to design, produce, distribute and interact with a range of print, audio, screen-based or hybrid artworks. Students explore, view, analyse and participate in media culture from a range of viewpoints and contexts. They acquire skills and processes to work in a range of forms and styles. Students learn to reflect critically on their own and others' media arts experiences and evaluate media artworks, cultures and contexts. They express, conceptualise and communicate through their media artworks with increasing complexity and aesthetic understanding.

Children today can and do gain access to mass media more readily than their parents could. Some even refer to today's students as 'screenagers'. American doctor and film-maker Delaney Ruston made a documentary about her own family's struggles with technology and she believes that we have accepted screens into our lives without questioning the effects (Maddox, 2017).

Link: Screenagers

So on the one hand, children may be more intensively targeted by commercial and inappropriate interests, but on the other hand they have the opportunity to take advantage of diverse and growing learning tools and participate actively in social change.

Kerckaert et al. (2015) suggest that more and more teachers are convinced that ICT in education provides multiple possibilities for children. This used to be a controversial topic, with some educators concerned that ICT use was a threat to playful learning and development; however, they go on to suggest that ICT use is no longer perceived as an innovative practice.

Nansen et al. (2012) found that research regarding use of ICT is focused on older children and this has meant that less obvious risks have not been addressed particularly those relevant for younger children. Their research showed that online risks to younger children's wellbeing are more ordinary and more often relate to interpersonal relationships and the content that they come across.

Marsh and Bishop (2014) suggest that there is a synergy between children's use of technologies online, off-line, digital and non-digital and this is becoming increasingly complex. Others suggest that apps used by preschoolers may foster play and creativity, especially those that engage children in creating texts in a variety of ways such as virtual constructions, drawings, paintings and stories.

Some suggest a digital wellbeing approach might be better for empowering children to be active, ethical and critical participants in digital culture. With this in mind, teachers have a very important role in ensuring that children develop the ability to critically analyse a range of media and to use it in a creative way. The inclusion of media arts in the Australian curriculum places the focus on the **creative and critical use of media**, not just learning

Creative use of media: not just the mastery of technical skills; it is more about using the technology in innovative ways to communicate ideas.

how to use technology, and in this sense media arts has strong links to the other Arts areas in terms of elements and principles.

In the 21st century, we often refer to media as the usage of the internet and devices that access it such as tablets, but we also need to recognise that media has been engaged with for over a century through radio, film, television and advertising. New technology has allowed greater access to view but also to create multiple forms of media.

> **Reflection activity**
>
> Make a list of the new media that have appeared in the past decade. Compare life for you as a child, or for your parents, with the lives of children now. What does this mean for children? Parents? Teachers? Curriculum designers?
>
> Watch two videos created in different years: one from 2013 and one from 2015.
>
> What do you think are the pros and cons of the new technology and how will you address the balance of digital and human/physical interaction?
>
> What do you think a similar video made in 2020 might be about?

Videos: 2013 and 2015

The term 'digital native' was introduced in 2001 by Marc Prensky (Joy, 2012). He defined the 'digital native' as those born in the age of digital culture and familiar with computers from an early age. Those who were born before the advent of digital technology he called digital immigrants (Prensky, 2001). Kirschner and De Bruyckere (2017), however, argue that 'digital natives' are a myth. They cite research undertaken in Hong Kong with first-year undergraduate students at university showing that students primarily use technology for personal entertainment and communication; they are not always literate in using that technology to support their learning (Kennedy & Fox 2013). Other research suggests that children now do not have the extraordinary talents and abilities that some teachers assume they possess and that they need to be taught the skills and competencies before they can be usefully applied (Kirschner & De Bruyckere, 2017). Tondeur et al. (2017) suggest that most beginning teachers have grown up with digital technologies and may be more open to using them in the classroom than in the past. However, it has been found that only a small number of beginning teachers are able to use technology in diverse and flexible ways (Gao et al., 2011).

> **Reflection activity**
>
> Do you consider yourself a 'digital native'? Or a 'digital immigrant'? Or are you something new?
>
> Do you have the skills and knowledge to use the latest technology and to be able to teach students to use it in a creative way?
>
> If not, how will you develop technological skills?

Valtonen et al. (2015) suggest that collaborating with peers provides a low-threatening environment to learn about technology integration.

Children learn the skills and understandings necessary to use various media to create media artworks and develop the ability to critically analyse available forms of media that are diverse and changeable.

The elements and principles of media in education

There are five key concepts in media education: media languages, media technologies, media institutions, media audiences, and constructed representations of reality. There are technical elements (for example, the way we use equipment such as cameras) and symbolic elements (such as use of light or sound to create meaning). Elements of media arts are combined and shaped using story principles of structure, intent, character, settings, points of view and **genre** conventions (ACARA, 2017). Children learn skills, techniques and processes to create media artworks and learn that meanings can be generated from different viewpoints. They develop skills in asking and answering questions in order to make critical judgments about their own work and media that they consume as audience.

Genre: a particular style, form or content.

Figure 6.1 shows the framework that can exist between the person(s) producing (making) media arts and the audience. Children learn that there is a relationship between the producer, the media, the message and the audience. We can see that the producer brings their own perspectives to the media 'text'. They may represent a media institution or someone or something (such as a TV station or a political party); they may have biases, for instance towards a particular race or gender; and they will have past experiences, cultural and social, that may affect the way they view things and present them. We need to think about reasons for producing media 'texts'; for example, to entertain, or inform, or change the audience's point of view.

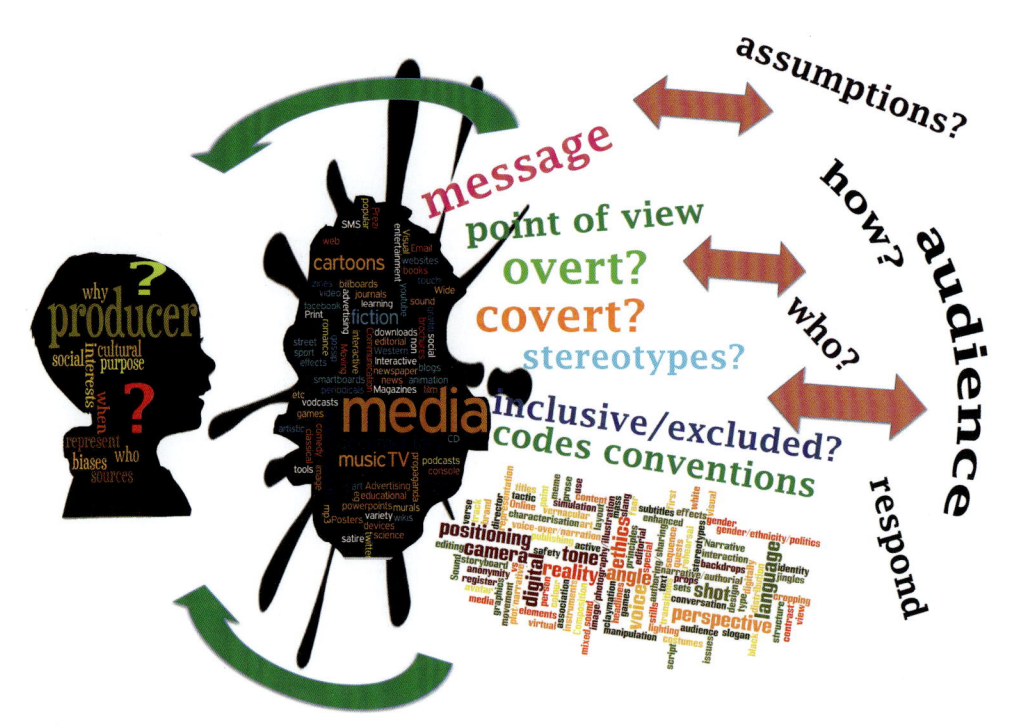

Figure 6.1 Media arts and audience

The producer of the artwork then selects the appropriate media product to communicate the message, which can present a point of view, which could have overt or covert meanings. We need to be clear in that the term 'producer' also has different specific context for drama and media (in particular film, television and radio) depending on the context used. The role of the title 'Producer' often relates to the supervisory/business side of the Arts, allowing the lead creatives to undertake an artwork production (such as financing and logistics) as part of the Producer's overall vision, but which is still part of the creative process.

Viewers could look for stereotypes and inclusions and exclusions; for example, has the producer assumed that all girls like to wear pink? Or the language may be used in a way that excludes children from non-English speaking backgrounds.

Video activity: Three little pigs ad

Key concepts in media arts (Australian Curriculum)

The key concepts are:

1 media languages
2 media technologies
3 media institutions
4 media audiences
5 media representations.

Making and responding through these five interrelated concepts gives children a deep understanding of their evolving world and prepares them for the future (ACARA, 2015).

1 Media languages

These are the technical and symbolic elements, such as **layout**, shot type, props and symbols used to tell stories (see Table 6.1). Figures 6.2 and 6.3 show two types of shots. Similar to drama, dance and visual art, the 'shot' allows the audience to be positioned and manipulated not only by what they see, but also by what they don't see, and *how* they see an idea.

> **Layout:** the spacing, size and placement of objects on a page (or a screen, if the work is digital). Effective layout helps the viewer find the message.

TABLE 6.1 MEDIA LANGUAGES

Language	Types	Definition	Considerations
Narrative	Prose	Ordinary writing	Voice: Whose voice is it? From what perspective or position? What language? What register or tone (e.g. anger, romance)? What is the purpose of the piece?
	Verse	Poems – literary art	
	Picture story	The use of images to tell a story	
	Movie	Moving image	
	Audio	Soundscape and narration	
	Journalism	Newspaper/magazine writing	
	Biographies	People's lives (from a perspective)	
Symbols	Religious Advertising Political Colour Words Safety Cultural Social Clothing (costume)	A symbol is something that represents something else, by association or by resemblance. It can be an object or a written sign used to represent something invisible. Language is a system of spoken or written symbols that we use to communicate with. Words are symbols.	Used to create meaning; e.g. a cultural symbol that is readily recognised and represents a concept with great cultural significance to a wide cultural group. For instance, the giant panda is a symbol of one of China's national treasures. It is also the symbol of eco-environmental conservation (two different meanings).
Composition	Layout	The way in which elements are placed, e.g. using visual language such as use of colour, placement of image and text together, size and shape, balance.	The layout helps the message to be communicated clearly. If it is well designed, the viewer will notice the important aspects.
Shot types	Close-up	A character's face and shoulders taking up the whole screen.	Focuses on the character.
	Extreme close-up	Focuses on one specific detail.	Gives extreme detail, e.g. expression in the eyes.

TABLE 6.1 (Cont.)

Language	Types	Definition	Considerations
	Extreme long shot	The object or character of interest is clearly visible but the background is also in view. Panoramic view.	Places the object or character in their environment. Often used to establish the setting.
	High angle	Camera at a downward angle.	Feels as if the viewer is watching from above.
	Low angle	Camera at an upward angle.	Feels as if the viewer is looking up.
	Medium shot	Balance between the background and the character.	Shows the object, but gives an impression of the setting too.
	Cut away	Shot of something other than the current action.	Shows something else happening – could represent a warning.
	Point of view	Shows what the character sees.	Gives us the character's perspective on what is happening.
Props	Small: hand props, e.g. weapons, food. Larger: tables, chairs etc.	Objects that are used on stage or in movies to further a plot.	They have to be meaningful, visible to the audience.

Figure 6.2 High-angle shot

The shot in Figure 6.2 appears to be looking down on the subject. It gives a feeling of surveillance, as if someone is checking on what the girl is doing.

Figure 6.3 gives a view of the work the girl is doing. It is a more open point of view, sharing the information and giving her perspective.

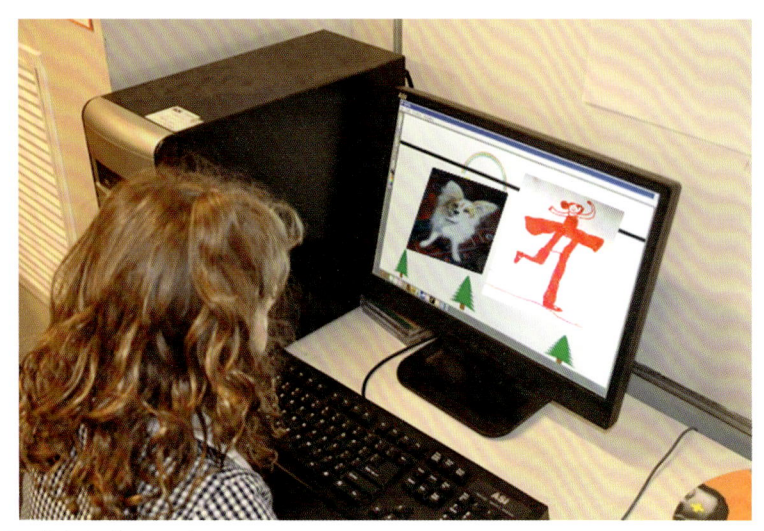

Figure 6.3 Point-of-view shot

2 Media technologies

Media technologies are essential for producing, accessing and distributing media; they perform social and cultural roles and serve many functions (see Table 6.2).

TABLE 6.2 MEDIA TECHNOLOGIES			
Media	**Form**	**Genre**	**Codes and conventions**
Print media	Magazines, newspaper, comics, books, cartoons, periodicals, journals, zines, brochures, pamphlets.	Fiction, non-fiction, entertainment, satire, editorials, cartoons, information, advertisements, poetry.	Narrative type and structure, prose, verse, narrative/authorial voice, perspective, positioning, headlines, issues of gender/ethnicity/politics, editorial, language and register, tone, mass media audience, publishing and distribution, use of image/photography/illustration.
Aural media	Radio, music CDs, mp3 downloads, sound effects, podcasts.	Wide variety of music (e.g. classical, popular), news and information, interviews, entertainment.	Sound, voice, tone, contrast, instruments, jingles, conversation, language.

TABLE 6.2 (Cont.)

Media	Form	Genre	Codes and conventions
Visual media	Posters, photography, billboards, graffiti, murals and street art.	Advertising, information, propaganda, artistic.	Composition, visual arts elements and design principles, digital manipulation, ethics, fear tactic, gender, brand, association, layout, graphics, text, camera angle, camera shot, cropping, positioning, slogan, black and white, colour, digitally enhanced.
Moving image	TV, film, animation, podcasts.	Western, documentary, romance, science fiction, advertising, sport, information, documentary, educational, comedy, reality TV etc.	Camera angle, camera shot, camera movement, editing, special effects, storyboard, soundtrack, positioning, rehearsal, characterisation, representation, stereotypes, sequence, transitions, plot/narrative, voice-over/narration, costumes, props, point of view, titles, subtitles, sets, lighting, script, stills, claymation, director, backdrops.
Interactive and social media	Email, Facebook, wikis, video and console games, blogs, websites, SMS, smartboards, YouTube, Twitter, PowerPoints, touch devices and apps, Prezi, other Web 2.0 tools.	Communication, information, gossip, interactive learning, entertainment.	Communication, information, gossip, interactive learning, entertainment.

3 Media institutions

These are various institutions that enable and constrain media production and use. Through identifying and studying the various institutions (such as broadcasters, corporate sponsors, magazine companies and websites), children, as audiences, acquire a basic understanding of the ways in which media representations structure our perceptions of the world, and the economic and cultural contexts within which mass media are produced and circulated. Children develop an understanding of the motives and goals that shape the media they consume and foster a critical understanding of media as one of the most powerful social, economic, political and cultural institutions.

This involves teaching children critical thinking skills for checking the quality of information. Once children enter cyberspace, where anyone can post anything, they need skills in evaluating the quality of different sources; for example, how the perspectives and interests of those who post definitions on Wikipedia can colour their representations. Children can also learn about the mechanisms by which misinformation is perpetuated or corrected. (Individuals can question or correct information.)

The increase in material aimed at young consumers demands that children be taught how to distinguish fact from fiction, a legitimate website from a hoax, argument from documentation, real from fake, and marketing from enlightenment. They can be taught the questions to ask about everything they see, hear and read.

4 Media audiences

Media arts products are made for audiences, who respond as consumers, citizens and creative individuals. This concept involves both developing a direct sense of 'target audience' in children and teaching the terms of responding as an audience to other media arts makers. According to Buckingham (2005), children are not particularly interested in how information is produced on the web. They see it as just a universal source of information without the human involvement of people, organisations and businesses. Therefore, children need to learn how to judge the quality of the information they find.

5 Media representation

The 'reality' that media arts show us is not reality itself. For example, the TV show you watched represents what life in a particular time in the future may be like but not what it is actually like for you. Advertisements are another example of constructed reality. How often does the food in the ad actually correspond to the food you purchase? As soon as we make an interpretation of the world around us, it is not reality but a constructed representation of the world, which relies on shared social values and beliefs. This idea addresses the sociocultural processes involved in the way we represent our 'reality'. Culture is not static. It is dynamic and changeable. Processes such as globalisation and the development of mass media have brought about dramatic changes to the way we view ourselves and others. A sociocultural approach focuses on the process (rather than the products) of creatively planning media arts, and children learn to find ways to work collaboratively to solve cognitive problems (Rogoff et al., 1995).

Traditionally, artists have been commentators on sociocultural issues such as human rights, social identity, ethics or what it means to be human. The new technologies provide dynamic ways for artists to construct their versions of 'reality' and amplify their voices. Children need to learn skills and knowledge so they can make their own meanings and convey their views effectively.

Media arts in early childhood settings

Children should be given opportunities to explore and experiment with a wide variety of media forms and technologies. Children can resource their own learning through a range of media, sounds and graphics and this is promoted when teachers introduce appropriate technologies and give children chances to develop skills in using and expressing ideas (DEEWR, 2009). The Early Years Learning Framework has many examples of ways that multimedia texts can be used to help children become effective communicators and to be positively engaged in in learning.

It is well established that play is an important aspect of young children's learning. As children discover, create, improvise and imagine, a synergy is provided that is more powerful than teacher-directed activity (Van Hoorn et al., 2011). Play can be child-initiated or teacher-initiated and while play is an important way to learn, children need to learn to follow processes as well, such as cleaning their hands before using equipment, and safely accessing the internet.

The revised Blooms Taxonomy provides a useful structure for thinking and planning for creating and responding to media arts from early childhood through the primary years, from the most basic level of recognising different forms of media and their purposes through to thinking critically and making judgments, and then creating new media.

Table 6.3 shows a development of skills and understanding using Bloom's Revised Taxonomy as a sequential framework for learning.

TABLE 6.3 DEVELOPMENT OF MEDIA SKILLS AND UNDERSTANDINGS

Skills	Different forms	Purposes of media	Use of key concepts and elements (C&E)	Responses
Recognise	Medium and genre, e.g. medium (PowerPoint or iMovie), genre (narrative or entertainment).	Recognise that there is a media-maker and an audience.	Make aesthetic choices (What looks good? Where?), camera angles, lighting etc.	Differences in response (e.g. this person felt moved by the movie; that person thought it was funny).
Understand	Describe advantages and disadvantages of a form: e.g. is a cartoon an appropriate way to tell a story?	What is the medium trying to do to me? Or the intended audience?	Noticing: look at media and identify and describe C&E, e.g. colours used for warning signs.	Personal meaning. Reflect on why (e.g. cultural background or experiences).
Apply	Choose a particular medium for a purpose and explain why.	Make a media product for an intended audience, e.g. create an advertisement.	Use appropriate equipment and use symbols such as sound (e.g. scary effect).	Share work with others – accept feedback.
Analyse	Explore the potential of different media. Analyse ways of manipulating media for a purpose.	Compare effectiveness of their own work and work of others.	Recognise and respond to basic media structures, e.g. genres, styles. Identify and articulate effective use of C&E.	Identify reasons for personal response to media products.

TABLE 6.3 (Cont.)

Skills	Different forms	Purposes of media	Use of key concepts and elements (C&E)	Responses
Evaluate	Critique a variety of media forms and discuss using appropriate vocabulary.	Make judgments about the quality and effectiveness of their work and the work of others.	Use a variety of equipment and judge which are best for a particular purpose. Experiment with various C&E, e.g. use of zoom, lighting, colour.	Confidently seek feedback. Understand that reactions from the audience may vary.
Create	Select the most effective medium and genre to create an innovative media product with a strong message.	Make deliberate choices of design elements and materials to plan an effective media product.	Creatively manipulate the C&E to generate a powerful personal statement.	Confidently use feedback to improve work. Create persuasive, purposeful media products that convey a message to the target audience.

Spotlight on Arts education

Benjamin Bloom and his colleagues (1956) created the original taxonomy of the cognitive domain for categorising the quality of learning that occurs in educational settings. His work was later revised by his colleagues Anderson and Krathwohl (2001). The taxonomy provides a comprehensive set of classifications for the quality of the learning being undertaken. Classifying instructional objectives using this taxonomy helps to determine the levels of learning included in an instructional unit or lesson. The lowest level is remembering or recounting knowledge and the highest level is demonstrated by the creation of something new and different using that knowledge.

Link: Bloom's Revised Taxonomy

While some educators criticise the use of 'new' media, such as computers, in early childhood (Cordes & Miller, 2000; Livingstone & Bovill, 2000), others such as Cook and Hess (2007), Clark (1999), Fasoli (2003), Couse and Chen (2010) and Prowse (2012) celebrate the use of various new technologies and identify skills that children develop through play and exploration with media. There are also some real concerns over 'screen time' with new technologies but there is no conclusive proof either way as to what impacts there might be, positively or otherwise.

Planning for learning in media arts needs to take into account a child's stage of development and past experiences. We cannot assume that all children have experience at home with new technologies. Some rules need to be established, such as storage (putting things back), clean hands and safe ways to hold equipment (using wrist straps and so on). Teachers need to be involved in the early exploration and play.

Teaching in media arts follows a spiral model, which introduces concepts, processes and strategies (such as camera angles, focus and editing) and then builds on them in increasingly complex ways. For example, young children could be given tablets and allowed to play, perhaps taking pictures of their friends or their families. Then the pictures can be shared with their peers and talked about. The teacher can demonstrate simple editing techniques and talk about concepts such as the close-up view. As children develop skills and understandings, they are gradually introduced to more complex forms and processes.

Lesson plan 6.1

AIM

To introduce children to simple children's stories from several cultures; for example, a European fairy tale, an Aboriginal Dreaming story or a Chinese tale.

OVERVIEW

Children work collaboratively to plan a **storyboard** using digital images that retell the story from a different cultural perspective.

Storyboard: an arrangement of images in sequence to organise a production; for example, a movie, an animation or a play.

OUTLINE/DESCRIPTION

Children will work in small groups to make characters with Lego (in costume, using paper, feathers, fabric and so on). They will learn to storyboard, then to make digital images of the beginning of the story, the events in the story and the end of the story. They will present their story to the class, identifying (on a map) which country their story came from.

INTENDED OUTCOMES

They will have successfully created a digital story with a beginning, events and an ending.

LINKS TO CURRICULUM

Foundation to Year 2 content descriptors
- Create and present media artworks that communicate ideas and stories to an audience (ACAMAM056).
- Respond to media artworks and consider where and why people make media artworks, starting with media from Australia including media artworks of Aboriginal and Torres Strait Islander peoples (ACAMAR057).

ASSESSMENT
- Children will demonstrate their understanding of different viewpoints by presenting various possible points of view in relation to one scene or incident.

Figure 6.4 A child's storyboard

Media arts in primary settings

Media arts is strongly connected to everyday culture for children. This makes it an interesting and engaging subject. During the primary years, children develop proficiency in the concepts and skills introduced in early childhood settings. Children learn individually and collaboratively in and through media arts by being actively involved in exploring and creating media products.

Media arts, just like any other art form, is about responding to and being creative with a range of media. To start with, children play, try things out and explore. Small children are very brave and don't hesitate to experiment with new materials of any sort. They are not concerned about 'breaking it'; they explore, experiment and try everything with complete freedom. This does require time allocation, but limits can be set at the discretion of the teacher. At some point a goal can be set – for example, to finish taking pictures in ten minutes.

Media products can be analysed in terms of narrative structure. Most media products have a storyline that can be mapped in some way. It could be a picture story, a series of photographs arranged in a way that tells a story, or a storyboard for a movie sequence.

Storylines could be mapped in the five media technologies listed in Table 6.2.

- Print media: by the arrangement of images, structure of layout, storyline (for example, the selling point, focus, or information in an advertisement).
- Aural media: by the playing order (music, voice), or the order of news items.
- Visual media: by the use of focus, the aspects that bring it all together (for example, the use of similar shapes), the use of line to direct the eye around the image.
- Moving image: the storyboard, the order of scenes, the structure of the movie (beginning, middle and end); the plot or the script tells a story.
- Interactive and social media: in the organisation of information – what do I want them to know about me? How do I progress in the game? What is the next step?

Children learn about how media arts are made and produced and then how to do this themselves. As with the other art forms, there is a distinct language to describe media arts and the discrete skills and processes to be learned.

Spotlight on Arts education

Teachers in Britain have been using film as a text to increase student literacy.

Researchers suggest that using film as a text provides opportunities to improve written expression as well as comprehension. They say this does not take away from traditional reading but adds communication and engagement. For more information on this initiative, find the video 'Teaching Literacy Through Film' by the British Film Institute.

Video: Teaching literacy through film

Children begin to realise that digital technology is a powerful tool for creating products, but to take these skills further than creating a mere product they need to understand aesthetics (see Chapter 1) and how making meaning and planning thoughtfully are essential. As children gain proficiency with the technology, they undertake more challenging units of inquiry using digital technologies in art-making.

The following example could be a unit of work done over several weeks and integrates media arts with visual art and history, with possibilities for other subject areas such as technologies and mathematics.

Lesson plan 6.2

AIM

To bring an artwork 'to life' using digital media.

OVERVIEW

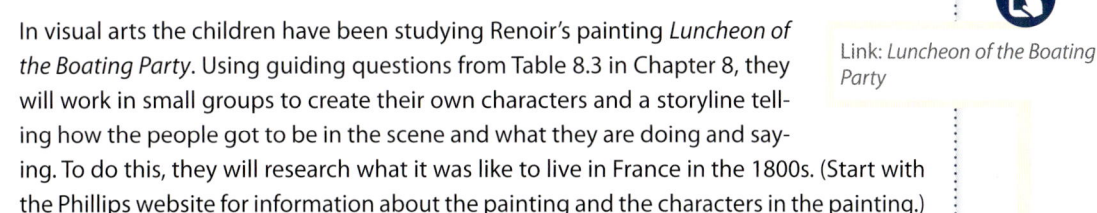

In visual arts the children have been studying Renoir's painting *Luncheon of the Boating Party*. Using guiding questions from Table 8.3 in Chapter 8, they will work in small groups to create their own characters and a storyline telling how the people got to be in the scene and what they are doing and saying. To do this, they will research what it was like to live in France in the 1800s. (Start with the Phillips website for information about the painting and the characters in the painting.)

OUTLINE/DESCRIPTION

The task is to bring the artwork to life in the form of a movie to explain the meaning of the artwork for the intended audience. To do this the children will develop skills in movie making. They will create a short story based on the characters in the painting and produce a storyboard that will be used to act out a story set in the scene in the painting.

There will be narrators who will introduce the painting and Renoir and explain who he was, and when and where the painting was made.

The story will be filmed for an audience.

INTENDED OUTCOMES

Children will develop skills in storyboarding and planning and making a movie that is informative and entertaining for viewers.

They will collaborate to develop a script using settings and story principles.

Australian Curriculum Media Arts: Achievement Standard Years 5–6

- By the end of Year 6, students explain how ideas are communicated in artworks they make and to which they respond. They describe characteristics of artworks from different social, historical and cultural contexts that influence their art making.
- Students structure elements and processes of arts subjects to make artworks that communicate meaning. They work collaboratively to share artworks for audiences, demonstrating skills and techniques.

STRUCTURE OF THE UNIT

As a class, children decide which roles to take: for example, painting a backdrop, creating characters (several characters and not everyone wants to be an actor), writing a script, being narrators, being the camera person, the music director, the editor(s), the props creator and the organiser. Once the roles are established, each child needs a 'contract' that outlines exactly what the role entails; an example appears below.

ROLE: PAINTING THE BACKDROP
- Research – find a good reproduction of the image and make a copy of it.
- Prepare the ground with fabric, cardboard, paper and so on; use undercoat.
- Draw it up, using a grid (links to mathematics – division of a rectangle and using grids to enlarge the image).
- Paint it, using an impressionistic style (link to visual arts – using pure colour and visible brushstrokes to capture shimmering light).

Everything needs to be carefully planned before beginning the filming.

There is a range of free software available to download for PC, such as Anim8or or Windows Movie Maker, and for Mac, which already has iMovie installed, there is FrameByFrame as a free additional download.

The editing team complete their task with music and titles added then the movie is presented to an audience.

ASSESSMENT

Children will be asked to keep a journal recording what they did and the decisions they made as they worked together. Each child will be asked specific questions about their participation and their understanding of media conventions such as use of space, time, movement and the use of storyboards.

This project has strong links to the other Arts subjects (visual arts, drama) and could easily be integrated with other subjects.

LINKS TO THE CURRICULUM
- **Drama:** Planning and creating the script and acting out the story with a narrator (ACADRM035, ACADRM036).
- **Health and physical education:** When collaborating to put the performance together, students consider how to work safely (emotionally and physically) (ACPPS055).
- **Geography:** Where is France? What was life like in the 1800s? How did French art influence Australian artists? (ACHASSK141)

Reflection activity

Think of a favourite television advertisement. Why do you respond to it? Try to analyse and interpret the advertisement. Do you know who produced the ad? Who were the intended audience? What key concepts and elements were used? What was the message? How was it conveyed?

To extend this activity, imagine you are from North Korea, where they have very limited access to information from outside their country. Would the message still be clear? Why? Why not?

The Australian Curriculum expects children to be taught to use various forms of media in a creative way as well as to learn to view media critically.

Media texts

No text is neutral, and no image is neutral. All texts and images are constructed for particular purposes: for entertainment, for procedural use, for economic gain, for political reasons.

The meaning of texts and images changes in different contexts. Competent consumers and producers of texts should use and evaluate signs and symbols in texts and what they communicate to their audience. Teachers need to understand how images present different meanings and need to teach students how to work effectively with images in complex relationships.

Critical analysis informs the reader or viewer of the different positions being presented and also empowers them to work with these communicative practices to take emancipatory positions. Students who gain a critical visual and multi-text proficiency will be able to select bits and pieces from many literacy types and use them to maximise communication effectiveness. To do this they need to understand how media works. They need to be literate across different texts and be able to engage with them critically.

TEACHER TIP

As teachers we can provide some guiding questions regarding the quality of the information students access, to help them critically evaluate texts.

Think of some open-ended questions that could be used to help students critically evaluate texts.

Teacher tip

Lesson plan 6.3

AIM

To introduce children to the idea that advertising materials have a purpose; that organisations enable media production; and that media languages are used to influence consumers.

OVERVIEW

This is an introduction to advertising and its effect on an intended audience.

OUTLINE/DESCRIPTION

Children will respond to advertising through guided questioning by the teacher. They will reflect on intentions of the creator of advertising and then they will plan and make their own advertisement for a product and a particular audience.

INTENDED OUTCOMES

1. Children will respond to printed and digital (for example, TV) advertising and talk about what they like and dislike, and identify reasons for their choices.
2. They will look at and talk about printed and digital advertising material aimed at children (such as toy catalogues or advertisements shown during children's TV time-slots) and identify what the makers of the material are trying to do. Who makes the advertisement and why?
3. Each child will design and talk about an advertisement for a particular audience. For instance, they can choose a food treat that they like and plan an audio and visual advertisement to sell it to their friends. This could simply be made on PowerPoint with sounds, or a short movie, or an animation, with their voice (a song?), or a picture drawn with colours that suit the product.

LINKS TO CURRICULUM

Years 3 and 4 Achievement Standard

- By the end of Year 4, students describe and discuss similarities and differences between media artworks they make and view. They discuss how and why they and others use images, sound and text to make and present media artworks.
- Students collaborate to plan and make artworks that communicate ideas.

ASSESSMENT

In this case the product is not the focus; rather, the focus is on the child's understanding of the use of advertising materials. The children could be questioned about their product or asked to write a critique of their product, or discuss the audience response to the product, which would indicate their understanding of purpose.

Lesson plan 6.4

AIM

To introduce the contexts within which information is produced and circulated.

OVERVIEW

This lesson aims to introduce children to the concept that there are different viewpoints behind media products

OUTLINE/DESCRIPTION

The children work in groups to report on an incident seen through various viewpoints. Each group takes on a different role. For example, show a scene or a video clip of children participating in carol-singing, going from door to door. Then think about different viewpoints, such as Christian (Oh lovely, celebrating the birth of Jesus), non-Christian (Nice singing), parents (Stranger danger!), other kids (Cool voices or uncool – what are they doing that for?), neighbours (Noisy little pests), council workers (They'd better pick up their litter), police (Better check out what they're up to) and so on …

INTENDED OUTCOMES

Children will understand that audience can have different viewpoints and respond in different ways to a particular event.

They will be able to describe differences and similarities between responses and identify reasons.

LINKS TO CURRICULUM

Years 3 and 4 content descriptors
- Identify intended purposes and meanings of media artworks, using media arts key concepts, starting with media artworks in Australia including media artworks of Aboriginal and Torres Strait Islander peoples (ACAMAR061).

ASSESSMENT

Children will demonstrate their understanding by talking about their viewpoint in a role and making comparisons between others.

Lesson plan 6.5

AIM

For children to become familiar with the ways in which materials can be manipulated to persuade or influence.

> ## OVERVIEW
> Children will learn about how images can be manipulated and then will change the meaning of a digital image to illustrate this.
>
> ## OUTLINE/DESCRIPTION
> Children will analyse images and identify meaning in them. They will observe the way images have been presented or manipulated to enhance their meaning. They will manipulate their own images to change or enhance their meaning.
>
> ## INTENDED OUTCOMES
> - Children will learn how to manipulate digital images.
> - They will learn how to change a photograph in ways that change the meaning.
> - They will think about why images, sound and textual representations are altered and what that means to them as consumers.
> - They will manipulate an image in order to create new meaning, for example using digital editing to 'cut' a character from a familiar scene and 'pasting' it into another very different scenario.
>
> ## LINKS TO CURRICULUM
> ### Years 5 and 6 content descriptors
> - Plan, produce and present media artworks for specific audiences and purposes using responsible media practice (ACAMAM064).
>
> ## ASSESSMENT
> Children present their images before and after and explain what they did to change the image and why they made the changes.

Making and responding in media arts

In the Australian Curriculum, 'making' in media arts involves using communications technologies to design, produce and distribute media artworks. 'Responding' in media arts involves students learning to explore, view, analyse and participate in media culture. In both 'making' and 'responding' students engage with the key concepts, story principles and elements of media (technical and symbolic) to use various forms of media in a creative way as well as learning to view media critically. Media arts is a discrete art form in itself, but it can also provide the link between traditional and contemporary art experiences, other art forms and across cultures.

The activities and examples in the previous section outlined a range of both making and responding activities. Through practical activities, children gain an understanding of the range of media available and they begin to understand the ways media can be used to shape and reflect the culture that made it. Children of all ages can begin to understand and interpret media products and artworks.

Simple questions are a useful starting point, such as: 'What are the makers of this TV program trying to do to you?'. It could be to amuse, to entertain, to inform, to teach, or to sell something. Children begin to recognise media products, such as PowerPoint and iMovie, and learn which products to use and when.

TABLE 6.4 KEY MEDIA ARTS CONCEPTS

Key concept	Explanation	Skills to learn
Media messages are constructed.	Choices involved in making media messages: • choice of picture • layout of newspaper • editing in news program.	Learning to notice. Awareness of choices and who makes them.
Media messages are representations of the world.	Media representations shape our views about the world and about ourselves and others.	Understanding that they may not represent reality. Questioning what is represented.
Individuals create meaning in media messages through interpretation.	The meaning an individual makes can be different from the meanings that others make, depending on past experiences.	Accepting difference. Recognising and critically analysing messages.
Media messages have economic and political purposes and contexts.	Films, TV programs, newspapers and magazines are produced in economic and political contexts.	Analysing and understanding political and economic purposes behind media messages. Who is making money? How? Who is making decisions?

We need to think about the messages we create ourselves and develop critical habits and skills to think carefully and wisely about the messages we receive.

> **Reflection activity**
>
> If you have a Facebook or Twitter account, consider the impression it gives to a viewer. How does this change depending on who the viewer is? Your family, friends or peers, or a stranger?
>
> Have you deliberately set out to appear in a certain way? Do you stop and think about what other people will think before you 'like' or 'share' anything? Does this affect what you do 'like' and 'share'? Why do you share information on social media?

Link: Social media

In the classroom

Most children enjoy music videos. A highly motivational way to teach technical skills with audio and visual media is to give children the opportunity to create their own videos. Software such as GarageBand and Audacity are used to create mp3 files, allowing music to be recorded and mixed easily. Then there are numerous ways to create movies, ranging from tablets or other digital movie cameras to iPads and smartphones which can be used to create a movie to accompany the soundtrack. There are various free editing apps such as Magisto, Splice and Videolicious, Apple's iMovie, and Camtasia.

The whole class can be involved and have fun and collaborate with each other as they learn about the production of music videos and production for an intended audience (their peers? their parents?). Codes and conventions (camera angles, props, lighting and so on) and narrative will be developed around a theme (my class, diversity, identity, my neighbourhood).

EXTENSION MATERIAL

The project could be extended by marketing a music video of the finished product. Posters, T-shirts and online advertisements can be designed to promote it to an intended audience/market.

Practicalities and possibilities for personal development in media arts

Recent literature suggests that students of today and the future will need to be able to take advantage of information and communication technology (ICT) (Valtonen et al., 2017). Supporting technology integration in schools has become an important issue globally as educators realise the importance of using technological tools and devices to facilitate teaching and learning processes (Saltan, Arslan & Wang, 2017). Valtonen et al. (2017) suggest that teachers need to support the development of their students' 21st-century skills and so must themselves be familiar with new and developing pedagogical approaches to using ICT. They can ensure this by taking part in professional development opportunities.

Links: Professional development

TEACHER TIP

You might think that, because you have minimal skills with ICT, you cannot teach it. Admiraal et al. (2017) suggest that most learning about how to teach with technology is done once pre-service teachers enter the profession.

As with all of the Arts, with just some basic skills, such as using a smartphone to capture and edit images, or creating drawings or paintings on a tablet, or using simple, seemingly dated, technology such as sound, images and animation functions in PowerPoint, you can expand your knowledge through participating in professional development opportunities.

As you begin planning your media arts program, you need to establish what equipment and facilities you have available. You should familiarise yourself with whatever technical support is available and how much funding there is for new equipment and software. Establish what the arrangements are for access to equipment and facilities (do you have to share?) and check out what software is installed on computers.

Link: How to record your computer screen

TEACHER TIP

Make a list of the skills you do have and think of ways to develop them. For example, if your school provides software such as 'Camtasia', which allows you to use your computer screen, you could create presentations that include various applications, such as PowerPoint, YouTube and Word, and then edit and add text, voice-overs and other effects.

How could you use such software in your teaching?

PowerPoint is a powerful tool and is on most computers. It can be used for display, or for movies with animation, or for hyperlinks (for instance, to make a simple game). As discussed earlier, posters and other media can be accessed cheaply as a starting point while you lobby for new equipment. Most children are familiar with tablets and many schools have access to iPads or similar. So as well as hard copy, posters, images, 3D and 4D media artworks, there are multiple ways of using digital technology to create media artworks.

Link: Digital storytelling apps

Equity and access to computers in the home is an issue to consider when planning activities for children to do in their own time. We also need to be aware that children will bring different experiences with digital media and so we have to allow for a range of skills and knowledge in one classroom. There may be some children who can teach you as well as the other children.

Relying on limited equipment and support, the following activity provides opportunities for children to play different roles in a production, not all involving equipment. As we suggested at the beginning of the chapter, it is best to start simply and to gradually build children's skills as they develop confidence and competence with materials and equipment.

In the classroom

A group of pre-service teachers prepared a 10-minute creative arts performance/product presentation and a 50-minute workshop for primary students at the zoo. This was an assessment task and they had to be sure to involve all five arts subjects and a zoo-related theme. There were five pairs of pre-service teachers and each pair prepared for one of visual arts, music, media arts, drama and dance. They knew the ages of the students they would be teaching but did not know anything else about them.

The pair with media arts brought iPads for the students to use and wanted them to create an animation about recycling at the zoo. They brought prepared blank storyboards for the students to use to plan their story and had a prepared example to show preparation and product. They downloaded a free animation app and thought they had it all covered.

The students were excited about the performance they had watched and about being at the zoo and were eager to participate in workshops – but they had not used iPads before. The pre-service teachers had 50 minutes and wanted the students to understand the use of media to influence people about recycling but realised that they would waste a lot of that time teaching the basics of the iPad and the app.

They introduced the concept of the storyboard and asked the students to create a comic on the blank sheet. The students had to use their imagination to tell a story about recycling at the zoo. The students spent the 50 minutes engaged in drawing their comics and then sharing what they had made with the rest of their group. On reflection, the pre-service teachers realised that the students had gained an understanding about how they could influence other people to recycle materials by telling a story through a comic.

The context of media in the Arts and in education

Digital citizenship is a term used to describe 'the self-monitored habits that sustain and improve the digital communities you enjoy or depend on' (Heick, 2013). It is about confident and positive engagement with digital technology. A digital citizen has skills and knowledge to use digital technologies effectively and safely and knows how to create and consume content.

Links: Digital citizenship

Emotional safety should be considered. Children should feel emotionally comfortable and as the teacher you need to be aware of negative behaviours. Often children will be asked to do things that they are not confident about, such as talking publicly about their work. They need to have a feeling of trust and a sense that their work is valued.

The other important aspect to be considered is the rise in online bullying and online grooming. The Office of the eSafety Commissioner reported an increase in these activities and that children as young as 10 were being targeted by bullies.

Link: Office of the eSafety Commissioner

Spotlight on Arts education

A new study has found that Australian children now spend more time using the internet than watching TV (Screen Australia, 2017). The internet is an excellent resource for children to use but parents and teachers need to educate them about how to use it safely. Children use the internet for a variety of reasons: for education, for communication with their peers and for entertainment. Recent research shows that children are exposed to a growing range of threats such as cyberbullying, sexting, identity theft and recruitment by various organisations (UNICEF, 2017). According to Gale (2017), up to 750 000 sexual predators are online and every nine minutes a web page shows a child being sexually abused. As younger and younger children are being allowed access to devices and the internet, they are unwittingly being exposed to sexual predators who are engaging with children online, often disguised as other child users (Wockner, 2017).

> Children are also at risk of sharing too much information about themselves and others. While obviously parents should take responsibility for their children's safety, teachers must also provide safety education to help children protect themselves online. Educating children often and early can greatly reduce risks.

Copyright is a major issue in media arts, and children need to understand the concept of ownership of an image or media product. Children need to be aware of how copyright is important to ensure 'creators' are recognised for their work. That includes the students' own work. Referencing and citing where materials, sounds and images are sourced is very important. It can also pay well. Students need to be taught the ethics of appropriation and the dangers of misusing others' work, particularly with the availability on the net. Being conscious of creative commons and free images available from certain websites is also important. Luckily, material used for 'educational purposes' is usually exempt.

Link: Smartcopying

There are general classroom safety considerations but there are also some particular issues to take into account in media arts. While there are few physical safety 'rules' other than electrical equipment safety, the concept of internet safety needs to be taught and monitored. There need to be rules and procedures for use and storage of equipment and about sharing and cooperating in equipment use.

Conclusion

New technologies have changed the way we think and behave and media has become an integral part of all Arts subjects, but it is a creative means of expression on its own. Digital technologies are increasingly the focus in media arts, but there are also traditional forms of media that should be considered, such as print. We can provide the opportunity for children to express their ideas and feelings aesthetically through media and to understand how others can influence audience perceptions using media codes and conventions. This informs and enriches young people as they move into an increasingly globalised world.

The inclusion of media arts in the Australian Curriculum places the focus on the creative use of media with a focus on five key concepts: media languages, media technologies, media institutions, media audiences, and constructed representations of reality. Making and responding through these five interrelated concepts gives children a deeper understanding of their evolving world and prepares them for the future.

REVIEW QUESTIONS

1 What important role do teachers have in supporting media arts learning?
2 Who are 'digital natives'?
3 What are the five key concepts relating to media education?
4 What assumptions must we be careful about, in regard to 'new' technologies?
5 How are media arts similar to other art forms?
6 How can students engage with making and responding in media arts?
7 What dangers do we have to be particularly aware of when engaging in web-based technologies in media arts?
8 While being aware of copyright issues, what is the good news for schools and teaching?
9 What must we remember about media arts, apart from it just being about technology?

RECOMMENDED READING

Allen, M. L., Hartley C. and Cain, K. (2016) 'iPads and the use of "apps" by children with Autism Spectrum Disorder: Do they promote learning?', *Frontiers in Psychology*, 7 [2016], 1305.

Tay, H. Y. (2016) 'Longitudinal study on impact of iPad use on teaching and learning', *Cogent Education*, 3(1). Retrieved from https://doi.org/10.1080/2331186X.2015.1127308.

7

Learning in music

> The best thing any teacher can do is to plant the spark of a subject in the minds of his students, so that it may grow, even if the growth takes unpredictable forms.

R. Murray Schafer

In this chapter

In this chapter we situate music education as 'praxis' (Alperson, 1991; Elliott, 1995; Regelski, 1998), encouraging personal agency and allowing children to become composers, performers and audiences as part of their daily lives. The importance of this approach is that musical learning and musical understanding occur in many ways: through listening, sharing, discussing, reflecting, performing, composing and recording. All of these processes should be conceived of culturally, socially and holistically in ways that enable children to explore connections between concepts, skills and understandings. In this approach, a music learning community of practice (Wenger, 2009) that encourages learning in multiple ways through learner agency can be established in your classroom.

By the end of this chapter you should have a clear understanding of:

- engaging with music in education
- the elements and principles of music in education
- music in early childhood settings
- music in primary settings
- making and responding in music education
- the context of music in the arts and in education.

Introduction

As a central part of human existence, music is a natural part of the worlds of children (Barrett, 2003; Pascoe et al., 2005; Russell-Bowie, 2002; Shilling, 2002). Music surrounds us in our daily lives (Barrett, 2003; Pascoe et al., 2005) and it can be found everywhere in our society, from a plane 12 000 metres in the air to a supermarket aisle, from a mobile phone to a concert hall. Music is part of being human (Gibson & Ewing, 2011) and, as Elliott (1995, p. 39) puts it, music 'at its root, is a human activity'. Every child has a right to a quality music education (Crittenden, 2009). As the *National Review of School Music Education* (Pascoe et al., 2005, p. 110) states: 'Every child has a right to have access to quality musical experiences within the school system.'

Reflection activity

We can engage in music in lots of different ways, ranging from listening to music when we exercise to singing or performing in a musical group. We have all had different experiences of music in our childhoods; some of us had great music experiences and others not so great.

Think back over your own music education experiences. What preconceptions and attitudes do you bring to your study of music in education now? Write a simple sentence that begins 'I want to be the sort of teacher who uses music in my classroom to help … '. Keep this 'resolution' in mind as you progress through this chapter.

In the classroom

Teaching music in a classroom or childcare setting does not require special 'talent'. You don't even need instruments. Go to YouTube and search for the video called 'Rain storm – Using the body to make sounds' by Julie Rogers.

These children are performing a 'soundscape' about a thunderstorm using nothing but their bodies – this is often referred to as **'body percussion'**. You could also make a nice connection through this activity to the Australian Curriculum's cross-curriculum priority of sustainability by discussing weather patterns. The topic for a soundscape could be anything: this one happens to be about a storm. Try composing and performing a soundscape when next you are working with children. Get them to work in groups of up to eight children and allow them to brainstorm their topic, experiment with making their sounds, and practise until they are happy with the outcome. Let them perform it for each other – you will be surprised how much fun this activity is and what students can achieve.

Body percussion: using our bodies to create sounds, such as by stamping our feet, clicking our fingers or clapping our hands.

Video: Rain storm

Music occurs in different ways according to the culture in which it is made: it is socially and culturally situated (Bamford, 2006; Elliott, 1995; UNESCO, 2006). Music is also temporally situated, meaning it reflects the time in which it was composed or performed. So, music that occurs as a part of Aboriginal or Torres Strait Islander cultural practice reflects the culture, place and time in which it is performed, in the same way that music by Mozart reflects European culture and society of the mid to late 18th century, or a Bob Dylan song reflects post-World War 2 American culture and society.

Reflection activity

Aboriginal music can often wrongly be thought of as music of the past. Today there is a rich and living culture of Aboriginal music to access for use in your classroom. With revival of Language, Aboriginal musicians are writing songs in Language.

Look up the video of Dewayne Everettsmith performing the song *milaythina nika*, written by Tasmanian Aboriginal community members. This is the first recording of a song in Tasmania's Aboriginal language (*palawa kani*) since Fanny Cochrane Smith's songs were recorded in the 1890s.

Read the English translation of the lyrics below the video and reflect on the importance of 'Country' to Tasmanian Aboriginal people. Reflect on the resilience of Tasmanian Aboriginal people.

Watch the video 'Wiradjuri Welcome' by Desert Pea Media.

In Wiradjuri language '*Yamandhu marang*' means 'welcome'. This performance, including local children and artists, is an example of living Aboriginal culture and an expression of what this means for these young people. Reflect on how this performance is a reflection of social (local), cultural (Wiradjuri) and temporal (past and present) considerations. Share your thoughts with a colleague.

Videos: Aboriginal music

It seems that everyone has access to music in the 21st century (Robinson, 1999), particularly because music can be shared faster than ever before in history (Cayari, 2011; Webb, 2007). Music written and performed today in Australia may be heard almost instantaneously anywhere else. How are we to view this digital transformation of access to music? Are children becoming merely passive 'consumers' of music? Robinson (1999) argues that young people actually appropriate new media for their own ends, an example of this being when we make choices about music by grouping musical items into a personalised 'playlist'. We suggest that, as educators, our role is to build on the musical worlds of children, such as that experienced through digital media, and to enable them to become 'musically literate': a notion that will be discussed later in this chapter. There are literally thousands of music and music education applications available on the internet, many of which are absolutely free.

In the classroom

As we have stressed, you don't have to have special musical 'talents' to use music in your classroom. Software and apps can make incorporating music into your classroom a fun and rewarding experience for everyone including you. But you need to experiment yourself and get to know some of the available digital resources first so that you can guide your students. Explore some free apps like Incredibox and MuseScore, and plan to use them in your classroom context.

Links: Music software and apps

One free digital resource that is available to all teachers is of course YouTube. With many hundreds of thousands of songs available for listening and performing, YouTube can be a great resource for any classroom. Nursery rhymes, pop songs, orchestral music, and music from specific cultures and countries are all there to be used. Go to YouTube now and type in 'Rain, Rain Go Away'. There are hundreds of versions of this simple nursery rhyme available. Listen to three different versions. Choose one that you think would be fine to use as a singalong in your classroom. Now take time each day to sing along with it. If you have access to an instrument you could also play this by experimenting until you work out the three notes it uses. Repetition is great in learning music; take time to do this every day. When you are ready try teaching someone how to sing it using the YouTube clip (or not) as you wish.

Reflection activity

Watch the video 'I'm Yours (ukulele)' by uke3453 on YouTube and consider what music means to this little musician. For us what is important here is that he doesn't seem to necessarily understand the words. What seems valuable for him is communicating through his voice and his ukulele.

Some would say this boy has musical 'talent' and this certainly aligns with Howard Gardner's (1993) multiple intelligences theory in which music is regarded as 'an intelligence'. People do possess certain intelligences or combinations of these. The question of 'talent' and the use of the word 'talent', however, are sometimes used as a convenient excuse to say, 'I can't do that because I know I am not "talented"'.

Video: I'm Yours (ukulele)

Looking at this little musician and thinking about what it means to use music in a classroom, it is worth considering Carol Dweck's work on mindsets (2006). She proposes a 'fixed' mindset in which our skills or qualities are 'dealt' to us at birth and can't be changed, and a 'growth' mindset in which our skills or qualities are 'just the starting point for things you can cultivate through your efforts' (p. 3).

Now think about your 'resolution' from the first Reflection Activity again – which mindset best supports your resolution and why?

Engaging with music in education

The Australian Curriculum defines music as a uniquely aural form and also specifically acknowledges the importance of engaging with a variety of sound sources in making and responding to music from diverse cultures (ACARA, 2014). This is an important statement about how music education should happen.

We understand and define music as a form of culturally situated, human expression and communication that uses sound and silence to express ideas. Most important in this understanding is that it is a unique, auditory form of *shared* human endeavour (Elliot, 1995). Music is as diverse as humanity and it continues to evolve every time a new piece of music is composed or improvised, performed or listened to. Music is often categorised according to style or genre, including Aboriginal music, 'classical' music, hip hop, jazz, grunge and opera, to name a few.

The status of music education in Australia is diverse and the quality of school-based experiences for children varies from region to region, school to school, and teacher to teacher. In Australia, this situation is described as 'patchy at best' (Pascoe et al., 2005, p. iii). Pascoe et al. (2005) also make an important observation, stating that 'There is widespread recognition that music is an important part of every child's education. There is also a general perception that Australian school music education is approaching a state of crisis' (p. 2). This highlights the disconnect between expectations and reality: music education is important, but the reality does not reflect this importance. Please note that Pascoe et al. (2005) also comment that, despite this, there are many examples of excellence in school-based music education in Australia. The value of music education to child development has again been acknowledged in Victoria where, following a Parliamentary Inquiry, the government has introduced a program to bring music to 1600 schools across the state by 2018 (Parliament of Victoria, 2013).

Pascoe et al. (2005, p. 39) also state that 'every Australian child is capable of learning music' and that 'while some children will make a specialised study of music, the majority of children learn music as part of a broad general education'. This is significant for you to understand, because it describes two important dispositions to music education: that every child can learn music, thus aligning with Barrett (2003) that every child is regarded as potentially musical; and that most children will engage with music as part of the general curriculum, thus rejecting the idea that music education should only be provided for an elite or 'talented' few. Everyone can do it!

> Reflect on each of these statements:
> - Everyone has the potential to be musical.
> - Everyone has the right to a music education.
> - Most children will engage with music as a part of their general education.
>
> What does this mean for you? In answering this you will need to think about how you approach teaching students and your expectations for them.
>
> What does this change in your thinking about music in education? If there are any changes or it reinforces your ideas, comment on why.
>
> Write down your responses, share these with a colleague and respond to their thinking about these statements. This is a useful activity to collaborate on with a partner and apply the critical thinking reflection required in the curriculum we teach to our students.

Reflection activity

In order to engage your own students in music education, it is first important to examine your own attitude towards music education. With such a diverse music education landscape it is perhaps unsurprising that while many children already value music in their lives, many initial teacher education students are often hesitant to engage in music education (Hennessy, 2000; Jeanneret, 2006; Pascoe et al., 2005; Russell-Bowie & Dowson, 2005; Russell-Bowie, 2002). A scanty or non-existent background in music, including the lack of a continuous formal music education, is certainly a contributing factor to the lack of confidence among many initial teacher education students when faced with the prospect of teaching music (Russell-Bowie & Dowson, 2005; Russell-Bowie, 2002). We have written this chapter with this in mind. *Be assured that it is possible to become competent at using music in your practice, despite your own background experiences.* Reflect on your 'resolution' and how using a 'growth' mindset can help you to achieve it.

> ### TEACHER TIP
>
> Set up a corner in your classroom with a selection of musical instruments. You may be able to borrow these if you have a music specialist at your school, you may buy them, or you and your students could make them.
>
> You could also have some generative resources nearby such as books, a laptop with lots of children's music on it, or posters that could generate ideas for music making such as *The Great Wave off Kanagawa* by Hokusai, which is in the National Gallery of Victoria (NGV) Collection.

Links: Making instruments and music

Throughout this chapter, several key music education concepts and approaches will be discussed in more detail. These may be difficult to understand without actually using them, but you will be given many opportunities to explore them through the lesson plans and teacher tips provided. These concepts and approaches are:

- The six elements of music (the ways by which we understand music) are one way of understanding music; others are as 'dimensions' (Wiggins, 2009) and 'student talking points' (Rose & Countryman, 2013). The elements are: rhythm, pitch, dynamics and expression, form and structure, timbre, and texture.
- The processes of music (the ways in which we engage with music) – listening, composing and performing.
- Approaches to music education, including Orff Schulwerk, the Kodaly method, Dalcroze Eurhythmics, Creative music education, and Teaching for Musical Understanding (TMU).
- 'Music 'literacy'; this is personally meaningful, culturally situated 'competence to participate' (Barrett, 2003, p. 75) in the discourse of music. Music literacy refers to having the knowledge and skill to engage meaningfully with music. Music literacy is more than just notes on the page.

The elements and principles of music in education

There are many different approaches to music in education, including Orff Schulwerk, the Kodaly method, Dalcroze Eurhythmics, Creative music education and Teaching for Musical Understanding (TMU). Each of these is quite distinct in its method, but they all position the child as an active learner with individual agency. It is difficult to do justice to these influential music educators and approaches here and it is really only possible to introduce you to their work. Please note that aspects of their methods feature in the activities provided in this chapter, and that in most cases there are professional associations in Australia that offer training and support in these approaches.

> **TEACHER TIP**
>
> Begin to build up a repertoire of recordings of children's music for use in your classroom. This could be in YouTube or on your phone – whatever you find is best for using with children. Some starters can be found on MuseScore.

Links: Children's songs

Creative music education

We have gathered a number of educators, theorists, philosophers and composers under the heading of 'Creative music education'. This is not a distinct approach, like that of the Orff, Kodaly and Dalcroze methods, but nonetheless this diverse group contributes much to the current practice of music education. These music educators include George Odham (UK), John Paynter (UK) and R. Murray Schafer (Canada). Through their unique contributions, they advocated a focus on children as 'creators' and 'composers' of music in their own right. These educators were particularly concerned with genuinely 'hearing' sound in its many sources, and highlighted the actual process of making music through techniques such as free improvisation and soundscapes.

Carl Orff

German composer and educator Carl Orff (1895–1982) developed a specific approach to music education called 'Orff Schulwerk' that foregrounds music as embodied learning; and uses a sequential, active approach using the voice and different percussion instruments. These percussion instruments include xylophones and metallophones, which many of you will have used in your own childhood.

Figure 7.1 Carl Orff

Zoltan Kodaly

Ethnomusicologist: someone who observes, records and works with music from different cultures in culturally embedded and sensitive ways, seeking to understand both music and culture.

Zoltan Kodaly (1882–1967) was a Hungarian **ethnomusicologist** and music educator who developed a sequential and highly structured approach to musical learning through singing. The Kodaly approach coincides with the natural development of the human voice and uses a system of mnemonic prompts or syllables known as solfege. Solfege relates each musical note to a corresponding sound: 'do', 're', 'mi', 'fa', 'so', 'la' and 'ti'. This approach includes the use of a system of hand signs pioneered by John Curwen (UK) and Sarah Glover (UK).

Émile Jaques-Dalcroze

Belgian music educator Émile Jaques-Dalcroze (1865–1950) pioneered an approach that privileges movement and embodied learning:. Children learn through responding to musical stimulus with their bodies. A simple example of this approach is to walk to the beat of a song, while clapping a different rhythm or moving arms in a certain pattern.

Figure 7.2 Émile Jaques-Dalcroze

Teaching for Musical Understanding

Teaching for Musical Understanding (TMU) grew out of David Perkins' Harvard Project Zero (Perkins, 2003) and the Teaching for Understanding (TFU) framework, and was pioneered by Professor Jacqui Wiggins (USA). TMU foregrounds a problem-solving approach through listening, composing and performing, with problems often including all three processes simultaneously. It positions children as active learners and problem-solvers with a sense of learner agency, and the learning process as socially constructed and **scaffolded**. Context is extremely important in a TMU approach, in which sequenced learning occurs in **multiple contexts**.

All of these different approaches have much to commend them and it is likely that you will use aspects of each as you develop your toolbox for music education. Some of the elements and principles of music in early childhood and primary environments, taken in part from these different approaches, include:

- understanding music through active engagement with the elements of music
- actively participating in music through listening, composing and performing
- engaging in sequential learning that is scaffolded over time, rather than as a 'one-off' lesson approach
- using embodied learning: actively engaging all the senses
- enabling learner agency, in which children are empowered to experiment and take risks
- providing opportunities to make music with instruments, body and voice
- engaging children's own lived musical experiences
- opening up multiple musical worlds through recognising and explicitly teaching about different musical practices from many cultures.

Scaffolding: the learning and teaching that occurs between what is known by a child and what could be known with the assistance of another person.

Multiple contexts: providing children with similar problems in multiple contexts, so that they are able to transfer understandings to new problems and hence deepen their learning.

A central principle of modern music education is that it is not predominantly about learning decontextualised musical terminology, such as melody or rhythm– although correct understanding of language is important – rather it is about encouraging understanding of music through **authentic** participation. Teaching musical elements such as pitch or rhythm through 'doing' music rather than just treating them as labels is a powerful approach. It is about 'music literacy' in the sense of knowing enough about music to engage in it with individual purpose and meaning. This is really about authentic music education, in which learning and teaching in music occur in similar ways to 'real' world music making.

Authentic learning: learning that not only has real-world relevance, but also occurs in the same way as it does in the real world.

In the classroom

Link: Haiku

Haiku is a form of poetry from Japan. It involves 17 syllables and three phrases, the first consisting of 5 syllables, the second of 7 syllables and the last of 5 syllables. In English these can be less rigid in their structure but still use three phrases. Generally, a Haiku focuses on one event or feeling of great intensity.

Read the following Haiku by Basho Matsuo (1644–1694):

An old silent pond

A frog jumps into the pond

Splash! Silence again.

Use this poem as a lyric to compose your own tune or melody. Experiment in lots of ways – you can use your voice, you could play it on an instrument such as a guitar, or a piano or a glockenspiel – it is up to you!

When you are next working with children give them the same task to complete in groups of about eight. Give them plenty of time to experiment. The process should be about brainstorming ideas, experimenting with sounds, rehearsing the final melody and performing this.

Note that this activity can link to the Australian Curriculum cross-curriculum priority of Asia and Australia's Engagement with Asia (Organising Ideas 3 and 4) and to the general capability of literacy.

Music in early childhood settings

As initial places of musical exploration and discovery, early childhood contexts have a vital role to play in music education. As Swain and Bodkin-Allen (2014) note: 'Music in early childhood contexts is about recognising and supporting the infant, toddler or young child as a musically aware individual who is keen to interact with the world around them through their sense of sound.'

The Early Years Learning Framework (DEEWR, 2009) has many connections to musical learning, through the ways in which they advocate that children learn such as play based and socially constructed learning. Music can be directly linked to each of the learning outcomes of the EYLF but is particularly relevant to Outcome 5: Children are effective communicators. As the Framework states:

> Communication is crucial to belonging, being and becoming. From birth children communicate with others using gestures, sounds, language and assisted communication. They are social beings who are intrinsically motivated to exchange ideas, thoughts, questions and feelings, and to use a range of tools and media, including music, dance and drama, to express themselves, connect with others and extend their learning (p. 38).

When the EYLF refers to 'a range of texts' and 'a range of media' they are referring to the Arts. Furthermore, interacting, 'expressing ideas' and using symbols and patterns are all musical activities (DEEWR, 2009, p. 39).

The Early Years Learning Framework emphasises the importance of community and family partnerships in the development of healthy children (DEEWR, 2009, p. 17). Encounters with music occur initially alongside and with primary care-givers, as children listen to and respond to sound stimulus through their own actions and sounds, such as 'cooing' at around eight weeks (Barrett, 2003, p. 70). In fact, a group of researchers from the University of Helsinki used recorded sound and electroencephalography (EEGs) to establish that babies hear sounds from the world outside from 27 weeks of gestation (Lethbridge, 2013).

Between the ages of around two and five, children interact with sound using all their senses through self-devised and familiar songs, the body, instrumental experimentation, and movement. They learn through exploring and experimenting with sound where they find it. The role for early childhood teachers in this process is multilayered and extremely important to the musical knowledge, skills and attitudes of the children in their care. Your role is that of a gatekeeper for positive, authentic and quality musical experiences, to plant a seed that will grow in your students' lives. This role includes the following aspects.

- *Environment:* to ensure a stimulating environment full of sound-making opportunities, in which children may naturally explore and discover through sound.
- *Learning through play:* creating an environment that reflects an understanding of play-based learning.
- *Community:* to ensure that primary care-givers participate in children's musical explorations and are aware of the importance of these.
- *Knowledge and sequence of learning:* to apply your knowledge of music from this chapter to provide regular musical engagement and a progression of experiences for children.
- *Relationships and attitude:* taking care to be positive and affirming about all musical exploration and particularly about singing, as children's voices develop and change over a very long period of time.

TEACHER TIP

Set up a learning centre in a corner of your childcare centre. A learning centre, sometimes called a learning station, is a place for independent or small-group learning. Have some pictures or drawings of animals such as kangaroos, lions, cats, or dogs on the table or wall nearby. Have a selection of tuned and non-tuned instruments handy. Ask the child to make the 'sound' of each animal.

Video: Preschool music lesson

There are many examples available online of music activities to undertake with very young children.

What musical experiences should be included in an early childhood setting? The following is intended as a guide to the types of learning experience that you can include in an early childhood setting.

Infants

- Provide and respond to stimulating sounds with the infant. Encourage the infant to respond to sounds you make.
- Provide auditory and physical stimulus; link sound to movement through such actions as rocking and bouncing.
- Provide musical stimulus by singing to the infant. This does not have to be a 'song' as such; it can just be the sound of a humming voice.
- Provide musical stimulus by playing music around the infant; use sources that include a diversity of beat, dynamic and timbre.

Toddlers

- Engage toddlers' natural energy and curiosity by providing a rich musical environment that includes diverse musical stimulus.
- Create opportunities for toddlers to 'find' the sounds of different musical instruments and other means of making sounds and allow them time to experiment.
- Sing familiar songs, such as nursery rhymes and name songs, with toddlers with animation and purpose.
- Provide opportunities to move with music, enabling toddlers to respond to changes in tempo, pitch and dynamics.
- Use music embedded in storytelling experiences.

Young children

- Continue building on the musical learning above, providing opportunities for musical experimentation through singing, moving, chants, rhymes, games and instruments.
- Introduce the child to more and more musical language including the elements and processes of music while they experiment.
- Provide a music 'corner' for musical experimentation including opportunities to listen, compose and perform.

Music in primary settings

One aspect of music education in primary settings is the need to acknowledge that children bring with them musical knowledge from their preschool lives. As Shilling (2002, p. 179) writes: 'They hear music on the radio, accompany sing-along tapes while riding in the car, and memorise commercial TV jingles.' One of the roles of primary educators is to ensure that these prior experiences and knowledge are used as a basis for engagement and expansion of children's understanding. The role of the primary educator is to ensure that music is taught in a sequential and integrated manner rather than in a 'one-off' lesson approach. Another important aspect of music in primary settings is your familiarity with not only the musical elements and processes, but with the structure and sequence of learning provided by curriculum documents.

Between the foundation year and year 6, primary children need to be given a sequential music education that is integrated with their classroom-based studies. The role of the primary educator in this process is multilayered and is of immense importance to the musical knowledge, skills and attitudes of the children in their care. As a primary educator you are the gatekeeper to positive, authentic and meaningful music education experiences, and your role is to spark your children's musical imaginations and to prompt their engagement. This role includes the following aspects.

- *Musical elements and processes:* creating opportunities for children to understand music through the elements and through opportunities to listen, compose and perform music.
- *Making and responding in music:* the language of making and responding to music should be explicitly taught as children take on the roles of composer, performer and listener.
- *Curriculum knowledge:* knowledge of the music curriculum and the relationships between Learning Areas, general capabilities and cross-curriculum priorities is essential to plan for and implement learning in music education.
- *Sequence of learning*: musical learning should be sequenced carefully in response to curriculum knowledge.
- *Relationships and attitude:* take care to be positive and affirming about all musical exploration and particularly about singing. Children should be encouraged to participate and engage without fear of failure, and thus be enabled to take risks.

- *Consultation:* discussions with parents, specialists and colleagues are essential to ensure that musical learning is valued, is integrated, and is carried forward through the primary years.

What musical experiences should be included in a primary setting? Below is a list of the types of learning experiences that you can include.

Foundation to year 2

- Continue to provide opportunities for play-based learning.
- Provide a music 'corner' with stimulating musical activities in listening, composing and performing.
- Engage in music chants and games in groups.
- Move to music as much as possible with known and self-devised dance as a means to respond kinaesthetically to the elements of music.
- Sing as much as possible, using known songs, and develop a repertoire of new songs.
- Use musical instruments (including body percussion) to listen, compose and perform, encouraging the development of musical language.
- Encourage children to record their compositions using graphic notation and begin to experiment with conventional notation.
- Access, listen and respond to diverse styles of music from world cultures.

Years 3 and 4

- Continue all of the above activities with increasing emphasis on expanded musical understanding and musical language.
- Begin the regular use of conventional musical notation.
- Diverse music styles provide increasingly useful contexts for musical experimentation and creation.

Years 5 and 6

- Continue all of the above activities, with increasing emphasis on the application of musical understanding and language in different musical contexts.
- These years should see children being able to form judgments about the music they make and respond to. Continue to use diverse music styles as a contextual backdrop to musical experimentation and creation.
- Develop opportunities for sharing musical compositions and performances.

In the classroom

Using found objects, and extending the idea of 'environment', children work in a small group to develop a soundscape that in some way represents a machine.

Brainstorm ideas for the machine: what sounds does it make?

Are they long or short (rhythm)? Loud or soft (dynamics)? Hard or smooth (timbre)? Experiment with making these sounds using found sounds in your space.

Now try combining sounds. This is 'layering' sound or 'texture'.

Children can experiment with giving their soundscape a sense of beginning, middle and end (form and structure). They may like to have a section where it runs smoothly and then breaks down.

They should now perform and notate their soundscape.

GarageBand is also a useful tool (as are other simple apps) for children to experiment with making sounds.

Video: GarageBand for Schools

Earlier in the chapter you were asked to watch a video of students performing a piece about a thunderstorm using just body percussion. This is a good example of a soundscape. A 'soundscape' is the organisation of sounds and silences – but never just 'noise'. Schafer (1967, p. 5) writes that 'Noise is any signal which interferes. Noise is the destroyer of things we want to hear'. The difference between sound and noise is 'intention'. If a sound is intended to be used as part of a piece of music, then this is 'sound', not 'noise'. Music is the organisation of sound sources, even if that organisation is random. Schafer (1967, p. 7) also writes about silence, stating that 'silence is a pocket of possibility. Anything can happen to break it'. Through soundscapes people can engage in the three main musical processes – listening, composing and performing – and can explore the six musical elements 'authentically' as listeners, composers and performers. Every soundscape is unique because those who create them are different; the sounds they find, use and manipulate are different each time, even if the soundscape is based on similar ideas.

Spotlight on Arts education

SOUNDSCAPES

R. Murray Schafer (b. 1933) was referred to earlier as one of the 'creatives' of music education. Schafer is a Canadian musician, composer, educator and environmentalist. Schafer's enduring legacies in music education include his approach to composing music from found sounds known as 'soundscapes', his use of graphic notation as a means of recording sound and his approach to music education that focused on 'ear-cleaning' and sonic discovery. Context, knowing something about the composer and their intentions, is an important part of listening to any music with students. As preparation for a soundscape activity do some preliminary research on R. Murray Schafer.

Links: R. Murray Schafer

→ Remember that the key to listening to music is thinking about the elements as you listen. For example, much popular music uses a drum kit to keep a steady beat (rhythm). In Schafer's song 'Minwanka', drums and the steady pulse of a beat is simply not there; rather the performers focus on timbre, defined as 'the particular tone, colour or quality that distinguishes a sound or combinations of sounds' (ACARA, 2017). Also of interest for the audience are the unusual sounds and colours that are a feature of this work.

Figure 7.3 R. Murray Schafer, pioneer of a creative approach to music education

An incredibly important component of any music-making activity is that children are engaged in a post-activity discussion about what they have learned through the making process. It is the oft-forgotten final step in the cycle of music making. This discussion values children as both artist and audience and empowers them to use evolving music language in conversation with their peers and with you. Thus, the discussion should be framed by the elements of music and the ways in which they have been used.

In the classroom

Ask the children to find their favourite sound. Allow them 3 or 4 minutes to wander around the classroom and experiment with different sounds. They might 'tap' something, such as a chair; or 'scrape' something, such as the floor; or blow into something, such as a water bottle. Encourage them not to settle on the first sound they make – this is about process and experimentation. Once they settle on their favourite sound ask them to experiment further with that sound. Can they make it longer or shorter (rhythm), higher or lower (pitch), louder or softer (dynamics)? Take on the role of a conductor for your class. Point to each student as an indication that they are to perform their sound. Start combining sounds one on top of another (texture). Use different agreed gestures to experiment with the sounds. You have just created and performed a soundscape with your class. You could go another step further now and record it using a mobile phone and listen back to it, thus allowing students to take on the role of audience.

TEACHER TIP

SOUNDSCAPES AND 'NOTATION'

Ask students to form groups of between six and eight, and to create a simple soundscape that tells a story. The topic could be anything that is relevant to your classroom at the time, but here are some suggestions: a haunted house, a day at the beach, in the jungle, a trip to the moon, or under the sea. The process is: brainstorm ideas, experiment with sounds, order and structure sounds using the elements, notate the sounds, rehearsal, performance and discussion. As notation, the students can use graphic notation (images) to draw the sounds in the order in which they occur.

Making and responding in music

The Australian Curriculum organises the Arts according to two overarching constructs: making and responding. The constructs of making and responding involve a knowledge and understanding of the elements of music and the processes of listening, composing and performing.

Lesson plan 7.1

AIM
Learning about how composers use the elements of music to express ideas.

OUTLINE/DESCRIPTION
In this lesson students listen to 'The Four Seasons' by Antonio Vivaldi. They identify how the composer used the elements to convey the idea or sound of each season. Students then compose and perform their own 'Seasons' soundscape/music representing two of the four seasons.

INTENDED OUTCOMES
Students identify
- musical elements in a piece of music
- the 'moods' created by the composer's use of elements.

Students understand
- that composers use the elements of music to create an effect or mood
- that they can use the elements as a composer.

Students are able to
- compose, rehearse, and perform two contrasting pieces of music using whatever instruments they have to hand
- talk about music using musical language.

LINKS TO CURRICULUM

Years 3 and 4 content descriptors
- Develop aural skills by exploring, imitating and recognising elements of music including dynamics, pitch and rhythm patterns (ACAMUM084).
- Practise singing, playing instruments and improvising music, using elements of music including rhythm, pitch, dynamics and form in a range of pieces, including in music from the local community (ACAMUM085).
- Identify intended purposes and meanings as students listen to music using the elements of music to make comparisons, starting with Australian music, including music of Aboriginal and Torres Strait Islander peoples (ACAMUR087).

ASSESSMENT
- Students compose, rehearse and perform their two 'Seasons' pieces for the class.
- Students complete the following questions in pairs.

QUESTIONS
- Spring: What instruments are used in this piece? It starts very 'happily'. What other words could describe how this sounds to you? Some people say they can hear birds calling to each other. Did you hear this?

- Summer: This piece starts very quietly. Which element of music refers to the louds and softs? What words could describe the speed or tempo of this piece at the start? Does the tempo stay the same? What instruments are used?
- Autumn: What words could you use to describe the tempo of this piece at the start? Are the dynamics always the same or do they change? What instruments are used?
- Winter: What instruments are used in this piece? Think of a word to describe the dynamics at the start? The solo violin makes little 'explosions' of sound that are fast and loud. What aspect of winter do you think this could be?

The elements of music

The notion of 'elements' of music is variously referred to as 'the basic properties of sound' (Barrett, 2003) and more recently as musical 'dimensions' (Wiggins, 2009). The Australian Curriculum articulates the use of six music elements; these are rhythm, pitch, dynamics and expression, form and structure, timbre, and texture. One way to understand music is to consider similarities between different styles of music, such as jazz and rock, or opera and hip hop. This leads to two key understandings about music: **elements** and the **processes**. As can be seen in Figure 7.4,

Elements of music: key components of a piece of music such as rhythm and pitch.

Processes of music: the ways in which we experience music – listening, composing and performing.

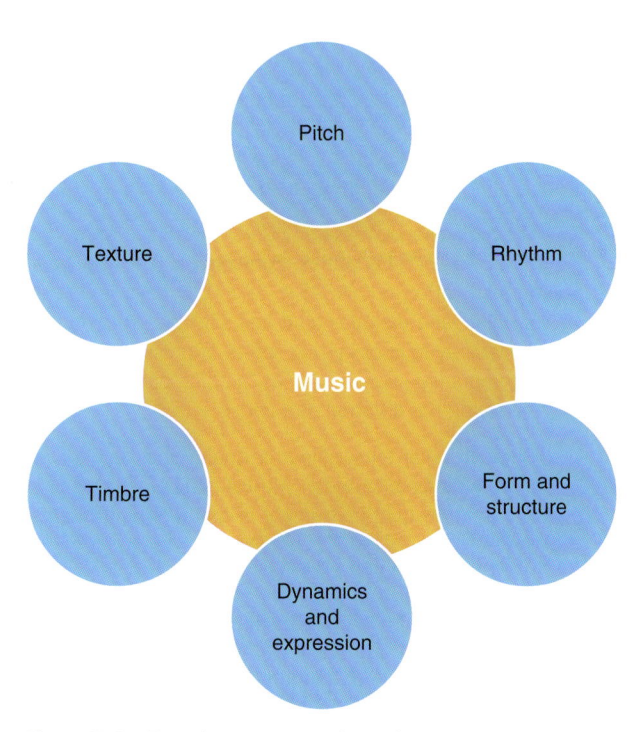

Figure 7.4 The six elements of music

these elements do not occur in isolation from each other; rather, each one impacts and relates to others to create the 'sound' of a piece of music.

Table 7.1 provides definitions of the six elements of music. Read this through with reference to Table 7.2, which provides examples of the six elements of music, and activities to increase your understanding of each. These tables are useful for gaining important knowledge and understandings about music in education. The activities provided should be worked through as you read, in order to gain experience to support your evolving skills and knowledge. These activities can also be used in early childhood and primary settings.

TABLE 7.1 THE ELEMENTS OF MUSIC: DEFINITIONS AND DESCRIPTIONS

Element	Australian Curriculum definition with a description
Pitch	'The relative highness or lowness of sound' (ACARA, 2017). A melody or tune is a combination of relatively higher and lower sounds. Harmony is the vertical alignment of pitch, or the simultaneous combination of pitches.
Rhythm	'Combinations of long and short sounds that convey a sense of movement subdivision of sound within a beat' (ACARA, 2017). Duration is the length of a sound, such as long or short. Rhythm is a combination of longer and shorter sounds. Beat is the underlying pulse of a piece of music.
Form and structure	'The plan or design of a piece of music described by identifying what is the same and what is different and the ordering of ideas in the piece' (ACARA, 2017). Structure refers to the ways in which a piece of music may be put together; it is the way in which the parts of a piece of music combine to make a whole. Form is often used to describe a certain type of structure such as 'song form' or 'binary form'.
Dynamics and expression	'Dynamics and expression refers to how the sound is performed, including sound qualities. For example, the relative volume and intensity of sound' (ACARA, 2017). Dynamics refers to the volume of music and includes loud and soft and gradations of these, such as moderately loud or getting softer. Expression refers to other ways of manipulating sounds such as 'holding back' or 'taking it a little slower', or varying the duration of a pause.
Timbre	'The particular tone, colour or quality that distinguishes a sound or combinations of sounds' (ACARA, 2017). Timbre is the overall sound that an individual instrument or group of instruments or voices makes.
Texture	'The layers of sound in a musical work and the relationship between them' (ACARA, 2017). Texture is the density of music or the 'thickness' or 'thinness' of a sound. A single instrument provides a thinner texture than does a full symphony orchestra, which has a thicker sound because of the number and variety of instruments it combines.

TABLE 7.2 THE ELEMENTS OF MUSIC: EXAMPLES AND ACTIVITIES

Examples	Activities for understanding
Pitch	
Certain instruments and voices have higher and lower pitches. A bass guitar has a 'low' pitch', while a piccolo is 'high'. 'Twinkle, Twinkle Little Star' has a well-known melody that many people can sing from memory. In some styles of music, such as choral music, the relationship between pitch (melody) and words is extremely important. The expression to 'sing in harmony' is often heard, and pitch includes harmony. A good example of harmony is several voices combining at different pitches to make a richer sound than just one. Harmony is often categorised as major or minor, which is known as tonality.	Infant: Sing to the child. Toddler: Find three high-pitched sounds and three low-pitched sounds. Young child–year 2: On a xylophone or metallophone play high and low sounds and ask the child to stand up for high sounds and sit down for low sounds. Years 3–4: With your voice, make a sound that goes from a low pitch to a high pitch. Years 5–6: Pitch conversations: Children set up opposite a partner with each having a tuned percussion instrument, such as a xylophone. Take it in turns to make up (improvise) a sequence of four pitches and copy each other's creations.
Rhythm	
A contemporary rock piece may have a steady beat underlying it; this is a 'back beat'. A rhythm can be as simple as four repeated sounds of the same duration, or it can be very complex, such as may be found in a song. Rhythm and pitch combine to create a 'melody'.	Infant: Bounce the child rhythmically. Toddler: Guide the child to clap along to the 'beat' of a song. Young child–year 2: Using any piece of music, 'walk the beat', keeping the pulse or beat in your feet. Years 3–4: In a circle, slap a simple beat on your knees as a group; take it in turns saying your name while the beat keeps going. Your name will be a rhythm. Years 5–6: Rhythm conversations: children sit opposite one another with a single drum in between. They take it in turns to improvise a short rhythm to be copied.
Form and structure	
A common contemporary music form is 'song form', which often includes sections such as an 'intro', 'outro', verses and a chorus. A more traditional form is 'binary form', which has two clear sections that are often referred to as sections A and B.	Infant: Play music for the child that features very different sections or emotions. Toddler: Play music for the child that features very different sections or feelings and work with them to change movements as each section is heard. Young child–year 2. Sing 'Twinkle, Twinkle Little Star'. Ask children if they can find anything that is the same and anything that is different in this song. The melody of the first and third lines is the same in pitch and in rhythm. This song has three parts to it: line 1, line 2 and line 3. But lines 1 and 3 are the same. This is a 'structure' called 'ternary form' or A-B-A form, in which the first and last sections are the same. Years 3–4: Ask children to create and perform a rhythm that has two sections to it. This is a binary structured rhythm. Years 5–6: Using any three current songs, ask children to listen to each song, identifying how many verses each one has and how many times the chorus is played. Is there any time when there is no voice? This is a structure known as 'song form'.

TABLE 7.2 (Cont.)

Dynamics and expression

Singing a lullaby to a baby would generally be at a softer dynamic, whereas a footy song is generally heard at a loud dynamic. Much of the language associated with dynamics is still in Italian, a hangover from earlier periods. For example, the Italian word 'piano' or 'p' is often used for 'soft' in a written piece of music. Expression refers to variations that individual composers or performers want in a piece of music. One performer may play a certain piece at a very fast tempo or speed, while another might play the same piece at a relatively slower tempo.	Infant: Play music for the child that features different dynamics, such as loud and soft. Toddler: Play music that features different dynamics and work with them to change movements as each section is heard. Young child–year 2. Draw these shapes on the board: Children should play or sing them. Ask children to select one that is to be sung or played loudly, one softly, and one that gets gradually louder. They are using dynamics. Years 3–4: Onomatopoeia describes a word that is spoken or sung according to the meaning of the word. Brainstorm words that are about dynamics, such as loud, soft, boom, bang, rumble, buzz, and tick-tock. Make up a sequence of words and perform them at appropriate dynamics. Years 5–6: Learn any football or sporting song or chant. Ask children to sing it two ways: once as if they were singing a baby to sleep (soft), and once as if they were at the football (loud).

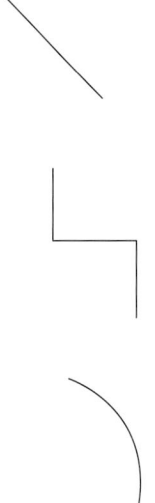

Timbre

A guitar, for example, has a certain tone colour or 'sound', and electric guitars and acoustic guitars have quite different timbres. Descriptive language is often used to talk about timbre; so, for example, a cello sound might be described as 'sweet' or 'rich'.	Infant: play music for the child that features different instruments and comes from a variety of cultures. Toddler–year 2: make up two signs, one with the word 'mouse' (thin texture) and one with the word 'lion' (thick texture) on it. Ask children to create a sound that matches each sign. Years 3–4: make up two signs, one with the word 'thick' and one with the word 'thin'. In groups of three, children experiment with instruments/voices to create one thick and one thin sound. Hold up the signs for each group to perform their sounds. Years 5–6: Listen to a recorder, which has a very 'thin' sound. Then listen to a full symphony orchestra and choir with a 'thick' sound: Ask children to identify and discuss why one is thick and one is thin. Answers may include the type and number of instruments/voices used. Videos: Thin and thick sounds

Texture

Music consists of 'layers' of sound. Some pieces of music have very simple textures, such as a solo voice which has just one layer of sound. Others are far more complex with many layers of instruments combining to make a thick, complex texture.	Infant – Years 5–6: play music for the child that features different textures, encouraging them to respond through movement and action and according to their developmental stage. There are different types of texture. Videos: Music suggestions

Lesson plan 7.2

AIM

Learning about Aboriginal music by making and responding.

OUTLINE/DESCRIPTION

In this lesson students listen to 'Songlines of the Moonbird' by Tasmanian Aboriginal artists Dyan and Ronnie Summers, understanding the story of the moonbird, reflecting on the elements of music and learning to sing the song.

Start by listening to the song.

As they listen to the song students can follow the lyrics.

'Songlines of the Moonbird' was written by Aboriginal poet Dyan Summers, who was born in Launceston and grew up on Flinders Island in eastern Bass Strait. It is about the relationship between the moonbird, commonly known as mutton bird or shearwater, Aboriginal Tasmanians and a tradition that has endured across the ages. Uncle Ronnie Summers wrote the music for this song, and we respectfully thank him for allowing us to transcribe and use this piece of music. 'Songlines include important information about creation and naming of natural features within the landscape. They identify landmarks and directions across travel and trade routes and ceremonial places. In English, Songlines are also described as codes, or dreaming tracks memorised and sung in a specific order' (Department of Education Tasmania, nd).

Using the MuseScore of 'Songlines of the Moonbird', children can sing the song, by pressing play you can sing or play along to the recording, or they could sing along to the song on YouTube.

Complete the questions provided.

INTENDED OUTCOMES

Students identify

- musical elements in a piece of music
- the intention of the artists to tell a story
- the artists and their cultural identity.

Students understand

- that Aboriginal and Torres Strait Islander music is part of a dynamic and living culture
- that Aboriginal and Torres Strait Islander peoples use music to tell stories
- that musicians use the elements of music when composing and performing.

Students are able to

- rehearse, sing and perform a melody
- talk about music using musical language.

> ### LINKS TO CURRICULUM
>
> **Years 3 and 4 content descriptors**
> - Develop aural skills by exploring, imitating and recognising elements of music including dynamics, pitch and rhythm patterns (ACAMUM084).
> - Practise singing, playing instruments and improvising music, using elements of music including rhythm, pitch, dynamics and form in a range of pieces, including in music from the local community (ACAMUM085).
> - Identify intended purposes and meanings as they listen to music using the elements of music to make comparisons, starting with Australian music, including music of Aboriginal and Torres Strait Islander peoples (ACAMUR087).
>
> **Cross-curriculum priority: Aboriginal and Torres Strait Islander Histories and Cultures**
> - OI.2 Aboriginal and Torres Strait Islander communities maintain a special connection to and responsibility for Country/Place.
> - OI.3 Aboriginal and Torres Strait Islander peoples have holistic belief systems and are spiritually and intellectually connected to the land, sea, sky and waterways.
> - OI.8 Aboriginal and Torres Strait Islander peoples' family and kinship structures are strong and sophisticated.
> - OI.9 The significant contributions of Aboriginal peoples and Torres Strait Islander peoples in the present and past are acknowledged locally, nationally and globally.
>
> ### ASSESSMENT
> - Students rehearse and perform the piece as a class.
> - Students complete the following questions in pairs.
>
> ### QUESTIONS
> - Find the highest note in the song (pitch).
> - Find the lowest note in the song (pitch).
> - Find all of the rests in the song (rhythm).
> - Find the longest note in the song (rhythm).
> - What is a 'songline'?
> - Where do Dyan and Ronnie live?
> - What is a 'Moonbird'?
> - What story does the song tell?

The processes of music

The processes of music are our ways of experiencing music. These are listening, composing and performing. Generally, in many schools and childcare centres, the valuing of these three processes can be a little unbalanced, with one process (performance) often being privileged over the others. Your approach needs to balance the three and should regularly combine the three processes of music within the same activity. Learning in music needs to connect the three processes as much as possible, enabling students to discover and explore the natural connections between the processes themselves.

Spotlight on Arts education

PATRICIA SHEHAN CAMPBELL'S STAGES OF LISTENING

Children commonly have listened to music using one of two approaches (both of which are relatively passive): by just listening to music (sometimes as background) or by listening to music while completing a worksheet. To be most meaningful, listening should be a far more active pursuit – a process that is more engaging and that is undertaken with direct links to the other two processes of composing and performing.

The six music elements provide a window into listening and the musical language to make meaning of listening experiences. Shehan Campbell (2005, p. 35) writes that 'Listening always has been and will continue to be the core of the musical experience ... it is the most direct route into music'. As seen in Table 7.3, Shehan Campbell (p. 31) proposes a three-stage framework for listening, including attentive listening, engaged listening and enactive listening. Attentive listening involves a relatively passive form of listening in which a worksheet may provide focus points for children. In engaged listening, children become 'participants' and may clap a rhythm or sing a melody. In enactive listening, the children become the performers, using the recorded piece as a springboard into their own composition or performance.

TABLE 7.3 PATRICIA SHEHAN CAMPBELL'S STAGES OF LISTENING

Attentive listening (Att-L)	Engaged listening (N-Gage)	Enactive listening (N-Act)
Att-L listening uses specific focus points that the teacher selects or creates to draw their attention to specific musical elements and events. 'Listeners' are purely 'listeners'.	N-Gage listening becomes more thorough as 'listeners' become 'participants'. N-Gage listening may include playing a beat or clapping while listening.	The 'listener' becomes the 'performer' in N-Act listening, using the performance as a 'springboard' into their own performance. N-Act listening includes creating and performing, such as listening to a piece, composing a piece with a similar theme or style, and then performing it.

Listen–Compose–Perform (L–C–P): a framework for quality musical experiences

Now apply your understanding of musical elements and processes to the practical early childhood and primary context. Learning that enables students to find connections between the three processes and to expand their understandings of musical elements can be the most profound for them. We will use excerpts from a piece for orchestra and pianos entitled *The Carnival of the Animals* by French composer Camille Saint-Saëns. However, we also provide a list of other music that can be used similarly in any classroom. It is the attention to elements and processes that is the key to such activities.

In the classroom

LISTENING FOR ALL AGES

Have children start by listening to 'The Swan' from *The Carnival of the Animals*.

For *infants*, play 'The Swan' and gently rock the child, encouraging any response from the infant, such as changes in facial expression or movement. The *toddler* could move in response to the music or 'draw' with their upper bodies, arms, hands and fingers as the music plays. *The young child* could initially respond solely through movement. Ask children to respond to the music by exploring movements that represent the swan, such as graceful or joined movements. Props such as scarves can be used to create a flowing sensation. With students from *year 1 and above* follow up with directed questioning. Question using the elements, such as: 'The tempo is important – how would you describe the speed. Is it relaxed? Is it fast? Is it slow?'. 'The cello sounds smooth and joined almost like a voice, can we sing along to it?'

Video: 'The Swan'

Such Listen–Compose–Perform activities enable natural and purposeful connections to other areas of the curriculum such as are evident through *The Carnival*. The role of the teacher in these activities is essential and involves scaffolding the listening to ensure that students have ample opportunity to identify the ways in which the composer uses the elements to create an effect or mood.

In the classroom

COMPOSITION FOR ALL AGES

Composition includes the skills of creating new music, improvising in the moment, and arranging an already existing piece of music for new instruments or voices. The process of composition is not only achievable in primary and early childhood environments, but should also be viewed as an essential process that contributes to musical understanding. Central to engaging children in composition is providing an environment in which there is no fear of failure: an environment that focuses on experimentation and participation. This is about 'process' and process is paramount in primary and early childhood settings. Unless children are encouraged to explore, create, collaborate, perform and reflect in music without fear, they may never participate with full agency. It is incredibly important to allow students to build on their initial responses as listeners, and composition is a perfect vehicle in this respect. Next time you are working with children engage them with composition through a simple soundscape activity.

These Listen–Create–Perform activities can be completed using any music; these are intended to be examples of this *process* rather than the only piece that you can use in this way. Each example provided above has advice for application of this process at each level.

TEACHER TIP

Many initial teacher education students think that composition is something that only other 'special' people (composers) do. While composition is a skill that some may choose to develop further, the aim of early childhood and primary music education is to authentically engage all young people in music *as* composers. Composition is about using the elements of music to express ideas. Students of all ages can create and perform their own piece of music about an animal, perhaps starting with 'The Swan'. The starting point for this is of course listening.

Other Listen–Compose–Perform (L–C–P) activities

In the previous L–C–P activities we used *The Carnival of the Animals* as a starting point. In fact, any music can form this starting point, and there are many pieces that have been tried and tested over generations as vehicles for musical understanding. If you apply the techniques discussed in the previous sections to a diversity of 'musics', your students will learn much.

Spotlight on Arts education

A REPERTOIRE OF ENACTIVE LISTENING PIECES TO USE IN L–C–P ACTIVITIES

Experiment with designing tasks using the following generative music in a similar way.

1. Gustav Holst: *The Planets Suite* for orchestra, particularly 'Mars, the Bringer of War'.
2. Bedřich Smetana: *The Moldau* for orchestra depicts the Vltava or Moldau River as it travels from its source to the city of Prague.
3. Peter Sculthorpe: *Small Town* depicts a typical small Australian town; listen for the 'Last Post'.
4. Antonio Vivaldi: *The Four Seasons* for string orchestra.
5. Sergei Prokofiev: *Peter and the Wolf* for orchestra.
6. Camille Saint-Saëns: *Danse Macabre* for orchestra and solo violin; a depiction of skeletons in a graveyard.

Videos: Generative music

The context of music in the Arts and in education

As will be explored in Chapter 12, there are many wonderful opportunities for you to work in partnership with community organisations, artists and industry partners in the delivery of quality experiences in music education. Likewise, there are many partnerships that can improve music learning opportunities for children, too many to be listed here, however you may like to consider these not-for-profit organisations:

1 Music: Count Us In

Anyone can register to download the resources and any school can participate. It is designed for generalist early childhood and primary teachers and is an amazing resource. According to the website, 'MCUI is Australia's biggest school initiative. With support from the Australian government, it has run since 2007 and is all about celebrating the value of music education for students' development, whoever they are, wherever they are'. It involves more than 600 000 students, teachers – and often parents – from schools all over Australia, who sign up to learn, rehearse, and then perform the same song, on the same day, at the same time. Music: Count Us In is for all schools – primary and secondary, state and independent, nationwide. It doesn't cost anything for schools to participate and all the support materials, including song charts and arrangements and classroom activity kits are freely available and downloadable.

Link: Music Australia – Count Us In

2 The Song Room

The Song Room is a not-for-profit organisation that works in partnership with schools to develop sustainable music and arts programs in schools where students may not otherwise have the opportunities for such learning. Their aims are social, educational and artistic; their website states that, 'Our aim is to bridge the education equity gap for all Australian children by facilitating learning through the arts, starting with our most vulnerable groups and reaching all communities that lack specialist music and arts education. We want every child to benefit from long-term school music and arts programs.'

Link: The Song Room

3 Symphony orchestras

Australia has a long history of magnificent symphony orchestras dating back to the early 20th century. Concerts for children have been a part of these orchestras and their missions for almost as long, however, in recent years the educational offerings of our orchestras have expanded incredibly, including: high-quality teaching resources, regional and rural activities, teacher support and training, community-led music projects and community outreach programs. We strongly encourage you to explore the possibilities of these programs.

Links: State symphony orchestras

4 Musica Viva in Schools

For over 30 years Musica Viva in Schools has demonstrated a genuine commitment to school music education in Australia. Their programs provide excellent teaching resources for primary and secondary schools, teacher training materials, and visits to schools around Australia by professional musicians.

Link: Musica Viva in Schools

TEACHER TIP

Children need time to rehearse and perform. Rehearsal is a key aspect of performance, and in a culture of musical consumption many young people do not have a genuine understanding of the symbiotic relationship between rehearsal and performance. Rehearsal and performance are intricately related and it is important to conceive of rehearsal and performance as a process and not as a product or end in itself. Furthermore, rehearsal involves critical listening. This is a good example of the interconnectedness of the musical processes. Rehearsal commences when a composition is essentially complete. In rehearsal students should collaborate in the refinement of a composed piece, and in so doing continue to refine the performance of that piece. Collaborative problem-solving of key questions such as 'What happens if we make this part of our piece softer, faster or smoother?' become significant. Rehearsal inevitably involves repetition, playing a composition over and over and reflecting on key questions individually and collaboratively. Repetition when linked to inquiry is a good thing in music. Active inquiry through dialogue, collaboration and questioning is a critical component of rehearsal.

Conclusion

Music is a central part of human existence and a natural part of the worlds of children. Early childhood and primary educators have a unique role in the delivery of quality music education experiences to the children in their care. It is you who will allow music to make a difference in children's lives. You will play a significant role in the musical development of children by developing an approach to music education that enables children to develop personal agency as part of a community of learners in which active engagement with the elements and processes contributes to musical understanding and literacy. Through an environment that allows free experimentation, children will develop their musical capacities and become musically literate, engaging with the value of music throughout their lives.

REVIEW QUESTIONS

1. Why is music an important component of the Australian Curriculum?
2. Name the six musical elements.
3. Next to each element write your understanding of that element.
4. Name the three musical processes.
5. How are the musical processes used most effectively in learning?
6. Describe an early childhood level activity in music that combines the three musical processes (L–C–P).
7. Describe a primary-level activity in music that combines the three musical processes.
8. What are three of the most important components of the role of the early childhood educator in providing music in education?
9. What are three of the most important components of the role of the primary educator in providing music in education?

RECOMMENDED READING

Allsup, R. A. and Baxter, M. (2004). 'Talking about music: Better questions? Better discussions!'. *Music Educators Journal*, 91(2), 29–33.

Baker, W. J. and Harvey, G. (2014). 'The collaborative learning behaviours of middle primary school students in a classroom music creation activity'. *Australian Journal of Music Education* [2014](1), 15–26.

Calogero, J. M. (2002). 'Integrating music and children's literature'. *Music Educators Journal*, 88(5), 23–30.

Dweck, C. S. (2006). *Mindset: Changing the Way You Think to Fulfil Your Potential*. London: Robinson Little, Brown.

English, R. and Wilson, J. (2004). *How to Succeed with Learning Centres*. Carlton South: Curriculum Corporation.

Kuzniar, M. (1999). 'Finding music in art'. *Teaching Music*, 7(3), 44–7.

Shehan Campbell, P. (2005). 'Deep listening to the musical world'. *Music Educators Journal*, 92(1), 30–6.

Summers, D., Gall, A. and Summers, R. (nd). *Songlines of the Moonbird*. Tasmania: Department of Education.

Wiggins, J. (2009). *Teaching for Musical Understanding*, 2nd edn. Oakland, MI: Center for Applied Research in Musical Understanding (CARMU).

Wright, S. (2003). *Children, Meaning-making and the Arts*. Frenchs Forest, NSW: Pearson.

8

Learning in visual arts

> Art is a line around your thoughts.
>
> Gustav Klimt

In this chapter

This chapter will provide a foundation for the provision of quality visual arts educational experiences in early childhood and primary years. Practical suggestions for planning a high-quality visual arts program are linked to recent theory in a way that helps you construct your own visual arts program. Visual arts concepts, language, elements and principles will be defined and explained, with examples of the progression in visual arts education from early childhood through the primary years. Practicalities such as classroom management, safety and materials are addressed and additional interactive material can be found through the icons.

By the end of this chapter you should have a clear understanding of:

- engaging with visual arts in education
- elements and principles of visual arts in education
- visual arts in early childhood settings
- visual arts in primary settings
- making and responding in visual arts
- the context of visual arts in the Arts and in education.

Introduction

We are surrounded by visual material in many diverse forms, from paintings in galleries to pictures on our mobile phones and the packaging on our foods. By learning through visual experiences, we find ways to describe and respond to our world. The visual arts are used to communicate, explain, decorate, influence, enquire and express ideas for particular aesthetic, practical and spiritual purposes. They can reflect the innovations of our times, or traditional methods and conventions, and inform our relationships with other people and with our environment.

The visual arts involve the creation of two-, three- and four-dimensional objects and images using a wide variety of traditional and contemporary materials. By engaging in visual arts children develop cognitively, emotionally, physically and socially as they learn the skills to perceive visual material and develop an ability to express their ideas and feelings. By studying the visual arts, they gain an understanding of themselves and of diverse perspectives and cultures.

To teach authentic art skills and knowledge, a teacher needs to know about the language of visual arts, understand the elements and principles of visual arts and have knowledge of visual arts concepts and some idea of visual arts histories and global cultures. It is useful to be aware of children's physical and cognitive developments in visual arts.

Engaging with visual arts in education

The visual arts involve the creation of works that are primarily visual in nature. Traditionally this comprised drawing, painting, printmaking and sculpture. There used to be a distinction between the fine arts (the traditional methods) and the applied arts (or crafts) and design, but there is no clear delineation now about what is deemed visual art. There are unlimited possibilities available for visual artists to express their ideas, and increasingly the borders between artistic disciplines such as performing arts, textile arts and media are becoming blurred.

The Australian Curriculum has two organising strands: making, which involves developing practical knowledge and skills to communicate ideas, and responding, which involves understanding the Arts in context and learning to interpret and evaluate them. All of the Arts have codes and conventions (like grammatical rules in English) and these vary across the Arts subjects.

> **Aesthetic knowing:** traditionally, aesthetics was associated with beauty. Now it tends to relate to a holistic and human awareness of whatever there is to be experienced on a certain occasion; for example, what you notice about a particular artwork informed by deep knowledge of Arts-specific ways of knowing.

In visual arts there are traditional and contemporary elements and principles to guide making in a wide range of materials and methods. We use **aesthetic knowing** to gain an understanding of the art that we make and experience and we learn about established conventions and ways of enquiring that reflect traditional and contemporary methods. Chapter 10 expands on this.

According to Mothersill (2004), there are several theories about aesthetic judgments and more than one could be applied at once. We could judge an artwork according to cultural criteria, such as technical qualities, as well as for its political message.

Because aesthetic judgments can be culturally conditioned, we may not agree that certain sculptures from another culture are beautiful, and our ideas of beauty are likely to change over time (such as the concept of the ideal female figure). Political, social and economic judgments may be linked to aesthetic values. For example, we may find something beautiful because we want to increase our social status by 'consuming' (buying) it (Korsmeyer, 1998). The factors shaping our aesthetic judgments are many and varied. They include, but are not limited to, our culture, emotions, subconscious, education, training, opinions, values and instinct. Indeed, our judgments can also be based on a combination of any of these factors.

Aesthetic knowing involves a deep appreciation of the meaning of the situation being experienced. This can be the immediate qualities of the experience felt through our senses. The experience can also be cognitive: the feelings and understanding we have in response to an artwork. The National Art Education Association (NAEA, 2009) suggests that the more we engage with new art experiences, the more we are able to accept diversity of thought and cultural expression.

Denac (2014) argues that one of the most important tasks of education is to develop the ability to enjoy the Arts and to perceive and experience aesthetic qualities as well as to develop creative capabilities and aesthetic judgments. She suggests that planned aesthetic education is essential in the development of the child's personality as a whole.

When the learner engages with a work of art, senses and emotions are conceptualised as important features of 'noticing', which takes the viewer beyond material exploration to engage with the meaning of the artwork in social and cultural terms (Greene, 2001).

Aesthetic noticing has been integrated into areas other than the Arts as a way to emphasise humanistic and holistic aspects of knowing; for example, medicine, which has a strong tradition of focusing on various ways of knowing in order to give excellent patient care. Doctors and nurses are trained to develop a high level of consciousness about what they see. They develop a fine attention to detail and form, noticing what is significant in a patient's behaviour (Carper, 1978). This involves the perception of relations – noticing harmony and discord – or nuance, such as important knowledge about colour and what changes of colour may mean.

Elements and principles of visual arts in education

Although other senses can be employed, visual art is predominantly about looking and seeing. Through looking at artworks, children learn to identify signs, symbols, narratives, social commentary and expression. By learning the 'language' of visual arts they learn to identify 'tools' that artists use. This in turn enables children to use the 'tools' to effectively express their own ideas.

There are many different reasons why visual artists make art. One common motivation is to encourage the viewer to reflect on what has been done in the artwork and why. Sometimes the artist wants us to appreciate the beauty in a landscape or a still life, or perhaps to influence our thinking about some issue, such as the environment. The artist may also want to tell a story or express a feeling. We can develop the capacity to view the world from perspectives other than our own by learning to 'read' what their art tells us. Ritchhart and Perkins (2008) suggest that learning to look for the invisible, or what is not at first obvious, in art helps us to think more clearly about the world around us. It is accepted that learning is an active process and children need to be actively involved in art-making in order to construct meaning (Gardner, 1999; Hein, 1991; Lombardi, 2007), but they also need to spend time appraising or responding to art in an informed and critical way in order to give educational validity to the activity (Ashton, 2008; Kolbe, 2001; Wright, 2003a).

In the classroom

Collect images of artworks that have been made for different purposes. Some examples are listed in Table 8.1.

Links: Table 8.1

TABLE 8.1 ARTWORK FROM DIFFERENT CULTURES AND THEIR PURPOSES

	Purpose or intention of artist
Ancient Egyptian art	Not meant to be seen. Designed to help a dead person communicate with the Gods
A range of Australian contemporary artworks	Narrative: to tell a story
Political artworks	Art about global warming
Expressionist	Expressing feelings

Use guided questioning to discuss the artists' intentions with the children. Following this you could note the characteristics of art for different purposes; for example, how artists have used colour, shapes or lines.

Visual arts tools

There are some 'tools' that can be used to both respond to and make art. These elements, principles and concepts apply to both traditional and new media, and are flexible and open to change. They form the basic language of art. Just as we use principles of grammar to combine words to make sentences, artists use art elements and principles to form compositions in many forms. These elements and principles are like building blocks, in

> **Appropriation:** the copying or quoting of an existing artwork to create a new artwork.

that they are used to construct artworks. Artists manipulate selected elements and principles and add additional concepts, such as **appropriation**, to compose their art. Not every artwork is made from every element and principle, but most have at least two within it (for example, colour and form). Artists now use many traditional and contemporary methods and materials, and a meaningful contemporary Arts curriculum emphasises contradictions and digressions and is full of surprises and complexity.

The language of the visual arts

The visual arts, like all the creative arts, has its own vocabulary, a language specific to the field that is used to speak about works of art. This technical vocabulary is extensive and is used to describe and analyse the techniques, styles and attributes of a piece of art. In this section we introduce a number of key terms and concepts, including traditional and contemporary, art forms, materials and methods, and art principles.

Traditional and contemporary

Traditional methods are methods that have been used for centuries, such as etching, drawing and sculpting; materials such as pens, charcoal and oil paint; and concepts such as linear perspective. *Contemporary methods* are newer, and include video art; performance art; materials such as digital media and the human body; and concepts such as appropriation and installation art.

Methods and materials

There are many art forms and each one has specific materials and methods. Table 8.2 defines and explains methods of various media that are used by artists and are appropriate for early childhood and primary years. The first column lists two-, three- and four-dimensional visual art forms and the second column describes materials used in creating the art form. The final column suggests examples of ways to employ each method. We have recorded both traditional and contemporary forms, but this list is likely to change over time.

Elements

Art elements

The elements of the visual arts refers to the vocabulary used to describe elements of artistic work. Key elements include line, colour, value, shape, space, texture, form, time and motion.

Principles

Principles such as unity, variety, balance, rhythm, emphasis, harmony, proportion and scale are used to arrange the elements. *Unity* refers to the way all parts of the work fit together; *variety* to the use of similar and different shapes, sizes, colours and so on. *Balance* is achieved if one part of the work does not overwhelm the rest. *Rhythm* can give life to an artwork by suggesting movement (perhaps through pattern). *Emphasis* draws the eye to a particular spot in the artwork. *Harmony* is achieved by using similar or harmonious

TABLE 8.2 ART FORMS

Art form	Media (material) used	Methods
Drawing	Pencils (soft/hard, coloured, watercolour), graphite sticks, charcoal, chalk, pastel, crayon, ink, felt tip pen, pens. Grounds: surfaces such as paper, wood, plastic, concrete. Digital 'tablets'.	From the imagination. From observation, scientific, life drawing. Realistic, abstract, cartoon/comic, storyboard, perspective, illustration, calligraphy. Mind-mapping, diagrams. Infographics conceptualising information.
Painting and digital media	Acrylic paint, watercolour, powder paint, fabric paint, painting mediums (e.g. to thicken or glaze). Grounds such as paper, card, canvas, fabrics, board, wall (outdoor/indoor). Photography, moving image. Digital 'tablets'.	Spatter, brushwork, sponge, rollers etc. Different artistic styles, e.g. cubist, abstract. Painting to music. Narrative painting. Thick (impasto); thin (washes, glazes). Collaboration (painting in public areas). Mixed media (paper, fabrics etc.). Digital manipulation, collage montage, bricolage, movie, animation etc.
Printmaking	Screen printing, intaglio, fabric printing, relief printing, monoprinting.	Monoprinting on different surfaces, with found objects, hands. Using stamps, playdough, drypoint etching/acrylic, styrofoam sheets, recycled materials, lino prints, card, string, fabrics, silkscreen, stencils. Aiming to create a series of the same image.
3D	Clay, playdough, modelling materials, found objects, recycled materials, wood, wire, paper, card etc.	Carving, modelling, rolling, slabs, mosaic. Tiles (outdoor/indoor), ceramics, construction, mobiles, sculpture (indoor/ outdoor), papier mâché, installation etc.
4D	Digital media, humans, sound, dance, voice, objects, actions, sites, audience.	Installation, kinetic art, performance art, video art.

elements, for example colours that work well together. *Proportion* is a measurement and relates to size, for example human proportions, which can be accurately measured. *Scale* refers to the relationship in size between one element and another; for example, showing a very small figure next to a very large, imposing figure suggests dominance.

Modern art is the term used for art made using traditional forms, such as painting and sculpture, from the later 19th century to the middle of the 20th century. This is different from the dictionary definition (which relates to the present rather than the past). Artists developed a variety of movements, theories and attitudes in an attempt to reject traditional, historical or academic forms and conventions and create an art that suited the changed social, economic and intellectual conditions of the time. Examples of modern art are cubism, impressionism, abstract expressionism and surrealism. Modernist artists you may be familiar with include Edvard Munch, Georgia O'Keeffe and Frieda Kahlo.

Postmodern art is art that has developed since modernism, often in contradiction to its aspects or theories. Postmodern art often recycles past styles and themes in a contemporary context and attempts to break down the barriers between 'high' or 'fine' art and 'low' or popular art/culture. Postmodernist artists you may be familiar with include Jeff Koons, Barbara Kruger and Roy Lichtenstein.

Content

Artists use the visual language to express and communicate *content*. Content refers to the subject matter and the underlying meanings of the art. These can take many *forms*, which is the total of what we see. For example, the form of a painting is paint on canvas. Artworks are made from a wide variety of media: the *medium* of a painting is paint and the medium of an installation may be found objects. Works of art often take on a particular *style*, such as *realism*, *abstraction* or *cubism*, which relates to the distinctive way in which the elements and the media have been used. The style may relate to a particular culture or period of time, or to an individual artist or group of artists.

TEACHER TIP

Link: *Maman*

Any work of art can be described using some of these elements and principles. Even if you don't know much about art you can use these concepts as a starting point for talking to children about artworks. For example, look up *Maman* by Louise Bourgeois.

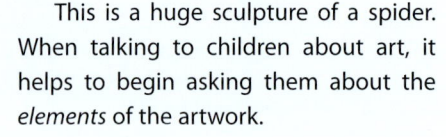

This is a huge sculpture of a spider. When talking to children about art, it helps to begin asking them about the *elements* of the artwork.

- Size (What space does it take up?)
- Colour (What colour is it?)
- Texture (What do you think it might feel like?)
- Line (What sorts of lines do you see?)

Then you can transition to more interpretative questions such as: How does the size make you feel? Does the spider look like it is moving? Why is that? It is called 'Maman', which is French for mother. Does this change your feelings about the spider?

Visual arts in early childhood settings

The visual arts are meant to be explored in early childhood programs in Australia but, as Terrini (2010) suggests, a more common practice is for exploration and artistic expression to occur through play-based programs. This approach reflects a traditional stance on 'no adult intervention' (see Lowenfeld & Brittain, 1975), that is, that teachers shouldn't interfere with children's art-making efforts. However, this doesn't take into account the capabilities of young children or the social and cultural contexts of learning (Isbell & Raines, 2013). McArdle (2005) likens learning visual arts to learning a language and asks:

> What if you really wanted to learn this language, so you could read, speak and write it … but nobody would teach you? Then you would experience the feelings of being illiterate … you would feel disempowered, foolish, constrained and inadequate. Eventually you would give up trying to communicate. You might even convince yourself that the language is silly, and that you have no interest in it. When you tried to become proficient in this language, people told you to just experiment and explore and you will naturally come to understand (p. 7).

She goes on to describe the way that young children are often simply provided with raw materials and told that all their attempts are brilliant. Any requests for help are refused in order to allow children 'freedom'. Without explicit teaching, children will not realise that they are learning in the Arts.

Play-based learning is not a frivolous activity but rather a serious learning opportunity where young children explore, use imagination, try things out and are interested in what they are doing. According to the Early Years Learning Framework, children learn through play.

> Play provides opportunities for children to learn as they discover, create, improvise and imagine. When children play with other children they create social groups, test out ideas, challenge each other's thinking and build new understandings. Play provides a supportive environment where children can ask questions, solve problems and engage in critical thinking. Play can expand children's thinking and enhance their desire to know and to learn. In these ways play can promote positive dispositions towards learning. Children's immersion in their play illustrates how play enables them to simply enjoy being (DEEWR 2009, p. 15).

Reflection activity

Compare learning visual arts with learning numeracy or literacy.

Do you think the approach McArdle (2005) describes, of leaving children to learn for themselves without adult interference, and praising their every effort regardless of result, would be acceptable in those areas? A suggested response might include comment on the place of primary skills, children constructing knowledge, and allowing children to learn through play.

Visual arts practices

The Australian Curriculum outlines the knowledge, skills and understandings that children can develop through visual arts practices. They are set out for each band and develop in depth and complexity across the years. These include various modes of *representation* such as *subject matter*; *forms*, for example painting, sculpture; *styles* such as realism and abstraction; *techniques* such as silkscreen printmaking and photo montage; *visual conventions* like design elements and principles; *materials* and *technologies*.

Also outlined are *practices*, including the actual *space* where artists work, for example the studio, exhibition spaces; various *skills* such as investigation, observation and practical; and *processes*.

Viewpoints in terms of both making and responding are considered. These include the contexts in which artworks are made and experienced by artists and audience. Key questions are suggested relating to art making, art history, art criticism and philosophical and ideological questions such as 'what political perspectives are evident in the artwork and how does this affect the audience's interpretation of it?'.

Representation in visual arts

There are many ways to create visual arts. Drawing is one of the most familiar and nearly all children will, at some stage early in life, pick up something within reach and start to make marks with it. Children master drawing easily and continue to enjoy drawing until they start to encounter difficulties, such as representing distance or human proportion. There are many types of drawing activities, such as observational drawing, imaginative drawing, diagrams, fantasy drawing, mind maps, cartoons, animations and scientific drawings.

Drawing from observation

Drawing from observation can be introduced once a child is able to manage the tools. Young children armed with a clipboard, paper and pencil can explore the garden or the school surrounds and begin to make drawings of particular objects; for example, different leaves or flowers. If they have the opportunity to draw regularly, the activity can become as natural as writing. Research shows that developing drawing skills enhances observational skills (Quillin & Thomas, 2015), particularly in science learning (Anderson, Ellis & Jones, 2014).

Drawing is a powerful and immediate way for children to explore ideas. Making thinking visible, for example, by drawing a diagram or trying to represent an idea in an image, is seen by some as a strategy to aid learning and encourage creativity (Pink, 2006). Incorporating drawing in day-to-day teaching is a possible way to improve learning in the classroom.

Drawing framework

TEACHER TIP

It is important to allow young children plenty of time to explore materials and develop skills. As they gain confidence with drawing tools, activities can be introduced. Children can be encouraged to draw what they see and do. Activities could include drawing themselves by looking in small hand mirrors or drawing collections of interesting objects. These drawings could then be made into a book. It is useful to have a collection of objects and sources of a wide range of images.

Teacher tip

A child asks for help drawing a chicken.

Taking into consideration what you've read in this chapter so far, how would you approach this?

Painting

Painting as a method focuses on the application of a painting material to a surface. This can be thick or thin, oil based or acrylic, or even homemade with ground pigment. There is an exciting range of non-toxic paints available to teachers teaching painting and a framework based on the one for teaching drawing can be used, beginning with exploration of materials and methods and developing techniques and concepts. With young children, the most popular activity seems to be using hands to explore paint. A safe and easily cleaned workspace is therefore essential. Gradually different surfaces and materials can be offered.

Surfaces of different textures and sizes and a variety of brushes (large, small, thick, thin, toothbrushes, kitchen brushes, hair brushes), sponges and rollers offer a good range of tools. The thickness of the paint can be adjusted by adding flour, sand or talcum powder. It can also be diluted with water or detergent. Food colouring and water makes cheap, safe 'inks' for dribbling and spattering.

The three primary colours – red, yellow and blue – are sufficient at this stage for young children. Children can learn to mix colours as they explore the paint, and guided discovery will teach them about deliberate colour mixing.

Figure 8.1 A 'palette' (foam tray) with small amounts of primary colours ready to begin

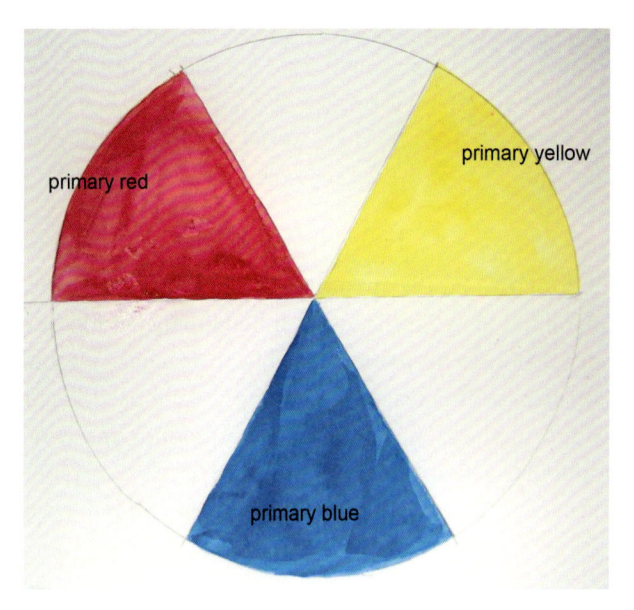

Figure 8.2 Primary colours 'palette'

Link: Colour mixing

Colour is one of the design elements. Colour can be used in many ways to create a response (emotional, physical or psychological) and can be exciting to experiment and play with and powerful as a mode of expression.

Figure 8.3 A colour wheel

A colour wheel is the easiest way to display colours. Divide a circle in half, then divide each half into thirds. Be sure to leave a space between each primary colour and carefully paint in red, yellow and blue.

Now mix a little of red and yellow to get orange, then blue and red to get purple, and blue and yellow to get green. These three colours are known as secondary colours.

Advanced colour exercises

Figure 8.4 Mixing secondary colours 'palette'

Colours that are opposite each other on the six-part colour wheel (see Figure 8.3) are called complementary colours (red/green, blue/orange and yellow/purple). When complementary colours are mixed together they create a greyish colour (tertiary colour).

Link: Colour theory

Tertiary colours are made by continuing to mix. Some artists, such as the Australian artist Ian Fairweather, use only tertiary colours.

Figure 8.5 Greys mixed with primary colours 'palette'

Some colours are understood to be *cool* colours and some to be *warm* colours (see Figure 8.7). A warm colour has more yellow or red in it and a cool colour has more blue or green in it. Colours can be both warm and cool; for example, you can find a warm red and a cool red, or a warm green and a cool green. When looking for the best colours to make primary colours, select cool red, cool blue and cool or lemon yellow. Warm colours tend to emerge from the surface while cool colours tend to recede. Look at a picture of a landscape. The colours in the distance look cool/bluer and the colours in the foreground seem warmer. In design, if you want a colour to appear to 'jump' out, use warm colours.

The *hue* of a colour is its classification; for example, decorating in hues of green and blue.

The *intensity* of a colour is the strength or purity of the colour; for example, a colour straight out of the tube is at its most intense.

Value refers to the lightness or darkness of a colour.

Figure 8.6 Mixing black 'palette'

Visual arts language can be introduced in painting in the same way as in drawing. Talking to the children about the colours they use, the lines they make or the texture they see develops their art vocabulary. Painting to music is a particularly good way to introduce the concept of difference. Even though every child has listened to the same piece of music, they all 'see' different colours and shapes. This reinforces the idea that there is no right and wrong way to express your feelings.

Different children will also associate different colours (and tone of colour such as warm or soft) to different emotions and ideas. Is red the colour of love or death or anger? Or indeed, could it signify all of those emotions in the context of an artwork? There are no right or wrong answers in this if an 'artist' can justify their use, which is why the development of critical thinking is important.

Figure 8.7 Warm/cool, receding. Look at this image. Even though the yellow and orange appear to be smaller (and therefore normally seem further away), because they are warm colours they seem to be jumping out of the square.

TEACHER TIP

Try this yourself. Find a palette (foam tray, for example) and get a small amount of blue, red and yellow paint, a jar of water and a brush.

Listen to some of your favourite music and just paint what you 'see'. Nothing 'real', just lines, shapes etc. Most people find this very relaxing and unthreatening as there is no expectation of reality.

Some people actually 'see' colours as they listen to music; this is called synesthesia. Kandinsky, a Russian artist, had synesthesia and was fascinated by the power of music and wanted to represent this in his art. He created a list of instruments to match colours for him.

Link: Wassily Kandinsky

In the classroom

Provide each child with the primary colours and a big sheet of paper, preferably at an easel. Tell the class that you are going to play some music (preferably without vocals) and ask them to spend a few moments with their eyes closed listening to the music. Ask them to think about what colours they see, what sorts of shapes, lines and so on. Then ask them to paint using only art elements (such as colour, lines, shapes) but no real or recognisable images.

When they have finished, display the works and view them with the class. There may be similarities in colours or other elements, but they will be able to see that they are all different and that there is no wrong or right way to express what they 'saw'. Guide discussion about what can be seen in the finished pictures, encouraging children to see colours, lines, texture and other elements.

You could teach directly about art elements and principles by viewing the finished pictures; for example, looking for patterns or rhythm. Children could look at the composition, and how lines suggest sound or movement. This activity could integrate music learning by selecting an artwork (such as a painting or sculpture) and making music to complement it.

The framework for drawing can be used for developing sequential learning activities in painting as children develop skills in mixing and applying paint. By looking at and responding to artworks, they begin to understand the reasons for making two-dimensional work, such as painting, digital imaging and printmaking.

Photography and digital media

There is an easily accessible source of images all around us. Supermarkets, shopping centres, movie theatres and sporting arenas are filled with images. Just as painting and drawing use art elements and principles, so do photographers. Children should plan for image making in the same way they would in media arts and in other visual arts practice. The drawing framework would again be useful for developing skills and knowledge in working with digital media and photography.

Providing students of any age with either a traditional or digital camera produces a rich source of images. Children could view their own images and those of others and look for art elements, or focus on signs or symbols. They can manipulate their images digitally and explore colour use or texture. This also links to media arts (Chapter 6).

Ashton (2008) reminds us of the value of books, which is sometimes lost in our digital world. Children enjoy looking at books and making books. Children writing and illustrating their own books is a great way to develop both visual arts and writing skills.

Colour mixing activity: 'Bob the Bilby'

> **Reflection activity**
>
> Books can be a rich source of ideas for classroom activities (for example, making illustrations in the style of Jeannie Baker and reinforcing art elements and principles, such as use of colour, and expression through line and texture). List some books that you are familiar with and suggest ways to teach visual arts concepts using the books as a starting point.
>
> Suitable books include:
> - Mem Fox and Judy Horacek, *Where Is the Green Sheep?*
> - Sarah Thomson and Rob Gonsalves, *Imagine A Day*
> - Jeannie Baker, *Mirror*.

Printmaking

Printmaking is the process of applying ink (or paint) to one surface and pressing it onto another surface. As with painting, there is a good range of non-toxic materials available. Children can make multiple prints or just one (**monoprinting**). Making prints is an excellent way for children to explore the sensory qualities of objects. This can be unpredictable and exciting, and can produce very sophisticated results. Printmaking is another way for children of all abilities to achieve success. Printmaking also links well to the maths curriculum, as it concerns patternmaking and tessellations using geometric and non-geometric shapes.

Monoprinting: making only one print.

Printmaking

Three-dimensional art

Three-dimensional art forms call on different skills and perceptions from those used for 2D art forms, and usually involve **kinaesthetic** activity. There are three common approaches to 3D art in the classroom: modelling, such as building with clay; carving, either into clay or other materials; and constructing, which usually involves joining different materials together, such as cardboard and pipe cleaners. There are many 3D materials available for purchase, such as clay, modelling wire and plaster strips. There are also endless possibilities with recycled materials from home.

Kinaesthetic: relating to the perception of movement.

Allowing children to play and explore different materials teaches them about form, size, weight, texture, mass and shape. They learn about manipulating materials and structure, and develop an understanding of balance and space.

Playdough is a good cheap material to start with. Children can manipulate it, stretch it, pull it, push it, or press into it, join it, or roll it. Extra-sensory experiences can be achieved by adding sand or rice, or even lavender oil. Children can make their own playdough and add food colouring for added attraction.

Clay is a terrific natural material that children enjoy working with. It can be preserved by firing (in a kiln perhaps at a high school or specialty art supplier or the studio of a local artist/parent), air-dried and painted, varnished or recycled. A nappy bucket with an airtight lid is perfect for storing clay in and a damp rag on top of the clay will ensure that it stays workable.

Papier mâché is a cheap and versatile medium. It is constructed around objects, most commonly balloons (although they can to be difficult for small hands to manage), but also cardboard structures or found objects like twigs, tubes and containers. Scrunched paper can be used to create shape and then layers of papier mâché over that. This process can be used to make a range of artworks such as sculpture, masks, musical instruments, frames.

Papier mâché: medium made using scrap paper and paste, usually some sort of acrylic glue or specialised papier-mâché paste powder.

Four-dimensional art

Four-dimensional art encompasses a wide variety of art practices, including performance art, kinetic art and installation art. These forms of art investigate interactions between artists, objects, actions, audiences and sites. Most other forms of art do not change: the artwork is the same before you look at it as it is after you leave. Four-dimensional art, however, changes while you are looking at it. Video art is an example of this. Four-dimensional art not only addresses time as a theme; it takes up our time as audience.

Kinetic art

Kinetic art is art that is made to move. It interacts with the audience and the space it is in. Movement may be mechanically powered (for example, by electricity, air or water motion) or started by the viewer moving past a work. Mobiles are movable 'sculptures' and can be constructed using wire and fishing line and paper or wooden objects that are designed to move in the wind.

Lesson plan 8.1

AIM
To introduce the concept of kinetic art and for children to design and make their own artworks.

OVERVIEW
Explain to the children what kinetic art is. Show examples (for example, on YouTube). Have the children work in small groups to experiment and plan their own kinetic art. They should make decisions about colour choice, container size and hole size, thickness of paint or ink.

OUTLINE/DESCRIPTION
Fill plastic bottles with paint (thick or thin) and suspend the bottles upside down from the branch of a tree. The wind moves the branch and the bottles, causing them to move around, forming a pattern. (This activity could connect to science activities, e.g. kinetics.) Paper or fabric can be placed under the bottles and when the lids are released or punctured the wind can move the bottles as they drip their contents onto the paper, creating an 'action painting'. The works will not represent anything 'real'; whatever we see in them comes from our imagination.

Invite other children to visit the display of finished works and ask them to give each work a title. Leave a sheet of paper next to each numbered painting. This could then be graphed (mathematics learning) to show diversity of response. Children will also be introduced to the concept of abstraction.

Each child will display the finished work to an audience. They will develop presentation skills and understand that audience members respond when looking at artworks.

INTENDED OUTCOMES
Students will
- understand the concept of kinetic art
- develop designing and making skills in planning and creating their own kinetic artwork.

> **LINKS TO CURRICULUM**
>
> **Early Years Learning Framework**
> - Outcome 4: Children are confident and involved learners.
>
> **Years 3 and 4: Making/Responding**
> - Use materials, techniques and processes to explore visual conventions when making artworks (ACAVAM111).
>
> **ASSESSMENT**
> - Early childhood – the teacher should note the child's interest and enthusiasm to participate and explore different media and try things out. Note ability to use equipment (scissors, tape, hammer) and children's development in ability to talk about what they are doing and demonstrate understanding of making artworks that move (kinetic art).
> - Older children – each child presents a folder showing designs and preparation and articulates the process of creating the work. The level of commitment and ability to plan and develop could be assessed. A child's understanding of the concept would be evident from discussion about their work.

Video: Theo Jansen – kinetic sculptor

Performance art

Performance art deals with the interaction of the artist's body with the audience. This could be through movement, sound or dialogue. It could also include other elements, such as artists interacting with objects, or costume or body art. It is live and tends to be experimental. Performance art is not usually for sale, although tickets could be sold to view the performance. It is not theatre. With new technologies there are no foreseeable boundaries for this form of art.

Performance art offers endless possibilities for bringing visual ideas to life. Children should start with a concept or issue, such as bullying or keeping the school clean. The concept should be clear and direct. It is predominantly visual but can have voice or sound. Make-up can be worn or props used to convey the message. Rather than being amusing or entertaining, the purpose of performance art is to encourage people to think. This is a good opportunity to integrate drama and dance learning to visual arts.

Installation art

Installation art usually involves 3D works that are site-specific. The artist's intention is to alter the perception of the space. It could be a collection of items that evoke complex and multiple associations and thoughts, or items that change the viewer's mood. The installation is usually set up in a particular space, such as the playground or a corner of the library, and the audience are invited to move among it and experience the arrangement.

> **Spotlight on Arts education**
>
> Brainstorm ways that visual arts, especially the less conventional styles that have just been discussed, could be used in health and physical education to meet this Australian Curriculum outcome:
>
> - Practise and refine fundamental movement skills in a variety of movement sequences and situations (ACPMP043).
>
> An example of this is a visual arts obstacle course.
>
> Set up easels at different locations with paper attached and labelled. Each one has a box of materials as set out below. You can use coloured tunnels or paths to connect the easels so the children can make their way around the obstacle course.
>
> ## EASEL 1 – COLOUR
>
> Have ready a box of torn, coloured paper (red, yellow and blue) and a brush with glue (or glue stick). Each child runs to the station and selects a primary colour and glues it on the paper. Then based on the colour paper they have chosen, they select the matching tunnel or path. At the end of the tunnel or path is another easel. Each easel contains a different activity for the children to complete. Some more ideas are listed below.
>
> - Texture: An easel is set up with texture written on it and another sheet of paper as well as a box of materials with different textures (feathers, corrugated card, alfoil, fabric, sandpaper, hessian etc.) and glue. Each child has to select a piece of textured material from the box and glue it onto the paper.
> - The child has to imagine what that texture would feel like on their bare feet and make their way to the next station as if they were walking on it.
> - Shape: An easel is set up with shape written on it. The child is presented with another sheet of paper and a box of materials with different shapes.
> - The child selects a shape (circle, square, star, octagon etc.) and draws it on the paper, then has to walk, making that shape either with their body or on the ground as they move to the next station.
> - Tone: An easel is set up with tone written on it, and a box contains materials of different shades.
> - The child decides on a light, dark or medium material and has to move in a heavy (dark), medium or light way to the next station,
> - Line: The next station will have line written on it and the child selects a particular type of line (wavy, zigzag, dots, straight etc.). They have to draw the line on the paper and make their way to the next station using the line as direction (i.e. walk or run in a zig-zag line).
> - Form: An easel is set up with form written on it and a box of different 3D shapes, balls, cubes, cones etc. The student has to build a sculpture using the different forms (might need a glue gun, foam balls, cardboard boxes etc.).
> - Space: The final easel has space written on it and each child has to draw the first letter of their name, deciding how much space to take up. For example, small and in the middle, large and over the whole piece, thin and down one side etc. They have to make their way to the finish/starting spot using their bodies to take up space e.g. a lot of space – arms legs stretched out, or a small amount of space – bodies scrunched up.

They might do this several times (depending on the numbers) and choose a different colour each time.

As a conclusion, gather the children and line the easels up to view the abstract artworks (with their labels i.e. colour, shape etc.). You can extend this by adding principles such as harmony, balance, rhythm and movement, variety, emphasis, pattern. This could also link beautifully to dance and choreography.

Making and responding in visual arts
Styles in visual arts

Visual artists represent their ideas in many different ways. These can be grouped into various styles or categories. Children of all ages enjoy looking at artworks and through guided questioning they can develop 'noticing' skills, so that they learn to notice different styles. Young children can draw and talk about what they see while older children learn to differentiate nuances and stylistic detail.

Lesson plan 8.2

AIM
Students will be introduced to the concept of self-portrait and explore ideas and practices used by artists.

OVERVIEW
Exploring self-portraits.

OUTLINE/DESCRIPTION
Visual artists make self-portraits for many reasons. Artists such as Frida Kahlo painted her own 'reality', making symbolic reference to her pain (Bersson, 1991), while others painted their own portrait because they could not find or could not afford a model. Some self-portraits help the artist to understand more about themselves or their identity. Figure 8.8 is an image of an artist's eye with a reflection of the artist in the iris and it is made up from words written about the artist's life. Artists make their portraits in many different ways and in different styles. One US artist, Pierson, uses portraits of other people to create his self-portrait (Rimanelli, 2002).

The Australian Curriculum has a link to 'Scootle' where, if you enter 'self-portrait' in the search engine, you will find a rich source of examples.

In groups of three, students will present three self-portraits made by artists from different times and cultures and identify visual conventions used, reasons for making them, and similarities and differences. Each student will display their self-portrait and provide a written description of their choice of materials, style and visual conventions.

→
INTENDED OUTCOMES

Students are able to

- understand reasons that artists make self-portraits
- research artists' self-portraits from different times and places
- learn how artists utilise visual conventions such as colour, shape, texture etc. in their artworks
- create a self-portrait and be able to identify and explain choices made.

LINKS TO CURRICULUM

Years 5 and 6 content descriptors

- Explore ideas and practices used by artists, including practices of Aboriginal and Torres Strait Islander artists, to represent different views, beliefs and opinions (ACAVAM114).
- Develop and apply techniques and processes when making their artworks (ACAVAM115).
- Explain how visual arts conventions communicate meaning by comparing artworks from different social, cultural and historical contexts, including Aboriginal and Torres Strait Islander artworks (ACAVAR117).

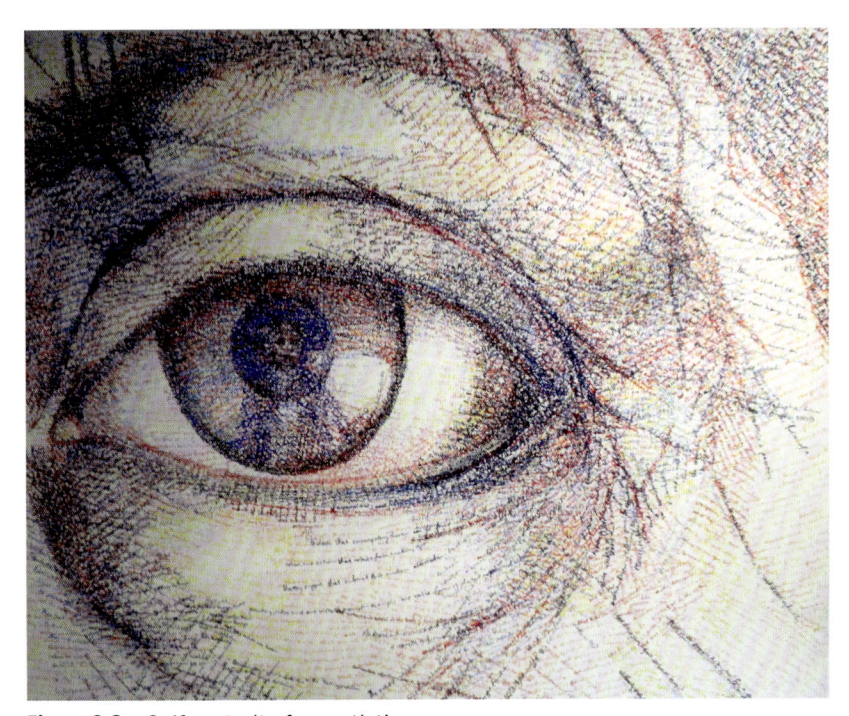

Figure 8.8 Self-portrait of an artist's eye

Responding to visual arts

To become visually literate, children should have the opportunity to make their own artworks and to view and experience artworks by others. Through guided looking, children start to understand about artists and what they do and have done in the past. They recognise different purposes for, and methods of, art-making. They gain an understanding of personal, cultural, social and historical contexts and develop skills in critical analysis and evaluation of their own work and the work of others. Theorists suggest that learning by looking at art in this way enables meaningful, deep learning in ways that traditional cognitive learning does not (Freire, 1970; Greene, 2001; Tisdell, 2008, Bell, 2012). Central to these views is the idea that the capacity to see more clearly the detail in things and to be able to detect nuance leads to discerning judgment (Tishman & Palley, 2010).

Opportunities for children to look at and think about art can occur in many ways. For example, visiting an art gallery or an artist studio, looking at postcards or other reproductions, and accessing digital images online. There are some things that teachers can do to enhance the experience. Allow plenty of time to stop and look carefully. It is important to remember that looking can involve other senses; for example, many sculptures are meant to be touched, and occasionally smell is an important factor (consider how a particular smell can trigger memories of past experiences). It can bring about an emotional response or make a connection to past experiences or knowledge. Children may need additional information to help them to make connections. Guided questioning is helpful in eliciting responses and in making connections and understanding.

Reflection activity

Use Table 8.3 to answer the following questions about Rebecca Hastings' painting (Figure 8.9).

1. What do you see?
2. How do the things in the image relate to one another?
3. Describe the painting using visual language.

TABLE 8.3 SUGGESTIONS FOR LOOKING AT ART: QUESTIONS TO ASK

Question	Child	Teacher
What do you see, hear or feel?	Describe what is visible. (Name what you see.) Perhaps walk around it if it is 3D. If allowable, touch it. It may be electronic media that can be watched repeatedly. There may be sound – describe what you hear. Are there things that you do not recognise?	Guided questioning. Help with unfamiliar objects or people.
Group or classification	How do the things you can see relate to each other? Are there any symbols or signs? Have you seen them before?	Explain: cultural, social background. Significant event. Meanings of symbols or signs.
Art elements Traditional and contemporary principles	Describe the painting using visual language. Elements: colour, shape, texture, line, space, value, form, time and motion. Principles: unity and harmony, variety, scale, balance, rhythm, repetition, emphasis, contrast, proportion. Use of juxtaposition, appropriation or time.	Look for ways visual language has been used to communicate, e.g. colour to express feeling, or line to show movement, balance or imbalance, subtle or dramatic. How has the artist borrowed from others?
The work	What do you know about the artist(s)? When was it made? How was it made? What style is the work? What is the title? Why was it created? Who is the intended audience?	What is the artist's background – cultural, social, political, gender? What was happening at the time? What materials (etc.)? Realist, abstract, appropriation (etc.)? Does the title give meaning? What is the artist's intention? How do you know? What are the artist's beliefs?
Personal response	How does it make you feel? Is it interesting? Is it relevant? How do you feel about the message?	Does everyone feel the same way? Does it make connections? Brainstorm ideas about the meaning and success of the artwork.

Figure 8.9 Rebecca Hastings, *Smell This*

4   Who is the artist? How does *Smell This* compare with her other work?
5   What do you think the message of the painting might be?
6   Do these questions help you to respond meaningfully to the work? Might questions like this have helped you interpret artworks at visual arts galleries or websites? Responses will vary – write a paragraph.
7   Does knowing what the author says the painting is about help you understand the image more?

The following are Rebecca Hastings' responses to questions about *Smell This*.

Q   What do you see?
A   A bald woman wearing a pretty dress is sniffing the finger of a hand which is poking through a hole in a wall.
Q   How would you describe the colours?
A   Pale pastel colours. The walls are pink and fleshy, like the characters in the scene. The green and blue floral dress provides a pretty contrast against the pink flesh.
Q   Can you see an adult's hand or a child's hand?
A   It is a child's hand. In fact, it is the hand of my (then) five-year-old son.

Q   Who is the woman?

A   The woman is me – his mother.

Q   Why is the hand coming out of the wall?

A   This is about the idea that no matter where I go, what I do, the children are always there; demanding something of me. Of course, it's an exaggeration of reality – my children don't really live in the walls of my house, but they're never far away and sometimes it really does seem as though they lurk within the very walls of my home.

Q   Where is this scene taking place?

A   This is a domestic space – the home – the place where the mother–child relationship is acted out, and where the mother is confined in her role.

Q   Why is the woman bald?

A   The bald head signifies 'masculinity' that belies the feminine ideal of the mother. When I painted this image my daughter was two and I decided to shave my head. It was an act of rebellion, pushing back against the feminine ideal that has been perpetrated through art for more than 200 years and more recently, in advertising and societal expectations.

Q   What is she doing?

A   She is sniffing a finger. Sniffing a finger seems to be something that is unpleasant. Unlike smelling someone's perfumed wrist, the finger implies filth ... poo even, something which a mother has to deal with constantly, and without complaint, in a world with small children.

Q   Does the dress have meaning?

A   The dress signifies 'femininity'. For me, the maternal role – being someone's mother – comes with the weight of society's expectations that mothers should behave and look a certain way.

Q   Is the woman angry, sad or happy?

A   She is neither. She has accepted her situation; she is resigned to it. She willingly performs strange and disgusting tasks that she never dreamed of before she had children.

Q   How does this painting make you feel? Is this a silly image? Is it serious?

A   The painting uses humour to make light of a serious topic. I didn't want to whinge or complain overtly about my role as a mother; instead, it was important that I present an image which is imaginative, and yet still based on truth.

The context of visual arts in the Arts and in education

Part 3 of this book discusses pedagogy in general, but there are some specific pedagogical skills and knowledge that relate to teaching visual arts.

Theories about the way children develop have always shaped Arts education (Gaitskill, Hurwitz & Day, 2006; Lowenfeld & Brittain, 1975; Wilson & Wilson, 1982; Winner, 1982).

There is general agreement that children's art-making develops in identifiable stages that are not age related but that appear to cease when children feel a need to draw realistically. The current approach contends that children need to be taught art skills and understandings (McArdle & Piscitelli, 2002; McArdle & Wong, 2010; The College Board, 2012, Chand, 2016).

Discovery, experimentation and play are important, but they work alongside explicit teaching. Tertiary students who are asked to draw say that they have not drawn since primary school and either cannot do it or draw at the level of an early primary school child (Hamilton, 2013). Research suggests that children learn through social and cultural processes. The child does not learn in isolation, but through relationships with others such as family, neighbours, community members and peers, and development takes place when the child participates in activities in their community (for example, in a childcare centre) (Fleer, 2010). Terrini (2010) suggests that children develop understanding in visual arts and a sense of belonging as they encounter cultural diversity in their Arts learning.

Figures 8.10 and 8.11 are artworks by the same child, one made in year 1 and the other in year 6. She was in a school that had a special visual arts teacher and enjoyed an authentic Arts education all through her primary years. The artwork by the child in year 6 was made after a unit of learning about the Dutch artist Piet Mondrian and his style of reducing objects to their simplest shapes.

Planning in the Arts should emphasise the importance of the students and take into account the diversity of abilities, cultural backgrounds and interests. The Australian Curriculum allows for flexibility and invites teachers to implement it in the way that bests suits the particular context of the school and community. It is also important to consider progression through learning rather than just a mix of different activities. Arts learning

Figure 8.10 Artwork by a child in year 1

Figure 8.11 Artwork by the same child in year 6

should be sequential so that children can build on their knowledge and the Arts learning is made explicit. For example, if the children are learning about books and illustrations, they need to understand that they are learning use of colour, composition, tone etc., as well as making a picture for their book.

Audience plays a vital role in all of the Arts and displaying children's artworks has many benefits. The concept of audience is important in that most artworks are made with the intention of expressing an idea to an audience. Sometimes the audience is the 'self'. Some artists make artwork as a way to understand themselves or others, and so their audience is purely personal. Others make artwork to be seen globally. In a classroom setting, the audience could be peers, the whole school, or even the community. The third content descriptor in the Australian Curriculum (F–6) is: Sharing artworks through performance, presentation or display (ACARA, 2017).

This should be considered as children make and respond to artworks. Some of the guiding questions in Table 8.3 relate to the artist's intentions and intended audience. Questions like 'Why did the artist make the work?' or 'Who is the intended audience?' are important in understanding the artwork and evaluating the success of the work.

Displaying children's work can also be used to reinforce what was learned, for example, use of perspective or use of design elements and images to influence people. Children's artworks can be used to raise awareness of issues, local and global, or to reinforce learning of ideas and concepts in other Learning Areas or as a starting point for discussion. By displaying children's art you show that you value their work. Children learn to use critical reflection and informed judgment when selecting best work for display. Their work could be displayed digitally as a movie or as an ebook, or on the school website for a wider audience. Recent studies have found that children rarely notice posters or information displayed that is made by others but they do notice informative posters and displays that they have created themselves (Hanley et al., 2017).

Most children enjoy displaying their work and can be involved in the creation of displays by selecting coloured mounts and making decisions about placements and so on. Organising an exhibition of themed work can be a good way not only to share the work with an audience and as a celebration of achievement but also as a community event or fundraising activity.

Children also learn about the function of art in the community and wider society by stepping into the role of artist and interacting with an audience.

Planning

Chapter 10 addresses specific approaches to Arts planning and it is important to consider both making and responding in the Arts. Rather than planning units of work around *making*, such as painting or printmaking, consider organising art-making activities to support learning the core elements and principles and concepts. For example, the focus could be on *texture*.

Unit plan: texture

Materials and classroom safety

Although a teacher does not have to be good at art to teach it, they do need to be familiar with materials and equipment and classroom safety. Art materials for children should always be non-toxic. Children should be taught to be responsible for the management of the materials they use, and some sort of storage system is essential. The most important tip for teachers is to keep the materials and equipment well organised so that children can find things easily and are able to return them when done.

Some materials and equipment need careful instruction on safe and appropriate use. Children can be involved in this by creating instructional posters for the classroom and by being responsible for the materials and equipment that they use. Children need to be familiar with rules and may need to be reminded by the posters. They should also be familiar with clean-up procedures and proper disposal of materials.

Some schools will have the luxury of an art room but many art lessons will be held in a general classroom. Organising storage well is essential, and some options for storing art supplies include large labelled containers or trolleys. Children need to be aware of procedures such as the distribution of paint and the care of brushes. A system of distribution of materials is useful, for example keeping collections of materials such as pencils in several large containers that can easily be distributed by one person from each shared workspace.

Supplies

You will find many lists of suggested supplies, but what you will need depends on your planned curriculum. For instance, if you are planning for 3D art you will need different materials to those required for printmaking. As you can see from the colour-mixing section, three primary colours, black and white acrylic paints are a good starting point. You can add media to these paints to create texture or to change their structure; for example, to thicken or to thin. A good range of paper sizes and pencils (soft 2B, 4B and HB pencils, coloured pencils), rollers and a range of brush sizes are good staples for an art classroom.

A well-planned curriculum based on student interests and needs that links to the Australian Curriculum does not need shelves stocked full of products, but rather an ability to think creatively about how to utilise what you do have.

Link: Classroom supplies list

Other useful materials can be collected from parents and local businesses, including containers, rags, paper offcuts, styrofoam sheets and so on.

Conclusion

This chapter gives a framework for teaching visual arts and provides some 'tools' that form the 'grammar and syntax' of visual arts. As with any language, there is so much more to be learned and the visual arts and Arts education are constantly changing, so readers are urged to read in more depth about visual artists and visual arts theories locally and globally.

Developing 'seeing' skills by learning to look at artworks and developing a personal understanding of concepts such as audience, or Arts elements and principles, will be rewarding both individually in terms of lifelong engagement and also for planning quality visual arts experiences for children.

REVIEW QUESTIONS

1. What does visual arts involve?
2. Note down some ways in which you might begin planning for teaching visual arts in the future.
3. Why might visual artists (and thus children) make art?
4. What are colours that are opposite each other on the six-part colour wheel called?
5. What is four-dimensional art?
6. List some opportunities for children to look at and think about art.

RECOMMENDED READING

Hanley, M., Khairat, M., Taylor, K., Wilson, R., Cole-Fletcher, R. and Riby, D. M. (2017). 'Classroom displays – Attraction or distraction? Evidence of impact on attention and learning from children with and without autism'. *Developmental Psychology*, 53(7), 1265–75.

Isbell, R. T. and Raines, S. C. (2013). *Creativity and the Arts with Young Children*, 3rd edn. Celmont, CA: Wadsworth Cengage Learning.

Quillin, K. and Thomas, S. (2015). 'Drawing-to-learn: A framework for using drawings to promote model-based reasoning in biology'. *CBE Life Science Education*, 14(1), 1–16.

Ritchhart, R. and Perkins, D. (2008). 'Making thinking visible'. *Educational Leadership*, 65(5), 55–61.

Wilks, S. (2003). 'The visual arts as a thinking tool'. *Australian Art Education*, 26(2), 27–33.

Wright, S. (ed.) (2003). *Children, Meaning-making and the Arts*. Sydney: Pearson.

PART 3

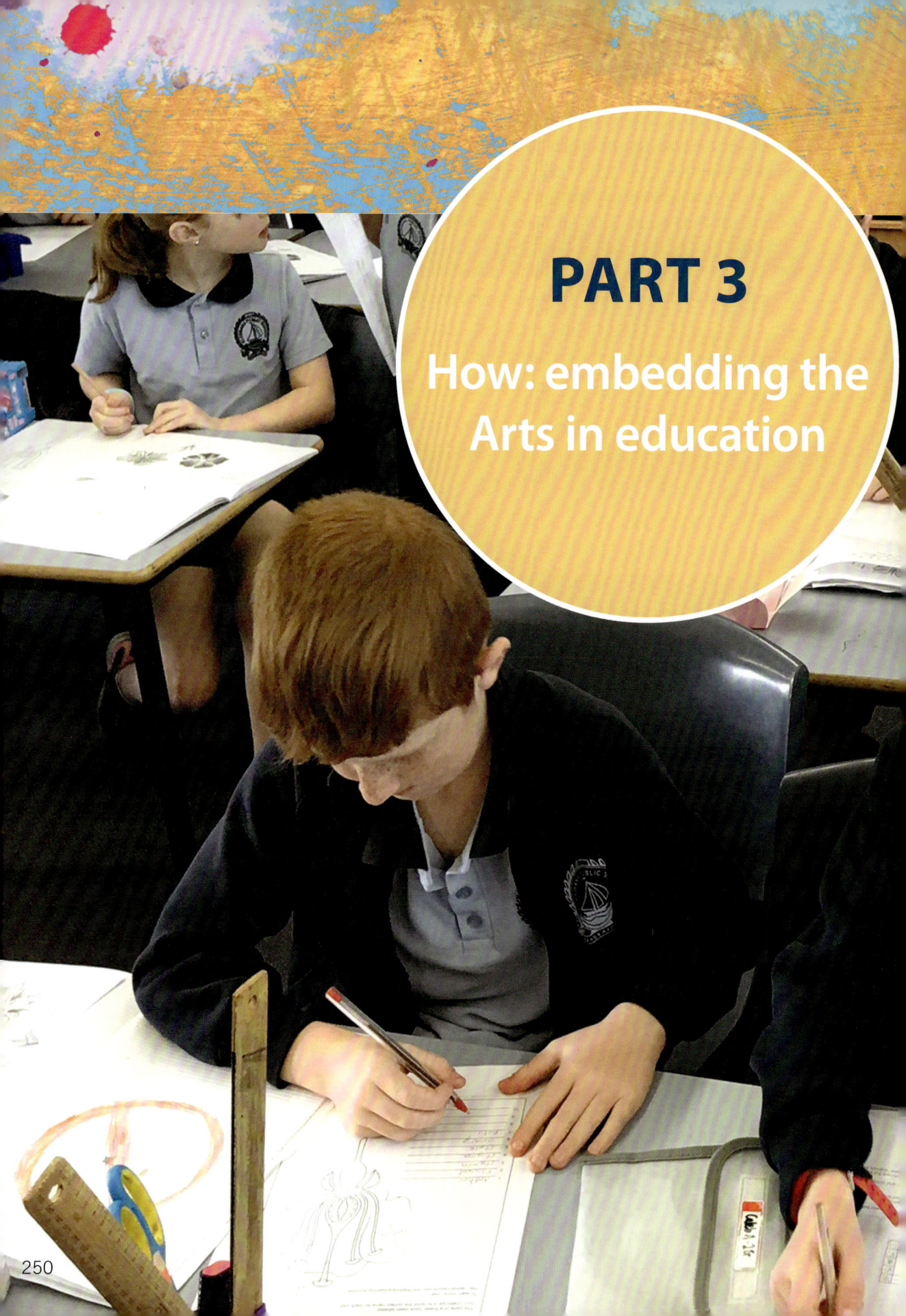

How: embedding the Arts in education

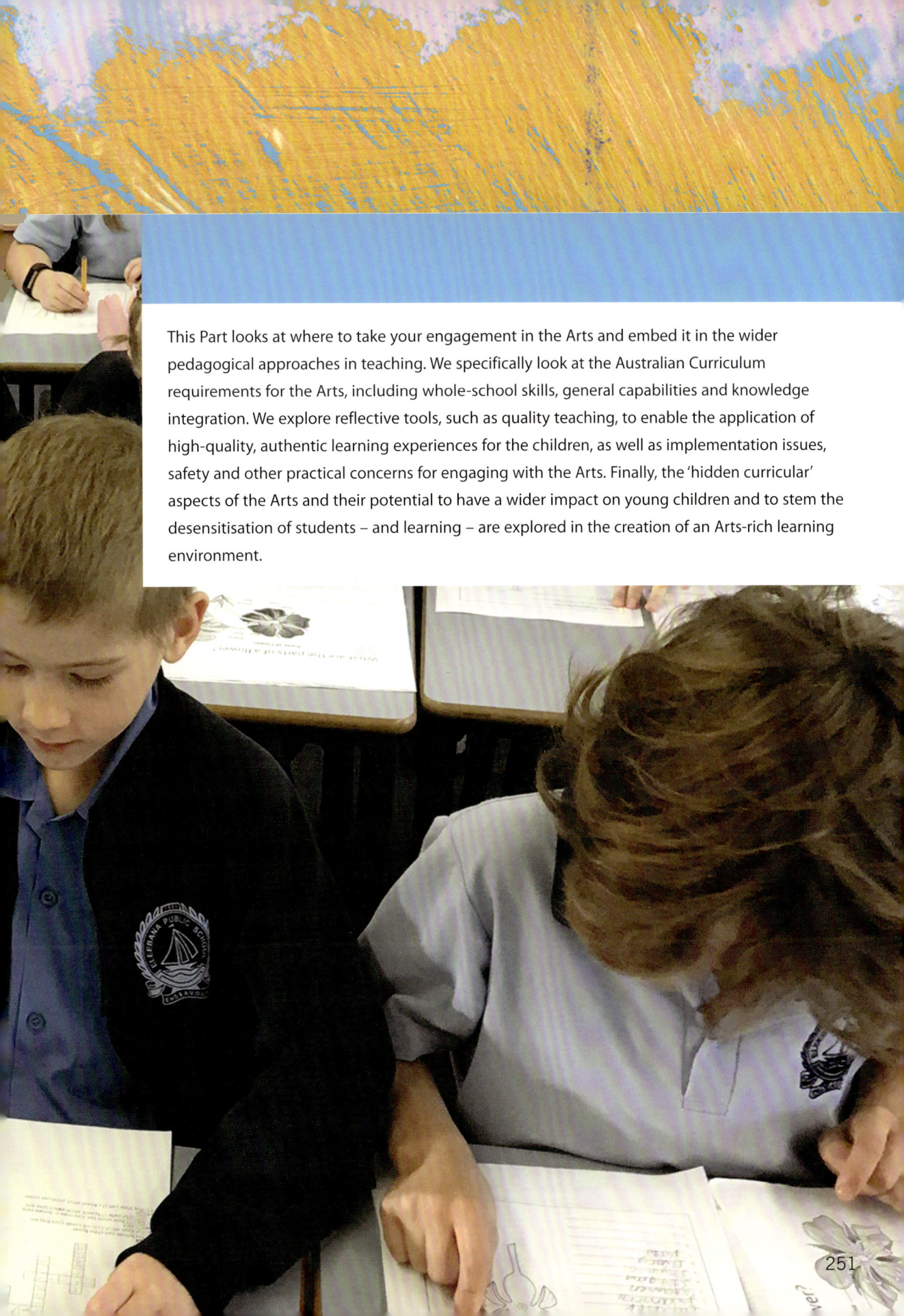

This Part looks at where to take your engagement in the Arts and embed it in the wider pedagogical approaches in teaching. We specifically look at the Australian Curriculum requirements for the Arts, including whole-school skills, general capabilities and knowledge integration. We explore reflective tools, such as quality teaching, to enable the application of high-quality, authentic learning experiences for the children, as well as implementation issues, safety and other practical concerns for engaging with the Arts. Finally, the 'hidden curricular' aspects of the Arts and their potential to have a wider impact on young children and to stem the desensitisation of students – and learning – are explored in the creation of an Arts-rich learning environment.

9

Integration and general capabilities

> Everybody lives, Rose. Just this once, everybody lives!
>
> David Tenant as 'The Doctor'

In this chapter

In this chapter we introduce and explain the key principles of integrated learning and outline ways in which it can be put into practice to provide quality Arts experiences, as well as quality learning in other areas. We suggest ways to achieve integrated learning that you can adapt to construct your own successful program.

We also move beyond the concept of curriculum integration to look at child integration as it should be applied in the classroom. Schools do exclude, both intentionally and otherwise. We explore the justifications offered for, and ways to remove, these barriers to engagement in the Arts by all. We argue in this chapter for the need for everyone to experience the Arts equally, no matter what their background or what form of diverse learning is brought to the classroom. For some children, this is the only pathway to success. In the Arts anyone can engage; everyone gets to live them.

By the end of this chapter you should have a clear understanding of:

- programming the Arts Curriculum
- the elements and principles of general capabilities
- integration of the Arts with other Learning Areas
- curriculum integration.

Introduction

Many educators agree that children learn best when they experience learning activities that relate to each other in a meaningful way. The 'integrated learning approach' is one way in which the curriculum can be organised to provide unifying learning experiences. An integrated learning unit is one in which several Learning Areas are linked together by relating them to a carefully selected theme or concept.

Programming the Arts curriculum

When approaching the integration of curriculum requirements, the first question is where to start. Within the new Australian Curriculum, each Learning Area has individual outcomes for each stage. Within the Arts this is further complicated as each of the Arts has a variety of outcomes to be met. The question is, therefore, where to start: visual art, dance, drama, media or music. In some school situations, the directive has been to choose one particular art and teach those outcomes until the strand has been completely covered and then move to another. The challenge with this is that later strands often have less time afforded to them as the year progresses. In addition, many strands have similar skill outcomes that are transferable. It is therefore perhaps better to integrate the teaching of various outcomes concurrently.

TEACHER TIP

A suggested methodology for integrating the teaching of various outcomes concurrently is to create a spreadsheet with outcomes listed in rows and subject areas in columns.

As outcomes are met, a tick can be placed in a box. It is important to recognise that outcomes can be met multiple times through the years when a stage is being applied, and so multiple ticks can be placed in the same box. We must also recognise that individual students will meet different outcomes at different times; thus, a spreadsheet can be made for each child as well as a whole class, and this can list not just what outcomes have been taught but what outcomes have been fully met by the whole class.

In individual activities, there are multiple outcomes that can be met at the same time. It is important as a teacher to have a focus on one or two, and these are the ones that can be recorded.

TABLE 9.1 PROGRAMMING

	Drama	English	Science	Visual art	HSIE	Dance	PE	Music	Maths	Media
2.1										
2.2										
2.3										
2.4										

The advantage of keeping such a record is that not only is it useful information for the reflective teacher (Chapter 11) but it is also a valuable document to share information with other teachers who may teach the class after you.

In the classroom

Wombat Stew (Lofts & Vaughan, 2005) is a children's story written by Marcia K. Vaughan and Pamela Lofts. It tells of a dingo that captures a wombat and decides to make a wombat stew. Various Australian animals offer suggestions to the dingo for flavouring the stew, which results in the stew being inedible and the wombat escaping. The book has lavish anthropomorphic visuals, rhythmic rhyme linguistics, as well as potential interpretation of dance, music and the humanities. As a text it can be explored for literacy or other Learning Areas.

Read the first six pages of the book where the wombat is caught and the platypus offers the first suggestion. Two students are then asked to be wombat and dingo. Re-enact the first page only. 'One day on the banks of a billabong, a very clever dingo caught a wombat.'

Suggested re-enactment:

Discuss with the class how a human-like wombat would move (a human with the movement characteristics of a wombat, slow, careful and fat) and a dingo-like human would move (quick, light-footed, sly) using stereotypes. Then discuss the types of food eaten (wombat: vegetarian, and dingo: carnivore). The two students will act like this, with their class offering advice to adapt movements.

Wombat can re-enact walking into a supermarket and looking at the fruit and vegetables. Narrate the line: 'One day on the banks of a billabong …' Enter dingo sniffing the air and suddenly seeing wombat. Narrate the phrase: 'A very clever dingo.' Have dingo creep up on wombat and touch the shoulder. Narrate the phrase: 'Caught a wombat!' Actors freeze with wombat looking shocked.

Now discuss the scene with the class. This discussion should be based on the Learning Area focus. Potential foci can be:

- literacy – interpreting the text/anthropomorphism/narrative/etc.
- drama – acting skills with the text as stimulus (characterisation or blocking)
- dance/PE – movement skills
- media – stereotypes/anthropomorphism
- visual art – images/anthropomorphism.

Students can then be asked to interpret the rest of the story in small groups using a method centred on the outcomes and Learning Area focus you wish to explore.

The elements and principles of general capabilities

The Australian Curriculum: The Arts has at its core a rationale to engage and develop creative learners for the future. However, learning for its own sake, while to some degree an ideal for individuals, is not an aspiration for society. Education is a large investment in a community. Thus, curriculum systems all over the world have a larger purpose and, in the developed nations, the same basic foci.

In Australia, the rationale of the curriculum in conjunction with the needs of society and the workplace has developed seven 'general capabilities'. These skills, though not directly related to discipline knowledge, are embedded in the learning in all subjects.

These general capabilities are:

- literacy
- numeracy
- information and communication technology capability
- critical and creative thinking
- personal and social capability
- ethical understanding
- intercultural understanding.

These are not just new names for essential skills; they demonstrate the links between skills, knowledge, attitudes and values. All of the core skills/competencies/ capabilities presented were based around the Programme for International Student Assessment (PISA) study, conducted for the large OECD countries in 1997. The report noted:

> Today's societies place challenging demands on individuals, who are confronted with complexity in many parts of their lives. What do these demands imply for key competencies that individuals need to acquire? Defining such competencies can improve assessments of how well prepared young people and adults are for life's challenges, as well as identify overarching goals for education systems and lifelong learning. A competency is more than just knowledge and skills. It

involves the ability to meet complex demands, by drawing on and mobilising psychosocial resources (including skills and attitudes) in a particular context. For example, the ability to communicate effectively is a competency that may draw on an individual's knowledge of language, practical IT skills and attitudes towards those with whom he or she is communicating (Rychen & Salganik, 2005).

Individuals need a wide range of competencies to face the complex challenges of today's world, but it would be of little practical value to produce long lists of everything that they may need to be able to do at different times in their lives.

Each 'key competency' must:

- contribute to valued outcomes for societies and individuals
- help individuals meet important demands in a wide variety of contexts
- be important not just for specialists but for all individuals (Rychen & Salganik, 2005, p. 4).

It is interesting to note that, while the media and government bulletins emphasise literacy and numeracy as key skills, within the balance of the 'competencies' and 'capabilities' the ability to understand oneself and others is key. When we consider Chapters 1 and 2, and the notion of praxis in Arts learning, it is clear that the Arts have a fundamental role to play. Table 9.2 highlights the exemplar of the Scottish education core skills, in part because Scotland has a national curriculum, unlike other English-speaking countries such as the United States or England. In the Scottish example, subject areas were linked to one key core skill, and all children were expected to meet these skills. Only one Learning Area met the core skill 'working with others' – the Arts. The Arts are fundamental to meeting the competencies/capabilities. Unsurprisingly, the DICE report (Cziboly, 2010) mentioned in Chapter 5 confirms exactly this.

Link: Scottish core skills

TABLE 9.2 EQUIVALENT COMPETENCIES IN AUSTRALIAN AND SCOTTISH CURRICULA

Equivalent Australian 'general capabilities'	Equivalent Scottish 'core skills'
Critical and creative thinking	Problem-solving
ICT capability	ICT
Literacy	Literacy
Numeracy	Numeracy
Ethical understanding	Problem-solving Working with others
Intercultural understanding	Problem-solving Working with others
Personal and social capability	Problem-solving Working with others

The capabilities, like the cross-curriculum priorities discussed in Chapter 3, are not individual subjects but are to be embedded in the learning of all the children we teach. This very concept will be explored further through quality teaching in Chapter 12.

ACARA(2012, pp. 21–2), defines the seven general capabilities as follows.

Literacy
Students become literate as they develop the skills to learn and communicate confidently at school and to become effective individuals, community members, workers and citizens. These skills include listening, reading and viewing, speaking, writing, and creating print, visual and audio materials accurately and purposefully in all Learning Areas.

Numeracy
Students become numerate as they develop the skills and confidence to use mathematics at school and in their lives beyond school. In the context of schooling, numeracy involves students recognising and engaging with whatever mathematical knowledge and skills are needed for understanding in all Learning Areas.

Information communication technology (ICT) capability
Students develop ICT competence as they learn to use information and communication technology effectively and appropriately to access, create and communicate information and ideas, solve problems and work collaboratively in all Learning Areas at school, and in their lives beyond school.

Critical and creative thinking
Students develop critical and creative thinking skills and suppositions as they learn to generate and evaluate knowledge, ideas and possibilities, and use them in combination when seeking new pathways or solutions. This includes learning to think deeply and broadly in activities that require reason, logic, resourcefulness, imagination and innovation in all Learning Areas.

Ethical behaviour
Students develop ethical understanding as they learn to recognise and understand matters of ethical concerns, make reasoned judgments and, in so doing, develop a personal ethical framework. This includes understanding the role of ethical principles and values in human life, acting with integrity and regard for the rights of others, and having a desire to work for the common good.

Personal and social capability
Students develop personal and social competence as they learn to understand themselves and others more fully, and to manage their relationships, lives, learning and work effectively. This includes recognising and regulating their emotions, establishing positive relationships, making responsible decisions, working effectively in teams and handling challenging situations constructively.

Intercultural understanding
Students develop intercultural understanding as they learn to understand themselves in relation to others. Students learn to respect and appreciate their own cultures and beliefs, and those of others. This includes engaging with people from diverse linguistic, social and cultural groups in ways that recognise differences and create connections and cultivate mutual respect, and coming to understand how personal, group and national identities are shaped by many different histories and experiences. In the context of schooling, this involves students learning about the diversity of languages, institutions and practices, and developing perspectives on complex issues related to global diversity.

Arts classrooms are ideal places for the exploration of critical and creative thinking, ethical understanding, intercultural understanding, and personal and social capability. There are few situations in the Arts where children are not encouraged to work together, to discuss and to plan for personal and social competence. Social support and cultural knowledge encourage ethical behaviour.

Tables 9.3a–e show practical examples of each of the general capabilities for each Art strand.

TABLE 9.3A GENERAL CAPABILITIES IN RELATION TO THE ARTS: DANCE

General capabilities	Dance skill	Practical example
Literacy	Responding to stimuli and initial planning of movements/space usage.	Watching a dust storm form in South Australia and researching how storms move across the landscape.
Numeracy	Using particular gestures/movements that carry meaning to the audience.	Holding arms up and hands above the head of a lower-placed body that is curled up, expanding out, signifying the fractal shape of lightning.
ICT capability	Working as an ensemble.	Using recorded sounds and music to represent the development of the storm.
Critical and creative thinking	Working as an ensemble.	Planning with fellow pupils, sharing ideas and building on an idea, e.g. how smooth/angular movements should be when representing lightning.
Ethical understanding	Working as an ensemble.	Planning with fellow pupils, sharing ideas and building on an idea, e.g. how our actions as people can effect the creation of storms, and how do we respond to others affected by storms.
Intercultural understanding	Responding to stimuli and initial planning of movements/space usage.	Considering the impacts of a storm and the harm and benefits to the environment and the peoples that are affected by it.
Personal and social capability	Working as an ensemble.	Planning with fellow pupils, sharing ideas and building on an idea, e.g. how smooth movements should be when representing lightning.

TABLE 9.3B GENERAL CAPABILITIES IN RELATION TO THE ARTS: DRAMA

General capabilities	Drama skill	Practical example
Literacy	Voice	Writing dialogue to a situation offered, such as an airport; children consider what they might be doing there.
Numeracy	Blocking	Suggesting where to place two characters hiding in the performance area so that the audience can see them but other characters cannot, considering space, and visual sight lines.
ICT capability	Reflection, logbook	Recording activities rehearsed during the day.
Critical and creative thinking	Group work	Sharing ideas on how to improve rehearsal.
Ethical understanding	Working as an ensemble.	Developing narrative to create purposeful meaning with clear themes.
Intercultural understanding	Group work	Planning with fellow pupils, to demonstrate variety of characters and equitable performer involvement.
Personal and social capability	Characterisation	Planning with fellow pupils, to demonstrate variety of characters and equitable performer involvement.

TABLE 9.3C GENERAL CAPABILITIES IN RELATION TO THE ARTS: MEDIA ARTS

General capabilities	Media arts skill	Practical example
Literacy	Recognising target audience.	Answering questions like 'What is this media product communicating (including semiotic language)?'
Numeracy	Using a media product with intent.	Costing/planning the time and resources needed to create media product.
ICT Capability	Using feedback to improve work.	Using design tools to influence a create a product audience, e.g. a poster.
Critical and creative thinking	Using feedback to improve work.	Applying feedback to edit a movie, to communicate meaning.
Ethical understanding	Recognising different viewpoint.	Answering questions like 'What is this media product communicating (including semiotic language)?'
Intercultural understanding	Recognising different viewpoints.	Sharing interpretations of an image; accepting different cultural and social points of view.
Personal and social capability	Characterisation	Sharing interpretations of an image; accepting different cultural and social points of view.

TABLE 9.3D GENERAL CAPABILITIES IN RELATION TO THE ARTS: MUSIC

General capabilities	Music skill	Practical example
Literacy	Listening to music of diverse cultural heritage.	Listening to 'Djarimirri' by Geoffrey Gurrumul Yunupingu. Reflecting on a rainbow and all that this means symbolically and metaphorically.
Numeracy	Translating sound into notation. Using symbols and notation.	Taking the time to record the pitch, rhythm and instrumentation of these ideas using a form of notation.
ICT capability	Composing	Using digital apps/programs to record ideas, musical concepts.
Critical and creative thinking	Exploring, selecting and combining musical ideas. Translating sound into notation. Using symbols and notation.	Individually developing a series of words from this thinking; e.g. 'arched', 'hopeful', 'colourful', 'dreams'. Improvising short pieces using voice and instruments that may represent these words.
Ethical understanding	Listening to music of diverse cultural heritage.	Listening to 'Djarimirri' by Geoffrey Gurrumul Yunupingu. Reflecting on a rainbow and all that this means symbolically and metaphorically.
Intercultural understanding	Listening to music of diverse cultural heritage.	Listening to 'Djarimirri' by Geoffrey Gurrumul Yunupingu. Reflecting on a rainbow and all that this means symbolically and metaphorically.
Personal and social capability	Working collaboratively to a shared musical goal.	Combining one's sounds and notations with those of two others in the class. Performing the finished piece. Listening to feedback and recording one's thoughts.

TABLE 9.3E GENERAL CAPABILITIES IN RELATION TO THE ARTS: VISUAL ARTS

General capabilities	Visual arts skill	Practical example
Literacy	Looking at artworks and discussing them.	Using visual arts language to talk about an artwork.
Numeracy	Exploring and playing with symbols.	Creating meaning by using symbols.
ICT capability	Designing a logo.	Sharing and accepting ideas for a classroom logo.
Critical and creative thinking	Working collaboratively to make an artwork.	Working together to print T-shirts.
Ethical understanding	Looking at artworks and discussing them.	Communicating interpreted meaning of art works.
Intercultural understanding	Designing a logo.	Sharing and accepting ideas for a classroom logo.
Personal and social capability	Recognising personal response.	Articulating feelings about artworks.

Integration of the Arts with other Learning Areas

Just as the general capabilities offer open opportunities to be embedded in the Arts, curriculum documents make specific links to other subject areas (ACARA, 2015). While useful, these can be somewhat limiting.

> Some Arts subjects have direct relationships with other subjects. All the Arts are relevant to history and geography studies, because the Arts embody some of the most significant and recognisable products and records of all cultures. Drama and media arts have a strong focus on language, texts and narrative, and aspects of these two Arts subjects are taught as part of English. Dance has links to health and physical education. Visual arts have links to design and technology. It is important that students can see connections to other learning areas within the curriculum (ACARA, 2015, p. 19).

The Arts have suffered in education as elements of each strand have been attached to Learning Areas with higher public prestige or 'academic' association (see Chapter 1). By now, the unique and powerful value of the Arts should be clear. Instead, with integration in the curricular sense, rather than being a servant to other subjects, the Arts should be used as a tool to allow children to access other subjects. In simple terms, the Arts can allow access for children to communicate understandings or enhance learning in all areas, including mathematics, English, humanities and science. The teacher, however, must consider the purpose behind using the Arts. To use them as a 'reward' devalues the learning experience and the actual art form. The purpose in using the Arts should be to enhance the learning by allowing the multiple **learning styles** of each child to be employed. Some children have visual learning styles, while others engage with sensory or verbal modalities.

Learning styles: the different methods by which each child learns best.

In addition, there is the manner in which we think. Children respond to ideas and concepts, in part, through the empathetic elements of the knowledge that they 'hook into'. Some children approach knowledge and learning through an environmental perspective, others with a physicality, and still others through methodologies of illustrating ideas. Through the Arts we give children access to these tools to allow them to demonstrate deep understanding.

In the following *Three Little Pigs* activity, the Arts are being integrated into a literacy lesson, but they are not being devalued or used as mere handmaidens. Instead, they are central to the activities in which children are given opportunities to demonstrate their comprehension skills.

In the classroom

Read the story of the *Three Little Pigs* to the class. Now offer a variety of opportunities to the class to respond to their understanding of the story and the underlying themes of planning, greed and betrayal. Set up four workstations/areas. At Workstation One, children can draw/

illustrate/paint a book cover for a printed version of the book. At Workstation Two, children have to write a letter of complaint from the wolf's mother, who believes the pigs were bullying her son. At Workstation Three, the group have to plan and rehearse a dramatic retelling of the story that will be performed in front of the class. Workstation Four contains simple musical rhythm instruments. Children have to create a soundscape of noise and movements that represents the final part of the story where the wolf gets to the brick house. They will have to perform their soundscape to the class and include body and hand movements that tell the story but use no words. Each group has 20–30 minutes at each station, then must move to another.

In the Arts, the different strands often support each other. However, if attempts to integrate learning with the Arts are forced in order to ease a crowded curriculum, they will not enhance learning. Creating a situation where the Arts are a barrier will distance children from all areas of learning in that activity.

The Arts are each embedded both implicitly and explicitly in different forms of intelligence. If we use various forms of them all to apply higher-order thinking, then we realise that to deny children access to the Arts is to deny them access to success and learning. To use an analogy, imagine telling someone that if they are hungry they can eat the chocolate on the shelf 4 metres above their head, and then providing them with no means to access the chocolate. If we then decide the person is not hungry and leave them, they will starve.

We use the same process in education with some children. We ask them to demonstrate their intelligence but deny them the appropriate methods to demonstrate it. We then communicate to them their failure. They eventually switch off school and learning and starve educationally. Why then do we wonder why children have behaviour management problems? Often it is due to their lack of engagement. By embedding learning within the Arts and thus allowing children access to their learning styles, we allow them to thrive and grow and become productive members of the school and the community. A well-resourced and relevant Arts lesson with authentic learning activities and outcomes, which offer opportunities for all, rarely has behaviour management problems. The Arts allow you to have fun teaching.

Bloom's Revised Taxonomy is a useful way to look at the difference between repeating facts ('lower-order thinking') and creating new meanings ('higher-order thinking'). Bloom's Taxonomy has six areas of activity, with various verbs attached. Research demonstrates that higher-order thinking tasks are required to improve achievement in schools. Lower-order thinking is required to enable higher-order thinking, but it is interesting to note where the Arts are easily placed within Bloom's Revised taxonomy. They are listed as the highest form of higher-order thinking.

TABLE 9.4 BLOOM'S TAXONOMY

Thinking skill	Activity	Verb
Lower-order thinking	Remembering	Tell, list, describe, relate, locate, write, find, state, name, identify, label, recall, define, recognise, match, reproduce, memorise, draw, select, write, recite.
Lower-order thinking	Understanding	Explain, interpret, outline, discuss, distinguish, predict, restate, translate, compare, describe, relate, generalise, summarise, put into your own words, paraphrase, convert, demonstrate, visualise, find out more information about.
Lower-order thinking	Applying	Solve, show, use, illustrate, construct, complete, examine, classify, choose, interpret, make, put together, change, apply, produce, translate, calculate, manipulate, modify, put into practice.
Higher-order thinking	Analysing	Analyse, distinguish, examine, compare, contrast, investigate, categorise, identify, explain, separate, advertise, take apart, differentiate, subdivide, deduce.
Higher-order thinking	Evaluating	Judge, select, choose, decide, justify, debate, verify, argue, recommend, assess, discuss, rate, prioritise, determine, critique, evaluate, criticise, weigh, value, estimate, defend.
Higher-order thinking	Designing	Create, invent, compose, predict, plan, construct, design, imagine, propose, devise, formulate, combine, hypothesise, originate, add to, forecast.

Curriculum integration

Multiliteracies: a model of literacy that recognises developments associated with globalisation, cultural diversity and changing technologies, and incorporates multimodal texts.

The Arts have a major role to play in **multiliteracies**. Literacy is not just the reading of words; it is also the ability to code, decode, reconstruct, and demonstrate cognition of and the use of symbols as communication. The most commonly recognised forms of such literacies are the written word and numbers. Written language is a system of communication in which visual symbols enable the creator of the 'image' and the viewer to communicate. Cuneiform, a scripting system that emerged in Sumerian culture around 3500 – 3000 BCE, is among the earliest examples of writing. It was a system of short markings in clay that represented words and numbers. Ancient Egyptian hieroglyphs, which included pictographic elements, are an obvious connection between the visual arts and literacy. Integrating curriculum subjects requires you as the teacher to make meaningful connections across curriculum areas. While integration in this context refers to knowledge and skills, inclusion is a separate matter that is fully explored in Chapter 11.

However, there are many more combinations of literacies. Drama and music engage with both oral and aural literacy through the use of instruments and voices to communicate ideas. The noises produced are symbols that we interpret. Drama, dance and media all create visual literacies through body language and gesture. Media adds a further dimension to this through the selection of frames that are chosen to place the 'reader' in (see Chapter 6). From the analysis of artworks through to the deconstruction of characters in drama and movements in dance, children are demonstrating their 'reading' of a communication form. These are forms of literacies through which the Arts can support learning. The Arts furnish children with tools that allow them access to the curriculum and fair assessment.

There are children who, because of their diverse learning needs, cannot access the education system as able-bodied and neurotypical children can. The Arts, therefore, can create a more level field, allowing equity in the educational experience. In many ways the Arts can be used to meet the *Disability Discrimination Act 1992* requirement for reasonable adjustments.

English and the Arts

Although English and drama are closely intertwined areas – Shakespeare, one of the most well-known figures of English literature, is perhaps best known for his plays, after all – English is not considered an Arts area according to the Australian Curriculum. The position of drama in English is more complicated. Drama is not explicitly an element of the English curriculum, but plays are identified as a literary text type that students engage with as part of their learning. Understanding a play necessarily entails an understanding of aspects of drama. The key to the integration of the Arts and English is how the Arts can add a depth in understanding of semiotics for even very young children.

Spotlight on Arts education

SEMIOTICS

- **Linguistic** – oral and written
- **Visual** – still and moving, media, animation, film (signs and symbols, colour, shape, movement etc)
- **Auditory** – music and sounds, genre styles (classical, jazz, popular), volume, pitch etc.
- **Gestural** – facial expression and body language
- **Spatial** – layout and organisation, proximity and direction
- **Mathematical number systems** – algebraic systems (letters and symbols)

Signs are graphical systems (numbers, graphs, charts etc) and we must note that imagery has complex historical and cultural carriers of meaning (as an image or object). Visual imagery as employed in the media, and in classrooms, employs the relationship between visual semiotic systems and text systems. Add to this the combination of auditory, gestural, spatial and linguistic systems and time as demonstrated through film, video and animation.

Video: *Presto*

A good example of signs and semiotics that create meaning without verbal speech would be that of short films without dialogue – for instance, the Disney/Pixar short film *Presto*.

Lesson plan 9.1

Lesson plan 9.1

AIM

Exploring literary concepts through performance. Focus on using movements to convey meaning in drama. In doing so you can actually meet English Curriculum outcomes.

OVERVIEW

Students will devise a performance/develop performance skills based on a children's text – responding to narrative.

For ACARA English Year 3 alone, this activity could support any of the following outcomes.

- Understand that successful cooperation with others depends on shared use of social conventions, including turn-taking patterns, and forms of address that vary according to the degree of formality in social situations (ACELA1476).
- Discuss texts in which characters, events and settings are portrayed in different ways, and speculate on the authors' reasons (ACELT1594).
- Draw connections between personal experiences and the worlds of texts, and share responses with others (ACELT1596).
- Create imaginative texts based on characters, settings and events from students' own and other cultures using visual features, for example perspective, distance and angle (ACELT1601).
- Identify the point of view in a text and suggest alternative points of view (ACELY1675).
- Listen to and contribute to conversations and discussions to share information and ideas and negotiate in collaborative situations (ACELY1676).
- Use interaction skills, including active listening behaviours and communicate in a clear, coherent manner using a variety of everyday and learned vocabulary and appropriate tone, pace, pitch and volume (ACELY1792).
- Plan and deliver short presentations, providing some key details in logical sequence (ACELY1677).

However, any such connections must be made meaningful and focused on in the lesson. Thus it is up to you as the teacher to decide if you are using literacy to teach in the Arts or the Arts to teach in literacy/English.

OUTLINE/DESCRIPTION

In this lesson students read *Wombat Stew* by Marcia K. Vaughan and Pamela Lofts. They identify how the authors have used the visual and prose elements of the text to convey relationship and characters through the anthropomorphism of animals. Students then create and perform their own interpretations of scenes from the text.

Link: *Wombat Stew*

INTENDED OUTCOMES

Students identify
- the movements of a dingo and wombat
- the way a human could represent animals in character (walking as quiet as a mouse, creeping cat-like, or muscular such as a gorilla).

Students understand
- that writers create characters to reflect us.
- that they can use the text as a narrative basis for a drama performance.

Students are able to
- create, rehearse, and perform a short scene in groups of three.

LINKS TO CURRICULUM

Year 3 and 4 content descriptors
- Use voice, movement and language to sustain role and relationships and create dramatic action with a sense of time and place (ACADRM032).

ASSESSMENT
- Through observation, students devise and work collaboratively to create meaning.
- Students create, rehearse and perform their scene for the class.

QUESTIONS
1. How do the animals move?
2. How would these characteristics be shown in a person who was described as 'dingo-like', etc.?
3. How will you show how the three characters in the section chosen interact?
4. Where is your audience positioned?

Maths and the Arts

Numeracy is a challenge for modern Western education systems. It has been placed as a key skill and competency that many government systems compare and contrast through standardised testing, such as NAPLAN. The challenge has always been to engage those students who feel challenged by numeracy. One methodology is to look for real-world applications of numeracy, and consider how we engage with numeracy in our everyday lives.

Reflection activity

We can engage in maths in lots of different ways, from using basic algebra when we shop to calculating the distance we can drive with a tank of petrol. Maths and numeracy are embedded throughout the Arts and the environment. Take **fractals**, for instance. Look at some images of lightning, gum tree branches, blood vessels and river deltas. Comparing the visual shape similarity, we see these are fractals. Fractals are never-ending repeating patterns. Look for other forms of repeating patterns in your day-to-day life. This can also be extended by looking at basic shapes in everyday objects. In doing this, mathematical concepts can be explored in the classroom through visual art, and visual art concepts can be explored through maths. What maths patterns can children find and share with the class?

Please note that 'maths' refers to the curriculum subject, while 'numeracy' is the skill.

Fractals: geometric patterns that repeat at progressively smaller sizes.

Science and the Arts

STEAM: the incorporation of Arts into the teaching of STEM, science, technology, engineering and mathematics.

Science and the Arts work wonderfully together, especially in the idea of STEM becoming **STEAM**. If we look at many of the great scientists of the past and present, they also had a key interest in the Arts. Leonardo da Vinci was a scientist and a painter/visual artist; Sir Isaac Newton was a musician and physicist; Professor Brian Cox was a pop star before he became a world leading astronomer. When understanding a musical instrument, frequency and physics come into play. Visual art and colour require chemistry and biology. Dance and drama have clear links to the biology of body as well as understanding space, mass and gravity in physics.

Consider any Arts or science concept and try to find no link between the two. If we truly want to encourage students in science, STEAM and not STEM should be the way forward. Only then might we have creative scientific solutions to the challenges our societies face (Roy, 2017).

TEACHER TIP

Working in science, it is important to ensure that students follow procedures for successful scientific exploration and recording. One way to introduce the discipline of method adherence is to introduce Science Safety Rules (such as putting bags away, cleaning equipment, no running). You should discuss the reason for each rule, and even have the class enact the rule being broken, or develop a media product highlighting the need, or have the class use the rules for stimulus for a visual art work or even a dance.

Links: Science safety

Lesson plan 9.2

AIM

Learn how to choreograph movement from nature and how to use the elements of dance to express ideas.

OVERVIEW

Students respond to stimulus, developing awareness of the movements of the environment and reflecting this in their choreography.

For ACARA Science Year 4 alone, this activity could support any of the following outcomes.
- Living things have life cycles (ACSSU072).
- Living things depend on each other and the environment to survive (ACSSU073).
- Forces can be exerted by one object on another through direct contact or from a distance (ACSSU076).
- Represent and communicate observations, ideas and findings using formal and informal representations (ACSIS071).

OUTLINE/DESCRIPTION

In this lesson students research the life cycle of salmon. They identify how the salmon travel up rivers, the obstacles faced, then the spawning, death and birth of salmon as the cycle begins again. Students then take movements from the journey (such as the river, calm at the source, wild and flowing at a waterfall) and compose and perform their own movements representing three aspects of the journey. They can reflect the environment and/or the fish in the movements that flow together for one extended piece of at least 5 minutes.

Links: Salmon

INTENDED OUTCOMES

Students identify
- potential movements to communicate from the source material

- the 'moods' created by the different movements and to apply the elements of dance.

Students understand
- that choreographers use the elements of movement to create an effect or mood
- that they can use the elements as a dancer.

Students are able to
- create, rehearse, and perform a dance reflecting several different movements from the spawning cycle of salmon.

LINKS TO CURRICULUM

Year 3 and 4 content descriptors
- Improvise and structure movement ideas for dance sequences using the elements of dance and choreographic devices (ACADAM005).
- Practise technical skills safely in fundamental movements (ACADAM006).
- Perform dances using expressive skills to communicate ideas (ACADAM007).

ASSESSMENT

Students create, rehearse and perform their movement piece for the class.

Expressionism: an art style that began in early 20th-century Germany, where artists seek to depict ideas or moods rather than physical reality.

Pop Art: an art style that began in the USA and Britain in the 1950s, where artists use popular imagery in an ironic or subversive way.

Humanities and social sciences and the Arts

Similar to science, the humanities and social sciences (HASS) is an area covering the wide variety of content relevant to the society that surrounds us, both physically as well as philosophically. It can actually be a challenge *not* connecting the Arts to the HASS curriculum! Films, paintings and music are often directly inspired by historical events, and all are influenced by the cultural context in which they are created. When talking about the Arts, it is important to consider the time periods and the geographical locations that influence each style. For instance, think about the history and the geography of different styles such as **expressionism** and **Pop Art**.

Spotlight on Arts education

POP ART

Andy Warhol (1928–1987) was a highly influential American artist, whose iconic images of Marilyn Munroe and soup cans you may recognise. He was a leading figure in the artistic movement of Pop Art, which deliberately and ironically took the idea of popular consumerism and used it to both question wider American society and embrace it. It was highly subversive. Musicians such as Lou Reed and The Rolling Stones arose as part of this movement, as did the Steppenwolf Theatre Company. The influence of Pop Art continues to today; for instance, Barack Obama's famous 'HOPE' poster for his 2007 presidential campaign uses Pop Art imagery.

Links: Pop Art

Physical education (PDHPE) and the Arts

There are clear links to the discipline of physical education (PE) in drama and dance. For drama in particular, through role-play and character development, students must concentrate on the control of coordination of their bodies, which transfers to physical athleticism and control in sport. Music, drama and dance all offer practical awareness of the application of health knowledge, and visual art life drawing creates awareness of the physicality of the self.

For all the Arts, personal development (PD) can be used as stimulus for creative works. In addition, the collaborative nature of the Arts allows students to develop deep understanding of social understanding in a 'praxis' method.

TEACHER TIP

Forming groups within a classroom can be a challenge. How do you create balanced groups without students feeling targeted or excluded? One method is to develop a culture of unpredictability. Randomising the process of putting children into groups can help to ensure that children don't feel targeted or excluded.

For instance, place students together in groups because they have similar hairstyles, or shoes, or birthdays. Vary it continually. You can create groups based on pedagogical purpose (e.g. because children each bring different skills or they have similar levels of ability) but use the random reasons as the justification. This way students will avoid creating limiting expectations of their potential success. It also allows you to ensure that no student is isolated through lack of friendship groups, or because of their ethnicity, disability etc. An added bonus is that it can create a sense of engagement and fun as the students try to find the 'silly' reason for the group formation despite the fact you have a more serious purpose behind it.

Technology and the Arts

Technology covers several creative domains: manufacturing, IT, food science and fashion design being just some examples. All have creative elements embedded and can easily have the skills from the Arts classroom applied. Technology can be seen clearly in visual art, in the designing of web pages to the video production of drama and dance performance skills. Music extends from the making of instruments as a highly specialised skill, to the emotion and mood created though soundscapes and composition in editing film, including the use of a wide variety of music apps and advanced digital recording capabilities.

Spotlight on Arts education

TIM BURTON AND SOUNDSCAPE

Tim Burton (born 1959) is probably best known as a director of movies such as *Batman* (1989), *The Nightmare Before Christmas* (1993), *Charlie and the Chocolate Factory* (2005) and *Alice In Wonderland* (2010). He started work as an animator for Disney, and then made short movies based on short stories and poems he had written. He is also an artist, with a particular 'gothic' style that has influenced the design of his major films. He is involved closely in the technical design of his films, including the settings, costumes and editing. He uses a variety of technology, from stop-motion animation to CGI. His design ideas and films are often fantastical and have an unreal element to them.

His most successful films are usually the ones where he has been given the greatest freedom to demonstrate his unique vision and style, such as *Beetlejuice* (1988) and *Corpse Bride* (2005). Burton's sketches and concept designs for his movies are available to view online. Look at them in relation to final stills from his completed movies. What elements does he use to create his own identifiable style?

Consider how the use of technology would have affected his approach to filmmaking. For instance, while Burton used stop motion for both *The Nightmare Before Christmas* and *Corpse Bride*, he also incorporated CGI into the latter film, due to advances in CGI technology between 1993 and 2005. How might technological advances affect films made in the coming decades?

Link: Tim Burton's goofy gothic

Language and the Arts

Languages are about the communication and expression of an indiviual, whether you are using your mother tongue or learning a completely new language. The Arts are core to language development as they can help children communicate subtlety of meaning or even offer a translation through visual semiotics. In support, new languages can be a way of developing a deeper understanding of all the Arts. Together they can lead to a fuller understanding of the cornucopia of cultures and societies across the world. Through clear communication, knowledge and understanding of different cultures, global society can thrive. Thus, language is embedded in the Arts and vice versa.

> **Reflection activity**
>
> We can engage with many different aspects of other cultures, but one that seems to work across languages is that of the 'comic' book. In particular, the French-language bande Dessinée of France and Belgium allow for comics that move beyond unrealistic (and often violent) images and use humour in visual art to understand other languages.
>
> Look at the two images from the Asterix book *Asterix and the Picts* (2013), one in French and one in English.
>
> Compare the images that create meaning without the need for dialogue.
>
> Now look at both the French and English versions; you'll see that word meanings can become easier to understand, as well as being contextual and fun.
>
> The Arts support communication and language development through the visual semiotics that offer contextual meaning to language that can be 'lost in translation'.
>
> Links: *Asterix and the Picts*

Conclusion

The need to express ourselves is one of the most important things in life. The Arts offer many opportunities for children to express themselves, to explore their identity and society and achieve individual transformation and liberation, as described in the praxial vision first introduced in Chapter 1. By embracing the freedom and challenges that the Arts offer, and by developing the fundamental core skills, the general capabilities and the key competencies, children can be nurtured to reach their fullest potential. Creativity is not just something innate; it can be taught. By interacting with the Arts and integrating the Arts fully and authentically into all that you do in the classroom, children will be engaged, focused and intellectually and emotionally stimulated, making your job easier as children take control and discover new paths to success. The children will enjoy learning; you will enjoy learning. Everyone reaches their potential. Everyone lives!

REVIEW QUESTIONS

1. Why has Australia introduced 'key competencies' in its curriculum?
2. What are main similarities between the Scottish 'core skills' and the Australian 'general capabilities'?
3. What are the dangers of 'curriculum integration'?
4. What are the benefits of 'curriculum integration'?
5. How can the Arts support behaviour management in a classroom?
6. Explain the role of the Arts in multiliteracies.

RECOMMENDED READING

Ashman, A. and Elkins, J. (eds), (2012). *Education for Inclusion and Diversity*. Sydney: Pearson.

Beane, J. A. (1995). 'Curriculum integration and the disciplines of knowledge'. *Phi Delta Kappa* 76(8), 616–22.

Ewing, R. (2010). *The Arts and Australian Education: Realising Potential*. Camberwell, Vic.: Australian Council for Educational Research. Retrieved from research.acer.edu.au/aer/11/.

Florian, L. and Black-Hawkins, K. (2011). 'Exploring inclusive pedagogy'. *British Educational Research Journal*, 37(5), 813–28.

Gardner, H. (1982). *Art, Mind and Brain: A Cognitive Approach to Human Development*. New York: Basic Books.

Haberman, M. (1994). 'The pedagogy of poverty versus good teaching'. In E. Hatton (ed.), *Understanding Teaching: Curriculum and the Social Context of Schooling*. Sydney: Harcourt Brace Jovanovich.

Keeffe, M. and Carrington, S. (2007). *Schools and Diversity*. Frenchs Forest, NSW: Pearson.

Macintyre, C. (2009). *Dyspraxia 5–14*. Abingdon: David Fulton Publishers.

Robinson, K. (2011). *Out of Our Minds: Learning to Be Creative*, 2nd edn. New York: Capstone.

Roy, D. (2016). 'Implementing a cross-curricular approach', *Teacher*, [2016](5).

—— (2017). 'Integrating Arts and Science in the classroom'. *Teacher*, [2017](10).

Sowell, T. (2001). *The Einstein Syndrome*. New York: Basic Books.

10

Organisation

> Ma te huruhuru ka rere te manu. (Without feathers the bird cannot fly.)
>
> Maori proverb

In this chapter

If we approach Arts education as we might approach literacy, we would aim to develop Arts literacy in students. We would teach students the tools of language, ways of constructing meaning, vocabulary, structures, forms, genres and shaping cultural and social contexts. In literacy we allow children freedom to gain confidence and experiment with creative writing, but we also intervene when necessary to correct, guide and teach them explicit skills and knowledge. If we apply this approach to the Arts, then, rather than stand back and 'let the child be free', we focus on developing proficiency in knowledge and skills as well as fostering creativity and imagination right from the start. As with any other Learning Area, child engagement and achievement in the Arts are determined by exposure to ongoing, sequential learning experiences. This chapter suggests ways in which teachers can achieve this in a way that is respectful of the needs and interests of the child.

By the end of this chapter you should have a clear understanding of:
- different approaches to planning for learning and teaching in the Arts, including quality teaching (QT) and an inquiry approach
- the value of colleagues, parents and the community and their contributions when organising learning and teaching in the Arts
- different approaches to the assessment of learning and teaching in the Arts in education
- different approaches to learning and teaching the Arts in early childhood and primary settings.

Introduction

This chapter presents a systematic approach to planning for Arts learning and teaching that incorporates the principles of quality teaching. Sotiropoulou-Zormpala (2012) describes three different approaches to learning and teaching in the Arts:

- teaching the Arts
- teaching through the Arts
- aesthetic teaching.

We outline these and discuss issues surrounding assessment in Arts learning and teaching. The unique characteristics of organisation for learning in the Arts in early childhood and primary settings are explored and we suggest practical ideas for managing space, materials, equipment and time.

Planning for learning and teaching in the Arts

Planning means deciding exactly what the children will learn and thinking about how you will know what they have learned. When you consider planning for learning and teaching in the Arts, it is important to have an understanding of what your curriculum documents require. The Australian Curriculum (ACARA, 2017), and the curriculum documents that have been shaped by it, provide organisers, which give a consistent structure for early and primary years. Making and responding are the broad organisers across the five arts subjects (dance, drama, media arts, music and visual arts) but each has its own specific language, concepts and processes.

To ensure quality outcomes for children, planning for learning and teaching in the Arts should be framed by the eight characteristics of quality Arts programs outlined in Chapter 1. Quality programs include:

- sequential learning planned to enable growth in Arts making and responding
- sustained learning from preschool
- substantial learning in the five Arts domains of dance, drama, media arts, music and visual arts
- child-centred teaching
- the child as an active learner
- authentic activities and processes
- inclusion of children of all abilities
- approaching the Arts from diverse cultural perspectives.

These characteristics are useful, as they provide you with a broad framework for planning and reflecting on both the content and processes of the Arts learning experiences you are providing your students. This list of characteristics may also be used as a checklist in your planning, as shown in Table 10.1. Please note that this planning checklist should be used when structuring learning over a period of time, such as for a unit of work, or over a term or semester of learning. Therefore, characteristic three – substantial learning in the five Arts domains of dance, drama, media arts, music and visual arts – may occur over a whole unit of work or period of learning. This list should not be regarded as a checklist for individual learning activities. Table 10.1 is based on an extended unit of learning.

TABLE 10.1 CHARACTERISTICS OF QUALITY IN AN EXTENDED UNIT OF WORK

Arts program characteristics	Present in unit
1 Sequential learning planned to enable growth in Arts making and responding.	Learning in media arts builds on existing skills and understandings, and includes making (the movie) and responding (to the mural and creating audio).
2 Sustained learning from preschool.	Building on the knowledge of using media to tell stories.
3 Substantial learning in the five Arts domains of dance, drama, media arts, music and visual arts.	Music: creating a soundscape and considering rhythm and pitch. Visual arts: observational drawing, using recycled materials to create a mural.
4 Child-centred teaching.	Children work individually and collaboratively on a range of tasks.
5 Treating the child as an active learner.	Children learn by making art and sharing their work with others. They learn about ecosystems as they research and create. They learn about using media to influence an audience.
6 Authentic activities and processes.	Each learning activity contains authentic processes.
7 Inclusion of children of all abilities.	Because tasks are open-ended, children of all abilities may work at these in their own time and space.
8 Approaching the Arts from diverse cultural perspectives.	Children explored traditional Indigenous stories from the area.

In the classroom

ANY AGE GROUP

Greg was asked to find a way to integrate the Arts and science. The children were studying ecosystems.

Year 1 content descriptor:
- Living things live in different places where their needs are met (ACSSU211).

Year 7 content descriptor:
- Interactions between organisms, including the effects of human activities can be represented by food chains and food webs (ACSSU112).

The unit was planned for lessons over seven weeks.

Greg chose to focus on media arts.

The aim was for the children to use arts-based pedagogies to observe and research a healthy local ecosystem and to create a video and soundscape that had a strong message about the way humans damage ecosystems and how to repair that damage. The outcome was to be a movie documenting the creation of a large mural that depicted a healthy ecosystem then gradual damage through to a dead ecosystem and then revival.

The materials used were to be all recycled fabrics, containers, paper etc.

The children started by taking digital images of a local ecosystem and drawing the plants and animals that they found. When drawing the subjects, they used observation to notice details.

They researched the heritage of the land and heard Aboriginal stories about the school site from a local Elder.

Greg sourced three large wooden panels (from a local timber store) and the children began designing and creating a mural.

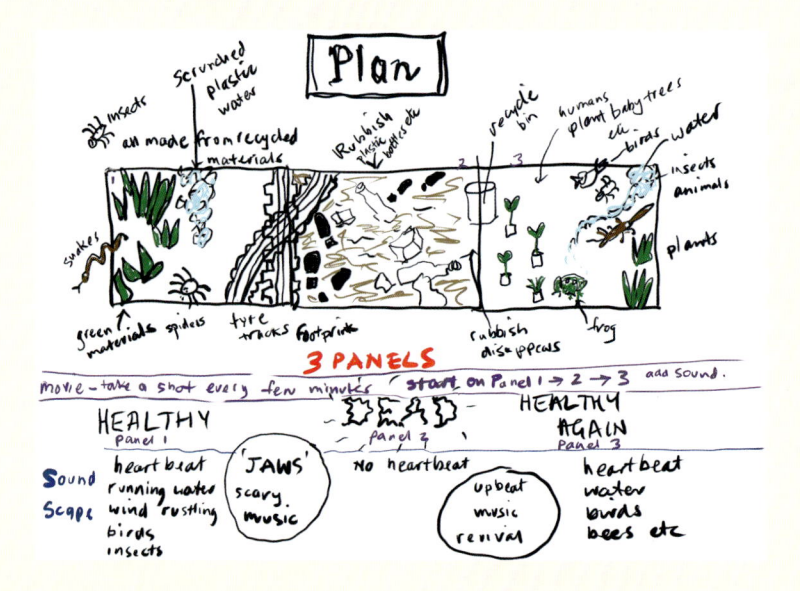

The first panel depicts a healthy ecosystem. They collaborated to use the recycled materials to create creatures and plants and environment such as water, rocks, holes etc.

As they developed the mural, the children recorded the progress of the mural (a still shot every few minutes). They built on previous learning in media arts about using digital media.

Gradually rubbish was added, then footprints then tyre tracks and finally the middle panel became a dead wasteland.

After brainstorming and researching ways to repair the damage, the students started to depict the removal of rubbish and gradual planting of new trees and grasses. By the end of the final panel the ecosystem was starting to look healthy again.

They worked collaboratively to edit the movie and then brainstormed and collected sounds to produce an audio track for the movie. The whole process involved responding as well as making. They recorded bird and insect noises, water noises and considered music elements such as rhythm and pitch, discussing what sort of sound expresses a dead ecosystem versus a healthy one. (One suggestion was a heartbeat for a healthy one and a scary rhythm for the damaged ecosystem).

When the movie was complete, they showed it to a school community audience.

Media arts:
- Plan, produce and present media artworks for specific audiences with awareness of responsible media practice (ACAMAM06).
- Plan, produce and present media artworks for specific audiences and purposes using responsible media practice (ACAMAM064).

Music:
- Develop technical and expressive skills in singing and playing instruments with understanding of rhythm, pitch and form in a range of pieces, including in music from the community (ACAMUM089).

The first thing to consider when planning is pedagogy that promotes intellectual quality and is deliberately designed to produce deep understandings of important concepts, skills and ideas. This deep learning is consistent with the Anderson and Krathwohl (2001) taxonomy of higher-order thinking.

No matter what the subject matter is, the way children learn is as important as what they learn. Regardless of the pedagogical approach a teacher uses, they have the responsibility to make every learning experience positive and productive for all learners. To do this, teachers need to take a systematic approach to planning. Short-term and long-term planning should incorporate principles of quality teaching (Killen, 2009). Most sources suggest three dimensions of quality teaching: teaching that is based on promoting high levels of intellectual quality, that promotes a quality learning environment and that makes explicit to students the significance of their work (Department of Education and Training, 2008; Gore et al., 2013; Yeigh, 2008).

The second thing to consider is the learning environment. The classroom should feel safe and comfortable, both physically and psychologically. There should be a focus on meaningful, challenging goals and there should be high levels of expectation in achievements and in behaviour that develops positive relationships between children and teachers, and between children and their peers. This involves explicit quality criteria so that everyone understands the difference between doing excellent and poor work. Child-centred learning and the child as an active participant and learner are the characteristics of quality Arts programs that are most evident when considering the learning environment.

To make learning significant for children, teachers needs to consider their own personal beliefs and ensure that they make connections with the children. Knowledge of the child prior to learning, any cultural and social differences, diversity of learning preferences, and the individual interests of children can all help you, as teacher, to make learning more meaningful to children. The characteristics of quality Arts programs most evident when striving to create a significant learning experience are the provision of learning that is 'inclusive' of all children and of learning that reflects cultural diversity. The knowledge and experience of the teacher should also be taken into account.

An inquiry approach

You should be familiar now with the various approaches to teaching the different art forms, and there is further discussion of these approaches in the next section of this chapter. Teaching inquiry focuses on the strategies that will best ensure that children learn what is intended. An inquiry approach to teaching and learning the Arts, therefore, should be based on the relevant curriculum documents and should be aligned with the relevant characteristics of quality Arts education, and your knowledge of your students and community.

An inquiry approach to learning the Arts is concerned with the *process* of the learning rather than the final product. Learning inquiry focuses on what has been learned, how it has been learned, and what needs to occur next. Assessment is therefore an imperative component of learning inquiry and will be discussed in more detail later in this chapter.

Child-centred learning and teaching begins and ends with the child and, as we discussed in Chapter 1, all children bring prior experiences to their learning in the Arts. There are therefore some important questions that should be asked before you start planning. Table 10.2 presents some of these for your reflection.

TABLE 10.2 WHAT YOU SHOULD KNOW OR FIND OUT ABOUT YOUR STUDENTS	
What are their interests and cultural backgrounds?	• Do they have an interesting cultural background to share? • Do any of the children have cultural reasons for not participating, e.g. religious? • What activities do they enjoy? • What arts, hobbies, games or sports do they already participate in?
What Arts skills do they have?	• Do they participate in Arts activities outside the regular timetable, e.g. music lessons, drama classes, dance classes or an art club? • Media: Do they have access to media, e.g. computer, iPad? Are they already familiar with technology? • Music: What music do they like to listen to? What do they like to sing? Do they have lessons in an instrument? Do they play in a band or sing in a choir? • Visual arts: Can they draw from observation? What materials are they familiar with? Can they handle the tools and materials, e.g. clay, construction or cutting? • Will the lesson be too easy so that they lose interest, or so difficult for them that they will be discouraged?
What do they know about artists?	• Which artists do they know about and like? • Do they have any historical and cultural knowledge about these artists and their art, or do they just like them?

TABLE 10.2 (Cont.)

What is their Arts vocabulary?	• Do they express their understandings in Arts language, such as 'rhythm' or 'shape'?
	• What art and design principles do they know?
	• Will they be able to understand the Arts concepts being taught?
At what stage of physical and cognitive artistic development are the children?	• Do they make typical pictures, sculptures etc. for their age?
	• How many are more advanced?
	• How many are less advanced?
	• How enthusiastic are they?
	• Are there different abilities that should be considered?
	• Do they have different preferred ways of working, e.g. visual, kinaesthetic or musical?

As discussed in Chapter 1, the Arts offer unique vehicles for the inclusion of parents and the community in the process of teaching and learning. Table 10.3 extends the process of establishing what you should know or find out in order to plan for Arts learning to the specific learning and teaching environment of your school or centre, and your parent and community stakeholders. Reflect on some of these questions and ways in which you may establish what these stakeholders could assist with.

TABLE 10.3 WHAT DO YOU KNOW ABOUT YOUR SCHOOL AND COMMUNITY?

What expertise do your colleagues possess?	• Is there a specialist(s) employed? • How often and for how long do they teach your students? • What are their aims for the year for your students? • How can you link in with what they are already planning? • How can you extend what they are teaching into your classroom? • Are there gaps in what is being provided in specialist classes? E.g. is there a music specialist, but no other Arts specialists? • Do your colleagues have skills and interests in any of the Arts? How can you use these skills with your students? • Are all the other teachers committed to teaching the Arts in their programs?
What are the facilities in the school, centre and community?	• Are there dance, drama, media arts, music or visual art spaces in the school or in the community that could be accessed? • Are there any musical instruments in the school that can be used? Is there a library of CDs and audio equipment available? • Is there a wet area, drying racks, storage space, a kiln; are there easels? • Is there paint, paper, brushes, printmaking equipment, clay, palettes, or rags? • Are there clothes and props that could be used in dramatic play? • What resources exist in the library: books, internet resources, CDs and CD-ROMs; are the computers media equipped?
Parents and the community	• Are there significant dates in the school or community calendar that may provide opportunities for your students to learn? • Is there somewhere in the school, centre or community where the children's work can be performed or exhibited? • Do any of the parents have Arts skills and interests and are they willing to visit the school or centre? • Are any of the parents from different cultural backgrounds and if so, are they willing to visit the school or centre? • Are there community groups and Arts or cultural organisations that provide education events or opportunities? Local galleries can provide an ideal opportunity. • What supplies can you ask parents to collect: paper, jars, CDs, books? Check with your school/state policy on using recyclable goods in school. • Are there any local businesses that could provide useful resources – scrap materials, donations, paint, brushes – or that would sponsor an Arts project?

Approaches to learning and teaching in the Arts

Teachers need to be reflective about their own past experiences and to be aware of the diverse backgrounds and needs of the children in their classroom. Consider that the different ways in which children like to learn this may vary according to personality, approaches to processing information or preferences for social interaction (Colak, 2015). Effective learning happens when the instructional process is compatible with these preferences.

There are three key underlying approaches to learning and teaching in the Arts: teaching the Arts (teaching specific arts content and skills such as role-play, or use of voice in drama); teaching through the Arts (the Arts are used as a way of teaching other subject area content as well as Arts content); and aesthetic teaching (Sotiropoulou-Zormpala, 2012). **Aesthetic teaching** is when children develop a way of thinking in the Arts and a deep understanding of what it means to have quality Arts experiences or an awareness of beauty or the quality in a work of art which evokes some sort of special awareness in the viewer. This involves using in-depth Arts knowledge to notice specific aspects about a work of art. This could be noticing the details of a well-executed leap in dance (i.e. noticing the line of the toes with the hip, and the location of the body's centre during the leap) or being aware of the way facial expression has been employed to express emotion in a dramatic play.

Aesthetic teaching: when children develop a certain method of thinking in and about the Arts; they develop a deep understanding of what it means to have quality Arts experiences and an awareness of beauty or appreciation of the quality in a work of art which evokes some sort of special awareness in the viewer.

Spotlight on Arts education

GARDNER'S THEORY OF MULTIPLE INTELLIGENCES

We should consider the way we tailor our teaching style to improve learning. Gardner's theory gives some useful examples of ways of learning that link closely with **Arts-based pedagogies**.

The Theory of Multiple Intelligences (MI) was developed by Howard Gardner in 1983. This theory suggests that the traditional idea of intelligence based on an IQ measurement is too limited. Gardner proposed eight different intelligences to account for a more diverse range of human potential. His theory helped to celebrate skills that were often undervalued in the traditional schooling system, where the focus tends to be on literacy, numeracy and logical thinking. MI encourages children (and adults) who have preferences for learning or demonstrating their knowledge in other ways, such as through images or diagrams, or music, or physically (for example, in role-play).

Arts-based pedagogies: a pedagogical approach where one or more art form is used to deepen understanding in a non-Arts subject as well as in the Arts subject. Children are engaged in learning the Arts content and skills at the same time as the non-Arts content. The focus is on how students learn and engage with material rather than on a product.

The eight intelligences are as follows:
- linguistic intelligence ('word smart')
- logical-mathematical intelligence ('number/reasoning smart')
- spatial intelligence ('picture smart')
- bodily-kinaesthetic intelligence ('body smart')
- musical intelligence ('music smart')
- interpersonal intelligence ('people smart')
- intrapersonal intelligence ('self smart')
- naturalist intelligence ('nature smart').

Gardner challenged the education system that assumed that everyone learns in the same way and that a universal testing system is the appropriate way to measure this learning (Gardner, 1993). Some academics challenge Gardner's theory of multiple intelligences

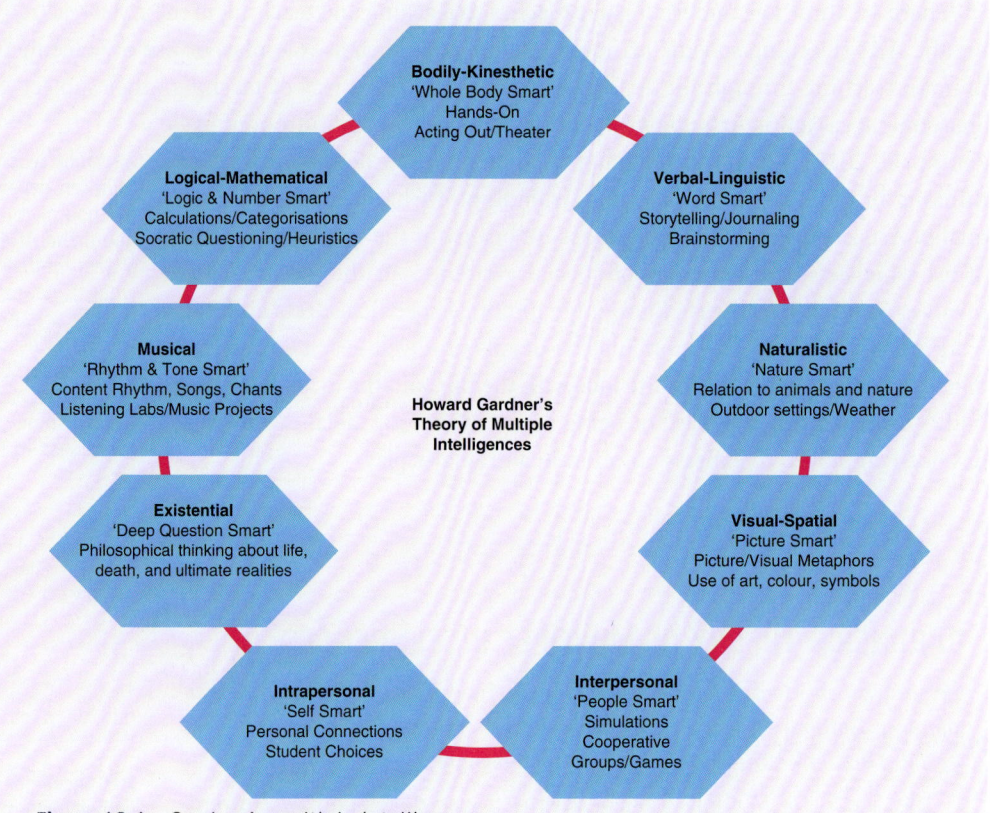

Figure 10.1 Gardner's multiple intelligences

(Jarrett, 2015; Weale, 2017; Goldhill, 2016), arguing that there is little strong evidence for the benefits of matching teaching style to preferred learning style.

The following articles discuss this:
- Multiple Intelligences theory by Gardner: myth, proven theory or philosophy?
- Howard Gardner: the myth of Multiple Intelligences
- 'Multiple intelligences' are not 'learning styles.'

What do you think of Gardner's theory? Do you have a preferred way of learning?

How could you use the MI theory in your teaching?

Even if it is a contested theory, it is still useful to be aware of different ways of learning and how the Arts offer a whole range of learning opportunities.

Links: Multiple Intelligences

It is important to be aware of these different ways of learning as you undertake your planning in Arts learning and teaching, because they are indicative of the ways your students learn.

Occasionally at the end of a semester packed with content and hands-on experiences, pre-service teachers ask: 'So how do I teach it?'. The simplest answer is, 'The same way you teach anything else.'

- You find out about the children, facilities, resources and curriculum requirements.
- Decide what you actually want to teach and think about what a successful learner would be able to do; for example, use Arts vocabulary to describe dance.
- Make decisions about how to record and report what they know (achievement).
- Look at different approaches to teaching and learning, such as teacher-directed or child-directed group work. Decide what approaches match the children's learning and abilities; for example, children enjoy doing individual research and are accustomed to discussing their findings in small groups.

Table 10.4 gives examples of good Arts teaching practice based on the Australian Curriculum. The curriculum documents suggest levels of achievement in each of the Arts, but does not state specifically *how* the Arts should be taught. These examples will be useful as you think and reflect about what you have learned so far and how you will implement your own Arts education program.

As children develop, confidence in their abilities to express themselves and respond to the Arts as well as their content and skill development become richer and more complex. Like any subject, the Arts can be taught in various ways and not every approach is appropriate for all activities. As professionals, one of the key decisions educators must make is 'how' they want children to learn. In Arts learning and teaching there is no silver bullet in this respect.

What is important is that you have a diversity of approaches from which you can draw, according to the Arts content and the individual needs and learning styles of your students. In this book you have already learned about many different types of learning activities that can be used in each art domain; Table 10.4 provides examples of some of these approaches.

TABLE 10.4 APPROACHES TO TEACHING THE ARTS

Teaching and learning approach	Example
Teacher-directed	While there is an overarching aim for Arts learning and teaching to be child-centred, there is still a role for teacher-directed learning activities as well. An example of this may be a teacher demonstrating a particular dance move, singing part of a song, or demonstrating safety instructions. These moments will always be followed up with opportunities for children to apply what has been demonstrated or presented. These should never be the norm in Arts learning and teaching; however, they are necessary even within a child-centred approach to learning in the Arts.
Child-directed	The bulk of learning that occurs in Arts education is child-directed, and occurs as the result of an open-ended task structure, often based on solving a problem. Children are given a question or a problem to solve; e.g. use dance to express the mood of a painting such as *A Sunday Afternoon on the Island of La Grande Jatte* (1884) by Georges Seurat. Children should work either individually or in groups to research, plan and develop ideas, then create their own visual artworks. Use drama to tell the story of the painting, and use music to accompany the performance of this dramatic piece.

TABLE 10.4 (Cont.)

Teaching and learning approach	Example
Group-based	As in the example above, group-based learning is a natural outcome of the process of much Arts making. Group-based learning offers opportunities for children to collaboratively solve Arts problems, share experimentations, and support each other's learning. For example, in the Arts corner of the early childhood centre, set up a prop and costume box, some musical instruments, such as xylophones, and a print of a sunset. Allow children to work collaboratively.
Whole class	Whole-class learning occurs most often when a single skill or group of skills is being taught, such as painting self-portraits or learning to sing a new song. Whole-class opportunities can also be framed as larger tasks, in which the aim is to produce an all-Arts performance or exhibition for a chosen audience; e.g. a local retirement village, or parents and friends, or schoolchildren.
Exploration	Individually or in groups explore, investigate and experiment with a concept: e.g. dance – energy; drama – role; media – technologies; music – pitch; visual arts – texture. The focus is not on the product but on the process. Materials can also be used as a starting point for the development of ideas; provide lengths of different fabrics and develop music or dance movements suggested by the colours and textures of the fabric; or, in visual arts, introduce a new material, such as marbling ink, and focus the learning on developing specific skills and understandings about how marbling works on fabrics and paper.
Integration	From your reading of Chapter 9, you will by now be familiar with the notion of integration in the Arts. Integration in the Arts is usually organised around a theme, such as healthy bodies (visual arts – human proportion/life drawing; music – rap music/ beat; dance – body as instrument; media – promoting healthy eating; drama – role-play; getting off the couch).
Learning centre	One way of ensuring musical participation in early childhood is to establish an Arts 'corner' or 'learning centre' in your space. Learning centres incorporate much of what we know about early childhood learning in music education. According to Barrett (1996), these are 'discreet physical spaces in the classroom set up to enable children to work independently of the teacher in the completion of self-paced tasks'. They have five characteristics: they are self-paced, able to allow connections to be made, self-directed, authentic and often framed as 'problem-solving'.
Guest artists and artists in residence	Guest artists can be invited to visit the school to talk about and demonstrate what they do, providing exciting and rewarding experiences for children and teachers. Also, businesses such as galleries and theatre companies provide an insight into the industry and can be invited to talk about what they do and may be interested in sponsoring an Arts activity (providing materials or prizes for fundraising activities).

Link: Musica Viva in Schools

Spotlight on Arts education

Teaching Through the Arts was an interesting initiative that was featured by the National Arts Council Education Programme in Singapore. The Council aimed to provide all students with access to quality Arts education programs.

The Teaching Through the Arts Programme saw other Learning Areas, such as maths and history, being taught through the Arts. This helped students to develop a deeper understanding of concepts in non-Arts subjects through a range of Arts-based pedagogies and gave the students the opportunity to learn through visualisation and by acting ideas out and being creative.

Video: Teaching Through the Arts Programme

288 ■ PART 3 HOW: EMBEDDING THE ARTS IN EDUCATION

Spotlight on Arts education

In Australia, the School Drama™ Classic – Primary Teacher Professional Learning Program developed by the Sydney Theatre Company involves a co-mentoring process where an actor works with a classroom teacher to develop drama-based strategies with a focus on improving student literacy and engagement.

Link: STC School Drama

Spotlight on Arts education

The US Department of Education provided funding to Wolf Trap Foundation to conduct independent research into the outcomes of students in STEM subjects who were exposed to learning in the Arts. The four-year study concluded that integration of Wolf Trap's Arts program enhanced students' ability in maths. The program was also found to enhance teacher practice.

Video: STEM Learning through the Arts

Assessment in learning and teaching in the Arts

Assessment: an imperative component of learning inquiry, providing teachers with information about the progress and development of a student's learning.

Assessment is an essential part of learning. It should provide teachers with continuous, detailed information about the development of children's knowledge, skills and understandings. This information is useful when planning appropriate learning activities. Assessment also gives feedback to children. Formative assessment, or assessment for learning, lets children know what they are doing well and what they could do to improve. Summative assessment, usually conducted at the end of learning, gives an indication of what the children have learned, but it is important that the assessment tasks are relevant, meaningful and appropriate to the Arts skills and understandings.

Another common question often asked by pre-service teachers at the end of a semester is 'How do I assess in the Arts?'. There seems to be a misconception among many pre-service teachers that, because artistic creations are personal expressions of an individual, they cannot be assessed – that it is somehow wrong to do so. This couldn't be further from the truth. As with any other Learning Area, children's progress in the Arts must be monitored and assessed rigorously in order to enable children to improve in their learning. The fact that artworks created by children are often intensely personal expressions of their own worlds does not make this any less important or any less possible. As in literacy or numeracy, what is assessable in the Arts includes:

- *Skills and understandings.* As you have learned, each art form has different skills and understandings that develop through learning and teaching. Elements, processes, codes and conventions and how these are used by children are central to this.
- *Products.* These refer to the completed pieces by children, including songs, dances, dramatic works, movies, paintings or drawings, just to name a few.
- *Individual dispositions.* How do children engage with the Arts activity? Are they collaborative? Do they share freely? Do they demonstrate application to the task? Do they demonstrate resilience with criticism?

As in any other Learning Area, there is much to assess in Arts learning and teaching, so the key decisions to be made by the professional educator are: 'What' do I choose to assess? and 'How' do I choose to assess it?

'What' is valued and important, and hence important to assess; it may be found in your curriculum documents and your own planning and program that are based on these. It is likewise extremely important that we do not 'over-assess' our children to the point where assessment leads learning. Assessment is an aspect of learning, not an end in itself. In the Arts, the artistic 'products' made by children lend themselves to assessment, because they are expressions of what has been learned and applied by the children. So, a musical composition created and performed by a child reflects what a child knows and can do at that time in music. Similarly, a painting by a child reflects what a child knows and can do at that time in visual arts. These products therefore offer teachers a multilayered means of assessment. For example, the musical composition and performance can assess children's use of all the musical elements and specific processes that comprise composing and performing. If an audience is involved, then listening can also be assessed. The importance of this example is that many different skills, techniques and understandings may often be assessed in the same task, and the danger of 'over-assessing' children can be avoided by using multidimensional assessment tasks.

'How' you choose to assess children's learning in the Arts includes consideration of the requirements of assessment: is it formative or summative? Formative assessment in the Arts often occurs through child–teacher informal interactions as learning is taking place. Summative assessment is usually more formal and includes some form of written feedback. Arts assessment requires a breadth of assessment techniques and strategies, and also requires learner agency in understanding and accepting assessment procedures. These strategies may include journal reflections on process, peer feedback on performance, visual diary work as a portfolio of process, a finished piece of art, a finished performance for an audience, audience feedback, and the child's self-assessment against criteria. This may be achieved through negotiated assessment tasks or by simply having a conversation about assessment and the criteria that may be used.

TEACHER TIP

Authentic Arts learning: learning in which the Arts concept or skill to be learned is explicit and Arts-specific. For example, the project may be painting a backdrop for a play. The Arts learning is learning how to use colour and lines (linear perspective) to create depth on a two-dimensional surface (canvas or paper).

Planning for learning should involve the development of clear aims and descriptive outcomes and ensure that the proposed learning and assessment is an **authentic** Arts skill or understanding. Once this is established, the teacher can describe what successful learning will look like. From this clear description, assessment criteria can be established. The case study in the next section demonstrates the ways in which criteria for assessment may be developed once the Arts learning is clear.

What is being assessed? – a case study

This case study looks at how a teacher can assess the development of two students through the Arts. It focuses on two students, Babz and Aimz, who were asked to draw a self-portrait each week for several weeks.

Figure 10.2 Babz

Figure 10.3 Babz's self-portrait

Figure 10.4 Aimz

Figure 10.5 Aimz's self-portrait

Preliminary assessment

A common question is 'How would you assess these drawings?'. You could first look at the artistic skills presented, such as:

- use of proportion
- observation skills
- use of expression
- colour mixing skills
- use of materials (pencils, computer)
- art history (development of portraiture)
- genre (type of artwork i.e. portraits)
- use of colour mixing.

As you can see, Aimz's drawing possesses more artistic skills, so she should be marked more favorably. But assessing only the artistic skills is not enough to fully assess the development of a student.

Second-level assessment

Other aspects to consider when assessing the arts:

Attitude to work
- How did they approach the work?
- Were they enthusiastic and engaged during the task or bored?
- Were they nervous about the task or confident?
- If there was group work, did they work well in a group?

Ability
- Were they able to follow processes and instructions?
- Were they happy to experiment?
- Did they use materials effectively and safely?
- Did their skills increase?

Reflection
- Were they able to talk about what they did and the choices they made?

As this task was conducted over a three-week period, only at the end can a full assessment be made. It looks like Babz developed her skills significantly over the three weeks, but Aimz's progression has faltered. Considering the progression of Babz and Aimz over the three weeks, would your original assessment change?

Observation and background are an essential part of assessment. The following graphic details what happened in the three weeks the task was set.

Figure 10.6 Babz's progression

Figure 10.7 Aimz's progression

They were sent to the library to do research on self-portraits.

Then they went to the computer lab to do an internet search about artists and their self-portraits.

They were asked to experiment with different media.

They were asked to explain what they did.

    With five minutes left Babz had completed a journal of reflections on what she had done and was just doing some finishing touches.

    Aimz had left it until last minute and quickly did a drawing of herself as she always does.

> Aimz's journal is empty.

This observation of the students over the three weeks provides a completely different assessment outcome from the original.

TABLE 10.5 ASSESSMENT OUTCOMES FOR BABZ AND AIMZ

Babz		Aimz	
Skill development	Good	Skill development	None
Exploration of materials	Excellent	Exploration of materials	None
Research skills	Excellent	Research skills	?
Arts response	Excellent	Arts response	?
Critical reflection	Excellent	Critical reflection	?
Motivation	High	Motivation	0

Reflection activity

Considering the above case study, what action do you think should be taken? Is the assessment of the two students fair? What should change?

Obviously Aimz has advanced skills in drawing but is totally unengaged. She needs to develop some research, writing and reflection skills.

Babz is highly motivated and is developing well in art skills and academically.

If you were the teacher what action would you take to help Aimz?

Often teachers expect children who are very good in a particular subject to help others who are struggling. This often leads to boredom and disengagement on the part of the exceptional student. It is fine for them to share what they are doing if they are comfortable, but they should not be seen as an assistant teacher.

The website 'We Are Teachers' has some useful tips for teaching students who are very good in particular subjects (often labelled 'gifted').

Lesson plan 10.1

AIM

Children in years 3–4 will understand the concept of patterns in nature and in art-making. They will learn about geometric and organic shapes. They will be introduced to Islamic art.

OVERVIEW

Children will learn about patterns and then use that knowledge to create their own.

OUTLINE/DESCRIPTION

Children will create patterns using geometric or organic shapes in their own work. Children will be introduced to artworks, in particular to patterns found in Islamic art and everyday objects, like fabrics and ceramics, that are decorated using patterns. They will find patterns in nature, collect natural objects, like leaves and shells, and draw them from observation. Then they will look for simple geometric and organic shapes and patterns and use a simple shape that is repeated to create tessellations.

Tessellation: a pattern made of identical shapes that fit together without any gaps and do not overlap.

INTENDED OUTCOMES

Students will be able to
- apply their knowledge to create patterns using geometric or organic shapes in their own work
- identify artworks and everyday objects, like fabrics and ceramics, that are decorated using patterns

- identify patterns in nature
- identify and describe Islamic artworks.

Students will
- use a simple shape that is repeated to create tessellations.

LINKS TO CURRICULUM

Years 3 and 4 content descriptors
- Use materials, techniques and processes to explore visual conventions when making artworks (ACAVAM111).

Cross-curriculum priorities – Asia and Australia's Engagement with Asia
- OI.1 The peoples and countries of Asia are diverse in ethnic background, traditions, cultures, belief systems and religions.

ASSESSMENT

To assess children's learning, describe what features an excellent outcome would have and what a satisfactory and hence unsatisfactory one would have. Table 10.6 provides an example of criteria related to this task.

TABLE 10.6 SUGGESTED ASSESSMENT CRITERIA FOR A TESSELLATIONS TASK

Understanding/ skill	Outstanding	Satisfactory	Unsatisfactory
Recognition of different shapes	Can recognise and name a variety of different geometric and organic shapes in nature and in artworks.	Can recognise and name some geometric and organic shapes in nature and in artworks.	Cannot recognise and name different geometric and organic shapes in nature and in artworks.
Drawing of objects	Demonstrates the ability to draw a variety of geometric and organic shapes.	Demonstrates the ability to draw some geometric and organic shapes.	Does not demonstrate the ability to draw geometric and organic shapes.
Understanding of tessellations	Demonstrates the ability to make a variety of different repeated patterns using shapes.	Demonstrates the ability to make some repeated patterns using shapes.	Does not demonstrate the ability to make repeated patterns using shapes.
Understanding of artist's/designer's use of pattern	Notices and describes a variety of different patterns in art/design works. Understands that most Islamic art involves patterns.	Notices and describes patterns in art/design works.	Does not demonstrate the ability to notice and describe patterns in art/design works.

Reflection activity

The Australian Curriculum provides some work samples to help teachers with assessments. Find The Arts: Dance work samples on the Australian Curriculum website. Go to the section on Choreography: Telling stories and watch the video of the students to see if you can identify the specific dance skills that are being assessed.

Link: Choreography: Telling stories

Organisation for Arts learning in early childhood settings

Teachers need to know about progression in children's development and how to support continuity in learning. Preschool children bring a wealth of learning experiences from their families and communities and are acquiring language and physical skills, but need strong emotional and practical support. Early childhood is a time of rapid growth and development. As children progress, their confidence grows and their skills develop. As they become more able to imagine and concentrate for longer periods, their ability to listen and talk increases and they become ready to extend their skills and persevere in problem-solving. Children of this age are eager for new experiences and learning, and the teacher should build on past experiences to reflect the children's needs, enthusiasms and interests.

To support progress, the early childhood educator needs to consider:
- ways to ensure continuity of learning and experiences, with each stage building on earlier knowledge and achievements

- what activities are appropriate to meet the stage of development and learning needs of the children
- how to provide a 'safe', positive environment that respects diversity and builds relationships
- what strategies are in place to encourage a positive sense of self and others.

In early childhood, the focus in Arts learning is on exploration and playful manipulation of materials, starting with the familiar: dance movements; drama roles and situations; media arts (digital and print media); music and sound, songs, chants and rhymes; and visual arts media, processes, experiences and observations. Table 10.7 provides examples for a sequential learning opportunity based on the Early Years Learning Framework and the Australian Curriculum: The Arts F–2. Three of the approaches to teaching referred to in the table are used, with suggestions for your role as teacher and general aims and outcomes for all Arts.

TABLE 10.7 SUGGESTED APPROACHES TO TEACHING THE ARTS: EARLY CHILDHOOD

Approach	Teacher	Aims	Outcomes/assessment
Exploration Making Responding	Provide opportunities for children to freely explore (sounds, movements, materials). Talk to the children as they explore.	Children use senses to explore and playfully manipulate (body movement, instruments). Children learn Arts language to describe what they do and see and understand their own preferences.	Children begin to make choices about materials, are able to talk about what they are doing, enjoy manipulating and playing creatively with various media. Children use Arts language to describe what they do and see and are able to discuss likes and dislikes.
Teacher-directed Responding	Show examples of art forms: play music, show a movie, go to a live concert, visit a gallery. Make a list of Arts language words.	Children understand that there are different art forms and that they can have an effect on our senses (enjoy the sound, make us happy, etc.). Children learn Arts language. Children learn to pay close attention to artworks.	Children can identify art forms. Children recognise difference in cultures (e.g. dance from India compared to Scottish dance). Children learn to use appropriate words to describe Arts. Children enjoy viewing Arts and describe their feelings.

TABLE 10.7 (Cont.)

Approach	Teacher	Aims	Outcomes/assessment
Group-based Responding Making	Show an artwork (e.g. a painting, cartoon, dance, music). Visit small groups and ask leading questions, such as: What do you see? What is happening? How do you feel? Record children's observations and display Arts language/words, e.g. beat, line, role. Guide children in making their own music or painting or media object or role-play or dance.	In small groups, children work together to identify simple elements in an artwork, e.g. shapes, colours, texture in a painting, different sounds/beats in music, movements in dance, camera angles in media arts, roles, props in drama.	Children use appropriate language to identify simple elements. Children work with others and share ideas. Children work with others to demonstrate their understanding of art forms and simple elements.

Reflection activity

There are many websites that provide ideas for Arts activities and exercises.

Evaluate each website and the Arts activity to see what Arts learning might take place.

Can you identify authentic Arts outcomes?

1 What to do with … Down by the Station

While this site has lots of good ideas for movement, can you identify any specific dance skills and knowledge? How could you add dance outcomes from the Australian Curriculum to this?

2 Introducing Preschool Children to Acting & Drama

Are the key drama outcomes clear? (setting, plot story etc.)

3 Pre-Kindergarten and Preschool Lesson Plans for Music Subjects

What are the children learning in this lesson? What could the explicit music outcome be? (E.g. beat?)

Links: Arts activities

Organisation for Arts learning in primary settings

Table 10.8 provides a demonstration of how Arts learning and assessment may be organised in a primary setting. The focus of this unit of work is on the concept of 'audience': how the Arts are a form of communication between artists and an audience. The role of 'audience' is a feature of both curriculum documents referred to in this book and is not a passive role, but rather has the role of a co-creator of artistic works, by observing, looking, responding or listening.

TABLE 10.8 UNIT OF WORK – ROLE OF AUDIENCE

Approach	Teacher	Children	Content
Week 1: Teacher-directed	Explain the task: record ideas (smart board). Describe the audience (e.g. other classes). Explain the time frame (10 weeks). Discuss the group work rubric.	Conduct a whole-class discussion. Brainstorm ideas. Come up with ideas for a message about sustainability. Discuss what excellent group work looks like; brainstorm possible issues and how to solve them.	Discuss 'sustainability', give examples, e.g. water use, pollution, recycling. Effective group work. Arts skills and understandings.
Week 2: Group work	Organise small groups.	Decide on a theme, e.g. cyberbullying	Storyboard: planning the 'story'.
Week 3: Group work	Organise roles and tasks.	Make group decisions about the form the performance will take, e.g. a movie clip with a song.	Discuss what the audience likes, what is interesting, what sort of message will appeal to them, what message will make them do something about the issue.
Week 4: Individual research	Help individuals to research and plan for their tasks.	Work on their own to develop their role in the performance, i.e. visual arts. (What will the performance look like? Colour themes, etc? What will the music or sounds be?)	What colours and textures fit the theme? What music or sound? What format? What media will be used? Appropriate media for the audience.
Week 5: Group work	Support groups in their preparation. Help to organise a storyline; check timing (not too long or too complex).	Develop and edit the storyboard; add details, e.g. props, sound.	Importance of editing and time awareness.
Week 6: Group work	Supervise rehearsals and provide advice as requested.	Run through the performance. Group discussion about feedback from teacher or other children.	Accepting feedback, keeping it simple.
Week 7: Group work	Make a roster for the technical equipment (tablets, etc.).	Rehearsing, editing, revising. Audience participation?	Keep refining, reviewing.
Week 8: Group work	Advise, observe.	Rehearsing, editing, revising. Audience participation?	How should the audience behave? Expected responses?

TABLE 10.8 (Cont.)

Approach	Teacher	Children	Content
Week 9: Group work	Introduce individual reflection sheets.	Rehearsing, editing, revising. Audience participation?	Preparation and rehearsal very important.
Week 10: Group work/Individual work	Organise timing for performance. Distribute reflection worksheet.	Performance. Reflect on personal achievement and response to group performance.	Reflection: what sort of response did you see/feel? How did you feel? How could you change what you did next time? What have you learned? What did you enjoy?

Lesson plan 10.2

AN INTEGRATED UNIT OF WORK AIMED AT PRIMARY YEARS 5–6

Children have been introduced to all Arts subjects in previous years and have an understanding of basic concepts and elements. For example, they can develop a dance, they have experience with movie-making and they have composed and performed many pieces of music.

The unit is designed for a class of 25 diverse Year 6 children: five groups of five to six children. Resources: five laptops, five iPads, musical instruments, basic visual arts materials, a smart board, a sound system. The unit will run over 10 weeks, allowing one hour per week with extra time as available.

AIM

Children will understand the role of the audience in art-making and responding. Children will use the Arts to express their ideas to an audience.

OVERVIEW

Children will prepare a performance with a message about cyberbullying. Their intended audience is their peers (the rest of the school).

OUTLINE/DESCRIPTION

The teacher will help the children plan a performance that encompasses all five of the Arts (music, media arts, dance, visual arts and drama) and has a message for a particular audience. They will write a script in drama (take on roles, and characterisation, use voice, movement etc.) use visuals (e.g. for a backdrop, or costume design), create music (could be simple percussion, or created on an app such as GarageBand), choreograph a simple dance that reflects cyberbullying (e.g. the shape of a bully, the swagger or sneaky walk, the feeling of being bullied). In media arts they plan a digital background with sounds.

INTENDED OUTCOMES

Children will work in small groups to prepare a short performance for a chosen audience, involving all five art forms. They will demonstrate their understanding of the role of audience as listener/viewer(s) and participant(s), and show their ability to make choices to target a specific audience. They will work collaboratively to express their ideas about a chosen theme (cyberbullying) through the five Arts subjects.

LINKS TO CURRICULUM

The Arts – Years 5 and 6 Achievement Standard

- Students structure elements and processes of arts subjects to make artworks that communicate meaning. They work collaboratively to share artworks for audiences, demonstrating skills and techniques.

> **Health and Physical Education – Years 5 and 6 Achievement Standard**
> - Students demonstrate fair play and skills to work collaboratively. They access and interpret health information and apply decision-making and problem-solving skills to enhance their own and other's health, safety and wellbeing.
>
> **ASSESSMENT**
> - The teacher records observations of child collaboration and the whole class will develop a rubric (self-peer-assessment) for effective group work.
> - Children will be able to justify their choices of materials (the content, storyline, ideas, images used) and form (role-play, mime, song, dance, comedy, news report and so on) to suit their audience.
> - This will be observed in children's individual reflections: How well did the audience respond? Did they understand the message? Did they enjoy the performance? Did they understand how to respond – clapping at the right time, observing clues? How could the performance be improved to express their idea to the audience?
>
>   At the end of the 10-week unit, the children will be able to reflect on the audience and their own responses to the performance. By writing a personal reflection, the teacher will be able to record the children's understanding of the concept of audience as both responder and maker of Arts. From teacher observations, a record will show how well each child participated and was able to express themselves individually and collaboratively in a performance setting.

Link: Sustainability

Conclusion

As in other Learning Areas, effective organisation is an important component of learning in the Arts. In this chapter you have become familiar with different approaches to planning for learning and teaching in the Arts, to learning and teaching the Arts and the assessment of learning and teaching in the Arts. Primary considerations are the characteristics of quality Arts programs and the requirements of the curriculum. Preparing an authentic Arts program requires good planning and the adaption of appropriate approaches to teaching. The importance of partnerships with colleagues, parents and the community when organising learning and teaching in the Arts has been discussed. The importance of knowing your students and school setting has been stressed as well as critical self-reflection on your own skills and knowledge and an awareness of the many excellent resources and support available to you.

When the approaches to organisation for learning outlined above are aligned with the development of your skills and understandings discussed in Chapters 4 to 8, you will be well prepared to develop a quality Arts program for your learning environment.

REVIEW QUESTIONS

1. As in any other Learning Area, child engagement and achievement in the Arts is determined by what?
2. What does effective planning mean?
3. List the two Arts organisers used in the Australian Curriculum.
4. List the five areas of knowledge about your students that should be established when organising for learning in the Arts.
5. Why is it important to know about what your colleagues, students' parents and community may contribute to the Arts in your environment?
6. Of the eight approaches to teaching the Arts in education, why are 'child-directed' and 'group-based' learning commonly used?
7. What three areas are assessable in the Arts?
8. What are the advantages of using multidimensional assessment tasks in Arts assessment?

RECOMMENDED READING

Burridge, S. (2003). *Arts-based approaches to creative teaching and learning*. Singapore: LASALLE-SIA College of the Arts.

Dorn, C. M., Sabol, R. and Madeja, S. S. (2014). *Assessing Expressive Learning: A Practical Guide for Teacher-directed Authentic Assessment in K–12 Visual Arts Education*. New York: Routledge.

Fleming, M. (2012). *The Arts in Education: An Introduction to Aesthetics, Theory and Pedagogy*. Florence, KY: Routledge, Taylor & Francis Group.

McLachlan, C., Fleer, M. and Edwards, S. (2010). *Early Childhood Curriculum: Planning, Assessment and Implementation*. Melbourne: Cambridge University Press.

Sotiropoulou-Zormpala, M. (2012). 'Aesthetic teaching: Seeking a balance between teaching Arts and teaching through the Arts'. *Arts Education Policy Review*, 113(4), 123–8.

11

Diverse learners, pedagogy and the Arts

> Education is not the filling of a pail but the lighting of a fire.
>
> William Butler Yeats

In this chapter

The previous chapters have explored the teaching methodologies and concepts related to different forms of the Arts, as well as methodologies for integration and organisation. However, in addition to being able to teach the Arts, we need to have in place a system for evaluating the teaching process to ensure that the outcomes and goals we wish to achieve are met for the learners. There has been a great deal of research to identify specific teaching practices that can improve children's outcomes. This chapter does not intend to analyse the validity or otherwise of these outcomes, as these are mandated by the various examination and education boards. In part, this is because it is difficult to isolate any specific technique or learning skill that works for individuals because all children have unique and individual learning styles. For these reasons, the focus of recent research has been to isolate general characteristics. This chapter looks at the application of reflective learning tools to enhance the teaching of the Arts, as well as inclusion and diversity in the classroom (specifically disability). Its focus, therefore, is to separate teaching from subjective assessment of teachers.

By the end of this chapter you should have a clear understanding of:

- reflective teaching
- implementing reflective practices
- valuation of quality teaching and reflective learning
- equality in the classroom and diverse learners
- how to T.E.A.C.H.

Introduction

As with any teaching area, the Arts classroom will have diverse teachers and diverse learners within it, and therefore it is important to adopt an inclusive approach. The role of a teacher is to create opportunity for learning and to allow demonstration of that learning to be made apparent so that the students can recognise their progression and development. There are multiple factors that impact upon this. A child's context and their individual disadvantages have a great impact, and as a teacher it is incumbent upon each of us to predict and prepare against potential barriers in order to support all children. Teachers also need to recognise the context of themselves that is brought to the classroom. Every individual, child and adult, has strengths, weaknesses and biases. Therefore, as a starting point, teachers need to recognise the perspective to education they bring and be reflective on the practice they present.

Reflective teaching

Before approaching the reflection of teaching practice, it is important to have an understanding of the teaching and **curriculum ideology** that a teacher has and is required to implement. A curriculum ideology (Ewing, 2010) is a set of values, attitudes and beliefs that knits together and represents the sort of vision that a person might hold in relation to curriculum. They go beyond the philosophical ('what should be') to the conceptual ('how one should behave'). Often, it is these influences that we have developed over a lifetime that support our own personal understandings of goals and expectations and often shape

> **Curriculum ideology:** a set of values, attitudes and beliefs that a person holds in relation to a curriculum.

actions and choices about teaching and learning. Here are some academic definitions of curriculum ideologies:

> 'A set of beliefs and practices that help an individual make sense of the world' (Ewing, 2010).
> 'A practical philosophy that influences educators day-to-day behaviors towards curriculum issues' (Schiro, 1992).

Schiro's (2008) four curriculum ideologies are as follows.

- *Scholar Academic:* is concerned with maintaining cultural literacy by having students study the content and modes of inquiry of traditional 'academic subjects'.
- *Social Efficiency:* conditioning students to learn the skills they need to perform as an efficient adult member of a society.
- *Learner Centered:* a 'progressive' approach that places the learner at the centre of the educational endeavour and is focused on their development into a unique individual who is healthy and has a positive self-concept.
- *Social Reconstructionist:* a 'socially critical' ideology central to which is the belief that society does not have the tools to address and fix the social problems that it faces. It believes in education's ability to change this, by developing a better vision of society and educating children to literally change the world.

Reflection activity

Complete the following multiple-choice quiz questions to help you to understand your approach to learning and pedagogy.

1 The most important task in teaching my area is:
   A teaching students core content and having them know it.
   B having students learn the skills they'll need to get a job and to fit into Australian society.
   C to help students become 'better' people – happy, confident and creative whether or not they master my course.
   D to guide students in adopting a questioning approach to social issues, using knowledge in my course to disrupt the status quo.

2 My attitude to testing/examinations is:
   A tests should always be used to measure student learning of content and that demonstration of mastery of content is important.
   B tests are an important means of sorting people and that people who do well on tests deserve better career opportunities.
   C testing is not the right method of assessing student performance in many cases and thus shouldn't be emphasised or used as the main method of assessment.
   D examinations are ok but, like any assessment, what's most important is that students have the opportunity to demonstrate independent thinking and propose creative solutions to problems.

3   Schools should be organised:

   A   into traditional subject areas, where expert teachers teach content that has been traditionally valued in the area and students master it.

   B   into traditional subject areas but more vocationally oriented than they currently are. Students should be preparing for a future career early and school subjects should teach the skills for this.

   C   so that subjects are much less strongly defined. They may still exist, but they cooperate much more with each other. Schooling should be more about the processes students go through and learning should be active and student-directed.

   D   so that a significant part of student learning in all areas is focused on social justice (making society more equal), critical thinking (independently informed, creative thinking) and proposing solutions to social, environmental and political problems (drug use, health inequalities, youth under-employment, gender inequality, Indigenous imprisonment).

Looking down your list, did you get:

Mostly 'A':   You're a *Scholar Academic* with a strong belief in the traditions of your subject area and the importance of students mastering its content and conventions.

Mostly 'B':   You like society how it is and want young people to keep that going. As an individual who applies the *Social Efficiency* ideology, you believe everyone has their place and students need to learn how to fit in and do their bit.

Mostly 'C':   You're a *Learner-centred* teacher, believing that traditional content and student knowledge of it is far less important than students becoming independent thinkers. You probably strongly believe in process-based curriculum.

Mostly 'D':   Society has problems and you want education to do something about them! *Social Reconstructionists* are focused on education's ability to produce critical thinkers who act in political ways to address society's problems.

Choose two articles from an education news website such as 'The Educator'. Read the articles and for each select two statements/ideas you agree with and two you question. Note the reasons why you agree or disagree and then consider what this tells you about your own perspective on teaching.

Link: 'The Educator'

Recent history of curriculum ideologies

1   Post 1970, as many curriculum documents and approaches have moved towards a more learner-centred model, there's been tension with those who hold academic-idealist beliefs.

2   The conservative governments in the UK, US and Australia during the late 1990s and early 2000s saw a return to conservative social values and with them, calls for curriculum to return to the content-centred approach that academic-idealists prefer.

3   Learner-centred approaches have most often been criticised as 'airy-fairy' – not clearly directed or defined. Such approaches have come under particular criticism as international testing and the comparison of education systems and student performance internationally have come into vogue.

4   Those whose major concerns are the economy and business (and the strength of these) will often have a preference for technical-rational approaches. Again, the reproduction of social values will also appeal to social conservatives – people who don't like change in society.

In Australia all educational curricula are based on the principles of **outcomes-based education (OBE)** and as such it's important that teachers understand the principles that underpin this approach, whether you feel it sits comfortably in the Arts domain or not.

The Arts use a mix of methods to implement an OBE curriculum. To fully apply **reflective teaching** skills we have to understand its context. There are three main approaches to structuring a curriculum.

Content-based: identifying the content that students have to learn; the closest model is probably Tyler's *Objectives* (Tyler, 1949).

Experience-based: identifying the experiences students will take part in, such as Stenhouse and Bruner's *Process* (Bruner, 1986).

Outcomes-based: asks 'What do we want students to be able to do by the end of their learning?'

> **Outcomes-based education (OBE):** an approach to teaching and learning in which all important decisions are guided by the outcomes we want learners to achieve (Spady, 1995).
>
> **Reflective teaching:** a teaching practice in which teachers self-assess their performance and continually strive to engage in learning and improving their teaching skills.

An outcomes-based approach:

- places emphasis on the end result of education
- leads to teachers making decisions such as, 'By the end of this lesson I want students to be able to …'
- means that all content is chosen for a particular learning purpose (and not because it seems to have inherent value).

There are four key ideas in outcomes-based education that (Spady, 1995) outlined.

- Outcomes are a statement of deep understanding. They list what a learner should be able to do or know. Outcomes are an agreed standard of achievement reached rather than a number or level in a test.
- Outcomes should recognise a significant level achieved, rather than a minor development. They should reflect required knowledge and skills to allow progression and should have a connection to the wider world and society outside of the classroom.
- Learners should demonstrate their achievements in appropriate contexts. Situations should be or at least simulate real-world settings in which learners will be expected to apply their knowledge and skills after they have finished school.
- All students should be expected to demonstrate high-quality learning – deep understanding, high levels of competence. Some criticisms of OBE suggest it is

a 'dumbing down' approach because it doesn't emphasise mastery of essential content. However, Spady's OBE stresses that all students should be capable of high performance, rather than assuming that some will fail (as is often the case in norm-referenced systems).

Implementing reflective practices

The Australian Institute for Teaching and School Leadership (AITSL) has mandated professional standards for all teaching staff. There are seven standards, all with different levels of accomplishment.

1 Know students and how they learn.
2 Know the content and how to teach it.
3 Plan for and implement effective teaching and learning.
4 Create and maintain supportive and safe learning environments.
5 Assess, provide feedback and report on student learning.
6 Engage in professional learning.
7 Engage professionally with colleagues, parents/carers and the community.

There is no question that in learning, teachers make a difference. John Hattie's study of factors involving teacher learning impact upon students found that teachers were the highest factor affecting student learning, after the students themselves being a factor (Hattie, 2008). Jeroen Imants' research into teacher development that impacts the classroom looked at inclusive and special education professional development and found that schools were the key to successful implementation of professional development, through supporting staff, and that the role of feedback and collaborative work between teachers allowed for more sustainable success in lasting implementation of development (Imants, 2002). It is therefore apparent that self-reflection combined with teacher-to-teacher collaboration, which engages teachers in action research, is important for teachers to continually develop their practice to achieve improvement in student learning.

Schnellert, Butler and Higginson (2008) demonstrated that the outcome potentials of projects and how teachers responded to professional development determine the success or otherwise experienced by the participants as to the relevance of their practical work and being given opportunities to engage in discussion and implementation. Beatrice Avalos (2011) reviewed research into teacher professional development, and confirmed that much of the research demonstrates that the professional development teachers find effective usually involves practical engagement, collaboration and application where the whole school is engaged in the reform/development, and progress is continually reviewed.

Ponte, Beijaard and Wubbels (2004) examined the development of teachers' professional knowledge through 'action research':

> Action research is geared to teachers' own practice and the situation in which they are practicing. In action research teachers engage in reflection based on information that they have systematically gathered themselves.

In this form of professional development, the teachers take responsibility for goals, as it is purposeful (Ponte et al., 2004). Ponte and her colleagues found that teachers respond with greater depth to professional development when facilitators asked open questions. All of this points to a need for teachers to embrace a pedagogical reflective tool such as Productive Pedagogies or Quality Teaching in conjunction with the development of their curriculum knowledge.

Observation

Planning will help. Make sure there is a clear understanding of what is going to be observed (such as how interactions with a student happen, or use of teaching materials). Try to have clear goals of what the observation is for. In addition, make sure you talk before the observation and set time as soon as possible afterwards to discuss the lesson observed. Participants must trust one another and feel comfortable with each other. It is worth investing time in having a coffee together (or equivalent) as a purely social activity before any observations are initiated.

> **TEACHER TIP**
>
> Observing others and being observed can be a stressful event for all involved. The key thing to remember is that it is intended to highlight how to be the best you can be. To be truly effective, teacher observation needs to be separate from performance management. The only purpose it plays is for those concerned to learn more about their teaching and to get better at it.

If you are observing, make sure any comments you make start with the strengths and positives of a lesson. Remember that every lesson has strengths and every lesson can be improved. Basically this is a formalising of the reflection that all teachers do after every lesson – 'What worked?' 'What could have been better?'. The more you partake in classroom observation, the easier it becomes. As teachers we should have nothing to hide. We are being observed by our own classes every minute already.

Jenlink and Kinnucan-Welsch (2001) found the same with their specific case studies. Those teachers who engage with reflective tools collaboratively also demonstrate greater change in practice and an ownership of the learning that they both implemented and adapted to achieve greater success with their students. The clear trend through all of this is the need for good communication between all colleagues, an openness and honesty with trust. These are the same precepts that professional learning communities also require (Bowe, Gore & Elsworth, 2010). Starkey's research found that a strong focus on needs of participants, understanding of participants, contexts, keeping people focused and preparing key program goals and objectives resulted in the most positive professional development experiences (Starkey et al., 2009).

Hilda Borko of the University of Colorado complements Starkey's research. She recognises the ultimate role of teachers needing to lead change through desire to have change (Borko, 2004). Borko places an emphasis on the need for strong professional learning communities. Professional learning communities are important tools to implement in collaboration because they can foster and grow teacher improvements, and the group as a unit can analyse, interpret and implement change from the findings of the action research. Borko also places emphasis upon records of classroom practice, case studies and staff feedback/discussion within the collaborative process.

Understanding quality teaching and reflective learning

Using a reflective tool to assess the quality of teaching in a classroom is not a panacea for schools and teaching. Rather, it is a tool or framework that enables direct reflection and allows teachers to engage in conversations about pedagogy and to codify elements of practice (Department of Education and Training, 2003a, 2003b). The goal is to create a system for teachers to target areas of teaching and learning in order to improve children's achievement (Gore, 2007). The real benefit of using a reflective tool is that it is not about teachers, but about teaching.

> If pedagogy is to improve significantly, teachers need a clear set of concepts as to what constitutes good practice with specific details about what that practice looks like and this set of concepts needs to be framed as support for teacher development, not as a system for judging relative performance (Gore, 2007, p. 16).

If we are to apply the learning in this text, it is useful to have a tool to measure the success of learning goals. One such study of looking at the quality of teaching in classrooms was the Systemic Implications of Pedagogy and Achievement (SIPA), conducted in New South Wales between 2003 and 2007 (Amosa et al., 2007; Ladwig et al., 2007). Creative and Performing Arts (CAPA) was one of the Key Learning Areas (KLAs) that was not commented on in detail. Another study, *Effective Implementation of Pedagogical Reform* (EIPR), explored the implementation of quality teaching as professional development (Bowe et al., 2010).

In many of these studies there have been clear areas of focus that are not always seen in classrooms but do appear to be engaged with to a greater extent when the Arts are taught.

Problematic knowledge

> To what extent are students encouraged to address multiple perspectives and/or solutions? To what extent are students able to recognise knowledge as constructed and therefore open to question? (Department of Education and Training, 2003a, p. 16)

Setting a problem is not problematic knowledge in itself. However, as soon as the basis of knowledge is questioned, then problematic knowledge is apparent. This may be in exploring issues and morals in media, or even in examining the differences between fact and fiction and the point of view in a film as shown in the way it is edited (Ellis, 1982). In *Toy Story 2*, the character Stinky Pete is seen as a bad character who tries to stop Woody and Jessie from being played with, as he doesn't like children. However, if we saw the film from a different perspective, we could say that Woody is being selfish, as he wants to be played with even though his owner Andy will grow up, whereas Stinky Pete knows they will be appreciated in a museum and not be thrown away. Neither viewpoint is wrong, but it is important to be aware of both of them.

Higher-order thinking

> To what extent are students regularly engaged in thinking that requires them to organise, re-organise, apply, analyse, synthesise and evaluate knowledge and information? (Department of Education and Training, 2003a, p. 18)

In most creative activities – those that do not just require the transportation of information (repeating given knowledge) – higher-order thinking is present. This can be as simple as synthesising tempo, rhythm and fingering (or breath) in performing a piece of music for an audience.

Spotlight on Arts education

Higher-order thinking is the basis of the Arts. We take multiple pieces of information and 'create' something new from it. If an Arts-based lesson does not have a high level of higher-order thinking, then the chances are it did not involve any meaningful Arts education. If you look at the revised Bloom's Taxonomy listed in Chapter 9, you will note that 'create, plan, compose, construct, design, imagine, devise, combine, originate, etc', are activities associated with higher-order thinking.

Student self-regulation

> To what extent do students demonstrate autonomy and initiative so that minimal attention to the disciplining and regulation of student behaviour is required? (Department of Education and Training, 2003a, p. 34)

In the Arts, we often have multiple learning situations happening at once, and therefore children need to have the skills to be able to work and behave autonomously. If children are using a variety of materials in visual arts, there needs to be strong organisation. As explored in Chapter 10, the teacher has to be willing to apply discipline where needed for the safety of all.

Student direction

> To what extent do students exercise some direction over the selection of activities related to their learning and the means and manner by which these activities will be one? (Department of Education and Training, 2003a, p. 36)

One of the joys of teaching in the Arts is that children will start to initiate the work to be undertaken or the pace at which they wish to work. In media creation, children will work at different paces as they film, edit and use IT and other resources. You will find that, with positive social support in the classroom and with engaging work, children can self-regulate, and as a teacher you will therefore be freed to facilitate their exploration of the Arts (Clay et al., 1998).

Inclusivity

> To what extent do lessons include and publicly value the participation of all students across the social and cultural backgrounds represented in the classroom? (Department of Education and Training, 2003a, p. 46)

Inclusivity is a teacher's responsibility: they have to ensure that all children can access the learning and that the teaching is not exclusive to only one group. If there are children with mobility issues, how can we as teachers ensure that children can partake in dance activities that are meaningful and of equal value to those who perhaps don't rely on a 'frame' to assist in walking? Inclusivity forces us to be creative as teachers and allows no child to avoid being challenged and realising their own potential.

Lesson plan 11.1

AIM

To recognise multiple cultural understandings using drama/dance/media/music or visual art (supported by, English and HASS).

OUTLINE/DESCRIPTION

In this lesson the students will be given a choice of four stimulus: four myths about animals from different cultures, which should include both images and text. Suggestions for myths include:

- stories about the 'Emu in the Sky' from various Aboriginal language groups
- the Chinese story of 'The Monkey King'
- the Chumash story of Hutash turning people into dolphins on the island of Limuw
- the Scottish legend of 'The Selkie Bride'.

Students, working either individually, in pairs or small groups, chose one stimulus and draw it, re-enact it, or develop music inspired by it.

Each student/group then presents their 'product' to the rest of the class, with a brief comment on the choices and reasons for the choices they made.

INTENDED OUTCOMES

Students identify

- representations of people/ideas
- meaning and interpretation in chosen art form
- appropriate and inappropriate use of images/techniques.

Students understand
- structure, intent, character and settings
- composition
- purpose and process when producing artworks.

LINKS TO THE CURRICULUM

Years 3 and 4 content descriptors

- Improvise and structure movement ideas for dance sequences using the elements of dance and choreographic devices (ACAADAM005).
- Explore ideas and narrative structures through roles and situations and use empathy in their own improvisations and devised drama (ACADRM031).
- Investigate and devise representations of people in their community, including themselves, through settings, ideas and story structure in images, sounds and text (ACAMAM058).
- Develop aural skills by exploring, imitating and recognising elements of music including dynamics, pitch and rhythm patterns (ACAMUM084).
- Explore ideas and artworks from different cultures and times, including artwork by Aboriginal and Torres Strait Islander artists, to use as inspiration for their own representations (ACAVAM110).
- Perform dances using expressive skills to communicate ideas, including telling cultural or community stories (ACADAM007).
- Shape and perform dramatic action using narrative structures and tension in devised and scripted drama, including exploration of Aboriginal and Torres Strait Islander drama (ACADRM033).
- Plan, create and present media artworks for specific purposes with awareness of responsible media practice (ACAMAM060).
- Create, perform and record compositions by selecting and organising sounds, silence, tempo and volume (ACAMUM086).

> - Present artworks and describe how they have used visual conventions to represent their ideas (ACAVAM112).
>
> **ASSESSMENT**
> - Students explore and develop ideas.
> - Students present artworks using conventions of art form to represent their ideas.
> - Assessment undertaken through observation and discussion.

All learning and teaching activities should aim to be a deliberate choice on the teacher's part. Take, for instance, in dance, when a new movement idea is being introduced; for safety reasons, it is highly likely that children's self-direction would be extremely low, because at this stage of the learning a clear control over the activities is needed until the children have grasped the skills to explore them safely themselves. Once children have knowledge, they are then encouraged to question the 'social construction' of that knowledge so that everything becomes problematic knowledge. This leads to higher-order thinking, deep knowledge and opportunities to demonstrate deep understanding. This is the beauty of the Arts.

It is important to remember that the reflective models do not dictate what to do. They cannot replace strong curriculum, lesson designs and task development. They are only a tool to analyse the quality of those efforts, and cannot be delivered meaningfully in isolation from a strong program focused on curriculum and pedagogy (Lewis, Perry & Murati, 2006). Reflective tools can be used to diagnose and refine the quality of classroom practice, the quality of assessment tasks, the quality of lesson plans, and the quality of units of work. As the teacher, you have to decide what you need to do next with your students to allow them to achieve success.

> Innovations often fail when educators focus only on the surface features of the innovation rather than the underlying mechanism[s] that will enable it to work (Lewis, et al., 2006, p. 5).

Brookfield (1995) presents educators with a 'critically reflective' approach to teaching. He maintains that what makes reflection 'critical' is the use of multiple 'lenses' to examine one's own teaching practice. He suggests four lenses: autobiography, colleagues, students and literature. Thus when reflecting on a teaching moment or observed lesson, Brookfield encourages the teacher to collect data from each of these sources in order to reflect critically on the meaning of that moment or lesson.

Equity in the classroom and diverse learners

Within the classroom there are a variety of children, each with individual needs and each having the right to engage fully with education, regardless of culture, ethnicity, physicality, neurology or gender. Schools should provide and promote a culture of inclusion. Discrimination is often based upon ignorance and is the antithesis of the purpose of early childhood and primary education. However, schools are a microcosm of society and there are children and teachers who will exclude students, either deliberately and maliciously or unknowingly. As a teacher, you have to actively find methodologies for inclusion.

> The objectives of the Australian Curriculum are the same for all students. The curriculum should offer students with special education needs (students with disability) rigorous, relevant and engaging learning experiences. ACARA is committed to the development of high-quality curriculum for all, while understanding the diverse and complex nature of students with disability. ACARA acknowledges the Disability Discrimination Act (1992 (DDA) and the Disability Standards for Education (2005), and its obligation as an education and training service provider to articulate the rights of students with disability to access, participate and achieve in the curriculum on the same basis as students without disability (ACARA, 2016).

Many forms of exclusion have been combatted and challenged successfully in schools. However, even though something like gender will rarely be brought up as an explicit issue, role modelling still exists for children as to how they view the different Arts in relation to their own gender (Keeffe & Carrington, 2007). As a teacher, your task is to challenge the sexist stereotypes that attach themselves to the Arts. Though this is rarely mentioned, a visit to any secondary school Arts class will often reveal an imbalance of numbers predominantly towards girls and against boys. While this issue needs to be addressed in the secondary schools, early childhood and primary teachers must also take some responsibility for not challenging some ingrained attitudes.

The Arts as an expressive force are formidable. They allow children to address taboo topics. Ideas of emotional depth and such issues as discrimination, bullying and exclusion will arise. As a teacher you need to be ready to deal with them. Through the use of cultural forms of Arts expression and stimuli, differing cultural knowledge can be valued and given equal space within the classroom.

There are four particular groups of divergent learners who are identified by policy-makers as having particular inequity in the classroom. Teachers of all subjects need to be aware of how to ensure that all learners are supported. Students who frequently face significant challenges in Australian classrooms are:

- children with a low social economic status (SES)
- children with a disability
- Aboriginal and Torres Strait Islander students
- children who have English as a second language (ESL)

While such labels may be of use in preparing to support individuals, it must be noted that labels should not define children, nor be used as justification for diminished expectations. All children have learning needs and all children need to be seen as individuals with individual circumstances and needs.

What must be remembered is that a different perspective on life is probably one of the main positives for individuals with specific and diverse learning needs. They clearly do see life differently compared to those who are not categorised as having specific, diverse learning needs. This can often lead them to become more understanding than most people, and they must be shown understanding and acceptance. We need to always consider the benefits that all children bring to the class.

Students with a low SES background

Multiple research programs have demonstrated that children who have a low SES background are fundamentally disadvantaged, in that they often have less access to books and cultural experiences, and generally have poorer nutrition and health. SES disadvantaged students often have fewer hours of early childhood education, throughout their school years will often have lower attendance at school, leave school early, and are less likely to go to university. Many schools have limited budgets, and it follows that where there is less wealth in a community, there is often less investment in schools. Any opportunity for teachers to offer alternative learning experiences to disadvantaged children can only be a benefit. If literacy is a challenge, communicating through drama or visual art may be a great option for many.

In wealthier communities there is often greater access to the Arts outside of the school environment; therefore creating opportunities within the classroom offers opportunity to those already disadvantaged by circumstances or place. While access to the Arts can be limited for children from low SES backgrounds, there are similar issues, for different reasons for children with rural communities, who are often considered part of this wider disadvantage circle.

> **Spotlight on Arts education**
>
> Desert Feet in an organisation that uses music to support remote communities in Australia not only to engage in the Arts but to find ways to express their ideas, concerns and bring mental health healing to many. Started in 2008 by two young musicians wanting to explore remote Western Australia, they began working with local communities when they recognised the impact music was having beyond simply performance.
>
> Link: Desert Feet

Supporting diverse learners and special needs

Early childhood is a time of paramount importance for cognitive and social development as well as the development of verbal, fine and gross motor skills. A sense of achievement or failure will be ingrained from children's early years in the school system. By applying the concepts of multiple intelligences, and therefore not prejudging a child's abilities with archaic assessment tools, children can be given opportunities to succeed. The Arts in all their forms offer many ways for children to access the curriculum.

The most obvious form of inclusion for children with diverse needs is for those with a visible physical disability. It is vital to create a working environment where these children can access the resources they require. It is a legal requirement of schools not to deny educational opportunities to any child. ACARA sums this up succinctly:

> Students with disability can engage with the curriculum provided appropriate adjustments are made, if required, by teachers to instructional processes, the learning environment and to the means through which students demonstrate

their learning. Adjustments to the complexity or sophistication of the curriculum may also be required for some students (ACARA, 2013, p. 18).

Children who struggle with intellectual challenges can have tasks developed to make them accessible. Children with neurological conditions, such as Autism Spectrum Disorder (ASD) and Attention Deficit Hyperactivity Disorder (ADD/ADHD), present additional challenges for themselves and the teachers. In Australia there is the added issue that some children may be diagnosed with these conditions when there may actually be other issues affecting them. This can lead a teacher to unwittingly supporting these children with methodologies that are completely inappropriate or counterproductive to their purposes (Dixon & Addy, 2004).

TEACHER TIP

Teacher tip Videos

Consider Michael, a student with cerebral palsy who uses a walking frame to help him move around. The class is performing *Does It Smell Nice?*, a small dance piece.

How would you include him? The inclusion has to be equivalent to that of the other students.

Consider the child in the video link performing to 'Let it Snow' who has cerebral palsy, and her sister who does not. She is able to be fully included and simply needs a support person to help her balance. Is there any other aspect of the recital that could have included her even further? Note all the children needed adult support at some point.

Now also consider the performance by the Latkovski sisters, and the deliberate interaction between able and differently abled sisters.

Dyspraxia

Dyspraxia is an example of a neurological disorder that impacts the classroom but is also one that the Arts can support. Concisely, dyspraxia (also known as developmental coordination disorder or DCD) is a miscommunication between the body and the brain as to where the body is physically in space, thus leading to coordination issues. This can affect speech, fine motor and gross motor movements. Given that the Arts are involved in using all of these forms of 'praxis', it might be a surprise to realise that many children with dyspraxia are drawn to the Arts as a Learning Area for these very reasons. In part this is because many traditional forms of assessment in schools are a challenge for children with dyspraxia (Brooks, 2007). The Arts, however, offer opportunities to practise and rehearse skills without competition, allowing children with barriers to communication to express themselves, and find success.

The Arts are particularly relevant for building on the inherent strengths that children with dyspraxia tend to develop because of the daily challenges they face. These include:

- powerful imaginations
- determined
- good long-term memory
- hard-working

- creative
- writing skills
- loyalty
- good language skills
- empathetic
- once a skill/ability is embedded, many people with dyspraxia appear to excel at those skills (Roy & Dock, 2014).

TEACHER TIP

Write your name copying the lettering shown and use your non-dominant hand (if you are right-handed, use your left hand). Consider how hard it is and how tiring. This is a demonstration of how difficult children with low muscle tone (such as those with dyspraxia or autism) find writing. Consider how you might help them.

ABCDEFGHIJ
KLMNOPQR
STUVWXYZabc
defghijklmnopqrs
tuvwxyz0123456
789!"$%?&*()

Autism Spectrum Disorder

Although commonly referred to as just 'autism', it is important to consider Autism Spectrum Disorder (ASD) as a *spectrum* because of the diversity of disability within its diagnosis. In simplistic terms, ASD is a developmental disorder that impacts the ability to communicate. For some children it acts like an intellectual disability, and for others it is more the inability to communicate their intellectual capabilities that is problematic. The key aspect in all these different disabilities is that while the labels offer a means for understanding and for seeking resource allocation, a teacher's focus should be on the learning challenges each individual child faces and how we can support them. As many of the symptoms of ASD match the symptoms of dyspraxia, which does have a genetic marker, the methodologies to support the challenges of dyspraxia also support children labelled on the autism spectrum.

Gifted and talented

Children identified as 'gifted and talented' are also identified as diverse learners. While there is some debate over the appropriateness of this terminology to describe intellectually 'advanced' students, the concept is commonly used in the education context. Although there is not a universally accepted definition of gifted and talented, in Australia Dr François Gagné's Differentiated Model of Giftedness and Talent is generally recognised by curriculum authorities, including ACARA, and education departments as an evidence-based model suitable for the education context. Gagné argues a gifted student demonstrates distinctly above average performance in at least one of the four domains of human performance. These domains include the intellectual, the creative, the social and the physical. Gagné's model recognises that giftedness is a potential and that talent requires learning to capitalise on that potential. Within this model, schools are recognised as having an important role in cultivating potential.

Children who have a disability as well as exceptional ability can sometimes be referred to as 'twice' or 'doubly' gifted. In the Arts, as teachers we regularly find that there are children who supersede our own skills in an area. It's important to remember that they still need to develop critical thinking skills; for while their technical skill may be outstanding, they are still children.

What is important to note is that all children benefit from interacting with other children who are not the same as themselves. Inclusion rather than segregation is the answer, and while a child with a label such as 'gifted and talented' may be outstanding in certain areas, they will still have other areas of need to develop (Bundy, Lane & Murray, 2002). Similar to many children with a disability, often children labelled 'gifted and talented' have social and emotional communication needs as they can be isolated at times by the peers because of the significant disparity in age and stage abilities.

If you have such children in the classroom, use the curriculum outcomes in the syllabus for the ages and stages above their own. One of the benefits of the Australian Curriculum: The Arts is that it is a learning progression. Year 4 outcomes are similar to Year 3, just a further development. In many ways those children who are labelled as 'gifted and talented' allow you as the teacher to apply Vygotsky's theory of Proximal Development in a real and practical way in the class (Kozulin et al., 2003).

Teachers, however, should be careful not to explicitly label children as 'gifted and talented' as this can set up false expectations. Part of the Arts learning processes should be to create opportunities for children not only to discover success but also to cope with challenges and failure in a safe space.

Aboriginal and Torres Strait Islander students

Over the last 40 years there has been increased recognition of the disadvantages faced by Aboriginal and Torres Strait Islander children. As has been shown throughout this text, the Arts are a key part of the communication basis for Aboriginal and Torres Strait Islander peoples. A lack of access to basic healthcare, housing, employment and infrastructure, and the intergenerational consequences of the Stolen Generations, in many remote communities can often lead to profound disadvantage. In addition, there are cultural differences in approaching education in terms of structure, as well as a lack of Indigenous teachers as leaders within schools. The combination of these factors can compound disadvantage and lower potential outcomes for many children. Some Aboriginal and Torres Strait Islander students may not have English as their first, or even their second language, and as such may face the same challenges as other ESL students. With cultural dominance from modern Australia, it is in engaging with the context of the Arts that increased opportunity for communication and expression of identity to help bridge educational inequities can be offered. We have to remember that Standard Australian English is not always the first language of Australia's First Nations peoples. There are multiple Indigenous languages that must be recognised and engaged with, depending on the land that a school is built upon.

One concern for all teachers, whether working with Aboriginal and Torres Strait Islander students or engaging in Aboriginal and Torres Strait Islander knowledges, is ensuring that we are being culturally appropriate. A simple way to be sure is to contact your local land council (often the Aboriginal and Torres Strait Islander community hub in an area) to seek expert advice and support, and to develop meaningful relationships with such organisations. To assist with making decisions, Sainty and Baker (2015) present a useful series of questions to consider when selecting material for inclusion in your classroom:

1. What is the purpose and intent for the selection of materials?
2. Is the material accurate and authentic?
3. Is the material respectful of Aboriginal people?
4. Are Aboriginal peoples and cultures presented in a positive way?
5. Does the material include appropriate terminology?
6. Who has produced/developed the material? If it was not an Aboriginal person, then has there been involvement and/or consultation with the relevant Aboriginal community?
7. Is the material endorsed by the relevant Aboriginal community?

> **Reflection activity**
>
> Read the news article 'Desert Feet bringing the healing power of music to remote Indigenous communities' on ABC News online.
>
> Consider how you use music to think about and deal with events and experiences in your life. Now think about the children you will reach and how you could use music or any of the Arts to support children with an Aboriginal and Torres Strait Islander Histories and Cultures background and heritage. What current songs or musical experiences might allow them to express feelings that are often difficult to express, and still be relevant to themselves?
>
> Link: Desert Feet article

One of the real issues teachers face in the classroom is the predominance of European and White Australian cultural reference points for engaging students, through stimulus or modelling. Too often there is commentary that the Arts (including film and television) in Australia and the wider world do not recognise the diversity of the people who listen and watch and engage with it. One solution is to continually reflect on the sources of Arts products being used and ensure that there is a wide variety of diverse groupings represented. For instance, the National Indigenous Television Network (NITV) offers a wide array of children's programming, called 'Jarjums'.

Link: NITV 'Jarjums'

English as a Second Language students

While English is the dominant language of Australia, there are multiple Indigenous languages, and with the Australian Bureau of Statistics stating that in 2016, 21 per cent of people spoke a language other than English at home, there is a continuing need for teachers to be conscious of the many children in a classroom who may be struggling with English communication at the most basic level, because their home life is in another language. As with all students who find barriers to the curriculum because of language and curriculum assumptions, multiple forms of semiotic systems can be applied. The Arts have a large role to play within this.

Semiotic systems may be:

- linguistic (oral and written)
- visual (still and moving, media, animation, film: signs and symbols, colour, shape, movement etc)
- auditory (music and sounds, genre styles, classical, jazz, popular, volume, pitch etc.)
- gestural (facial expression and body language)
- spatial (layout and organisation, proximity and direction)
- mathematical number systems, (algebraic systems – letters and symbols).

Successful communication through the visual semiotics of visual arts, or the performance arts of dance and drama, can be a core tool in allowing students to develop relationships and demonstrate deep understanding of themselves and the world around them, as can the international language of music through auditory communication and in symbols (notation).

328 ■ PART 3 HOW: EMBEDDING THE ARTS IN EDUCATION

Lesson plan 11.2

Lesson plan 11.2

AIM

Learning about emotions and communication across linguistic barriers, using media (supported drama, English and visual arts

OUTLINE/DESCRIPTION

In this lesson the students will use emoji as a stimulus for communicating in pairs.

Each student is paired up (or in groups of three if required) and each student is given a sheet of '**emoji**'. Part of the purpose of working in small groups is so that those students with linguistic differences can support each other.

Emoji: small images, used in electronic communication, to demonstrate emotion to accompany written statements.

Each student takes turns in choosing an emoji and using only noises (not words) and facial and body gestures to communicate what they believe the emoji to mean. It may be useful to have a written description of what each emoji is underneath depending on the background knowledge of each student.

If students think that an emoji means something other than its intended meaning, that in itself would be a useful discussion at the end.

As a closing element to the lesson the class should discuss the issues, challenges and fun things they learned while undertaking the task.

Extension activities could be for students to then argue for or against the use of emoji in school written work or if they think they are a good thing or not. There are also connections to visual arts in this lesson, and also history, in regard to pictures being used as a foundation to language communication (consider hieroglyphics).

INTENDED OUTCOMES

Students identify
- themselves as audiences and explore other audience groups
- meaning and interpretation in media
- appropriate and inappropriate use of images.

Students understand
- structure, intent, character and settings
- composition
- purpose and process when producing media artworks
- meaning and interpretation, and forms and elements of media artworks.

LINKS TO THE CURRICULUM

Years 3 and 4 content descriptors
- Investigate and devise representations of people in their community, including themselves through settings, ideas and story structure in images, sound and text (ACAMAM058).
- Identify intended purposes and meanings of media artworks, using media arts key concepts, starting with media artworks (ACAMAR061).

ASSESSMENT
- Students communicate understanding of different emoji.
- Students perform emoji in a physical way and work collegially.
- Assessment undertaken through observation and discussion.

How to T.E.A.C.H.

One solution to support all children with recognised disadvantage is to **T.E.A.C.H.**

When a child is learning a new task or having difficulties with daily activities, T.E.A.C.H. is a helpful framework to guide you in helping a child. T.E.A.C.H. is an acronym for five things that can be done to better match an activity to a child's abilities.

- T – Talk to the student
- E – Expect success
- A – Achievable, challenging and realistic goals
- C – Chunk the activity
- H – Harbour the learning area

Talk to the student

Key to trying to support children, whatever their learning needs, is to talk with them first, or communicate to recognise they have aims, goals and often know the challenges they face. Rather than assuming this is the difficulty or need, speak with the child and listen their thoughts. Then apply your skills as a teacher to work with the child for success.

Expect success

Expect any children you have responsibility for to be able succeed even if they require support. This is all about attitude, yours and that of the other children in the classroom, as well as the wider school community, including parents. A label, such as ethnicity, disability, or any other potential disadvantage that society comments on, does not mean that a child does not have the potential to succeed – it only means the route they take to get there may be different.

Achievable and goals

Consider carefully what you are asking a child to do. Activities should be achievable. The student must be able to see the potential for success, but at the same time it should not be easy – it should challenge the student with skills and supports provided to do so. The goal must be realistic, and not so challenging that it disengages the student. Vygotsky's theory of Proximal Development suggested activities to be not what a student can already do, nor what a student cannot do but instead what a student can do with guidance or support, aiming eventually for them to be able to eventually achieve tasks independently.

Chunk the tasks

Chunking the task is, in effect, breaking a task, activity, knowledge or skill into smaller parts that build to a whole. By allowing students to tackle each component, they find success and can build upon this. Basically, you are creating mini achievable goals until a full task in completed, and the child is not overwhelmed. This may include clear written steps in instruction. For example: 1. Draw picture 2. Cut out shape 3. Glue shape 4. Stick shape to collage.

Harbour the learning area

A harbour is a secure, safe place for a child to develop in. To allow there to be significance and depth in learning, a learner needs to feel they are in a place where they can learn without distraction, judgment or condemnation. For many children, changing slight elements in the learning space can create an environment where they can thrive. This may be in allowing a child to work in a different position such as lying down. It may be allowing a child to be in a quieter area, or one that has brighter light or is more shaded.

Other pedagogical approaches

There are multiple 'systems' available to apply pedagogically in the classroom – particularly for learning diversity. Many have both passionate proponents and fierce critics. There is no one system that is a panacea (Allen & White, 2017). Serious research into some of these systems, such as the 'Universal Design for Learning' (UDL), has begun to question any benefit. 'Differentiated Instruction' (DI) as a model has been shown to have some impact but that is balanced by those who advocate for 'Direct Instruction' as a method. Expert teachers will try multiple techniques and vary them as they find pedagogical methods that work for each individual child (Scott, 2015). What we do know is that children do not have specific 'learning styles' and that theories such as Gardner's 'Multiple Intelligences' (Gardner, 1993) have often been wrongly applied in the classroom. The best solution is to continue to independently read research and find what works for the individual children in your classroom (Hudson, 2013).

TEACHER TIP

Some children need to 'stim' (stimulate) themselves while working – such as chewing a pencil or tapping a finger.

Some strategies to support this need include:
- providing a piece of foam on the desk for quieter pen/finger tapping
- putting a photosensitive child beside a window with the blind drawn down
- allowing children to move in the classroom, with clear rules about not disturbing others. Some children have low muscle tone and have to move or change position to keep awake.

For all the above five areas of T.E.A.C.H, the key is communication – talk 'with' students not just 'at' them.

Conclusion

The Arts allow children to develop fine motor skills through visual arts, media and musical instrument control. Even the usage of 'apps' on iPads is beginning to be researched and understood to be a successful method allowing children with fine motor skill issues to access classroom activities and share their understanding. Drama and dance offer opportunities to develop balance and other gross motor skills from an early age. Drama is a key intervention strategy for dyspraxia and autism. Drama is an effective and engaging learning opportunity for children with dyspraxia, as it encourages and develops speech and gross motor skills, while for autistic children it can provide engagement, socialisation and the assistance of empathetic understandings.

The Arts are a means of communication. They can be used to give a voice to those who can't access the usual tools of classroom communication. They give expression to the emotional resonances deep within us, consciously or otherwise. They allow us to voice our understandings of other knowledges and demonstrate our clarity of thought in multiple curricular areas. By placing the Arts at the core of the learning experience, more so than anything else, we allow higher-order thinking to bloom through creativity and diverse modal methods, to question, to experiment and to explore the full possibilities of knowledge and identity.

REVIEW QUESTIONS

1. What are Schiro's four curriculum ideologies?
2. What principles are the Australian Curriculum based upon?
3. What are the seven professional standards set by AITSL for all teaching staff?
4. Why might using a reflective tool be important for a teacher?
5. What law states that children with a disability must be able to access education?
6. What are the four main groupings of disadvantage for children in Australia?
7. What are the dangers of misdiagnosis?
8. How can the Arts support children with disabilities in their learning?
9. What do you see as the greatest challenge for teachers to include children with physical and/or intellectual/neurological disabilities in Arts activities? Why?
10. What is does the acronym for T.E.A.C.H. stand for?

RECOMMENDED READING

Department of Education and Training (2003). *Quality Teaching in NSW Public Schools: A Classroom Practice Guide*. Ryde: NSW Department of Education and Training Professional Support and Curriculum Directorate.

Gardner, H. (1993). *Multiple Intelligences: The Theory in Practice*. New York: Basic Books.

Gore, J. (2007). 'Improving pedagogy'. In J. Butcher and L. McDonald (eds). *Making a Difference: Challenges for Teachers, Teaching and Teacher Education*, pp. 15–32. Rotterdam: Sense.

Haberman, M. (1994). 'The pedagogy of poverty versus good teaching'. In E. Hatton (ed.), *Understanding Teaching: Curriculum and the Social Context of Schooling*, pp. 17–25. Sydney: Harcourt Brace.

Hattie, J. (2008). *Visible Learning*. London: Routledge.

Ladwig, J. G. (2010). 'Beyond academic outcomes'. *Review of Research in Education*, 34 (March), 28.

Newmann, F. M. & Associates (1996). *Authentic Achievement: Restructuring Schools for Intellectual Quality*. San Francisco: Jossey-Bass.

12

Quality Arts education and rich learning

> All you need is love.
>
> The Beatles

In this chapter

Throughout this book you have been challenged to look at the role the Arts play in society and in education. Various methodologies have been suggested and each specific Arts area has been broken down for you. The tools are now in place for you to organise Arts learning and teaching in your classroom. You also have reflective tools to apply to the learning and teaching you undertake. In this final chapter, we challenge you to imagine your Arts-rich classroom. What do you want the Arts to look like and how do you want your students to engage in them? These decisions will reflect your vision and rationale for teaching the Arts and your many experiences in working with the Arts as you have progressed through this book. These decisions are best made by the person who decides the 'what' and 'how' for their students every day – YOU.

By the end of this chapter you should have a clear understanding of:

- the characteristics of quality Arts education
- Arts-rich learning
- Arts-rich teaching.

Introduction

To teach effectively, we need to continually consider our own professional learning and reflect on what we do each day as teachers. Part of this process involves recognising that our professional knowledge must continually evolve and that, as effective teachers, we must also continually reframe what we know and can do. What will you do to ensure that your teaching is reflective and critical?

TEACHER TIP

Reflection is a key characteristic of quality teaching. One way to reflect on your own teaching is to keep a journal of significant events in your teaching practice. When important events occur in your classroom (both positive and negative), describe them in your journal, reflect on why they are important, and think about how you will react next time a similar event occurs.

Video: Critical reflection

In this chapter we invite you to apply all that you now know and can do. We revisit quality Arts education and offer ways to ensure that opportunities for sequential, sustained and substantial Arts learning are embedded in your classroom. We will discuss the notion of the 'Arts-rich' learning context, in which the Arts are at the core of learning experiences, and offer examples of what Arts-rich learning should include. Here we will explore and review activities that are inspired by the Arts and that embed and integrate the Arts with other areas of learning. These activities and ways of thinking, doing and learning are multimodal: they combine two or more art forms and they encourage you to use the Arts as a thinking and self-determining professional educator. Finally, you will be challenged to reflect on your role and your vision for the future of the Arts in your practice.

> **Reflection activity**
>
> In Chapter 1 you were asked to prepare a personal vision for the Arts in education. Go back to that vision now, and consider what has changed as you have read this book; what you now know; and what this means for the children you teach and for your practice. Take the time to update your vision, now focusing on what you have learned. You may focus on one or two of the components of quality Arts education listed below or may choose to make your vision very personal and talk about the learning 'leaps' that you have made through this book.

Characteristics of quality Arts education

In Chapter 1 you were introduced to the notion of quality in Arts education and the importance of being aware of such elements as praxis, learner agency, and cultural diversity.

Quality Arts education includes:

- the Arts experienced as praxis
- sequential learning planned to enable growth in both Arts making and responding
- sustained learning from preschool
- substantial learning in each of the five Arts domains of dance, drama, media arts, music and visual arts
- child-centred teaching
- active learning
- authentic activities and processes
- access
- inclusion of Arts from diverse cultural perspectives
- continuous teacher reflection about the effectiveness of learning Arts opportunities provided for children.

The importance of each of these characteristics was discussed in some detail in Chapter 1, so in this chapter we want to focus on the ways in which you can embed these principles into your teaching practice. We will now elaborate on these key attributes of quality Arts education.

> **Spotlight on Arts education**
>
> ### HARVARD PROJECT ZERO: THE QUALITIES OF QUALITY
>
> Project Zero was founded in 1967 at the Harvard Graduate School of Education and recently celebrated 50 years of operation. In 2009, Project Zero released the results of a wide-ranging investigation into what constitutes quality Arts education.
>
> Link: Harvard Project Zero
>
> Some of the major findings of this investigation were as follows.
>
> - Quality Arts education has many different purposes. The report lists seven of these, including the generation of important dispositions and skills in learners in addition to the actual Arts techniques that are learned.
> - One approach to investigating Arts programs is to look at them through four lenses: student learning (what happens in the room), pedagogy (how this happens and how the teacher positions themselves in the learning process), community dynamics (the relationships in the classroom) and environment (the decisions taken about how many hours of Arts will be taught, the resources allocated to this teaching, and the value placed on that learning). These lenses also provide a framework for what is important in establishing quality.
> - Reflection on what constitutes quality and how the Arts learning is trending in relation to quality is a constant and cyclic conversation that is important not only in the provision of quality but also in understanding what constitutes quality.
> - If an Arts program is achieving two or more of the characteristics of quality then this is a great outcome; to achieve all would be impossible – rather, quality is about process.

Arts taught as praxis

An indicator of quality Arts education is the approach to learning and teaching in the Arts and how that approach is implemented in the classroom. As you know Arts education as praxis focuses on authentic making and responding activities in which the child is central and through which they gain a sense of agency. Praxis refers to the 'doing' of the Arts in your classroom and physical engagement with the Arts as a human activity.

Sequential, sustained learning for growth in Arts making and responding

If we are to enable our students to engage deeply in the Arts, we must provide them with opportunities for learning that allow them to grow as Arts makers and responders, that are carefully sequenced over time and that are pedagogically sound. Chapters 4 to 8 outlined the important learning to be included in your teaching for each of the Arts domains and also provided different approaches to teaching them. These chapters should therefore provide you with the tools to ensure that students in your care grow in and through Arts making and responding. Following on from Chapter 9, where ways of integrating the Arts were presented, and Chapter 10, where organisational aspects of Arts learning were discussed, you now need to learn how to embed the Arts into your continuous thinking, planning and reflection.

Sequential Arts education: student learning in the Arts that occurs in a logical order or sequence over time.

Sustained Arts education: Arts learning that proceeds from early childhood through high school without any breaks or gaps.

When you are planning your program of work over a term, and more importantly on a weekly and daily basis, you need to consciously ask yourself, 'Have I regularly used the five Arts where I can?'. These Arts should be included in every week of your teaching program. This means that students are learning **sequentially** and in a **sustained** way.

TEACHER TIP

SEQUENTIAL ARTS EDUCATION

When you are next working in an early learning or classroom setting, ask your colleagues to elaborate on any Arts-based learning that the children have engaged in. If the response is 'little' or 'nothing', ask if you could use your skills in Arts education at different points in your placement.

This should include varieties of learning tasks that involve both making and responding, and explicit use of Arts language. For example, in term 1 of a year 6 class, the focus is on exploring 'me', and ideas of identity and individuality continue to be explored throughout the curriculum. How can you incorporate the Arts into this? Table 12.1 has some suggestions for a term of Arts engagement within this theme and provides examples of how quality Arts education may occur in a themed area of learning.

The Arts have a key role to play in children's identity formation in allowing expression of the subconscious inner self (explored in Chapters 1–3). If we recognise that engagement

TABLE 12.1 ENGAGING THE ARTS IN EXPLORING IDENTITY

Art form	Exploration	Example
Dance	Children work in small groups to explore the ideas of space, tension and release. Each group needs to prepare a finished dance piece by the end of the term to include in the drama piece, which relates to the story.	Children form groups of five and reach forward, imagining they are pulling and being pulled against another team in a 'tug of war'. They move rhythmically back and forth and then after several repetitions fall forward letting go in slow motion, all landing apart.
Drama	The class work collaboratively to write and perform a story about valuing diversity.	Children, in small groups, discuss their positive differences and when these have been noticed, choose one idea from their group about which to devise a short scene that shows the 'difference' having a positive effect.
Media arts	Each child makes a short film about their life to date, sharing the use of the video over the term and learning basic editing features in iMovie.	Children create a short animation showing their changing appearance over time from baby to now. They add audio to match their interests over time.
Music	In small groups, children explore and extend their use of the elements of music by composing and performing an extended work that illustrates one important characteristic of their own unique personality, such as 'fun' or 'perseverance'. They can use any form of music making they want.	Children compose a piece of music based on the idea of 'fun' as a representation of an aspect of their own personality. They use 'pitch' in composing a tune that is expansive and happy. Their tune uses a 'jumpy' rhythm and a fast 'tempo'.
Visual arts	Children represent their identity through the construction of a self-portrait. They research and explore the use of a variety of contemporary image-making media to create self-portraits.	Children take a series of 'selfies' and manipulate them, considering colour, texture, line and tone, using a program such as Photoshop Elements. They use a range of materials (photographs, wrappers, small objects, labels etc.) to create a bricolage [something constructed from a variety of materials] that represents their interests.

is a key tool in supporting student achievement and that identity development in all its forms underlies this engagement, the importance of any pedagogical tool that can embrace both these concepts of engagement and identity, like the Arts, needs to be recognised, implemented and valued.

In the classroom

Select one of the activities presented in Table 12.1. When you are next engaged in teaching children resolve to teach that activity. When you have finished the teaching task, reflect on that experience. Reflect on what you did, what the children did, what the children learned, what feedback you received, and what you would do differently next time. Then try one of the other activities in Table 12.1 and repeat.

Finally, to ensure quality learning and teaching in the Arts you need to make sure that other teachers are aware of the ways in which you are using the Arts and the importance that you and your students attach to these. One of the great concerns about Arts education, as discussed in Chapter 1, is the need to ensure that children's Arts engagement is continuous between their years of learning. Therefore, your use of curriculum documents in planning and the ways in which you inform other teachers about this are vital.

In the classroom

Go to the Early Years Learning Framework or to the Australian Curriculum: The Arts (whichever is your focus). Select one element from the document to focus on in one of your teaching opportunities when you are next working with children. For example, the EYLF advocates play-based learning.

How can you set up opportunities for children to learn the Arts through play?

Substantial learning in the five Arts domains of dance, drama, media arts, music and visual arts

Substantial Arts education: Arts learning that is of 'substance' or 'quality'. Authentic making and responding as artists and significant use of Arts language, along with the other attributes of quality Arts education.

Arts learning must be '**substantial**' if it is to be of quality. If we take the theme of identity from Table 12.1 and the visual arts component as an example, we see that the self-portraits will require engagement with many visual arts skills and much visual language. Responding activities could involve viewing contemporary self-portraits that utilise traditional as well as new and emerging technologies. Children come to understand how artists use materials and techniques to communicate individual characteristics in innovative ways. Over the term, they will engage with many art codes and conventions, including visual arts elements, time and movement and appropriation. They will explore making through different techniques, such as drawing or installation. This is learning of substance, learning that not only relates well to the theme, but is also authentic in both process and product.

Child-centred teaching and the child as an active learner

Learner agency, or the sense that you can have an effect on your own learning and that it is important, is significant in developing a child-centred Arts program. This means that children must have licence to explore, experiment and make mistakes without any fear of condemnation. The child as an active learner is the one who is encouraged to 'do' the Arts. So the child learns about self-portraits, not just by responding to the works of others, but also by engaging in the process of making self-portraits themselves. The Arts are intensely personal, and therefore individuals will express themselves uniquely through their Arts creations. For children in a child-centred Arts context, what is important in the process of Arts making is not necessarily mastery but engagement and self-efficacy. Children have years to learn more about the self-portrait and to refine their skills and techniques; what is important in early childhood and primary classrooms is that they are engaging with authentic Arts making and responding and that their relationship with the Arts is positive and self-affirming.

TEACHER TIP

As Stephen Brookfield (1995) writes:

> of all the pedagogic tasks teachers face, getting inside students' heads is one of the trickiest … When we start to see ourselves through students' eyes, we become aware of what Perry (1988) calls the 'different worlds' in the same classroom. Next time you are planning a lesson or interacting with your students ask yourself the question 'If I was a student how would I respond to this?'.

Authentic activities and processes

Authentic activities and processes refer to Arts learning that occurs in the same ways as it does in real life. In the example of identity and individuality shown in Table 12.1, children engage in each art form as artists, grappling with the same problems that artists do and having multiple opportunities to use Arts elements, processes, codes and conventions. Central to the process of making for an artist is the opportunity to exhibit or perform works to an audience. In the learning described in Table 12.1, this would mean that a day or night of exhibition and performance for friends and families may be appropriate.

> **Reflection activity**
>
> Remember that the Arts is about both 'process' and 'product'. All too often in classrooms and childcare centres it is the product that is the focus and unfortunately this misses the point! A performance or an exhibition is the final stage of arts making, and the point at which the audience 'responds'.
>
> Why do you think performance or exhibition is an important part of the process of making art?

Children of all abilities and Arts from diverse cultural perspectives

As was discussed in Chapter 1, access to Arts education includes access for all, and Chapter 11 discussed some of the strategies for inclusion that can be applied in your teaching context. Inclusion of Arts from a diversity of cultural contexts – particularly Australian Aboriginal and Torres Strait Islander peoples, and the cultures of our Pacific and Asian neighbours – is an important part of learning in the Arts. Through exploring the Arts of these different cultures with respect and understanding, children grow in other understandings of diversity and, consequently, as individuals. The theme of individuality and identity in Table 12.1 could feature many opportunities for community elders and family members to demonstrate aspects of their cultural heritage. Children could be inspired to listen widely to the music of all children in their class, to respond to the visual arts of the cultures of fellow class members, and to experiment with applying these to their own musical or art creations. Their self-portraits, in whatever form, could show aspects of their cultural backgrounds; for example, Islamic repeat patterns or Japanese calligraphy.

Continuous teacher reflection

One of the characteristics of quality teaching is the ability to reflect critically on your own practice as a teacher. When considering the Arts, you should continually reflect on the effectiveness of the Arts learning opportunities you have provided for your students. For reflection to be 'critical', reflection on multiple sources of information about your teaching practice is required. Steven Brookfield (1995) offers us four 'lenses' for critical reflection: the autobiographical lens, the student lens, the colleague lens, and the lens of literature. The autobiographical lens focuses on you and why you do what you do; the student lens is concerned with how your students interpret your intentions as a teacher and how effective your teaching is for them. The colleague lens includes data about your teaching from a trusted other; and the literature lens focuses on what is common from our practice when aligned with research. There are other approaches to reflection, such as John Smyth's (1992) four-stage approach to reflection, consisting of: describing, informing, constructing, and reconstructing; and, Gibbs' (1988) six-stage approach, consisting of: description, feelings, evaluation, analysis, conclusion, and action. Whatever approach you use, critical reflection is an indicator of quality.

In the classroom

Ask students to listen to the song 'The Children Came Back' by Aboriginal rapper Briggs, featuring Gurrumul and Dewayne Everettsmith. Ask students to write down some of the names referred to in the song of important Aboriginal and Torres Strait Islander people and to discuss why they are famous.

Videos: Protest songs

Talk about the importance of protest songs, such as the original song by Archie Roach entitled 'Took the Children Away'. How could these songs be linked to the cross-curriculum priority of Aboriginal and Torres Strait Islander Histories and Cultures, the EYLF section or 'The Journey for Educators: Growing Competence in Working with Aboriginal and Torres Strait Islander Cultures'?

Quality Arts education involves using your professional judgment to pay attention to all of these characteristics with integrity. Integrity is the key to this; the Arts must not become just an 'add-on' to thematic learning. One way of achieving this integrity is through developing an Arts-rich learning context.

Arts-rich learning

The expression 'Arts-rich learning', also referred to as 'Arts enriched' education (Anderson & Gibson, 2004) or Arts-infused learning (Hanley, 2003; Snyder, 2001), is starting to appear in common usage; however, its meaning is neither clear nor well articulated. According to the Arts Education Partnership (2011) in the United States, Arts-rich education is 'an essential tool in children's achievement and whole school reform', but there is no clarity about what this may be. Elster (2001) writes that 'an Arts-rich curriculum can provide a vehicle for self-expression, self-understanding, self-confidence, creative problem-solving and motivation' – once again, a definition of 'Arts-rich' is not provided, although the author refers to an 'Arts-infused' curriculum. According to MCEETYA (2007, p. 5): 'An Arts-rich education can help young people make sense of the world and enhance their awareness of diverse cultures and traditions and the wider global context in which they live.' However, again what this entails is not really made clear. Gardiner (2003) writes broadly about the benefits of Arts-rich education, stating: 'When the Arts become central to the learning environment, schools and other educational settings become places of discovery.' For Gardiner (2003), the Arts as embodied learning, engaging minds, hearts and bodies, is a part of Arts-rich learning. She writes:

> While learning in other subjects often focuses on development of a single skill or specific understanding, the Arts regularly require children to multi-task – engaging and nurturing their cognitive, social and personal competencies simultaneously.

The expression 'Arts-infused' learning is somewhat more common, but again is not clearly distinguished from, for example, **Arts-rich learning** or Arts integration (Hanley, 2003; Snyder, 2001).

Arts-rich learning: places Arts learning at the centre of an integrated approach, in which children engage authentically in and through the Arts with other domains of learning. It is a means of developing learner agency, and places the child at the centre of the learning and teaching process.

Arts-rich learning includes attention to quality Arts education, but it is more than this. In Chapters 4 to 8, you learned about each Arts domain and how to engage the children authentically and meaningfully with each one. The principles outlined in these chapters provide you with the tools to implement Arts learning of quality in each area. To ensure that you provide an 'Arts-rich' learning context, you need to go beyond the question 'Have I regularly used these five Arts?' and also ask: 'Have I provided opportunities for each of these five Arts to be fully integrated and explored with integrity?' 'Integrity' refers to the quality of the learning and to the authenticity of making and responding alongside genuine Arts language development.

Spotlight on Arts education

MELBOURNE GRADUATE SCHOOL OF EDUCATION: ARTS-RICH PROFESSIONAL LEARNING FOR TEACHERS

In conjunction with the Musical Futures program and primary schools in Victoria, academics from the Melbourne Graduate School of Education explored different approaches to providing generalist teachers in schools with 'arts-rich' professional learning (Wright et al., 2014). The professional learning included drama, visual arts and music, and also included intensive sessions followed by mentoring. What is of particular interest here is the focus on 'immersive' experiences for teachers, through which teachers learn intensively and authentically *as* artists. The importance of the intensive component of these Arts-rich learning experiences is significant, in that immersion over time may be a component of Arts-rich experiences. This also supports our assertion that Arts-rich or quality Arts learning positions the learner *as* an artist with personal agency in the creative process.

An Arts-rich learning context responds to both of these questions affirmatively.

An Arts-rich environment pays attention, in and through the Arts, to each of the following:

- integration of the Arts into all domains of learning, as both content and pedagogy
- the characteristics of quality Arts education
- 'key competencies' and 'general capabilities'
- children with disabilities
- cultural diversity, Indigenous, Maori, Pacific and Asian Arts and cultures
- sustainability
- partnerships and the contributions of colleagues, parents and the community.

Most of these characteristics of Arts-rich learning have been explored in some detail throughout this book. The one area that requires further exploration is partnerships and the contributions of colleagues, parents and the community.

> Constructing an Arts-rich environment in your classroom that pays attention to all of the above characteristics may at first seem daunting. As with so many things in life, starting with just ONE of these characteristics and working with it offers you a 'doorway' into Arts-rich learning. Select one of the characteristics listed above and note the ways in which this characteristic could be highlighted in your classroom to effect Arts-rich learning.
>
> Take, for example, the characteristic of cultural diversity. Focusing on cultural diversity in your classroom could involve a number of Arts learning opportunities through which learning can occur. Listening and responding to music from different cultures, making Art inspired by other cultures, or engaging with dance from other cultures, are some very simple ways to place Arts-rich learning at the centre of learning about cultural diversity.

Reflection activity

Partnerships and the contributions of colleagues, parents and the community

The importance of creating partnerships with colleagues, parents and the community was referred to in Chapter 2. Hunter (2005) makes particular reference to the value of this engagement. Arts learning is not restricted to the classroom. Within the community, there are many opportunities to engage with the Arts and bring new Arts experiences into the classroom. The community of your school, both within and without, are not separate from the learning in the classroom. There will be artists, performers and educators living locally, and also within the parent body of the school, who may be able to partner with you and your students in developing an Arts-rich environment.

Engaging with such people can be a sensitive issue. Parents may be reluctant to 'show up their children', and professionals in the community may be caught between their desire to serve the community and a concern not to undersell their personal living. In addition, working in the Arts is about opening your emotional self to others. Some in the profession will regard this as a form of risk-taking and exposure; others will take it as an excuse to allow their already engorged egos to run rampant! Always remember: You are the educator in the classroom, it is you who makes decisions about what is valued in your classroom. While members of the community may have much to offer, and invaluable skills in different Arts strands, you are the pedagogical expert. You must champion the children's needs so that learning experiences are engaging and authentic, as described in Chapter 12. With these caveats in place, bringing in outside practitioners to share with children – whether as visitors to the school or on excursions – can be one of the richest Arts experiences they can enjoy. Such experiences can literally change a child's life in a positive way. Examples of partnerships with the community can include welcoming Aboriginal and Torres Strait Islander peoples into your classroom to build reconciliation and understanding, working with local museums or theatre groups, or engaging with music organisations such as symphony orchestras.

If you are basing your students' Arts activities on specific community stimulus, we would encourage involving members of the community in other fields to share their experiences and depth of knowledge. It brings a relevance and connectivity to the classroom practice. When engaging in Aboriginal and Torres Strait Islander activities, contact the local land council and/or the local elders or community leaders and invite them to be part of the children's learning experience. As the teacher, you need to forge these links.

When we talk about partnerships and collaboration in Arts education the possibilities are endless, and opportunities for collaboration through partnerships abound. Collaboration through 'partnerships' refers to working with organisations such as:

- international groups – via websites such as the Kennedy Center's 'Arts Edge' (US)
- national groups – may be touring your area, such as a visiting exhibition or performance, or contact them through their websites
- local groups – your local or capital city art gallery or symphony orchestra
- local individuals – Aboriginal elders or local artists
- members of your school community – other teachers or support staff with an interest in the Arts, and parents/grandparents with particular skills.

Link: Arts Edge

Link: Music: Count Us In

Spotlight on Arts education

Music: Count Us In is an Australia-wide, annual music experience for students and teachers of all musical abilities. Music Count Us In features one song composed by Australian school students working alongside a mentor, usually a professional musician, such as Marcia Hines or Katie Noonan. The song is then released to schools around Australia, with wonderful support materials such as AUSLAN support, inclusion support materials, lesson plans and song files. On a given day towards the end of the year students get together all around Australia to sing the song at the same time. Importantly, all of these materials are absolutely free. Also, each state provides support workshops for teachers in addition to the online support that is available. This program is a wonderful example of how your classroom can partner with an organisation to make for great learning outcomes.

Lesson plan 12.1

AIM
To engage in quality, Arts-rich learning in the early childhood context.

OVERVIEW
Learning through play about using sounds and visual materials for effect.

OUTLINE/DESCRIPTION
In this activity students are enabled to learn through play. A corner is set up in the childcare centre or classroom. At this learning corner are a variety of visual materials including: paints, crayons, paper, cardboard, safe scissors, coloured paper and safe glue. Musical instruments are also located at this learning corner, including a variety of tuned and non-tuned percussion instruments, such as claves, tambourines, xylophones, glockenspiels and drums. Other stimulus at the learning corner may include pictures of planets and solar systems. Students are asked to design their own planet using the visual materials available. Once finished, students are asked to play with the instruments available to compose music for their planet.

INTENDED OUTCOMES
Children identify
- ways to use music to express an emotion or idea
- ways to use visual arts to express an emotion or an idea.

Children understand
- that music can be used to express their feelings and ideas
- that visual arts can be used to express their feelings and ideas.

Children are able to
- use the materials available to express personal preferences
- use music to express an idea or emotion.

Children
- express ideas and make meaning using a range of media (DEEWR, 2009, p. 42)
- begin to understand how symbols and pattern systems work (DEEWR, 2009, p. 43).

> **LINKS TO CURRICULUM**
>
> **Early Years Learning Framework**
> - Outcome 5: Children are effective communicators.
> - Children interact verbally and non-verbally with others for a range of purposes.
> - Children engage with a range of texts and gain meaning from these texts.
> - Children express ideas and make meaning using a range of media.
>
> **ASSESSMENT**
> - Students should be provided with positive, formative feedback throughout their engagement.

Arts-rich learning contexts for early childhood and primary

When children enter your classroom, what visual impact does it have to engage the creative mind? Does it have an abundance of stimuli? Are children's Arts creations performed and displayed, and is the child's voice recognised and valued? Are their senses engaged? A classroom can have a multitude of images to enhance learning. There can be aural stimulation from music and sound. The furniture can be arranged so as to encourage group work, or to encourage a variety of uses of space, even with the most limited of resources. All such choices that you make can either encourage or smother engagement with learning.

This is, of course, additional to the critical element in creating a powerfully engaging learning environment, which is you – the teacher. Your beliefs and attitudes and your verbal and visual signals, implicit and explicit, will guide the children as to the importance and purpose of activities and experiences. Classrooms and materials that are maintained and cared for are valued by children because of the value that you demonstrate. A four-year-old will treat a colouring pencil as important and valuable if the purpose it is used for and your attitude demonstrate that the pencil, and the process of creating a visual artwork, are valuable.

In the classroom

Ask a child to write a letter/word/sentence/paragraph, depending on their literacy, age or ability. Now ask the child to illustrate their writing with a large, clear picture to represent what they have written. Emphasise that the picture must cover most of the paper and, depending on the age/level of the child, should demonstrate the visual arts skills they have previously learned. Thus, a child may write a letter K, or a paragraph on why they love kangaroos, and then draw a kangaroo. Such an activity allows children to communicate, with depth, their level of understanding of kangaroos, and also supports and embeds the literacy activity they have undertaken.

Children engage in the Arts continually, whether consciously or subconsciously. As teachers, we should engage the children in sharing their experiences. Talk to your class. Substantive communication and narrative application are core pedagogical tools to allow for authentic teaching experiences. Share with the children your experiences and fears in engaging with the Arts. Share moments such as attending an art gallery, listening to music, dancing at a wedding, or dressing up. Of course, it is important to remember to maintain the teacher–child relationship, but your honesty will encourage the children to share their experiences and also to discover unrealised experiences. Even in sharing experiences, the Arts can be used as the tools for communication.

In the classroom

This activity can be developed and extended for all primary children, though some preschool children may need support.

Give each child four pieces of blank paper. This is a timed activity. Tell the children this. Each task uses one side of each piece of paper.

Task 1: In one minute, children are to draw an image of themselves in their favourite place.

Task 2: Using a fresh piece of paper, they are to write in one minute one word that describes how they feel the night before Christmas or another important event.

Task 3: They close their eyes and think of their favourite outfit; the one they like to wear and that makes them feel special. Then, with their eyes still closed, zoom in on one detail of that clothing. Then they quickly open their eyes and draw that zoomed-in image on a new piece of paper. They have one minute.

Task 4: On the centre of a new piece of paper, they write their favourite activity from this list: drawing, singing, acting, dancing and watching. Draw six lines coming out from the word like an ant's legs. Now, in one minute, they write the first six words (one beside every line where the ant's foot would be) that come to their minds when they think about the word in the centre.

Your students have just written a reflective journal of their Arts experiences. Now have them share their four-page logbook with a partner and talk about their pages. They have one minute each (two minutes total). Invite anyone who wants to share their reflective logbook with the whole class. This can be the start of a journal that can follow them through all of their learning.

The Arts are a form of communication that allows a variety of learning styles to be used to access and share the curriculum. The concept of 'learning styles' has begun to be significantly questioned, with experts arguing that children do not have preferred learning styles. However, there are a variety of differing learning methods that allow multiple forms of access and communication of ideas. As has been previously noted, the Arts are a 'primary' form of learning and communicating the conscious and subconscious self. This development of communication methods supports identity development.

Reflection activity

Table 12.2 shows the core curriculum areas (except the Arts) on the left-hand side. Think of an Arts strand (dance, drama, media arts, music or visual arts) and an activity that can support each curriculum Learning Area.

For example, Health and PE could be supported through dance and music. Students could participate in any number of well-known dances (that simultaneously impact on HPE) such as 'The Wheels on the Bus' action song or 'The Hokey Pokey'.

TABLE 12.2 CORE CURRICULUM AREAS

Curriculum area	Arts strand	Activity
English		
Mathematics		
Science		
HASS		
Technologies		
Health and PE		
Languages		

In the classroom

Clear an open space in the classroom where each child can have an individual space to sit in. Give each child a wooden stick or object. Have the children hit a rhythm in unison (led by teacher modelling) and then have them stop together on command with the word 'Freeze'. Once the children have mastered this, offer the children real-life situations, such as being given a plate of broccoli to eat. Children have to tap out a rhythm that reflects how they feel about the broccoli they have to eat. This rhythm does not have to be in unison. Between each situation they must freeze, then return to the unison rhythm before another freeze and another situation. Each situation should be followed by an opposite. Thus, after broccoli the situation may be a plate of chocolate cake. Situations can become more emotionally complex as the activity progresses and depending on the age/stage of the children. Table 12.3 provides some suggestions.

TABLE 12.3 SUGGESTIONS

plate of broccoli to eat	having a friend over to play
bar of chocolate	being on your own at recess
losing a toy	a tooth falling out
being given a present	getting money from the tooth fairy
doing well in a test	being given a merit award
losing a game of soccer	being called names

If the class can cope with more subtle differences and challenging ideas, then the following suggestions may be attempted. The response can also be adapted to include movement.

no-one checking your homework	giving a gift that the other person doesn't like
being congratulated for something you didn't do	feeling lucky you didn't get bullied, even though your friend did
getting a gift you don't like	helping a friend who is being bullied, even though you get involved

The Arts help children safely explore complex emotions that are hard to express by other means. The Arts can allow us to distance ourselves from direct emotional involvement in a situation by exploring it as an observer or from the viewpoint of another. This can be done by painting a situation, performing it as part of an ensemble, or creating an image/soundscape reflecting the situation and its emotional content.

Arts-rich teaching

In Chapter 1 you were asked to prepare your vision for the Arts in education, and at the start of this chapter you were asked to revisit it. Throughout this book you have also been challenged to develop your understandings of what this means in both early childhood and primary contexts. This vision and your understandings stand you in good stead as you move forward. Consider: if we are to allow children to explore their identity and society – to allow the transformation and liberation of the individual as suggested by Freire (1993) and the Melbourne Declaration (MCEETYA, 2008) – the Arts have to be moved to a core place in learning. In Chapter 1, a praxial vision for Arts education was proposed (Alperson, 1991; Bernstein, 1999; Elliott, 1995; Freire, 1993). Arts education as praxis has a dual meaning. First, it is about the Arts as individual practices wherein authentic, culturally specific learning occurs in all of its diversity in both process and product. Second, it is about learner agency and the importance of doing this in ways that foreground making and responding in the Arts. Arts education as praxis is important in achieving the goal of the Arts being positioned at the centre of learning.

To achieve this, though, will require a fundamental change in the industrialisation of education: from producing mere functional bodies that feed the needs of society, to sending out enlightened and successful members of society who can lead the future to change through the application of creative and diverse thinking (Robinson, 2011). We need to remember that, as teachers, we must allow creativity and diverse thinking to flourish (Gardner, 1995). However, we should also be aware that we can inadvertently stifle growth and smother children's ability to express and communicate their individuality. It is through the Arts that children flourish rather than remain at the level of lower-order thinking (Eisner, 1998).

Lesson plan 12.2

AIM

To engage in quality, Arts-rich learning in the primary context.

OVERVIEW

Learning how to tell a story through music and drawing.

OUTLINE/DESCRIPTION

Program music: narrative music or music that is composed to tell a story.

In this lesson students listen to a piece of **program music**, compose and perform a piece of music that tells a story, and draw a story, adding text to the finished sequence of drawings.

Students should listen to the 'Little Train of Caipira' by Hector Villa-Lobos, using the listening points below as a guide.

0'–40': You can hear the steam engine at different dynamics and tempo, the whistle blaring, and a folk song. In the beginning you hear the train moving and the whistle.

40': You can hear the 8-bar folk song melody played by strings. Sliding and descending sounds in trombones and other instruments. It goes higher and higher up the mountain.

At 2.00' the train suddenly stops. To pick up more passengers, or does it just reach the top of the mountain?

At 2.15' the train is moving smoothly along; more folk tune.

3.40': starting to slow down to stop.

Ask students to use whatever instruments they have available to compose a piece of program music. The choice of story is entirely theirs; but it should be a 'journey' of some sort, in a boat, a plane, a car, a train or a rocket! Students should perform their finished composition. They should explain their use of the elements of music to create their narrative composition. Ask students to draw the story they just composed in music. It should have several 'pages' of images that when combined tell the story. They should experiment with techniques of drawing using different materials such as pencil, charcoal, pastel, markers etc. Now they should add text to each or some images if needed, remembering that the focus for this activity is on their visual storytelling. The text will elaborate the meaning from each image and would be suitable for a child to read. Students talk about how they have used the elements of visual art to create their narrative drawings.

INTENDED OUTCOMES

Students identify
- the different elements used in a piece of programmatic music.
- the different elements used in a piece of narrative visual art.

Students understand
- that composers and artists use the elements of music to create an effect or mood.
- that they can use the elements as an artist and composer.

Students are able to
- compose, rehearse and perform a piece of music using whatever instruments they have to hand
- design and draw a sequence of narrative artworks that tell a story.

LINKS TO CURRICULUM

Year 3 and 4 content descriptors
- Develop aural skills by exploring, imitating and recognising elements of music including dynamics, pitch and rhythm patterns (ACAMUM084).
- Practise singing, playing instruments and improvising music, using elements of music including rhythm, pitch, dynamics and form in a range of pieces, including in music from the local community (ACAMUM085).
- Identify intended purposes and meanings as they listen to music using the elements of music to make comparisons, starting with Australian music, including music of Aboriginal and Torres Strait Islander peoples (ACAMUR087).
- Use materials, techniques and processes to explore visual conventions when making artworks (ACAVAM111).
- Present artworks and describe how they have used visual conventions to represent their ideas (ACAVAM112).

ASSESSMENT

Students can be assessed in multiple ways in this learning activity. Their finished compositions and visual artworks could be assessed, *or* their collaborative skills, or their application could be assessed.

Conclusion

Throughout this book, it has been shown that the Arts are an integral part of a child's academic and vocational development, as well as an ongoing learning process for adults. No one Learning Area can be complete without the support of other knowledges. It must also be remembered that while 'the Arts' have a particular definition for curriculum and education in Australia, the Arts as a whole encompass literature, science, mathematics and the wider humanities. While the Arts do not 'teach' creativity, they do offer children access to knowledges and skills that allow creativity and creative expression to thrive. A quality, arts-rich education benefits the child, the school community and wider society both intrinsically and extrinsically.

We are happier people when we engage in the Arts, and that is what we all want for the children we teach. Through the Arts, if we can instill a love of learning, then we can all learn to love.

REVIEW QUESTIONS

1. What makes critical reflection 'critical'?
2. How would you define 'sequential' Arts education?
3. How would you define 'sustained' Arts education?
4. How would you define 'substantial' Arts education?
5. Identify any three of the characteristics of quality Arts education.
6. How would you define Arts-rich learning?

7 List any three of the characteristics of an Arts-rich learning environment.

8 List three individuals or organisations that could be good partners for learning in your Arts-rich classroom.

RECOMMENDED READING

Anderson, M. and Gibson, R. (2004). 'Connecting the silos: Developing Arts rich education'. *Change: Transformations in Education*, 7(2), 1–11.

Clay, G., Hertrich, J., Jones, P., Mills, J. and Rose, J. (1998). *The Arts Inspected*. London: Heinemann.

Dewey, J. (1980). *Art as Experience*. New York: Perigee.

Gardner, H. (1982). *Art, Mind and Brain: A Cognitive Approach to Human Development*. New York: Basic Books.

Ladwig, J. G. (2010). 'Beyond academic outcomes'. *Review of Research in Education*. 34 (March), 28.

Pinar, W. F., Reynolds, W. M., Slattery, P. and Taubman, P. M. (1995). *Understanding Curriculum*. New York: Peter Lang.

Seidl, S., Tishman, S., Winner, E., Hetland, L. and Palmer, P. (2009). *The Qualities of Quality: Understanding Excellence in Arts Education*. Cambridge, MASS: Project Zero. Retrieved from http://www.wallacefoundation.org/knowledge-center/Documents/Understanding-Excellence-in-Arts-Education.pdf.

Vygotsky, L. S. (1986). *Thought and Learning*. Cambridge, MA: The MIT Press.

Wright, S., Sinclair, C., Jeanneret, N., Sallis, R., Watkins, M., Adams, R. J., Stevens-Ballenger, J., Grant, G. and McLennan, R. (2014). *Teachers' Application of Arts Rich Practice Teaching In and Through the Arts: Executive Summary*. Melbourne: Melbourne Graduate School of Education.

References

ACARA. See Australian Curriculum, Assessment and Reporting Authority.

Admiraal, W. et al. (2017). 'Preparing pre-service teachers to integrate technology into K–12 instruction: Evaluation of a technology-infused approach', *Technology, Pedagogy and Education*, 26(1), 105–20.

Agin, M. C., Geng, L. F. and Nicholl, M. J. (2003). *The Late Talker*. New York: St Martins Press.

AITSL. See Australian Institute for Teaching and School Leadership Ltd.

Allen, A. and Coley, J. (1995). *Dance for All*. London: David Fulton Publishers.

Allen, J. and White, S. (2017). *Learning to Teach in a New Era*. Melbourne: Cambridge University Press.

Allen, M. L., Hartley C. and Cain, K. (2016). 'iPads and the use of "apps" by children with Autism Spectrum Disorder: do they promote learning?', *Frontiers in Psychology*, 7 [2016], 1305.

Allsup, R. A. and Baxter, M. (2004). 'Talking about music: Better Questions? Better discussions!'. *Music Educators Journal*, 91(2), 29–33.

Alperson, P. (1991). 'What should one expect from a philosophy of music education?'. *Journal of Aesthetic Education*, 25(3), 215–42.

Amosa, W., Ladwig, J. G., Griffiths, T. and Gore, J. M. (2007). 'Equity effects of quality teaching: Closing the gap'. Paper presented at the Australian Association for Research in Education Annual Conference. Fremantle, 25–29 November 2007.

Anderson, J. L., Ellis, J. P. and Jones, A. M. (2014). 'Understanding early elementary children's conceptual knowledge of plant structure and function through drawings'. *CBE – Life Sciences Education*, 13(3), 375–86.

Anderson, L. W. and Krathwohl, D. R. (eds). (2001). *A Taxonomy for Learning, Teaching, and Assessing: A Revision of Bloom's Taxonomy of Educational Objectives*. New York: Longman.

Anderson, M. (2012). *Master Class in Drama Education*. London: Continuum.

Anderson, M. and Dunn, J. (eds). (2013). *How Drama Activates Learning: Contemporary Research and Practice*. London: Bloomsbury.

Anderson, M. and Gibson, R. (2004). 'Connecting the silos: Developing Arts rich education'. *Change: Transformations in education*, 7(2), 1–11.

Arts Education Partnership. (2011). 'Arts-Rich Learning Helps Students Succeed – Experts Convene in San Francisco for National Forum on *"Transforming Urban School Systems Through the Arts"'*. Retrieved from https://www.aep-arts-org.

Ashman, A. and Elkins, J. (eds). (2012). *Education for Inclusion and Diversity*. Sydney: Pearson.

Ashton, L. (2008). *Creativity: The chameleon in the curriculum*. Paper presented at the AEV Conference, Melbourne University, Victoria, Australia.

Australia Council (2014). *Arts Facts*. Retrieved from artfacts.australiacouncil.gov.au/overview.

Australian Curriculum, Assessment and Reporting Authority (ACARA) (2012). The Shape of the Australian Curriculum. Sydney, ACARA.

—— (2013). *Shape of the Australian Curriculum: The Arts*. Sydney: ACARA

—— (2014). *Cross-curriculum Priorities*. Sydney: ACARA. Retrieved from https://www.acara.edu.au/curriculum/cross-curriculum-priorities.

—— (2015). *General Capabilities*. Sydney: ACARA. Retrieved from https://www.australiancurriculum.edu.au/f-10-curriculum/general-capabilities/.

—— (2016). *Student Diversity*. Sydney: ACARA. Retrieved from http://acara.edu.au/curriculum/student-diversity.

—— (2017). *Australian Curriculum: The Arts*. Retrieved from https://www.australiancurriculum.edu.au/f-10-curriculum/the-arts/.

Australian Government Department of Education, Employment and Workplace Relations (DEEWR) (2009). *Belonging, Being and Becoming – The Early Years Learning Framework for Australia*. Produced for the Council of Australian Governments. Retrieved from https://docs.education.gov.au/documents/belonging-being-becoming-early-years-learning-framework-australia.

Australian Institute for Teaching and School Leadership Ltd (AITSL) (2017). *Australian Professional Standards for Teachers*. Retrieved from https://www.aitsl.edu.au/teach/standards.

Avalos, B. (2011). 'Teacher professional development in teaching and teacher education over ten years'. *Teaching and Teacher Education*, 27(1), 10.

Baim, C., Brookes, S. and Mountford, A. (eds) (2002). *The Geese Theatre Handbook: Drama with Offenders and People at Risk*. Winchester: Waterside Press.

Baker, W. J. (2012). 'The arts pale behind literacy and numeracy'. *Education Review*, pp. 1. ISSN 1834–7967. [Professional, Non Refereed Article].

Baker, W. J. and Harvey, G. (2014). 'The collaborative learning behaviours of middle primary school students in a classroom music creation activity'. *Australian Journal of Music Education* [2014](1), 15–26.

Bamford, A. (2006). *The Wow Factor: Global Research Compendium on the Impact of the Arts in Education*. Berlin: Waxmann Verlag.

Banks, R. A. and Marson, P. (1998). *Drama and Theatre Arts*, 2nd edn. London: Hodder & Stoughton.

Barrett, M. S. (1996). *Learning Centres in Music Education*. Launceston: Uniprint.

—— (2003). 'Musical children, musical lives, musical worlds'. In S. Wright (ed.), *Children, meaning-making and the Arts*. Frenchs Forest, NSW: Pearson.

Barrett, M. S. and Smigiel, H. M. (2003). 'Awakening the "Sleeping Giant"?: The arts in the lives of Australian families'. *International Journal of Education and the Arts*, 4(4). Retrieved from www.ijea.org/v4n4/index.html.

Barrett, M. S., Everett, M. C. and Smigiel, H. M. (2012). 'Meaning, value and engagement in the Arts: Findings from a participatory investigation of young Australian children's perceptions of the Arts'. *International Journal of Early Childhood*, 44, 185–201.

Beane, J.A. (1995). 'Curriculum integration and the disciplines of knowledge'. *Phi Delta Kappa*, 76(8), 616–22.

Bell, D. (2012). 'Talking about art with young people: Conversational strategies for aesthetic learning in early childhood settings'. *International Art in Early Childhood Research Journal*, 3(1). Retrieved from http://artinearlychildhood.org/journals/2012/ARTEC_2012_Research_Journal_1_Article_1_Bell.pdf.

Bernstein, R. J. (1999). *Praxis and Action: Contemporary Philosophies of Human Action*, 2nd edn. Pennsylvania: University of Pennsylvania Press.

Berry, C. (1992). *The Actor and the Text*. London: Virgin.

Bersson, R. (1991). *Worlds of Art*. London: Mayfield Publishing.

Biasutti, M. (2017). 'Strategies adopted during collaborative online music composition'. *International Journal of Music Education*, 36(6). Retrieved from: http://journals.sagepub.com.ezproxy.utas.edu.au/doi/pdf/10.1177/0255761417741520.

Bloom, B. S. and Krathwohl, D. R. (1956). *Taxonomy of Educational Objectives: The Classification of Educational Goals, by a Committee of College and University Examiners*. NY: Longmans, Green.

Blumenthal, E., Taymor, J. and Monda, A. (2007). *Julie Taymor*, 3rd edn. New York: Abrams.

Boal, A. (2002). *Games for Actors and Non-Actors*, 2nd edn. London: Routledge.

Bourdieu, P. and Passeron, J. P. (1977). *Reproduction in Education, Society and Culture*. Beverly Hills: Sage.

Borko, H. (2004). 'Professional development and teacher learning: Mapping the terrain'. *Educational Researcher*, 33(8), 3–15.

Bowe, J., Gore, J. M. and Elsworth, W. A. (2010). 'Rounding out teacher professional learning: Professional learning community, instructional rounds and Quality Teaching'. Paper presented at the Australian Association for Research in Education Annual Conference.

Bradley, K. K. (2009). *Rudolf Laban*. Abingdon: Routledge.

Braun, E. (1995). *Meyerhold: A Revolution in Theatre*. London: Methuen.

Brookfield, S. (1995). *Becoming a Critically Reflective Teacher*. San Francisco, CAL: Jossey Bass.

Brooks, G. (2007). *Dyspraxia*, 2nd edn. London: Continuum.

Brouillette, L., Childress-Evans, K., Hinga, B. and Farkas, G, (2014). 'Increasing Engagement and Oral Language Skills of ELLs through the Arts in the Primary Grades'. *Journal for Learning through the Arts*, 10(1).

Bruner, J. (1986). *Actual Minds, Possible Worlds*. Cambridge, MA: Harvard University Press.

Bryce, J., Mendelovits, J., Beavis, A., McQueen, J. and Adams, I. (2004). *Evaluation of School-based Arts Education Programmes in Australian Schools*. Camberwell, Vic: Australian Council for Educational Research.

Buckingham, D. (2005). 'The media literacy of children and young people: A review of the research literature'. London: Centre for the Study of Children, Youth and Media Institute of Education, University of London. Retrieved from eprints.ioe.ac.uk/145/1/Buckinghammedialiteracy.pdf.

Bundy, A. C., Lane, S. J. and Murray, E. A. (2002). *Sensory Integration: Theory and Practice*. Philadelphia: F. A. Davis.

Bunting, M. (2009). 'The rise of climate-change art'. *The Guardian*, UK, 2 December. Retrieved from https://www.guardian.co.uk/artanddesign/2009/dec/02/climate-change-art-earth-rethink.

Burridge, S. (2003). *Arts-based approaches to creative teaching and learning*. Singapore: LASALLE-SIA College of the Arts.

Burton, J. M., Horowitz, R. and Abeles, H. (2000). 'Learning in and through the Arts: The question of transfer'. *Studies in Art Education*. 41(3), 228–57. In R. Deasy (ed.), *Critical Links: Learning in the Arts and Student Academic and Social Development*. Washington, DC: Arts Education Partnership and National Endowment for the Arts.

Butzlaff, R. (2000). 'Can music be used to teach reading?' *The Journal of Aesthetic Education*, 34(3), 167–78. In R. Deasy (ed.), *Critical Links: Learning in the Arts and Student Academic and Social Development*. Washington, DC: Arts Education Partnership and National Endowment for the Arts.

Calogero, J. M. (2002). 'Integrating music and children's literature'. *Music Educators Journal*, 88(5), 23–30.

Campbell, J. (1969). *The Masks of God: Primitive Mythology*. New York: Penguin Compass.

Campbell, P. S. (2005). 'Deep listening to the musical world'. *Music Educators Journal*, 92(1), 30–6.

Carper, B. A. (1978). 'Fundamental patterns of knowing in nursing'. *Advances in Nursing Science*, 1(1), 13–24.

Catterall, J. S., Chapleau, R. and Iwanaga, J. (1999). 'Involvement in the Arts and human development: General involvement and intensive involvement in music and theater arts'. In E. Fiske (ed.), *Champions of Change: The Impact of the Arts on Learning*, pp. 1–18. Washington, DC: The Arts Partnership and the President's Committee on the Arts and Humanities.

Catterall, J. S. and Waldorf, L. (1999). 'Chicago Arts Partnerships in Education Summary Evaluation'. In E. Fiske (ed.), *Champions of Change: The Impact of the Arts on Learning*, pp. 47–62. Washington, DC: The Arts Partnership and the President's Committee on the Arts and Humanities.

Cayari, C. (2011). 'The YouTube effect: How YouTube has provided new ways to consume, create, and share music'. *International Journal of Education & the Arts*, 12(6). Retrieved from www.ijea.org/v12n6.

—— (2016). 'Connecting music education and virtual performance practices from YouTube'. *Music Education Research*, 20(3), 360–76.

Chand, A. (2016). 'Why is teaching kids to draw not a more important part of the curriculum?'. *The Conversation*. Retrieved from https://theconversation.com/why-is-teaching-kids-to-draw-not-a-more-important-part-of-the-curriculum-60379.

Clark, C. D. (1999). 'The autodriven interview: A photographic viewfinder into children's experience'. *Visual Sociology*, 14, 39–50.

Clay, G., Hertrich, J., Jones, P., Mills, J. and Rose, J. (1998). *The Arts Inspected*. London: Heinemann.

Colak, E. (2015). 'The effect of cooperative learning on the learning approaches of students with different learning styles'. *Eurasian Journal of Educational Research*, 59, 17–34.

Cook, T. and Hess, E. (2007). 'What the camera sees and from whose perspective: Fun methodologies for engaging children in enlightening adults'. *Childhood*, 14(1), 29–45.

Cordes, C. and Miller, E. (eds). (2000). *Fool's Gold: A Critical Look at Computers in Childhood*. College Park, MD: Alliance for Childhood.

Couse, L. J. and Chen, D. W. (2010). 'A tablet computer for young children? Exploring its viability for early childhood education', *Journal of Research on Technology in Education*, 43(1), 75–98.

Craig, E. G. (1956). *On the Art of the Theatre*. New York: Theatre Arts Books.

Cremin, T., McDonald, R., Goff, E. and Blakemore, L. (2009). *Jumpstart! Drama: Games & Activities for Ages 5–11*. London: Routledge.

Cremata, R. and Powell, B. (2017). 'Online music collaboration project: Digitally mediated, deterritorialized music education'. *International Journal of Music Education*, 35(2), 302–31. Retrieved from http://journals.sagepub.com.ezproxy.utas.edu.au/doi/pdf/10.1177/0255761415620225.

Crittenden, S. (2009). 'Who stopped the music?' *Background Briefing*, ABC Radio National. Retrieved from https://www.abc.net.au/radionational/programs/backgroundbriefing/who-stopped-the-music/3055612.

Curtis, D. J., Reid, N. and Ballard G. (2012). 'Communicating ecology through art: What scientists think'. *Ecology and Society*, 17(2), 3. http://dx.doi.org/10.5751/ES-04670-170203.

Cziboly, A. (2010). 'The DICE has been cast'. In A. Cziboly (ed.), *Research Findings and Recommendations on Educational Theatre and Drama*. Hungary: DICE Consortium. Retrieved from www.dramanetwork.eu.

Davies, M. (2003). *Movement and Dance in Early Childhood*. Thousand Oaks, CA: Sage Publications.

Davis, D. (2008). *First We See: The National Review of Visual Education*. Canberra: Department of Education, Science and Training.

Deasy, R. J. (ed.) (2002). *Critical Links: Learning in the Arts and Student Academic and Social Development*. Washington, DC: Arts Education Partnership and National Endowment for the Arts.

DEEWR. See Australian Government Department of Education, Employment and Workplace Relations.

Denac, O. (2014). 'The significance and role of aesthetic education in schooling'. *Creative Education*, 5, 1714–19.

Department of Education and Training (2003a). *Quality Teaching in NSW Public Schools: A Classroom Practice Guide*. Ryde: NSW Department of Education and Training Professional Support and Curriculum Directorate.

—— (2003b). *Quality Teaching in NSW Public Schools: An Assessment Practice Guide*. Ryde: NSW Department of Education and Training Professional Support and Curriculum Directorate.

—— (2008). *Quality Teaching to support the NSW Professional Teaching Standards*. Professional Learning and Leadership Development Directorate. NSW Department of Education and Training.

Department of Education, Tasmania (nd). *Songlines of the Moonbird Learning Resource*. Hobart: Aboriginal Education Services.

Dewey, J. (1980). *Art as Experience*. New York: Perigee.

—— (2007). *Democracy and Education*. Teddington: Echo Library.

Dixon, G. and Addy, L. M. (2004). *Making Inclusion Work for Children with Dyspraxia: Practical Strategies for Teachers*. London: RoutledgeFalmer.

Dixon, J. (2011). *Delivering Authentic Arts Education*. Melbourne: Cengage Learning Australia.

Donaldson, J. and Scheffler, A. (1999). *The Gruffalo*, 6th edn. London: Macmillan Children's Books.

Donelan, K. (2012). Arts education as intercultural and social dialogue. In C. Sinclair, N. Jeanneret and J. O'Toole (eds), *Education in the Arts: Teaching and Learning in the Contemporary Curriculum*. South Melbourne: Oxford University Press.

Dorn, C. M., Sabol, R. and Madeja, S. S. (2014). *Assessing Expressive Learning: A Practical Guide for Teacher-directed Authentic Assessment in K–12 Visual Arts Education*. New York: Routledge.

Duma A. and Silverstein, L. (2014). 'Cross-study findings: A view into a decade of Arts integration', *Journal for Learning through the Arts*, 10(1). Retrieved from https://escholarship.org/uc/item/3pt13398.

Duncum, P. (2001). 'Visual culture: Developments, definitions, and directions for art education'. *Studies in Art Education*, 42(2), 101–12.

Dweck, C. S. (2006). *Mindset: Changing the Way You Think to Fulfil Your Potential*. London: Robinson Little, Brown.

EATSIPS (2011). *Embedding Aboriginal and Torres Strait Islander Perspectives in Schools: A Guide for School Learning Communities*. Retrieved from www.deta.qld.gov.au/indigenous/pdfs/eatsips_2011.pdf.

Edson, G. (2005). *Masks and Masking: Faces of Tradition and Belief Worldwide*. Jefferson, North Carolina: McFarland.

Edwards, C. P., Gandini, L. and Forman, G. E. (eds). (1993). *The Hundred Languages of Children*. Norwood, NJ: Ablex.

Edwards, L. (2014). *The Creative Arts: A Process Approach for Teachers and Children*. Harlow, Essex: Pearson.

Eisner, E. (1998). *The Kind of Schools We Need*. Portsmouth, NH: Heinemann.

Elliott, D. J. (1995). *Music Matters: A New Philosophy of Music Education*. New York: Oxford University Press.

Ellis, J. (1982). *Visible Fictions*. New York: Routledge.

Elster, A. (2001). 'Learning through the Arts program goals, features, and pilot results'. *International Journal of Education & the Arts*, 2(7). Retrieved from www.ijea.org/v12n6.

English, R. and Wilson, J. (2004). *How to Succeed with Learning Centres*. Carlton South: Curriculum Corporation.

Ewing, R. (2010). *The Arts and Australian Education: Realising Potential*. Camberwell, Vic.: Australian Council for Educational Research. Retrieved from research.acer.edu.au/aer/11/.

Fasoli, L. (2003). 'Reading photographs of young children: Looking at practices'. *Contemporary Issues in Early Childhood*, 4(1), 32–47.

Fawcett, A. (1976) *John Lennon: One Day at a Time – A Personal Biography of the Seventies*. New York: Grove Press.

Fiske, E. (ed.) (1999). *Champions of Change: The Impact of the Arts on Learning*. Washington, DC: The Arts Partnership and the President's Committee on the Arts and Humanities.

Fleer, M. (2010). *Early Childhood and Development: Cultural–Historical Concepts in Play*. Melbourne: Cambridge University Press.

Fleming, M. (2012). *The Arts in Education: An Introduction to Aesthetics, Theory and Pedagogy*. Florence, KY: Routledge, Taylor & Francis Group.

Florian, L. and Black-Hawkins, K. (2011). 'Exploring inclusive pedagogy'. *British Educational Research Journal*, 37(5), 813–28.

Fontana, T. (2018). *25 Best Guitar Websites in 2018*. Retrieved from https://www.theguitarlesson.com/guitar-lesson-blog/guitar-lesson-review/best-guitar-websites/.

Foreman, J. (2000). *Maskwork*. Cambridge: The Lutterworth Press.

Freire, P. (1970). *Pedagogy of the Oppressed*. New York: Herder and Herder.

—— (1993). *Pedagogy of the Oppressed*, 3rd edn. London, UK: Pearson.

Gaitskill, C., Hurwitz, A. and Day, M. (2006). *Children and Their Art*, 8th edn. New York: Harcourt Brace Jovanovich.

Gale, L. (2017). World Congress speech: Global realities of child exploitation. Retrieved from https://www.afp.gov.au/news-media/national-speeches/world-congress-speech-global-realities-child-exploitation.

Gallagher, S. (2000). 'Philosophical conceptions of the self: Implications for cognitive science'. *Trends in Cognitive Sciences*, 4(1), 14–21.

Gao, P., Wong, A. F., Choy, D. and Wu, J. (2011). 'Beginning teachers' understanding performances of technology integration'. *Asia Pacific Journal of Education*, 31(2), 211–23.

Gardiner, G. (2003). 'Creative engagement: The place of arts-rich education in Australian schools'. *Curriculum & Leadership Journal*, 9(2).

Gardner, H. (1982). *Art, Mind and Brain: A Cognitive Approach to Human Development*. New York: Basic Books.

—— (1983). *Frames of Mind: The Theory of Multiple Intelligences*. New York: Basic Books.

—— (1993). *Multiple Intelligences: The Theory in Practice*. New York: Basic Books.

—— (1995). *The Unschooled Mind: How Children Think and How Schools Should Teach*. New York: Basic Books.

—— (1999). 'The happy meeting of multiple intelligences and the Arts'. *Harvard Education Letter*, 15(6). Retrieved from www.hepg.org/hel/article/440.

Garvis, S. and Pendergast, D. (2011). 'An investigation of early childhood teacher self-efficacy beliefs in the teaching of arts education.' *International Journal of Education and the Arts*, 12(9). Retrieved from www.ijea.org/v12n9.

Gibbs, G. (1988). *Learning by Doing: A Guide to Teaching and Learning Methods*. Oxford: Further Education Unit.

Gibson, R. and Ewing, R. (2011). *Transforming the Curriculum Through the Arts*. Melbourne: Palgrave Macmillan.

Goldhill, O. (2016). 'The concept of different "learning styles" is one of the greatest neuroscience myths'. *Quartz Private Key*. Retrieved from https://qz.com/585143/the-concept-of-different-learning-styles-is-one-of-the-greatest-neuroscience-myths/.

Gore, J. (2007). 'Improving pedagogy'. In J. Butcher and L. McDonald (eds). *Making a Difference: Challenges for Teachers, Teaching and Teacher Education*, pp. 15–32. Rotterdam: Sense.

Gore, J., Bowe, J., Mockler, N., Smith, M., Ellis, H. and Lyell, A. (2013). *Investigating 'Quality Teaching Rounds' to support teacher professional learning: Research report*. Newcastle, NSW: University of Newcastle.

Goss, P. (2017). *Towards an adaptive education system in Australia*. Grattan Institute Discussion paper No. 2017–01, November. Grattan Institute. Retrieved from https://grattan.edu.au/report/towards-an-adaptive-education-system-in-australia/.

Greene, M. (2001). *Variations on a Blue Guitar: The Lincoln Center Institute Lectures on Aesthetic Education*. New York: Teachers College Press.

Grishin, S. (2015) *Australian Art: A History*. Vic: The Miegunyah Press.

Guterres, A. (2017). 'The Sustainable Development Goals Report'. Retrieved from https://unstats.un.org/sdgs/report/2017/.

Haberman, M. (1994). 'The pedagogy of poverty versus good teaching'. In E. Hatton (ed.), *Understanding Teaching: Curriculum and the Social Context of Schooling*, pp. 17–25. Sydney: Harcourt Brace Jovanovich.

Habibi, A., Damasio, A., Ilari, B., Veiga, R., Joshi, A., Leahy, R., Haldar, J., Varadarajan, D., Bhushan, C. and Damasio, H. (2017). 'Childhood music training induces change in micro and macroscopic brain structure: Results from a longitudinal study'. *Cerebral Cortex*, 28(12), 4336–47.

Hallam, S. (2010). 'The power of music: Its impact on the intellectual, social and personal development of children and young people'. *International Journal of Music Education*, 28(3), 269–88.

Hamilton A. (2013). *Preparing pre-service primary school teachers to teach cross-curricular priorities and the Arts through 'big ideas' and the zoo. Uncharted territory? Navigating the new Australian Curriculum*. ACSA Biennial Conference.

—— (2014). *School Drama Evaluation*. Unpublished review.

Hanley, B. (2003). 'The good, the bad, and the ugly: Arts partnerships in Canadian elementary schools'. *Arts Education Policy Review*, 104(6), 11–20.

Hanley, M., Khairat, M., Taylor, K., Wilson, R., Cole-Fletcher, R. and Riby, D. M. (2017). 'Classroom displays – Attraction or distraction? Evidence of impact on attention and learning from children with and without autism'. *Developmental Psychology*, 53(7), 1265–75.

Harland, J., Kinder, K., Lord, P., Stott, A., Schagen, I., Haynes, J., with Cusworth, L., White, R. and Paola, R. (2000). 'Arts education in secondary schools: Effects and effectiveness'. In R. Deasy (ed.), *Critical Links: Learning in the Arts and Student Academic and Social Development*, pp. 76–7. Washington, DC: Arts Education Partnership and National Endowment for the Arts.

Hattie, J. (2008). *Visible Learning*. London: Routledge.

Heathcote, D. and Bolton, G. (1994). *Drama for Learning: Dorothy Heathcote's Mantle of the Expert Approach to Education*. Portsmouth, New Hampshire: Heinemann.

Heick, T. (2013). 'The Definition of Digital Citizenship'. Retrieved from https://www.teachthought.com/the-future-of-learning/the-definition-of-digital-citizenship/.

Hein, G. (1991). 'Constructivist Learning Theory'. *Institute for Inquiry*. Retrieved from https://www.exploratorium.edu/IFI/resources/constructivistlearning.html.

Hennessy, S. (2000). 'Overcoming the red-feeling: The development of confidence to teach music in primary school amongst student teachers', *British Journal of Music Education*, 17(2), 183–96.

Hetland, L. and Winner. E. (2001). 'The Arts and academic achievement: What the evidence shows'. *Arts Education Policy Review*, 102(5), 3–6.

Hodge, A. (ed.) (2010). *Actor Training*, 2nd edn. Abingdon, Oxon: Routledge.

Horowitz, R. and Webb-Dempsey, J. (2002). 'Promising signs of positive effects: Lessons from the multi-Arts studies'. In R. Deasy (ed.), *Critical Links: Learning in the Arts and Student Academic and Social Development*, pp. 98–100. Washington, DC: Arts Education Partnership.

Hudson, P. (ed.) (2013). *Learning to Teach in The Primary Classroom*. Melbourne: Cambridge University Press.

Hunter, M. (2005). *Education and the Arts: Research Overview*. Sydney: Australia Council.

Imants, J. (2002). 'Restructuring schools as a context for teacher learning'. *International Journal of Educational Research*, 37(8), 715–32.

Inoa, R., Weltsek, G. and Tabone, C. (2014). 'A study on the relationship between theater arts and student literacy and mathematics achievement'. *Journal for Learning through the Arts*, 10(1). Retrieved from https://escholarship.org/uc/item/3sk1t3rx.

Isbell, R. T. and Raines, S. C, (2013). *Creativity and the Arts with Young Children*, 3rd edn. Celmont, CA Wadsworth: Cengage Learning.

Jarrett, C. (2015). 'All You Need to Know About the "Learning Styles" Myth, in Two Minutes'. *Wired*. Retrieved from https://www.wired.com/2015/01/need-know-learning-styles-myth-two-minutes/.

Jeanneret, N. (2006). 'The National Review of Music in Schools and the endless debate about music in primary schools'. *Australian Journal of Music Education*, 1, 93–7.

Jefferson, M. and Anderson, M. (2017). *Transforming Schools: Creativity, critical reflection, communication, collaboration*. London: Bloomsbury.

Jenlink, P. M. and Kinnucan-Welsch, K. (2001). 'Case stories of facilitating professional development'. *Teaching and Teacher Education*, 17(6), 705–24.

Joy, O. (2012) 'What does it mean to be a digital native?' Retrieved from https://edition.cnn.com/2012/12/04/business/digital-native-prensky/.

Keeffe, M. and Carrington, S. (2007). *Schools and Diversity*. Frenchs Forest, NSW: Pearson.

Kelly, M. (1998). *Encyclopedia of Aesthetics*. New York: Oxford University Press.

Kennedy, D. M. and Fox, B. (2013). 'Digital natives': An Asian perspective for using learning technologies'. *International Journal of Education and Development using Information and Communication Technology*, 9(1), 64–79.

Kerckaert, S., Vanderlinde, R. and van Braak, J. (2015). 'The role of ICT in early childhood education: Scale development and research on ICT use and influencing factors'. *European Early Childhood Education Research Journal*, 23(2), 183–99.

Killen, R. (2009). *Effective Teaching Strategies: Lessons from Research and Practice: Australia–New Zealand Edition*. Melbourne: Cengage Learning.

Kirby, A. and Peters, L. (2007). *100 Ideas for Supporting Pupils with Dyspraxia and DCD*. London: Continuum.

Kirschner, P. A. and De Bruyckere, P. (2017) 'The myths of the digital native and the multitasker', *Teaching & Teacher Education*, 67, 135–42.

Kolbe, U. (2001). *Rapunzel's Supermarket: All About Art and Young Children*. Sydney, NSW: Peppinot Press.

Korsmeyer, C. (ed.) (1998). *Aesthetics: The Big Questions*. Oxford: Blackwell Publishing.

Kozulin, A., Gindis, B., Ageyev, V. S. and Miller, S. M. (eds). (2003). *Vygotsky's Educational Theory in Cultural Context*. New York: Cambridge University Press.

Kuzniar, M. (1999). 'Finding music in art'. *Teaching Music*, 7(3), 44–47.

Ladwig, J. G. (2010). 'Beyond academic outcomes'. *Review of Research in Education*, 34 (March), 28.

Ladwig, J., Smith, M., Gore, J. M., Amosa, W. and Griffiths, T. (2007). 'Quality of pedagogy and student achievement: Multi-level replication of authentic pedagogy'. Paper presented at the Australian Association for Research in Education Annual Conference.

Lethbridge, J. (2013). 'Language learning begins in the womb'. *The Conversation*. Retrieved from https://theconversation.com/language-learning-begins-in-the-womb-17450.

Lévi-Strauss, C. (1982). *The Way of Masks* (S. Modelski, Trans.). Seattle: University of Washington Press.

——(1995). *Myth and Meaning*. New York: Schocken Books.

Lewis, C., Perry, R. and Murati, A. (2006). 'How should research contribute to instructional improvement? The case of lesson study'. *Educational Researcher*, 35(3), 3–14.

Lewis, M. and Rainer, J. (2005). *Teaching Classroom Drama and Theatre*. Abingdon: Routledge.

Livingstone, S. and Bovill, M. (2000). *Young People and New Media*. London: Sage.

Lo, C. and Hew, K. (2017). 'A critical review of flipped classroom challenges in K–12 education: Possible solutions and recommendations for future research'. *Research and Practice in Technology Enhanced Learning*, 12(4). Retrieved from: https://telrp.springeropen.com/track/pdf/10.1186/s41039-016-0044-2?site=telrp.springeropen.com.

Lofts, P. and Vaughan, M. K. (2005). *Wombat Stew*. Sydney, Australia: Scholastic.

Lombardi, M. M. (2007). 'Authentic learning for the 21st century: An overview': ELI Paper 1. Educause Learning Initiative. Retrieved from http://www.lmi.ub.edu/cursos/s21/REPOSITORIO/documents/Lombardi_2007_Authentic_learning.pdf.

Lorenzo, O., Herrera, L., Hernández-Candelas, M. and Badeac, M. (2014). 'Influence of music training on language development. A longitudinal study'. *Procedia – Social and Behavioral Sciences*, 128, 527–30.

Lowenfeld, V. and Brittain, W. L (1975). *Creative and Mental Growth*, 6th edn. New York and London: Macmillan Publishing Co., Inc.

Macintyre, C. (2009). *Dyspraxia 5–14*. Abingdon: David Fulton Publishers.

Maddox, G. (2017). 'The documentary *Screenagers* shows how to overcome our obsession with screens'. *The Sydney Morning Herald*, 8 April. https://www.smh.com.au/entertainment/movies/the-documentary-screenagers-shows-how-to-overcome-our-obsession-with-screens-20170406-gvewgx.html.

Marsh, J. and Bishop, J. C. (2014). *Changing Play: Play, Media and Commercial Culture from the 1950s to the Present Day*. Maidenhead: Open University Press/McGrawHill.

Marsh, J., Plowman, L., Yamada-Rice, D., Bishop, J. C., Lahmar, J., Scott, F., Davenport, A., Davis, S., French, K., Piras, M., Thornhill, S., Robinson, P. and Winter, P. (2015). 'Exploring Play and Creativity in Pre-Schoolers' Use of Apps: Final Project Report'. Retrieved from www.techandplay.org.

Martin, A., Mansour, M., Anderson, M., Gibson, R., Liem, A. and Sudmalis, D. (2013). 'The role of arts participation in students' academic and nonacademic outcomes: A longitudinal study of school, home, and community factors'. *Journal of Educational Psychology*, 105(3), 709–27.

McArdle, F. (2005). 'What if …? Art as language in early childhood'. *Every Child*, 11(2), 6–7.

McArdle, F. and Piscitelli, B. (2002). 'Early childhood art education: A palimpsest'. *Australian Art Education*, 25(1), 11–15.

McArdle, F. and Wong, K. B. (2010). 'What young children say about art: A comparative study'. *International Art in Early Childhood Research Journal*, 2(1), 1–17.

McCarthy, K., Ondaatje, E., Zakaras, L. and Brooks, A. (2004). *Gifts of the Muse: Reframing the Debate about the Benefits of the Arts*. Santa Monica, CA: RAND.

McDowall, A. (2018). '(Not)Knowing: Walking the terrain of Indigenous education with preservice teachers'. *The Australian Journal of Indigenous Education*, 47(2), 100–8.

MCEECDYA. See Ministerial Council on Education, Early Childhood Development and Youth Affairs.

MCEETYA. See Ministerial Council on Education, Employment, Training and Youth Affairs.

McLachlan, C., Fleer, M. and Edwards, S. (2010). *Early Childhood Curriculum: Planning, Assessment and Implementation*. Melbourne: Cambridge University Press.

McLennan, D. P. (2008). 'Kinder-caring: Exploring the use and effects of sociodrama in a kindergarten classroom'. *Journal of Student Wellbeing*, 2(1), 74–88.

Ministerial Council on Education, Early Childhood Development and Youth Affairs (MCEECDYA) (2010). *Aboriginal and Torres Strait Islander Education Action Plan 2010–2014*. Melbourne: MCEECDYA.

Ministerial Council on Education, Employment, Training and Youth Affairs and the Cultural Ministers Council (MCEETYA) (2007). *National Education and the Arts Statement*. Melbourne: MCEETYA.

—— (2008). *Melbourne Declaration on Educational Goals for Young Australians*.

Mokak, G. (2017). 'How much First Nations' culture, history and perspectives were you taught at school – are Australian students getting adequate access to Indigeneity?' *NITV*. Retrieved from https://www.sbs.com.au/nitv/article/2017/05/09/do-our-teachers-care-enough-about-indigenous-australia-bring-it-classroom.

Moloney, R. and Saltmarsh, D. (2016). '"Knowing Your Students" in the culturally and linguistically diverse classroom'. *Australian Journal of Teacher Education*, 41(4).

Moreton-Robinson, A., Singh, D., Kolopenuk, J. and Robinson, A. (2012). *Learning the Lessons?: Pre-Service Teacher Preparation for Teaching Aboriginal and Torres Strait Islander Students*. Queensland: QUT Indigenous Studies Research Network.

Morgan, N. and Saxton, J. (1987). *Teaching Drama: A Mind of Many Wonders*. Cheltenham: Stanley Thornes.

Mothersill, M. (2004). 'Beauty and the critic's judgment'. In P. Kivy (ed.), *The Blackwell Guide to Aesthetics*. Oxford: Blackwell.

Nakamura, J. and Csikszentmihalyi, M. (2002). 'The concept of flow'. In C. R. Snyder and S. J. Lopez (eds), *Handbook of Positive Psychology*. New York: Oxford University Press.

Nakata, M. (2002). 'Indigenous knowledge and the cultural interface: Underlying issues at the intersection of knowledge and information systems', *IFLA Journal*, 28(5/6), 281–91.

Nansen, B., Chakraborty, K., Gibbs, L., MacDougall, C. and Vetere, F. (2012). 'Children and digital wellbeing in Australia: Online regulation, conduct and competence', *Journal of Children and Media*, 6(2), 237–54.

National Advisory Committee on Creative and Cultural Education. (1999). *All Our Futures: Creativity, Culture and Education*. London, UK: Department for Education and Employment. Retrieved from https://www.creativitycultureeducation.org/publication/all-our-futures-creativity-culture-and-education/.

National Art Education Association (NAEA) (2004). *Beginning Drama 11–14*, 2nd edn. London: David Fulton.

—— (2009). 'Professional standards for visual arts educators'. Retrieved from http://www.arteducators.org.

Neelands, J. (2002). *Making Sense of Drama*. Oxford: Heinemann.

—— (2004). *Beginning Drama 11–14*, 2nd edn. London: David Fulton.

Newmann, F. M. & Associates (1996). *Authentic Achievement: Restructuring Schools for Intellectual Quality*. San Francisco: Jossey-Bass.

O'Toole, J. (2012). 'Art, creativity, and motivation'. In C. Sinclair, N. Jeanneret and J. O'Toole (eds), *Education in the Arts*, 2nd edn, pp. 7–14. Melbourne: Oxford University Press.

Pascoe, R., Leong, S., McCallum, J., Mackinlay, E., Marsh, K., Smith, B., Church, T. and Winterton, A. (2005). *National Review of Music Education: Augmenting the Diminished*. Canberra: Department of Education, Science and Training.

Parker, J., Heywood, D. and Jolley, N. (2012). 'Developing pre-service primary teachers' perceptions of cross-curricular teaching through reflection on learning'. *Teachers and Teaching*, 18(6), 693–716.

Parliament of Victoria. (2013). *Inquiry into the extent, benefits and potential of music education in Victorian schools*. Author. Retrieved from https://www.parliament.vic.gov.au/file_uploads/Music_Education_Final_041113_FJWsJhBy.pdf.

Paterson, A. B. and Lindsay, N. (1970). *The Animals Noah Forgot*. Melbourne: Lansdowne Press.

Perkins, D. (2003). *The Intelligent Eye: Learning to Think by Looking at Art*, 6th edn. Occasional Paper Series (Book 4). Los Angeles: J. Paul Getty Museum.

Perso, T. (2012) *Cultural Responsiveness and School Education: With particular focus on Australia's First Peoples; A Review and Synthesis of the Literature*. Darwin, NT: Menzies School of Health Research, Centre for Child Development and Education.

Phillips, J., Harper, J., Lee, K. and Boone, E. (2014). *Arts Integration and the Mississippi Arts Commission's Whole Schools Initiative: A Stennis Institute Study for Decision-Makers*. Mississippi: John C. Stennis Institute of Government.

Pierse, L. (2006). *Improvisation: The Guide*. Sydney: Improcorp Australia Pty Ltd.

Pinar, W. F., Reynolds, W. M., Slattery, P. and Taubman, P. M. (1995). *Understanding Curriculum*. New York: Peter Lang.

Pink, D. H. (2006). *A Whole New Mind: Why Right Brainers Will Rule the Future*. New York: Riverhead Books.

Pitts, S. E. (2016). 'Music, language and learning: Investigating the impact of a music workshop project in four English early years settings'. *International Journal of Education & the Arts*, 17(20). Retrieved from http://www.ijea.org/v17n20/.

Ponte, P., Ax, J., Beijaard, D. and Wubbels, T. (2004). 'Teachers' development of professional knowledge through action research and the facilitation of this by teacher educators'. *Teaching and Teacher Education*, 20(6), 571–88.

Posten-Anderson, B. (2008). *Drama: Learning Connections in Primary Schools*. Melbourne: Oxford University Press.

Prensky, M. (2001). 'Digital natives, digital immigrants, part II: Do they really think differently?' *On the Horizon*, 9(6), 1–6.

Prowse, S. (2012), 'How does media play and ICT fit in the early childhood context? In S. Wright (ed.), *Children, Meaning-making and the Arts*, 2nd edn. Frenchs Forest, NSW: Pearson Education Australia.

Quillin, K. and Thomas, S. (2015). 'Drawing-to-learn: A framework for using drawings to promote model-based reasoning in biology'. *CBE Life Science Education*, 14(1), 1–16.

Reimer, B. (1989). *A Philosophy of Music Education*, 2nd edn. New Jersey: Prentice Hall.

Regelski, T. (1998). 'The Aristotelian bases of praxis for music and music education as praxis'. *Philosophy of Music Education Review*, 6(1), 22–59.

Rickard, N. S., Bambrick, C. J. and Gill, A. (2012). 'Absence of widespread psychosocial and cognitive effects of school-based music instruction in 10–13-year-old students'. *International Journal of Music Education* 30(1), 57–76.

Rimanelli, D. (2002). 'Jack Pierson, Regrets'. *Artforum International Magazine*, November.

Ritchhart, R. and Perkins, D. (2008). 'Making thinking visible'. *Educational Leadership*, 65(5), 55–61.

Robinson, K. (1999). *All Our Futures: Creativity, Culture and Education – The Report of the NACCCE Committee*. London: National Advisory Committee on Creative and Cultural Education.

—— (2005). 'Do Schools Kill Creativity?' Retrieved from https://www.ted.com/talks/ken_robinson_says_schools_kill_creativity.html.

—— (2011). *Out of Our Minds: Learning to Be Creative*, 2nd edn. New York: Capstone.

Rogoff, B., Baker-Sennett, J., Lacasa, P. and Goldsmith, D. (1995). 'Development through participation in sociocultural activity'. In P. Goodnow, P. Miller and F. Kessel (eds), *Cultural Practices as Contexts for Development*. San Francisco: Jossey-Bass.

Rose, D. (1996). *Nourishing Terrains: Australian Aboriginal Views of Landscape and Wilderness*, Canberra: Australian Heritage Commission.

Rose, L. and Countryman, J. (2013). 'Repositioning 'The Elements': How students talk about music'. *Action, Criticism & Theory for Music Education*, 12(3), 44–64.

Rose, M. (2015). 'The "silent apartheid" as the practitioner's blindspot'. In K. Price (ed.), *Aboriginal and Torres Strait Islander Education: An introduction for the teaching profession*, 2nd edn, pp. 66–82. Cambridge University Press, Melbourne.

Roy, D. (2008). *How to Pass Standard Grade Drama*. Paisley: Hodder Gibson.

—— (2009). *Nelson Drama for Secondary Students*. Melbourne: Cengage.

—— (2011). 'Helping the invisible children'. *Education Review* (November), 24–5.

—— (2012). 'Opening the curtains to thinking'. *Education Review* (February), 19.

—— (2016). 'Implementing a cross-curricular approach'. *Teacher* [2016](5). Retrieved from https://www.teachermagazine.com.au/articles/implementing-a-cross-curricular-approach.

—— (2017). 'Integrating Arts and Science in the classroom'. *Teacher*, [2017](10). Retrieved from https://www.teachermagazine.com.au/articles/integrating-arts-and-science-in-the-classroom.

Roy, D. and Dock, C. (2014). 'Dyspraxia, drama and masks: Applying the school curriculum as therapy'; *Journal of Applied Arts & Health,* 5(3). DOI: 10.1386/jaah.5.3.369_1.

Rudd, K. (2008). *Apology to Australia's Indigenous Peoples, House of Representatives, Parliament House, Canberra*. Retrieved from https://www.australia.gov.au/about-australia/our-country/our-people/apology-to-australias-indigenous-peoples.

Russell-Bowie, D. (2002). 'Where in the world are we? How the perceptions of Australian primary teacher education students differ from those from four other countries in relation to their background and confidence in music education'. *Australian Journal of Music Education*, 1, 33–44.

Russell-Bowie, D. and Dowson, M. (2005). 'Effects of background and sex on confidence in teaching the creative arts: Tests of specific hypotheses.' Proceedings of the *Australian Association for Research in Education Conference, Sydney*. Retrieved from https://www.aare.edu.au/05pap/rus05351.pdf.

Rychen, D. S. and Salganik, L. H. (2005). *The Definition and Selection of Key Competencies: Executive Summary*. Paris: DeSeCo.

Sainty, T. and Baker, W. J. (2015). 'Aboriginal Music in your Classroom: A Tasmanian Perspective'. Unpublished paper presented at the 2015 Australian Society for Music Education (Tasmania) State Conference.

Saltan, F., Arslan, K. and Wang, S. (2017). 'A comparison of in-service and pre-service teachers' technological pedagogical content knowledge self-confidence'. *Cogent Education*, 4(1). DOI:10.1080/2331186X.2017.1311501.

Schafer, R. M. (1967). *Ear Cleaning: Notes for an Experimental Music Course*. Ontario, Canada: Berandol Music Ltd.

Schiro, M. (1992) 'Educators' perceptions of the changes in their curriculum belief systems over time'. *Journal of Curriculum & Supervision*, 7(3), 250–86.

—— (2008). *Curriculum Theory: Visions and Enduring Concerns*. Los Angeles: Sage.

Schnellert, L. M., Butler, D. L. and Higginson, S. K. (2008). 'Co-constructors of data, co-constructors of meaning: Teacher professional development in an age of accountability'. *Teaching and Teacher Education*, 24(3), 25.

Scott, C. (2015). *Learn to Teach: Teach to Learn*. Melbourne: Cambridge University Press.

Screen Australia (2017). 'Online and On Demand 2017: Trends in Australian online viewing habits'. Retrieved from https://www.screenaustralia.gov.au/getmedia/f06697b8-07be-4a27-aa8b-bc3ad365238c/OnlineOnDemand_2017.pdf.

Scripp, L. and Paradis, L. (2014) 'Embracing the burden of proof: New strategies for determining predictive links between arts integration teacher professional development, student arts learning, and student academic achievement outcomes'. *Journal for Learning through the Arts*, 10(1), 1–17.

Seidl, S., Tishman, S., Winner, E., Hetland, L. and Palmer, P. (2009). *The Qualities of Quality: Understanding Excellence in Arts Education*. Cambridge, MASS: Project Zero. Retrieved from: http://www.wallacefoundation.org/knowledge-center/Documents/Understanding-Excellence-in-Arts-Education.pdf.

Shehan Campbell, P. (2005). 'Deep listening to the musical world'. *Music Educators Journal*, 92(1), 30–6.

Shilling, W. A. (2002). 'Mathematics, music, and movement: Exploring concepts and connections'. *Early Childhood Education Journal*, 29(3), 179–84.

Sierra, J. (2000). *The Gift of the Crocodile. An Indonesian Cinderella Story*. New York, Simon & Schuster.

Sinclair, C., Jeanneret, N. and O'Toole, J. (eds). (2009). *Education in the Arts*. Melbourne: Oxford University Press.

Smith, L., Munzenrider, C., Raphael, B. and Bakker, K. (1993). 'Cultural aesthetics and conservation in New Mexico'. *WAAC Newsletter*, 15(1), 23–6.

Smith-Autard, J. M. (2001). *The Art of Dance in Education*. London: A&C Black.

Smyth, J. (1992). 'Teachers' work and the politics of reflection'. *American Educational Research Journal*, 29(2), 267–300.

Snoeyenbos, M. H. and Knapp, C. A., (1979), 'Dance theory and Dance education'. *Journal of Aesthetic Education*, 13(3), 17–30.

Snook, B. (2004). *Count Me In*. Sydney: McGraw Hill.

Snyder, S. (2001). 'Connection, correlation, and integration'. *Music Educators Journal*, 87(5), 32–9, 70.

Somers, J. (1994). *Drama in the Curriculum*. London: Cassell.

Sotiropoulou-Zormpala, M. (2012). 'Aesthetic teaching: Seeking a balance between teaching arts and teaching through the arts'. *Arts Education Policy Review*, 113(4), 123–8.

Sowell, T. (2001). *The Einstein Syndrome*. New York: Basic Books.

Spady, W. (1995). *Outcomes-based Education: Critical Issues and Answers*. Alexandria, Virginia: The American Association of School Administrators.

Stanislavski, C. (1981). *Creating a Role* (E. R. Hapgood, Trans.). London: Methuen.

Starkey, L., Yates, A., Meyer, L. H., Hall, C., Taylor, M., Stevens, S. and Toia, R. (2009). 'Professional development design: Embedding educational reform in New Zealand'. *Teaching and Teacher Education*, 25(1), 181–9.

Summers, D., Gall, A. and Summers, R. (nd). *Songlines of the Moonbird*. Tasmania: Department of Education.

Swain, N. and Bodkin-Allen, S. (2014). 'Can't sing? Won't sing? Aotearoa/New Zealand 'tone-deaf' early childhood teachers' musical beliefs'. *British Journal of Music Education*, 31(3), 245–63.

Tay, H. Y. (2016). 'Longitudinal study on impact of iPad use on teaching and learning', *Cogent Education*, 3(1). Retrieved from https://doi.org/10.1080/2331186X.2015.1127308.

Terrini, L. (2010). 'Adding new possibilities for visual art education in early childhood settings: The potential of interactive whiteboards and ICT'. *Australasian Journal of Early Childhood*, 35(4), 90–4.

The College Board, *Child Development and Arts Education: A Review of Recent Research and Best Practices*, New York, January 2012.

Thomas, K. M., Singh, P. and Klopfenstein, K. (2015). 'Arts education and the high school dropout problem'. *Journal of Cultural Economics*, 39(4), 327–39.

Thwaites, J. (2016). 'Australia ranks 20th on progress towards the Sustainable Development Goals'. *The Conversation*. Retrieved from https://theconversation.com/australia-ranks-20th-on-progress-towards-the-sustainable-development-goals-62820.

Tisdell, E. (2008). 'Critical media literacy and transformative learning: Drawing on pop culture and entertainment media in teaching for diversity in adult higher education'. *Journal of Transformative Education*, 6(1), 48–67.

Tishman, S. and Palley, B. (2010). 'Why teach the arts: Views from the field'. *Min-Ad: Israel Studies in Musicology Online*. 8(I, II). Retrieved from https://www.biu.ac.il/hu/mu/min-ad/10/index.htm.

Tondeur, J., Roblin, N., van Braak, J., Voogt, J. and Prestridge, S. (2017). 'Preparing beginning teachers for technology integration in education: Ready for take-off?'. *Technology, Pedagogy and Education*, 26(2), 157–77.

Tyler, R. (1949). *Basic Principles of Curriculum and Instruction*. Chicago: The University of Chicago Press.

UNESCO (2006). 'Road Map for Arts Education'. The World Conference on Arts Education: Building Creative Capacities for the 21st Century. Lisbon, 6–9 March. Retrieved from http://portal.unesco.org/culture/en/files/40000/12581058115Road_Map_for_Arts_Education.pdf/Road%2BMap%2Bfor%2BArts%2BEducation.pdf.

—— (2010). 'Seoul Agenda: Goals for the Development of Arts Education'. The Second World Conference on Arts Education. Retrieved from http://www.unesco.org/new/fileadmin/MULTIMEDIA/HQ/CLT/CLT/pdf/Seoul_Agenda_EN.pdf.

UNICEF (2017). 'The state of the world's children 2017: Children in a digital world'. Retrieved from https://www.unicef.org.au/Upload/UNICEF/Media/Documents/SOWC-2017-Full-report.pdf.

Valtonen, T., Kukkonen, J., Kontkanen, S., Sormunen, K., Dillon, P., Sointu, E. (2015). 'The impact of authentic learning experiences with ICT on pre-service teachers' intentions to use ICT for teaching and learning'. *Computers & Education*, 81, 49–58.

Valtonen, T., Sointu, E., Kukkonen, J., Kontkanen, S., Lambert, M., Mäkitalo-Seigl, K. (2017). 'TPACK updated to measure pre-service teachers' twenty-first century skills'. *Australasian Journal of Educational Technology*, 33(3).

Van Hoorn, J. L., Nourot, P. M., Scales, B. R. and Alward, K. R. (2011). *Play at the Center of the Curriculum*, 5th ed. Upper Saddle River, NJ: Pearson.

Vaughn, K. (2000). 'Music and mathematics: Modest support for the oft-claimed relationship' In R. Deasy (ed.), *Critical Links: Learning in the Arts and Student Academic and Social Development*. Washington, DC: Arts Education Partnership.

Voogt, J. and Pareja Roblin, N. (2012). 'A comparative analysis of international frameworks for 21st century competences: Implications for national curriculum policies', *Journal of Curriculum Studies*, 44(3), 299–321.

Vygotsky, L. S. (1986). *Thought and Learning*. Cambridge, MA: The MIT Press.

Waller, T. and Bitou, A. (2011). 'The sociology of childhood: Children's agency and participation in telling their own stories'. In T. Waller, J. Whitmarsh and K. Clarke, *Making Sense of Theory and Practice in Early Childhood*. Maidenhead: Open University Press.

Weale, S. (2017). 'Teachers must ditch "neuromyth" of learning styles, say scientists'. *The Guardian, Australian edition*, 13 March. Retrieved from https://www.theguardian.com/education/2017/mar/13/teachers-neuromyth-learning-styles-scientists-neuroscience-education.

Webb, M. (2007). 'Music analysis down the (You) tube? Exploring the potential of cross-media listening for the music classroom'. *British Journal of Music Education* 24(2), 147–64.

Wenger, E. (2009). 'Communities of practice: A brief introduction'. Retrieved from neillthew.typepad.com/files/communities-of-practice.pdf.

Wiggins, J. (2009). *Teaching for Musical Understanding*, 2nd edn. Oakland, MI: Center for Applied Research in Musical Understanding (CARMU).

Wilks, S. (2003). 'The visual arts as a thinking tool'. *Australian Art Education*, 26(2), 27–33.

Wilsher, T. (2007). *The Mask Handbook: A Practical Guide*. Abingdon: Routledge.

Wilson, M. and Wilson, B. (1982). *Teaching Children to Draw: A Guide for Parents and Teachers*. Upper Saddle River, NJ: Prentice Hall.

Winner, E. (1982). *Invented Worlds: The Psychology of the Arts*. Cambridge, MA: Harvard University Press.

Winston, J. and Tandy, M. (2009). *Beginning Drama 4–11*, 3rd edn. Abbingdon: Routledge.

Wockner, C. (2017). 'Online sexual predators: How to keep your kids safe'. *The Courier-Mail*. Retrieved from https://www.couriermail.com.au/news/national/online-sexual-predators-australian-federal-police-officer-exposes-the-grim-reality-threatening-our-kids/news-story/2d703c5fa9ae2edf260e32a280e4b199?memtype=anonymous.

Wright, S. (2003a). 'Ways of knowing in the Arts'. In S. Wright (ed.), *Children, Meaning-making and the Arts*. Frenchs Forest, NSW: Pearson.

—— (2003b). (ed.). *Children, Meaning-making and the Arts*. Sydney: Pearson.

Wright, S., Sinclair, C., Jeanneret, N., Sallis, R., Watkins, M., Adams, R. J., Stevens-Ballenger, J., Grant, G. and McLennan, R. (2014). *Teachers' Application of Arts Rich Practice Teaching In and Through the Arts: Executive Summary*. Melbourne: Melbourne Graduate School of Education.

Yeigh, T. (2008). 'Quality teaching and professional learning: Uncritical reflections of a critical friend'. *Australian Journal of Teacher Education*, 33(2). Retrieved from http://dx.doi.org/10.14221/ajte.2008v33n2.2.

Index

Pages in **bold** denote tables. *Italics* denote figures

4Cs, 10–11

Aboriginal and Torres Strait Islander Histories and Cultures
    cross-curriculum priority, 61, 62, 63–5, 208
Aboriginal and Torres Strait Islander peoples
    Aboriginal students, 326–7
    Acknowledgment of Country, 68
    art, 18, 66, 67, 74
    in the classroom, 66, 74
    colonialism, 66, 67, 74
    culture, 65, 66, 342, 327
    dance and drama, 97, 124
    equity and representation, 64–5
    lesson plans, 74
    music, 18–19, 186, 343
    partnerships, 277–9, 346
    role of teacher, 65–6, 326
    Aboriginal Education Consultative Groups, 68
action research, 312, 313
active learning, 277
Adelaide Declaration (1999), 125
advertising, 165, 172, 174, 178
aesthetic knowing, 217–18
aesthetic teaching, 283
aesthetics, 12, 98, 110, 170
Alperson, P., 22
Anderson, L. W., 167, 279
Anderson, Michael, 6, 8, 10–11, 15, 40, 36
Anderson, Peter, 65
appropriation, 68, 182, 220
apraxia, 99, 131
artists in residence, 286
Arts
    aesthetics, 12
    characteristics, 11, 31
    culturally determined, 12
    different domains, 16
    equity, 14, 15–16
    as language, 13, 272
Arts education
    hierarchies of curricula, 15–16, 40
    intrinsic and instrumental benefits, 40–3, 44, 45, 46, 50, 51–53, 54
    role in children's lives, 31
    role of teacher, 24–6
    see also quality Arts education
Arts Education Partnership, 343
Arts-rich education, 36, 343–5, 351
Arts-rich schools, 46
Arts specialists, 26, 27, 282
Asia and Australia's Engagement with Asia
    cross-curriculum priority, 61, 62, 63, 74–5, 194, 297
Asia Education Foundation, 81
Asia literacy, 75
AsiaLink, 81

Asian music, 75–7, *97*
Asian puppetry, 79–81
assessment, 280, 288–96
    case study, 290–6
Attention Deficit Hyperactivity Disorder (ADD/ADHD), 322
audience, **110**, 246
    impact of technology, 8, 34
    media arts, 159, 160, 165
    primary settings, **300**, 301–2
aural media, **163**, 170
Australia Council for the Arts, 32, 48
Australian Curriculum, 23, 125, 246, 325
    cross-curriculum priorities, 61–3, 64, 75, 78, *82*
    dance, 95, 115
    diverse learners, 321
    drama, 121, 130
    general capabilities, 255, 257–8
    integration, 253, 261, 265
    making and responding, 93, 127, 176, 201, 217, 224
    media arts, 156, 157, 160, 171, 172, 182
    music, 188, 203, **204**
    objectives, 319
    teaching practice, 285, 299
    visual arts, 226, 239, 245
Australian Institute for Teaching and School Leadership (AITSL), 61, 64, 311
authentic learning, 18, 20–2, 23, 36, 84, 193, 277, 290, 341
Autism Spectrum Disorder (ASD), 322, 323, 324, 332

Bamford, A., 17, 20, 25, 44, 48, 54
Barrett, M. S., 31, 189
Bernstein, R.J., 22
blocking, 137
Bloom, Benjamin, 167
Bloom's Revised Taxonomy, **166–7**, 263–4, 315
body
    principles of movement, 107
    and space, 132–3, 136, 147, 271, 332
    warm-ups, 141
body awareness, 100, 102
body percussion, 186, 199
books, 234, 246
Borko, H., 313
Braun, E., 138
breathing, warm-ups, 141
Brookfield, S., , 318, 341
Brouillette, L., 44
Bryce, J., 20, 45
Buckingham, D., 165
Burton, J. M., 46
Burton, Tim, 272
Butzlaff, R., 46

Catterall, J. S., 46, 47
cave paintings, 96
Champions of Change: The Impact of the Arts on Learning, 46
Changing Education through the Arts (CETA) program, 44
checklists, 276
Chicago Arts Partnerships in Education (CAPE) program, 47
child-centred approaches
    dance, 97, 103
    drama, 125, *126*
    music, 21
    quality education, 276, 277, 279, 280, 285, 341
Chinese opera, 97
choreography, 95, 109, 111, 239–268, 269, **269**
class discussion, 134, 200
clay, 235
codes and conventions, 54, 143, 163–4, 217, 341
collaboration, 11, 84, 213, 313, 346
colonialism, 64, 66, 67, 74, 124
colour, 227, 9, 230, 231–231, 232, 238–9
commedia dell'arte, 122, 123
communication, 11, 13, 41, *126*, 194, 331, 332, 349, 350
contrast, 135
coordination, 100, 101, 113, 271
copyright, 182
'Country', 64
crafts, 12, 217
Creative and Performing Arts (CAPA), 314
creative music education, 191
creativity, 11, 46, 157
critical and creative thinking, 164, 256, 257
    dance, 258
    drama, 259
    media arts, **259**
    music, **260**
    visual arts, **260**
Critical Links: Learning in the Arts and Student Academic and Social Development, 46
critical reflection, 11
cross-curriculum priorities, 60–90
    and the early years, 63
    meaning, 62–3
    the Arts, 62–3
    see also Aboriginal and Torres Strait Islander peoples; Asia and Australia's Engagement with Asia; sustainability
cultural appropriation, 68
cultural diversity, 342
    intercultural understanding, 56, 256, 258, 259, 260
    and learner agency, 17–18
    lesson plans, 168, 345, 316–18
    and the Arts, 12, 219, 277
    see also Aboriginal and Torres Strait Islander peoples; Asia and Australia's Engagement with Asia
cuneiform, 264
curriculum ideologies
    approaches, 310
    types, 308, 309

curriculum integration, 252–74, **286**
    in the classroom, 253, 254, 61–262
    general capabilities, **255–61**
    English, 265
    methodology, 253–4
    multiliteracies, 264–70
    other Learning Areas, 261
    programming, 45, 47, 253
    the Arts and
        humanities and social sciences, 270
        language, 272
        mathematics, 267–8
        physical education, 271
        science, 268
        technology, 272
cyberbullying, 181, 303–4

dance, 16, 94–119, 332
    choreography, 95, 109, 111, 239–268, 269
    concepts, 107, 110–11
    context, 115, 117
    and drama, 96, 99
    in early childhood settings, 97, 99
    elements and principles, 98, 101–2, 111–14
    engaging with, 96–8
    exploring identity, 339
    general capabilities, 258
    in the classroom, 100–1, 102, 104, *107*, 109, 115, 118
    learning in and through the Arts, 56
    lesson plans, 100–1, 103, 106–268, 269
    and literacy, 117, **258**
    making and responding, 98, *107*, 111
    in primary education, 103–4
    and physical education, 107, 115–17
    safety, 97, 98, 115, 318
    styles, 105, 106, *114*
Denac, O., 218
Desert Feet, 321
Differentiated Instruction (DI), 331
digital citizenship, 181
digital media, 171–2, 221, 233
digital natives, 158
digital technologies, *see* technologies
Direct Instruction, 331
director, 150
Disability Discrimination Act 1992, 265, 319
Disability Standards for Education, 319
diverse learners, 306–33
    equity, 318–20
    lesson plans, 328–9
    other pedagogical approaches, 331
    special needs, 98, 99, 107, 131, 265, 321–2
    T.E.A.C.H., 329–31
    see also Aboriginal and Torres Strait Islander peoples; cultural diversity; English as a second language (ESL); socioeconomic status (SES); students with disability
domain-centred learning, 36
Donelan, D., 61

downstage, *137*
drama, 16, 124
   assessment, 150
   in the classroom, 132, 135, 138, 140, 142, 145, 149, 151
   context, 151, 160
   and dance, 96, 99
   in early childhood and primary settings, 126–8
   elements, 56, 130–9
      body and space, 132–3, 136, 147, 271, 332
      contrast, 135
      focus, 138
      mood, 139, 140
      stage settings, 137–8
      symbol, 135
      tension, 135
      time, 136
      voice, 131
   and English, 43–4, 265
   exploring identity, 18, 339
   general capabilities, 259
   and literacy, 49–50, 259, 264
   making and responding, *127*, 142–5
   masks, 122, *123*, 147, 148
   meaning, 121
   role of teacher, 124–5, 126–8
   safety, 128, 140
   stimulus, 129–30
   theatre arts, 149, 150
   theories and theorists, 122–3
   warm-ups, 140–2
Drama Improves Lisbon Key Competencies in Education
     (DICE), *126*, 256
drama programs, 43–4, 288
drawing, 221, 226, 227, 271, 352–3
Duma, A., 44
Dweck, C., 188
dynamics, 112, 114, 204
dyspraxia, 98, 131, 322–3, 324, 332

early childhood settings
   approaches, 299–300
   cross-curriculum priorities, 63
   dance, 97, 99
   drama, 126–8
   educator role, 23–6
   media arts, 165–6
   music, 194–7
   organisation, 298–300
   visual arts, 223–4
Early Years Learning Framework for Australia (EYLF), 19, 23, 38, 50, 63, 70, 79, 80, *126*, 165, 194, 223, 224, 237, 299, 340
Effective Implementation of Pedagogical Reform (EIPR), 314
Eisner, E., 2, 30
El Sistema orchestra education system, 32
Elliott, D. J., 22, 185
Elster, A., 343
embodied learning, 8, 40, 115, *191*, 192, 193, 343
emoji, 328–9

emotional safety, 181
English, 25, 43–4, 265, 266
English as a second language (ESL), 326, 327–9
equity, 14–17, 61–2, 64–5, 265, 320
   see also diverse learners
ethical understanding, 256, 257
   dance, 258
   drama, 259
   media arts, 259
   music, 260
   visual arts, 260
Ewing, R., 18, 35, 40, 44, 308
exploration, 286, 299
expressionism, 270

fine arts, 217
fine motor skills, 95, 332
flipped classroom, 35
focus, 138
folk dances, 97, 103, 118
Fontana, T., 34
formative assessment, 288, 289
four-dimensional art, 221, 235
four lenses, 337, 318
fourth wall, 138
fractals, 268
Freire, P., 22, 352

Gagné, Françoys, 324
Gale, L., 181
Gardiner, G., 343
Gardner, H., 42, 188, 283, 284, 331
Garvis, S., 25
gatekeepers, 25
Geese Theatre, 45
gender stereotypes, 115–17, *160*, 319
general capabilities, 115, 194, 252–74
   dance, 258
   drama, 259
   elements and principles, 255–61
   equivalent competencies, 256
   media arts, 259
   music, 260
   visual arts, 260
genre, 143, 159–65, 188
Geography, 172
Gibson, R., 35
gifted and talented students, 324–6
Grattan Institute, 10
group-based learning, 271, 286, 300, 301, 302
guest artists, 286
guided questioning, 174, 219, 239, 241, 242
Guterres, António, 81

Haiku, 194
Hallam, S., 43, 48
Hamilton, A., 43
arvard Graduate School of Education, 337
Harvard Project Zero, *193*, 337
Hattie, John, 311

health and physical education, 172, 238, 271, 304
health and safety, *see* safety
Heathcote, Dorothy, 124
higher-order thinking, 263–4, 279, 314, 318
Horowitz, R., 46
humanities and social sciences (HASS), 270
Hunter, M., 45, 345

identity, 339
Imant, Jeroen, 311
improvisation, 145
inclusivity, 277, 316, 318
information and communication technology (ICT), 157, 178, 179, 256, 257
    dance, 258
    drama, 259
    media arts, 259
    music, 260
    visual arts, 260
installation art, 237
instrumental benefits, 40, 42–3, 44, 45, 46, 50, 51–53, 54
interactive and social media, 164, 170
intercultural understanding, 256, 258
    dance, 258
    drama, 259
    media arts, 259
    music, 260
    visual arts, 260
internet, 34–5
internet safety, 181, 182
intrinsic benefits, 40–2, 45, 54
iPads, 179, 180, 181, 332

Jaques-Dalcroze, Émile, *192*
Jefferson, Miranda, 6, 8, 10–11, 15, 40, 36
Jenlink, P. M., 313
John F. Kennedy Center for the Performing Arts, 44, 346

Kerckaert, S., 157
kinaesthetic activity, 234
kinetic art, 236
Kirschner,. P. A., 158
Kodaly, Zoltan, *192*

Laban, Rudolf, *107*, *108*, 109, 132, 133
language
    dance, 110
    media, 161–2
    and the Arts, 13, 272, 275
    visual arts, 220
layout, 161
learner agency, 17–18, 23, 193, 289, 341
learner-centered approach, 308, 309
Learning Areas, 13, 16, 92, *253*, 261
learning corners, 14, 40, 195, 286, 347
    music, 26, 190, 197, 198
learning in the Arts, 40, 54, 56–58, 70
learning styles, 261, 263, 350, 331
learning through the Arts, 40, 54–8, 70
Lewis, C., 318

Listen–Compose–Perform (L–C–P), 209–11
listening, 200, 209, 213
literacy, 17, 43–4, 117, 256, 257, 275
    dance, 115, 258
    drama, 49–50, **259**, 264
    media arts, **259**
    multiliteracies, 264–70
    music, 260, 264
    visual arts, 260
Living Kaurna Cultural Centre, Marion, SA, 68
Lo, C., 35
lower-order thinking, 263–4

making and responding, 93, 98, 217, 276
Manga, 75–7
Marsh, J., 157
masks, *122*, 123, 147, 148
mathematics, 46, 47, 234, 267–8, 288
McArdle, F., 223
McCarthy, K., 25, 40, 41
media arts, 16, **155–83**, 221
    in the classroom, *178*, 180, 277–9
    context, 160, 181
    copyright, 182
    development of media skills and understandings, 166–7
    in early childhood settings, 165–6
    engaging with, 156–8
    exploring identity, 339
    general capabilities, 259
    key concepts, 159, 160–5, 177
        audiences, 159, 160, 165
        institutions, **164–5**
        languages, 161–2, 163, 174
        representation, 165
        technologies, 156, **163–4**, 170, 178
    learning in and through the Arts, 57
    making and responding, 176
    media texts, 159, *173*
    personal development, 178
    in primary settings, 169
    safety, 166, 168, 181–2
    social media, 164, 170, 178
    medical profession, 218
Melbourne Declaration on Educational Goals for Young Australians (2008), 61–2, 63, 74, 81, 125, 352
Melbourne Graduate School of Education, 344
Meyerhold, V., *122*, *123*, 152
Mnouchkine, Ariane, 123
mobiles, 236
modern art, 221
Monash University, 65
monoprinting, 221, 234
mood, 139, 140
Mothersill, M., 218
motor skills, 95, 332
moving image, 164, 170, 272
multiliteracies, **264–70**
multiple contexts, 193
MuseScore, 36, 187, 191, 207
music, 16, 21, 39, 46, 184–249, 321
    Aboriginal music, 18–19, 186, 343

Asian music, 75–7, 97
in the classroom, 187–8, 194, 199, 200, 210–11
composition, 56, 211, 289
in early childhood settings, 194–7
elements and principles, 22, 143, **190–1**, 203–6
   definitions and descriptions, 204
   examples and activities, 205
engaging, 48, 188–9
equity, 17
exploring identity, 339
general capabilities, 260

learning corners, 26, 190, 197, 198
learning in and through the Arts, 56
Listen–Compose–Perform (L–C–P), 209–11
listening, 200, 209, 210
making and responding, 201
music education in Australia, 188–9
and neuroscience, 31–3
music literacy, 187, 190, 193, 264
processes, 203, 208
in primary settings, 197–8
soundscapes, 186, **199–200**, 201, 272
technology, 34–5, 178, 187, 272
Music Count Us In, 346
Music Viva, 213
Musical Futures, 344

Nansen, B., 157
NAPLAN, 267
National Advisory Committee on Creative and Cultural Education, 11
National Art Education Association (NAEA), 218
National Arts Council Education Programme, Singapore, 287
National Education and the Arts Statement, 18
National Educational Longitudinal Survey (NELS), 17, 46
National Indigenous Television Network (NITV), 327
National Review of School Music Education, 185
neutral position, 147, 149
new media, 34, 35, 36, 58, 158, 165, 167, 182, 187
noticing skills, 239
numeracy, 17, 117, 256, 257, 267–8
   dance, 258
   drama, 259
   media arts, 259
   music, 260
   visual arts, 260

observation, 312–13
Odham, John, *191*
OECD, 255, 310
Office of the eSafety Commissioner, 181
Orff Schulwerk approach, *191*
Orff, Carl, *191*
organisation, *see* planning
O'Toole, J., 8, 40, 125
outcomes-based education, 310–11

painting, 221, 227–31
papier mâché, 235
parents, 282, 345–7
Parliament of Victoria, 189
Partnership for 21st Century Learning, 10
Partnership for 21st Century Skills, 10
partnerships, 45, 47, 277–9, 345–7
Pascoe, R., 17, 189
Paynter, John, *191*
pedagogy, 279
   approaches, 283, 285–6, 299–300, 301–2
   Arts-based pedagogies, 278, 283
   other pedagogical approaches, 331
   see also T.E.A.C.H.
performance art, 237
Perkins, David, *193*
personal and social capability, 256, 257
   dance, 258
   drama, 259
   media arts, 259
   music, 260
   visual arts, 260
personal development (PD), 178, 271
Phillips, J., 47
photography, 233
physical education, 107, 115–17, 118, 172, 238, 271, 304
pitch, 204
planning, 275–305
   approaches, 282, 285–6, **299–300**
   assessment, 288, 290–6
   and audience, 300, 301–2
   in the classroom, 277–9
   in early childhood settings, 298–300
   inquiry approach, 280–1
      school and community, 282
      students, 280–1
   pedagogy, 283
   in primary education, 300, 303–4
   quality characteristics, 276, 277
   units of work, 301–2, 303–4
play-based learning, 40, 110, 126, 166, 194, 195, 223, 340
playbuilding, 144, 149
playdough, 235
Ponte, P., 311
Pop Art, 270
postmodern art, 222
PowerPoint, 179
praxis, 98, 107, 256, 271, 337, 352
   vision for the Arts, 22–3
Prensky, Marc, 158
primary education, 23–6, 300, 301–2
   dance, 103–4
   drama, 126–8
   integrated unit of work, 303–4
   learning environment, 348–50
   media arts, 169
   music, 197–8
   organisation, 300
   visual arts, 224
print media, 163, 170
printmaking, 221, 234

Index   375

problematic knowledge, 314, 318
producers, 160
professional development, 179, 311, 312, 344
    problem of time, 16, 24
Professional Standards for Teachers (AITSL), 61, 64, 311
program music, 352
Programme for International Student Assessment (PISA), 255, 310
props, 150, 162
puppetry, 79–81

quality Arts education
    arts-rich learning, 36, 343–5, 351
    Arts-rich learning, 36, 343–5, 351
    in the classroom, 339–40, 343
    continuous teacher reflection, 335, 342
    Harvard Project Zero, *193*, 337
    identity theme, 339
    inclusive, 342
    partnerships, 345
    principles, 20–2, 276–7, 336–42
    research, 44
    Queensland government, 67

reflective teaching, 307–8, 310, 318
    implementing, 311–12
    observation, 312–13
    quality teaching and reflective learning, 313
Regelski, T., 22
rehearsal, 213
remote communities, 321
rhythm, 99, 101, 102, 204, 220
Rickard, N. S., 39
Ritchhart, R., 219
ritual, 2, 96
Robinson, K., 15, 35, 40, 187
Rose, D., 18
Rose, Mark, 64
rural communities, 321
Russell-Bowie, D., 25
Ruston, Delaney, 157
Rychen, D. S., 256

safety, 279, 299, 331
    dance, 97, 98, 115, 318
    drama, 128, 140
    internet safety, 182
    media arts, 166, 168, 181–2
    science safety rules, 269
    visual arts, 227, 247
Sainty, T., 326
Saraceno, Tomás, 87
scaffolding, 193, 210
Schafer, R. M., 184, *191*, 199, 200
Schiro, M., 308
Schnellert, L. M., 311
scholar academics, 308, 309
School Drama program, 43, 288
science, 117, 152, 268
Scottish curricula, 256

Scripp, L., 47
self-portraits, 20–2, 239–40, 290–6, 342
semiotics, 265, 327–9
Seoul Agenda: Goals for the Development of Arts Education (UNESCO), 45
sequential learning, 19–22, 193, 197, 233, 246, 277, 299, 337–8
sexual predators, 181
Shehan Campbell, Patricia, 209
Shilling, W. A., 197
shot types, 161, 162
Sibley, Frank, 98
social efficiency ideology, 308, 309
social media, 164, 170, 178
social reconstructionism, 308, 309
socioeconomic status (SES), 17, 47, 61, 320–1
Sotiropoulou-Zormpala, M., 276
soundscapes, 186, 199–200, 201, 272
South Australian School Drama program, 43
space
    body and space, 132–3, 136, 147, 271, 332
    dance, 113
Spady, W., 310
special needs, *see* diverse learners
stage settings, 137–8, 139
Stanislavski, Konstantin, *122*, 152
Starkey, L., 313
State Theatre Company SA Education Program, 43
STEAM, 268
STEM, 268, 288
stereotypes, 115–17, 132, 133–4, 160, 319
stimulus, 129
storyboards, 168, 169, 171, 181
storylines, 170
structure, 143, 204, 205
students with disability, 95, 319, 321–2
    Attention Deficit Hyperactivity Disorder (ADD/ADHD), 322
    Autism Spectrum Disorder (ASD), 322, 324, 332
    dyspraxia, 98, 131, 322–3, 324, 332
substantial learning, 20, 276, 277, 340–1
summative assessment, 288
sustainability, 81–9
    in the classroom, 277–9
    cross-curriculum priority, 61, 62, 63, 186
    environment and the Arts, 84
    in and through the Arts, 83
    lesson plans, 87
    materials, 86
sustained learning, 19–22, 277, 337–8
Swain, N., 194
Sydney Theatre Company, 43, 288
symbols, 135, 161

tableaux, 142, 144, 145
Tasmanian Aboriginal Centre, 19
Taymor, Julie, 123
T.E.A.C.H., 329–31
    achievable and goals, 330
    chunk the tasks, 331
    expect success, 330

harbour the learning area, 331
talk to the student, 329, 331
Teaching for Musical Understanding (TMU), 193
Teaching Through the Arts, 287
technologies, 272
    and audience, 8, 34
    impact on Arts education, 34, 224
    media arts, 156, **163–4**, 170, 178
    music, 34–5, 178, 187–8, 272
tension, 135
Terrini, L., 223
tessellations, 234, 296, 297
texture, 204
theatre arts, 149, 150
Theory of Multiple Intelligences (MI), 188, 283–4, 321, 331
three-dimensional art, 221, 236
timbre, 204
time, 16, 19, 24, 36, 236
    dance, 113
    drama, 136

UNESCO, 7, 14, 16, 20, 31, 45
United Nations, 81
United Nations Sustainable Development Goals Report, *81*
Universal Design for Learning (UDL), 331
University of Helsinki, 195
University of Melbourne, 81
University of Southern California, 31
University of Sydney, 48
upstage, *137*
US Department of Education, 288

Vaughn, K., 46
viewpoints, 142, 143, 168, 175, 226
visual arts, 16, 216–49
    assessment, 290–6, 297
    in the classroom, 219, 225, 232
    colours, **227**, 9, 230, 231, 232, 238–9
    content, 222
    context, **244–8**
    cultural diversity, 219
    curriculum integration, 264, 268
    displaying children's artwork, 245–7
    in early childhood settings, 223–4
    elements and principles, 218–22
    engaging, 217–18
    exploring identity, 339
    general capabilities, 260
    language, 220
    learning in and through the Arts, 57
    looking at art, 218, 242
    making and responding, 219, 239, 241
    materials, 220, 221, 222, 227–31, 234, 235, 247–8
    methods, 221
    planning, 245, 247
    in primary education, 224
    safety, 227, 247
    styles, 222, 239, 270
    tools, 219–22
    visual arts practices, 226–7
visual arts forms, 221
    digital media, 171–2, 221, 233
    drawing, 221, 227, 271, 352–3
    four-dimensional art, 221, 235
    installation art, 237
    kinetic art, 236
    painting, 221, **227–31**
    performance art, 237
    photography, 233
    printmaking, 221, 234
    representation, 226
    three-dimensional art, 221, 236
voice, 131, 141
Vygotsky, L. S., 326, 330

warm-ups, 97, 115, 140–2
whole class learning, 286
Wiggins, J., 17, 193
Wolf Trap Foundation, 288

YouTube, 188

zone of proximal development, 326, 330